Aspen's Fund Raising Series for the 21st Century
Edited by James P. Gelatt, PhD, CFRE

Capital Campaigns

Strategies That Work

Aspen's Fund Raising Series for the 21st Century
Edited by James P. Gelatt, PhD, CFRE

Fund Raising Basics: A Complete Guide
Barbara Kushner Ciconte, CFRE and Jeanne G. Jacob, CFRE

Planned Giving Essentials: A Step by Step Guide to Success
Richard D. Barrett and Molly E. Ware, CFRE

Strategic Fund Development: Building Profitable Relationships That Last
Simone P. Joyaux, ACFRE

Capital Campaigns: Strategies That Work
Andrea Kihlstedt and Catherine P. Schwartz

Successful Special Events: Planning, Hosting, and Evaluating
Barbara R. Levy, ACFRE and Barbara H. Marion, CFRE

Corporate and Foundation Fund Raising: A Complete Guide from the Inside
Eugene A. Scanlan, PhD, CFRE

Donor Focused Strategies for Annual Giving
Karla A. Williams, ACFRE

Aspen's Fund Raising Series for the 21st Century
Edited by James P. Gelatt, PhD, CFRE

Capital Campaigns

Strategies That Work

Andrea Kihlstedt
Fund Raising Counsel
The Kihlstedt Group
Lancaster, Pennsylvania

Catherine P. Schwartz
Former Development Officer
The Alban Institute, Inc.
Bethesda, Maryland

AN ASPEN PUBLICATION®
Aspen Publishers, Inc.
Gaithersburg, Maryland
1997

8 -21-98

This publication is designed to provide accurate and authoritative information in regard to the Subject Matter covered. It is sold with the understanding that the publisher is not engaged in rendering legal, accounting, or other professional service. If legal advice or other expert assistance is required, the service of a competent professional person should be sought. *(From a Declaration of Principles jointly adopted by a Committee of the American Bar Association and a Committee of Publishers and Associations.)*

Library of Congress Cataloging-in-Publication Data

Kihlstedt, Andrea.
Capital campaigns: strategies that work/Andrea Kihlstedt, Catherine Schwartz.
p.   cm.—(Aspen's fund raising series for the 21st century)
Includes bibliographical references and index.
ISBN 0-8342-0794-X (pbk.)
1. Nonprofit organizations—Finance.   2. Fund raising.
I. Schwartz, Catherine P.   II. Title.   III. Series.
HG4027.65.K55   1997
658.15'224—dc21
96-48720
CIP

Orders: (800) 638-8437
Customer Service: (800) 234-1660

About Aspen Publishers • For more than 35 years, Aspen has been a leading professional publisher in a variety of disciplines. Aspen's vast information resources are available in both print and electronic formats. We are committed to providing the highest quality information available in the most appropriate format for our customers. Visit Aspen's Internet site for more information resources, directories, articles, and a searchable version of Aspen's full catalog, including the most recent publications: **http://www.aspenpub.com**
Aspen Publishers, Inc. • The hallmark of quality in publishing
Member of the worldwide Wolters Kluwer group

Editorial Resources: Brian MacDonald
Library of Congress Catalog Card Number: 96-48720
ISBN: 0-8342-0794-X

Printed in the United States of America

2 3 4 5

Life shrinks or expands in proportion to one's courage.

Anaïs Nin

Table of Contents

Foreword

In the case of fund development, there are no short-cuts to increasing gift support. With few exceptions, increases come as a result of investing resources, . . . good planning and hard work.
—Fred A. Matthews and Patricia Lewis
"Long Range Planning in a Short-Term Environment"

Although the terms "development," "fund raising," and "advancement" are often used interchangably, the philosophical underpinnings are clearly those of development. "Development" was at one time paired with "planning" to form the name of many fund-raising offices or departments. The idea was—and is—sound: effective development is the result of good planning. As the authors of the epigraph above write:

> One reason for long-range planning is that it challenges us to start thinking concretely about the future. An organization needs to start planning how it is to get the resources—human and financial—to make a reality of the vision it has created. This requires a serious assessment of its current situation, the probable costs of the future it has projected and how the bridge to that future will be built. (Matthews and Lewis, 1988, 14).

A Look at Some Trends

To build a successful fund-raising program, one must be cognizant of major external trends (Gelatt, 1992):

(1) *The nature of the donor is changing.* As we enter the 21st century, the median age of the American population will be 36 years; it was about 28 years in 1970. The superannuated (the "old old") will be a burgeoning part of the population.

One in three persons will be from a minority background. Fund-raising approaches that might have worked for a predominantly white, Protestant population in one part of the country may be singularly ineffective in another part that is multicultural, multilingual, and multi-denominational.

One in two persons within the workforce will be women. Women with their own earning power also make their own decisions about which causes they will support.

(2) *The level of sophistication in fund raising continues to rise.* Fund raising may always be an art, but it is increasingly becoming a science. Successful fund raisers are becoming market-driven, asking "who wants, who needs" the services that the nonprofit organization provides, or might provide.

(3) *The scrutiny of fund raising is likely to increase.* Public scrutiny is being driven by two forces: concern about nonprofits in general and fund raising specifically (both influenced by unfortunate incidents such as that of William Aramony and The New Era Fund); and the public sector's need for ways to raise money without raising the traditional tax base.

At every level—federal, state, and local—the scrutiny is likely to increase. And much of it will focus on the raising and use of funds.

(4) *Increased competition for funds appears inevitable.* Some 100,000 new nonprofit organizations were created between 1975 and 1990. Virtually all of them seek funding. They will be joined by new entrants.

(5) *Overall, there should be a continued growth in philanthropy.* Even allowing for inflation, philanthropic contributions continue to rise.

(6) *Some things don't change:*

- People give to people, not places or things
- At base, fund raising is people who believe in what they are doing, who ask others to share in that belief

Capital Campaigns

If you have built castles in the air, your work need not be lost; that is where they should be. Now put the foundation under them.
—Henry David Thoreau
Walden Pond

Capital campaigns are among the most exciting, invigorating, challenging—and terrifying—of fund raising activities.

Planning the campaign is not unlike building "castles in the air," for by their very nature, capital campaigns call on us to think ambitiously. They often demand that we set fund raising goals that far exceed what the organization has typically raised. If that were not challenge enough, we then go public (at least to our institutions' publics) by announcing the goal that we have set. Reach that goal, and we look like heroes. Fall short of the mark, and everyone knows it.

Fortunately, we now have a friend who can help. That friend is Kihlstedt and Schwartz's *Capital Campaigns: Strategies That Work.* The book is aimed at those who most need it. Not the multi-million dollar institutions; they can afford to retain a big named consulting firm. *Capital Campaigns* is targeted to the vast majority of nonprofits—small to mid-sized, community-based, making a difference. The authors, Andrea Kihlstedt and Cathe Schwartz, have extensive experience as both staff and consultants on capital campaigns. The result is a book filled with insight, practical experience, and assurance that with it, your own capital campaign can succeed.

James P. Gelatt, PhD, CFRE
Prentice Associates
Nonprofit Management Consulting
Adjunct Professor
Graduate School of Management and Technology
University of Maryland
Editor, *Aspen's Fund Raising Series for the 21st Century*

References

Gelatt, J.P. 1992. *Managing nonprofit organizations in the 21st century.* Phoenix, AZ: Oryx Press.

Matthews, F.A. & Lewis, P. 1988. "Long-range planning in a short-term environment." *Journal of Contemporary Issues in Fund Raising, 13* (Spring): 14.

Preface
Lessons from Life

Our capital campaign funded the new building, but more than that, I had a great time! The experience of that campaign built my professional and personal confidence. I learned to ask for major gifts without getting sick to my stomach. I learned to trust my instincts. I figure that if I could do this successfully, then I can do just about anything . . .
— Development director, on having completed a successful campaign to raise $3 million

In the life of a small organization, a capital campaign occurs only once in a very great while. Many executive directors, development directors, and board members of small nonprofit agencies, who are very experienced in running their agencies and in conducting annual-giving programs, are campaign neophytes, first-timers, tyros.

This book has been written for development directors, executive directors, and board members of small-to-midsized community-based nonprofit organizations that are considering a capital campaign. It is the distillation of many capital campaigns undertaken by such organizations. The authors have gathered stories—both inspiring and excruciating—from more than a dozen professionals in the field who have gone through the campaign process. We have worked with many of these individuals throughout their campaigns—from the early, tentative questions about how to get started to the capstone decisions about the design of donor plaques and the planning of campaign celebrations.

To prepare for writing this book, we invited friends and clients who have been in the campaign trenches to gather for a workshop to share their campaign experiences and to reflect on what they have learned. As we prepared for this meeting, we worried about how willing the participants would be to share their stories. We found, however, that everyone who attended our meeting was hungry for the chance to talk. For all of these people—executive directors, development directors, and board members—their capital campaigns had been ma-

jor events not only for their organizations, but in their lives as well. Each capital campaign had moved the organization ahead in a major way, while also expanding each individual's abilities. They gained increased confidence in how much they could accomplish in their lives, they learned to trust more fully their instincts about human nature, and they learned how to use campaign design and group process to help volunteers function at their very best.

Every one of the workshop participants was eager to share stories about what had happened in their campaign, and they listened enthusiastically to the stories of others. We spent an entire day telling campaign tales, and these stories reminded us that this form of fund raising—the capital campaign—brings out the best in people: Staff members work to capacity and beyond, volunteers find that they have the inner resources to accomplish miracles, and donors are inspired to get in touch with their generosity and those feelings of civic responsibility and love for their fellow human beings that motivate them to decide to make a difference in their community.

Although we heard tales of anxiety, fatigue, and overwork, it was stories of human accomplishment, empowerment, persistence, heroism, and enthusiasm that prevailed and shaped a memorable and spirited day. The authors are pleased to share with you through this book the concepts, practices, and ideas that made the capital campaigns succeed in these people's organizations. We have spiced our theoretical framework with quotations and tales from the front lines in the hopes that our readers will see the very human and often humorous aspects of capital-campaign fund raising. We hope that our stories will inspire others to find the courage, wisdom, and good humor to guide their organizations through successful campaigns.

Because the original meaning of the word *campaign* is that of a military operation, it is not surprising that much that is written about capital campaigns, just as with political campaigns, uses militaristic terminology to describe the campaign process. Indeed, after giving the military definition of the word, the Oxford English Dictionary informs us that the word *campaign* can be figuratively "applied to any course of action analogous to a military campaign, either in having a distinct period of activity, or in being of the nature of a struggle, or of an organized attempt aiming at a definite result." So, while campaigns in some of their aspects resemble military operations, they are not warfare. Campaigns have been likened to raging battles fought by the troops in trenches, soldiers with powder-stained faces called to arms by a powerful and wealthy ruler whose generals engage in planning and carrying out mighty expeditions to overcome an enemy. While the imagery of the capital campaign as warfare stirs some people, we prefer other more positive, constructive imagery.

The authors believe that capital campaigns provide some of the best opportunities for staff, volunteers, and donors to work together around the shared excitement of helping a worthy organization reach new heights and accomplish important community goals. Such cooperative work most certainly is not warfare. It is hearts, not territory, that are conquered. People's wealth is not plundered, rather they share their resources voluntarily with an organization that is carrying out their will.

A capital campaign is not a military campaign, but the preparation and execution of these two types of campaigns have much in common. Campaigns are labor-intensive, requiring both broad vision (strategy) and attention to detail (tactics). They require strategic thinking, specific action, and punctilious follow-through. As development director or executive director your role as the key staff member in the campaign will demand that you work effectively at many levels. You will need to be clear, crisp, and focused on the tasks at hand. You will need to model the behavior that you wish to see in your campaign workers—kindness, follow-through, responsibility, and timeliness. You will need to be well organized, tough, and assertive. At the same time, you will need to be compassionate, encouraging, and supportive. You will need to expand your communications skills in every area—and as you reach out through your organization to the larger community, you will make new friends and learn many valuable lessons.

Through the demands of a campaign, you will learn an enormous amount about yourself and about all the individuals who work with you on the campaign. You will learn some lessons of life and motivation that, if learned well, will make you stronger and more effective in everything you do. You will forge genuine friendships with a surprising variety of people. You will request and receive gifts of more money than you ever thought possible. You will learn not to underestimate people's capacity for generosity in the service of creating a better world. You will learn what motivates people and how to create a climate that supports people and helps them to do their best. You will be reminded of the power of positive thinking, the importance of clear and effective organization, and the rewards of follow-through. These lessons will take you far beyond the campaign itself, for they are truly lessons for life.

Acknowledgments

This book would not have been possible without the people whose campaigns and campaign experiences seeded many of its ideas and stories. Douglas Atkins, Mary Barnard, Louise Huntley Brown, Sally Bures, Cassandra George, Baird Hansen, Mary Lerner, Bonnie Light, Terry Nolen, Rosemary Richie, and Charlie Troutmann shared stories with us as we prepared to write. Their tales and many others have been adapted for this book.

Special thanks goes to David Kramer for his attentive and insightful heavy editing. His clear eye, sharp intellect, and ability to turn a good phrase helped shape this book!

Marian Joyce and Bev Hesterberg provided excellent office support. Chuck Thompson, Paula Sidle, Bob Pierpont, and John Synodinos helped answer questions and offered ideas and insights when we asked for them.

Andrea Kihlstedt acknowledges her husband, Tyko, whose good humor and understanding supported her through months of long hours and tension. She would also like to thank Blake Albright, Louise Huntley Brown, and Cassandra George of the Kihlstedt Group for their feedback, insight, and encouragement.

Cathe Schwartz thanks Leslie Buhler and her colleagues at the Alban Institute, H. Judith Jarrell, Ph.D., Chris Silk, CPA, and John Squire, CPA at Sarfino and Rhodes, Inc., and the reference librarians at the National Society of Fund Raising Executives. She also thanks her husband, Dan, and sons Benjamin and Nathaniel for their encouragement, patience, and understanding during the writing of this book. She also thanks Andrea Kihlstedt, since this book would not have been possible without her wisdom, experience, and insight.

And finally, the authors acknowledge Robert Berendt who introduced them to one another.

Chapter 1

Is Your Organization Ready for a Capital Campaign?

Chapter Outline
- What Is a Capital Campaign?
- The Power of Capital Campaign Fund Raising
- Familiar Fund-Raising Principles
- Fund-Raising Practices
- Special Characteristics of Capital Campaigns
- Campaign Anxiety
- Requirements for a Successful Campaign
- Patterns of Giving
- Managing Campaign Announcements
- Estimating Campaign Costs
- The Phases of a Campaign
- Timing Considerations
- The Campaign Plan
- A Time for Heroes

What Is a Capital Campaign?

A capital campaign is a particular method of building an organization's assets through fund raising. A campaign enables an organization to raise a significant amount of money in a limited time for a special project designed to improve that organization's service to its community.

Capital campaigns are major fund-raising episodes in the life of a nonprofit organization. While organizations rely on annual giving and special-events fund raising to nourish them as they evolve, organizations undertake capital campaigns when they are ready to take a major step forward—building a new facility, renovating current offices, adding equipment, or developing a major new program.

Compared to the staff time and expense of special events or direct-mail programs, the capital campaign is one of the most efficient, cost-effective ways to raise funds for a nonprofit organization. Although such a campaign demands extensive planning and preparation and requires the best skills and fullest commitment of everyone close to the organization, the returns on these investments far outstrip those from other types of fund raising. The following characteristics are typical of capital-campaign fund raising.

- Capital campaigns have goals far in excess of annual giving goals.
- Capital campaigns enable an organization to accomplish specific project goals.
- Capital campaigns have clearly defined, often tight timetables.
- Capital campaigns are occasional (or even unique) events in an organization's life.
- Capital campaigns are challenging—perhaps scary—but always exciting.
- Capital campaigns are volunteer intensive.
- Capital campaigns boost an organization to a higher level of effectiveness and significance in the life of the community.

The Power of Capital Campaign Fund Raising

Capital campaigns provide opportunities to expand the "family" and are by nature volunteer intensive. They draw people closer to an organization, extending and strengthening the organizational family. A campaign provides numerous opportunities to involve volunteers in authentic and meaningful short-term tasks. Campaign volunteers help plan the campaign process, oversee the consultant's work, share information about prospective donors, cultivate prospects, and solicit gifts. At every step of a well-executed campaign, volunteers are actively involved and deeply engaged.

Capital campaigns focus on major gift fund raising. Most smaller nonprofit organizations do little to organize a program of major-gift fund raising and rely instead on smaller gifts from a broad base of donors. In fact, many development staff members and executive directors not only have

> *Involved volunteers are often a campaign's best donors. By creating opportunities for involvement throughout the campaign, the organization extends and strengthens its donor base.*

little or no experience in soliciting major gifts, but they have little confidence in their ability to do so. Capital campaigns force organizations to explore the *terra incognita* of major-gifts fund raising.

Capital campaigns strengthen an organization's ongoing fund-raising program. Through the campaign process, both staff and board members gain experience and confidence in their ability to build strong relationships with donors and to solicit major gifts. These new skills and the confidence that comes with them help reshape the organization's ongoing development program.

Capital campaigns increase an organization's visibility, and there are few things quite so effective as a successful capital campaign to boost an organization's stature in its community. Not only does a campaign provide many opportunities for media attention, but word of mouth among donors and volunteers also tends to build confidence in an organization and to spread word of its accomplishments.

A capital campaign is hard work—for staff, for board members, and for other volunteers. Yet, when successful, it enables an organization to expand and strengthen its financial resources, its volunteer base, its family of donors, and its visibility in the community.

Familiar Fund-Raising Principles

Many development staff members who are called on to conduct a capital campaign have never before been involved in such an enterprise. They may have cut their teeth on annual fund giving or special events and so may feel out of their depth when faced with a capital campaign. However, the lessons of annual fund giving and special events are excellent preparation for a capital campaign. Capital-campaign fund raising provides the opportunity to apply many of the principles of other forms of fund raising in a way that can yield big results. The following three principles are fundamental to the success of any fund-raising activity.

Fund-Raising Principle #1: People Give to Make Their World Better

Every year most development directors struggle to frame their annual giving letter around a specific and compelling need. Year after year they are reminded that the more compelling the reason to give and the more effectively they can show prospective donors how their gifts can make a real difference, the better the response. This is because people don't make gifts in order to fund organizational needs. Rather, they give money to make a difference in their world—to help other people, to save the whales, to support children in after-school programs, to teach illiterate adults to read, to feed and clothe those who have been stricken by disaster, or to subsidize the cost of shelter for the homeless. In short, they use their gifts to help address particular problems in their community or in society at large that they find important.

Fund-Raising Principle #2: People Give to People

In addition to the desire to make a difference in the world, an individual's decision to support an organization depends on a complex set of personal relationships. Most development professionals have heard the axiom that people give to people. Special events coordinators rely on this principle by enlisting committee members to call on their friends to send gifts, contribute goods, and attend the event. If the events committee members don't reach out to friends and colleagues, a development director may well experience the frustration and the heartbreak of an event to which only a few people come.

People are motivated to give for many reasons, but one of the most powerful motivators is the personal relationship between donor and solicitor. Some people give to a cause to honor and support the person who has asked for the gift. Some gifts are made in payment for an obligation to an individual in the organization. Still others give because they trust the judgment and recommendations of their friends who are involved in the organization.

Even when a contribution is made without a personal solicitation, some donors will give simply because they know and believe in the people who serve on that organization's board. At a time when many no longer trust large institutions that for so long were regarded as pillars of dependability, people are increasingly giving to organizations that involve people whom they know.

The larger the gift, the more important are the strong personal relationships among the donor, the organization's leadership, and the gift solicitors. The power of personal relationships is an important concept in all areas of fund raising—it's just more important in the context of a capital campaign.

Fund-Raising Principle #3: The More Involved the Donors, the Larger Their Gifts

People give generously to organizations they care about, and their level of caring increases with their level of involvement. As that involvement grows, the history, activities, and mission of the organization claim a place of genuine meaning and importance in that individual's life.

> *The power of personal relationships is an important concept in all areas of fund raising—it's just more important in the context of a capital campaign.*

A campaign's success depends on how well it is able to build relationships with people and involve them in the organization. Throughout the planning and implementation of the campaign, the development staff will use every possible opportunity to build a team of volunteers who accept the campaign and the project it will fund as their own. Volunteers may already be involved with the organization in identifying, cultivating, and soliciting prospects for the annual fund-raising program. For a capital campaign, volunteers may help plan the campaign, screen prospects, host receptions, give presentations about the organization's work, solicit gifts, plan campaign events, and recognize other donors.

Myriad opportunities for involving volunteers in an organization emerge during the project planning that occurs prior to the campaign or during its early phases. By opening the planning efforts to key volunteers in the community, an organization builds ties that will prove invaluable during the campaign itself and lead to gifts far larger than those given by the same donors at an earlier time.

Fund-Raising Practices

Not only do the same simple principles underlie all types of fund raising, but the basic processes of fund raising also remain unchanged. Every effective development director is always working on prospect identification, research, cultivation, solicitation, and recognition.

Prospect Identification

Fund raising begins with the process of identifying people who might become donors to an organization. One accomplishes this task by looking first at those who are closest to the organization and then gradually extending the search out into the community. Prospects worth learning more about will have an interest in the organization's work. They may have had an experience or found themselves in a situation that creates a natural interest in the organization's mission. They may have a general interest in the field. They may have a history of giving to similar organizations. And, although it is sometimes hard to know, they may have the financial ability to make a significant gift. Organizations that have never developed a major gifts program are often surprised to find that many major gift prospects already have a history of giving smaller gifts to the organization but have just never been asked for a large gift.

Research

Research is the method by which one discovers whether hunches about prospects are accurate. The more an organization can learn about its donors, the more it will know about how their interests might overlap with the organization's mission and programs. And the more donor information that is assembled in the files and put to use in soliciting gifts, the stronger the fund-raising programs will become.

Cultivation

Cultivation is the process by which organizations involve donors in their mission and institutional life. New prospects are introduced to an organization and are gradually turned into long-time friends. Cultivation activities include acts as simple as inviting a prospect to a reception, as far-reaching as asking someone to serve on the board, or as direct as asking someone for a gift. Every contact that an organization has with the donor further cements and strengthens the relationship.

Asking for and receiving a gift from a donor in no way signifies the end of the process of cultivation. Solicitation is simply a different level of cultivation in the ongoing process of strengthening an organization's relationship with its donors. By making a gift, the donor reinforces a belief in an organization's mission, taking that interest a step further—from interest to investment. And each gift the donor makes sets the stage for a further level of involvement.

Solicitation

There are only a few ways to ask people for money. One can be asked in person, on paper, over the telephone or other electronic media, or by a combination of these methods. Well, perhaps there are other methods, such as billboards, megaphones, and skywriting, but we shall confine ourselves to the less esoteric modes. Although the solicitation field is populated by anxiety-ridden staff members and volunteers, the reality of soliciting gifts is no more complicated than an honest request of any sort—honestly asked and honestly responded to. We ask people to give advice, to serve on committees, to help clean up, to work the ticket desk, to join us for dinner—and they either agree or they decline, depending on their desires, priorities, schedules, energy level, or other circumstances. In principle, asking people for money is no more and no less. The only real difference is that discussion of personal finances is generally a taboo subject in our culture. There are only two ultimate answers—yes and no. And no matter which answer is given, the solicitation process, if done honestly and with sensitivity, builds the relationship between an organization and a donor.

Recognition

Last, but certainly not least, we recognize donors. We send them thank-you notes, we list their names in public places, we ask their advice because of their importance, and we find ways to let them know that because they are donors, they are members of our organization's family. The simple act of recognizing donors' importance to an organization and appreciating the value that they bring to its work continues the cultivation process.

These basic, familiar principles and practices of fund raising are precisely those that are applied to capital campaigns. So, for those who have been in the development field for a while, it is likely that an understanding of these principles and a reliance on well-developed instincts are just what are needed to conduct a successful campaign.

Special Characteristics of Capital Campaigns

While fund-raising techniques on the whole do not vary across the different areas of the fund-raising business, certain elements are unique to capital campaigns.

Campaign Goals Are Bigger

Those development directors who have been running annual fund programs and haven't yet done any major-gifts fund raising will have to adjust the way they think about money. Whether a capital campaign's goal is $500,000 or $5 million, in general the numbers will be much larger than those raised during the annual giving program. It might shock both a staff and a board who have only dealt with four-figure gifts to have to begin thinking about asking people for five- and maybe even six- or seven-figure gifts.

Although such large numbers are intimidating for an organization that is conducting its first capital campaign, donors' giving histories are often not accurate predictors of their giving capacities. If donors have never been invited to give major gifts to help fund large projects, there is no reason that they should ever have given at higher levels.

Campaigns Fund Special Projects

Unlike annual giving, capital campaigns generally do not fund operations. Campaigns for smaller organizations often raise funds for special, turning-point projects that take the organization to a new level of operation. A hospice might build a new administrative facility with an in-patient unit; a library might go on-line, automating all of its collections and providing access to the information highway for its users; a day-care center might build a new wing for an infant-care program; a private school might build a new gymnasium. Each of these projects represents a new, unique leap in the size and function of the organization. And while leaps can be frightening, they are also exciting opportunities that generate larger gifts.

Campaigns Are Rare Occurrences

Campaigns have become regular occurrences for many large organizations such as hospitals or universities, with

> *Capital campaigns are strategic moments in the evolution of long-term fund-raising programs. The philosophy and values that support a capital campaign should be consistent with the goals and values of the organization.*

the next campaign in the planning stages even before the current one has been completed. It is uncommon for smaller, community-based organizations, however, to conduct capital campaigns more than once in any ten-year period. And because smaller organizations often have a high turnover of staff and board, many development directors, executive directors, and board members have never been involved in a capital campaign before. Capital campaigns of this kind are very special events indeed!

The unique excitement that permeates organizations as they begin to contemplate a capital campaign helps motivate both staff and volunteer leadership to take the necessary preparatory steps. Once the plunge has been taken it's hard to turn back, and the staff and volunteers are drawn almost inexorably into the vortex of the campaign, committing an extraordinary amount of time and energy to make it a success. Throughout the period of intense effort, the certain knowledge that when they declare victory there will not be another campaign around the corner enables them to find the motivation and energy to continue to the end.

Campaigns Usually Result from Long-Range, Strategic Planning

Because most capital campaigns are organized to fund major new initiatives—building projects, automation, endowment development, and so forth—they often emerge out of an extensive organizational planning process. In this process, the organization has paused to review its mission, evaluate its strengths and weaknesses, assess its current resources, and determine where it hopes to go during the next few years. If an organization is "working smart" it will bend over backward to involve key volunteers and those with the ability to give major gifts in the planning process, providing opportunities for these individuals to have a voice in determining the organization's future. Capital campaigns build on the sense of excitement and enthusiasm for the new directions that have been developed through the planning process.

Campaign Anxiety

Those who have never managed a capital campaign before, or perhaps even those who have, are likely to be anxious about an upcoming campaign. After all, the stakes are much higher and the risks are greater. The goals are larger, many people are involved, and the development professional's job will become even more demanding. The campaign may seem like a storm cloud looming over an otherwise peaceful development experience.

Several fears are common among development professionals, directors, and board members as they begin planning a campaign.

Fear of Failure

"I was really worried we wouldn't be able to reach our goal. In fact, I was petrified!"

No matter what size the campaign goal, staff members, who have been responsible for raising only a fraction of that amount in their annual fund program, are likely to be intimidated by such a large goal.

There are ways to protect an organization from aiming too high. A professional feasibility study, the focus of chapter 4, can help an organization evaluate its potential to raise funds for the project it has in mind. Among other things, a well-done feasibility study will assess the organization's readiness and make recommendations about a realistic campaign goal. The recommendations about a campaign goal that are presented in the feasibility study will provide an objective expert opinion on which to base the campaign goal. The consultant's informed opinion will establish a sense of credibility and reality for the goal and will help to allay fears.

Fear of Inadequacy

"I don't really know very much about running a capital campaign. In fact, I don't know a darn thing about it!"

Any successful development director probably already understands enough about development to manage a capital campaign. It is possible to learn campaign basics from a variety of sources—books like this one, colleagues, and consultants. In chapter 2, we look at how a campaign consultant can help guide staff members through the process, how to find a consultant, and how to make the best use of a consultant once one has been engaged.

Every organization makes mistakes as it feels its way through the campaign process. However, by learning about campaigns beforehand, an organization can lessen the severity and impact of those mistakes.

Fear of Making Errors

"I'm terrified that we might make a strategic error that would cost us the loss of a big gift."

The fear of losing a major gift is the fear of every development director, executive director, and solicitor, whether or not they are involved in a campaign. There is always a chance that something may happen to change the donor's mind about making a major gift to an organization. Occasionally that something is controllable, but sometimes it's not. Chapter 5 discusses techniques that

will help fund raisers learn as much as possible about prospects and donors. Research will diminish the chance of strategic errors that stem from not having enough information. Chapter 7 reviews the gift-solicitation process, explaining what motivates a donor to make a gift and the best ways to ask for gifts. In capital campaigns, as in all fund raising, a little preparation goes a long way toward ensuring success!

Fear of Not Having Enough Time and Resources

"How can we—the board, the volunteers, and I—stay focused on the campaign when there is so much else to do?"

Campaigns require time, effort, and a great deal of energy from people already loaded down with multiple, ongoing responsibilities. A development director may well wonder how the added campaign tasks will get done. However, those who have been through campaigns learn that because the stakes are high and the time period limited, campaigns are not so easy to let slide. In fact, once a campaign planning process begins, an organization's other priorities tend to slip onto the back burner. Well-conceived, clear, and thorough campaign plans that have been developed before the campaign gets rolling help everyone stay focused. A good plan improves staff efficiency, reassures volunteers that they are all moving together in an organized way, and enables board members to see how the campaign fits into their other leadership responsibilities.

Fear of Not Having Enough Stamina

"I have a really big job as it is. How can I possibly keep my own energy level and enthusiasm up through the campaign?"

Campaigns take a lot of energy, particularly from the staff. Development staff members must work with the board, volunteers, and other staff members. They must be the cheerleaders, radiating confidence and encouraging everyone else. How can they keep from becoming discouraged and tired during the periods when the campaign lags?

Again and again, campaign directors report that "it's lonely at the top," and loneliness can be distressing. Although this is a very real problem, there are solutions. If campaign directors find ways to take care of themselves from the very beginning of the campaign, they are likely to be more effective throughout. They might identify a support system of people in whom they can confide. A friend, a spouse or partner, perhaps even a neighbor can be available to talk through fears and anxieties and provide needed encouragement. The best supporters are those not related to the organization, and perhaps not even active members of the fund-raising community. They should be neutral people who will listen, keep the

> *In China, the concept of chi, or life force, is fundamental to understanding health and medicine. We might understand capital campaigns better if we thought of them as the process of directing the chi of people to stimulate new levels of accomplishment and generosity. The flow and excitement of this collective chi often takes an organization far beyond what had been considered possible.*

conversations to themselves, and provide emotional support. Chapter 2 looks at how an effective consultant can provide encouragement, and chapter 8 suggests some other ways to connect with colleagues who are in similar situations.

Everyone has fears about campaigns, but campaigns are the most exciting, challenging, and fast-paced type of development work there is. Well-planned and executed campaigns do succeed, and staff members emerge from them with a deeper understanding of their organization, their volunteers, their donors, and themselves—in spite of their fears!

Requirements for a Successful Campaign

Although capital campaigns vary in size, scope, and timing, there are some elements that characterize every successful campaign. Some of these elements should be in place prior to the start of the campaign, and some emerge through the campaign process. For a campaign to maximize its chances of success, fifteen elements must be in place.

Compelling Needs and a Credible Plan

Every successful campaign is driven by a compelling need in society or the community and an organization's plan to meet those needs. Those needs are identified through an organizational planning process that gives the leadership focus and direction. The needs must reflect those of the community, not those of the organization, although the project may also serve organizational needs. To convince donors to help meet those needs, this plan must be realistic for both the organization and the community.

A plan at its most basic level requires solid, realistic answers to the following questions:

- **What** is the community need that the organization is seeking to fill through this project?
- **Why** has the organization elected to undertake this project?
- **How** does the organization plan to carry out the project?

- **Who** is going to make it happen?
- **When** will it happen?

The answers to these questions will form the nucleus of the *case for support*, which is discussed in chapter 3.

A Strong Case for Support

The organization must be able to write a case for support that describes the compelling needs and the plan for the project in a way that is concise, clear, and easy to read. An effective case for support focuses on the needs of the community rather than on the needs of the organization.

A Realistic Goal

Successful campaigns have goals that make sense—both for the organization and for the community. There are dreamers in every organization who build castles in the air as they plan how to spend the vast sums of money that donors will give, but these hyper-optimists forget that both organizations and communities have tolerances and patterns of giving that determine reasonable goals. A pie-in-the-sky goal (fresh from the ovens of that castle in the air, no doubt) may sound impressive, but it will hurt the organization's credibility in the end if the goal is not reached. If an organization sets a goal that is too low, however, it artificially limits the amount of money that might be raised through a campaign. The right goal stretches an organization beyond what is easily accomplished, yet it is a goal that is achievable!

Previous Fund-Raising Success

Although in special circumstances it is possible for a new organization to run a successful startup campaign, most campaigns rely on prior donor relationships as the springboard for giving. Campaigns depend on well-developed annual giving programs to help identify campaign prospects and volunteers.

A Sufficient Number of Qualified Prospects

Because contributions to campaigns fit into predictable patterns, it is possible to estimate how many gifts it will take to reach a certain goal. Applying the generally accepted estimate that the campaign will get one gift for every four donor prospects, it is possible to estimate the number of prospects needed for a successful campaign. Not everyone who lives in the community is a qualified prospect. Qualified prospects are those who either are already donors to the organization, have a reason to give to the organization (perhaps they have benefited from its services), or are part of the community leadership base that is known for giving to campaigns of similar organizations. For a campaign to be successful, an organization will need to identify enough such people so that it can see the potential of raising its funds from that constituency.

A generally accepted campaign rule states that the top ten prospects will produce eighty to ninety percent of the gifts, with the remainder coming from a considerably larger group of donors of relatively small gifts. This rule illustrates the supreme importance of the top donors to the success of the campaign.

Strong Staff Support and Resources

Successful campaigns depend on strong staff leadership to organize and manage every aspect of the campaign. This role might be played by the executive director, the development director, or someone brought in specifically for the campaign, but it is a role that must be filled if a campaign is to flourish. A campaign director will need an adequate budget for promotional material, cultivation activities, and campaign events. Organizations new to the campaign scene must take to heart the advice, "Spend money to make money."

Full and Early Commitment by the Board

A committed board is critical to a campaign's success. Although many small organizations do not have fundraising boards, even these "working" boards must fully support the campaign financially to the extent of their abilities. For some boards, collective giving of $20,000 might be far more impressive than a $1 million commitment from another board. Beyond the dollar value, there is a symbolic value in board gifts as well. Other donors look to see whether the board wholeheartedly supports the campaign.

Effective Volunteer Leadership

Campaigns are made or broken by the quality of their volunteer leadership. The configuration of this leadership comes in many forms. Some campaigns have one chair and several division heads. Others have honorary co-chairs and managing co-chairs as well as a campaign steering committee. Whatever the design, at least some of the volunteers in leadership positions must have stature in the community, the ability to make a lead gift, and a willingness to follow through on their jobs.

Clear Campaign Organization

Because capital campaigns rely on a great many volunteers to solicit the most important gifts, clear and effective organization is of primary importance. Volunteers have only limited tolerance for ineptitude. They operate at their best when they know what they are supposed to do, how to do it, how their work fits into the larger project, when their work will begin, and when it will end. Good campaign planners take great pains to provide such organization and structure for their volunteers.

Clear Campaign Policies

Before venturing very far into planning a capital campaign, a great many policy questions for guiding key areas of the campaign must be answered. Questions such as what will count toward the campaign goal, what kinds of gifts will be accepted, how will gifts that are not immediate cash or pledges be valued, what sorts of naming opportunities will be available to donors, and a whole host of other questions must be answered before an organization begins soliciting gifts.

A Realistic Timetable

There are few things more calming than knowing that a big job has a beginning, a middle, and finally an end. Both staff and volunteers function more effectively if they know how long their efforts will be needed on the campaign. Realistic campaign timetables provide impetus for getting the job done. They help in planning for what's ahead, and they reassure staff and volunteers that the campaign will proceed according to schedule. It is a great comfort for all participants in the campaign to be able to envision a time for a jubilant celebration of the campaign's successful completion.

Identification and Early Solicitation of Major Gift Prospects

The success of most campaigns is determined by the top ten gifts. And successful campaigns keep their focus on those gifts from the beginning. Not only are these top ten donors extremely important because of the gifts they can make but also because they are usually the people who have the clout, commitment, and ability to solicit the next fifty gifts. By identifying the top ten donors early and involving them in the key decisions that will shape the project and the campaign, one builds ownership in the campaign and sets the stage for success.

Written Proposals Suggesting Specific Requests

Campaigns rely on well-written proposals that invite people to consider making gifts of specific amounts. Because in capital campaigns people are always being invited to make gifts that are significantly larger than their usual donations, it is helpful to the donor when the solicitor suggests a specific amount or range. This must be accomplished in a nonpressuring way, but it must be done if the campaign is to succeed. Written proposals are the mechanisms by which organizations present a formal request for a gift. Leadership gift proposals are always followed up by one or more personal visits by trained volunteer solicitors.

Personal Solicitations by Trained Volunteers

Personal solicitations are the most effective way to raise money. In the best of all campaign worlds, every donor would be visited by precisely the right person asking for precisely the right amount of support for something the donor is vitally interested in. In the real world most of us live in, this can only happen some of the time. Often our knowledge of the donor is incomplete, or the right person is unavailable or cannot be identified. Nonetheless, in campaign times, an organization must do its very best to see every donor as an important individual and to have committed volunteers take the time and energy to visit them personally to ask for their gift.

A "Top-Down, Inside-Out" Order of Solicitation

Campaigns are like trains. When they begin, they slowly chug out of the station using lots of energy and creating much smoke. The people who have the most stamina and the strongest interest in moving the campaign train are the insiders—board members, committed volunteers, founders, and staff. The people who can help build a head of steam the fastest to get to the top of the first hill before energy flags are the lead donors. Successful campaigns use their insiders and lead donors to get the train out of the station and up that hill. Once the going gets easier, when success seems within reach, those who are less committed to the organization are often willing to jump aboard to help the train into the next station.

Proceeding with the solicitation from the inside-out and the top-down—beginning with those closest to the organization and those who have the ability to make the largest gifts—allows the organization to engage the people who are closest in the early stages of the campaign. These insiders and leaders are the people who can move the campaign forward. Their early commitment and involvement is critical to the campaign's success. If they are unwilling to become involved, the unspoken message they send speaks louder than anything else.

Exhibit 1–1 will help an organization assess its readiness for a campaign. The more responses of "no," the more cautious an organization should be about moving ahead with a campaign. In assessing its readiness, an organization should remember that it is possible to strengthen itself over time, and, in so doing, the number of affirmative answers will increase.

Patterns of Giving

Campaign after campaign reveals patterns of giving that are remarkably consistent and from which we

---

Exhibit 1–1 Are You Ready for a Capital Campaign?

The Basics

	Yes	No
❏ Does your organization have its 501(c)3 status?	___	___
❏ Is your organization registered with the bureau of charitable organizations (if necessary) in your state?	___	___
❏ Do you have a full and committed board?	___	___
❏ Is your board actively involved in setting policy in your organization and working to implement it?	___	___
❏ Do the majority of your board members make regular financial contributions to your organization?	___	___
❏ Is your organization well-regarded in the community?	___	___
❏ Is your organization widely recognized in the community?	___	___

Capital Project

❏ Have you decided what special project(s) you want the campaign to fund?	___	___
❏ Do you have a reasonable estimate of the project's budget and timetable?	___	___
❏ Does the campaign project move the organization to a new level?	___	___
❏ Does your project fit into a recent long-range plan?	___	___
❏ Has the long-range plan been accepted by the board?	___	___
❏ Is the organization's leadership excited about the project?	___	___
❏ Will the project make a difference in your community?	___	___

Fund Raising

❏ Does your organization have a history of reaching its fund-raising goals?	___	___
❏ Do you have accurate donor records from the past 5 years?	___	___
❏ Are your donor records computerized?	___	___
❏ Are you willing to work hard and stay the course?	___	___

can learn important principles of capital-campaign fund raising.

The 90/10 Rule

Ninety percent of the total raised in the campaign will come from ten percent of the campaign's donors. It seems hard to believe that so few people could contribute so much, but time and again this rule has been proven true. Most campaigns, no matter what their size, raise most of their money from only a few donors.

Just Ten Donors

The just ten rule is closely tied to the 90/10 rule. The campaign's success will depend on its top ten donors, no matter how large or small the campaign goal. The lead gift should constitute at least 10 to 15 percent of the campaign goal—although in some cases the lead gift may be much higher. These top ten gifts are often referred to as "strategic" or "leadership" gifts. They set the pace for the campaign and act as magnets for other donors. Together, the top ten leadership gifts, given early in the campaign, create a sense of optimism and a belief that the campaign will be successful. And of course, people are much more likely to become part of a campaign when they believe that it will succeed.

The Secret of the Pyramid

Because people have different financial capacities and giving patterns, the gifts that make up a campaign range from large to small. Although it is tempting to think about raising $500,000, for example, from 500 donors who give $1,000 apiece, it is also unrealistic. That's not how actual campaign gifts come in.

The pattern of giving in virtually all capital campaigns looks like a pyramid. At the very top are the few leadership donors whose major gifts secure the success of the campaign. In the middle is a larger number of donors, many of whom are individuals, businesses, or foundations, who have given at relatively low levels over the years but who have stretched their giving budgets for the campaign. Many people in this middle category, even though they are not lead gift donors, are opinion setters in the community, and their generous giving is extremely important. At the base of the pyramid is the largest number of donors. This group of donors is the bread and butter of the organization—the many people who believe in the organization but do not have the resources or inclination to make a large gift. For a person in this category, his or her gift of $300 may be every bit as meaningful as the lead gift of $50,000 is to its donor.

The width and height of the giving pyramid varies from organization to organization in patterns that are somewhat predictable. A young institution with a small number of donors must rely more heavily on leadership gifts—a tall pyramid with a narrow base. Mature institutions with many donors and constituents are likely to have a broader-based pyramid.

Giving patterns are also determined by the organization's culture, history, and constituency. Some institutions are afraid to solicit leadership gifts, either because they are afraid of the power that large donors wield or because they lack the self-confidence, vision, and training needed to think big. Other organizations have relied on a small number of leadership gifts to support many aspects of their programs. Some organizations, like private schools, have clearly defined constituencies, resulting in a narrow base, while others, like community libraries, have a broad-based constituency.

Each organization has its own giving pyramid (Figure 1–1). Clear thinking about the culture, donor base, and giving histories of an organization will help predict the pattern that a campaign's gifts are likely to form. These patterns of giving, often referred to as the table of gifts or the giving pyramid, projected early in the campaign, are tools that help clarify and plan the campaign.

Sometimes, because they are unable to believe that leadership gifts of the size needed for a campaign are available for their organization, campaign leaders believe that they will be able to conduct a flat-topped campaign. They are convinced that their campaign will follow all the patterns of every other campaign except that it will not have leadership gifts. They believe that their campaign will look like a truncated pyramid. Experi-

Number of Gifts

Campaign pattern for young organizations or organizations with limited constituencies

Campaign pattern for organizations that are more mature and have a moderate reach in the community

Campaign pattern for well-established organizations that have a broad appeal in their community

Figure 1–1 Giving Pyramids

ence has shown, however, that virtually all campaigns are pyramidal in shape and that lopping the top off the pyramid simply results in lowering the amount of money raised, as shown in Figure 1–2.

Managing Campaign Announcements

Campaign success seems likely before the public kickoff. Because of the strategic power of the top ten gifts, these leadership gifts are solicited before the campaign is made public. In fact, the process of identifying, cultivating, and soliciting major gift prospects constitutes the largest and most important part of any campaign. It is a quiet process, done before hosting a kickoff party and printing and mailing campaign brochures. It is also the process that determines the outcome of the campaign. During this period, commonly referred to as the "quiet phase" of the campaign, major donor prospects develop a sense of ownership of the project and the campaign and are solicited for their gifts.

Announce the campaign kickoff only after half the money has been committed. Although it is tempting to share an organization's needs with the world from the beginning in the hopes that new donors will respond generously, successful campaigns tightly control the flow of information. Successful campaign planning requires that an organization wait before publicly announcing the campaign and its goal until success seems likely. A public kickoff event, staged at just the right time, celebrates the generosity and commitment of a campaign's leaders and insiders, prepares other donors to be solic-

ited, and gives the solicitors courage and confidence to complete the campaign.

Estimating Campaign Costs

Capital campaigns are efficient ways to raise money. While direct-mail fund raising or special events can have costs that approach or even exceed half of their total revenue, the cost of running a capital campaign to raise $750,000 to $3 million need not exceed 10 percent of the campaign goal. Because many campaign costs are fixed no matter what the size of the campaign, that per-

Jumping the Gun

We planned to build a new children's museum. We knew that we needed to get the entire community working together, both as donors and as construction volunteers, so once we had our building plans, we staged a kickoff event. In retrospect, it was a great way to build community enthusiasm for the building part of the project but a lousy strategy for fund raising. Because we hadn't raised any of the money yet, people just didn't believe we would be able to do so. That sort of took the wind out of our sails and we had to take a step back to solicit leadership gifts before we could move ahead.

—Museum Executive Director

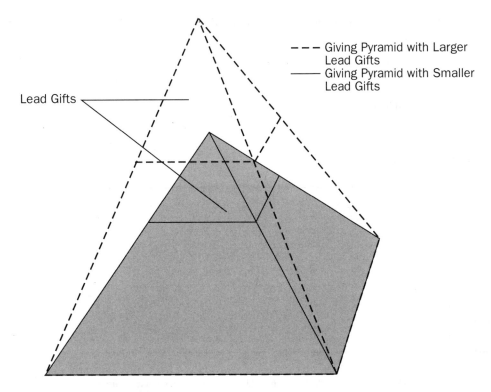

- - - Giving Pyramid with Larger Lead Gifts
— Giving Pyramid with Smaller Lead Gifts

Figure 1–2 Expanding Giving Pyramids

centage is likely to be larger for smaller campaigns and smaller for larger campaigns. A campaign to raise $500,000 might cost 12 or even 13 percent, but a campaign to raise $5,000,000 should run no more than 5 percent of the total.

Campaign expenses are likely to break down as follows:

- 55% Personnel costs: consultants, campaign director, and support staff
- 15% Office expenses: supplies (including stationery, etc.), telephone, duplication, postage, travel and entertainment for donor cultivation, committee expenses
- 25% Public relations and materials: design and printing for brochures, direct-mail pieces, other presentation materials, and events
- 5% Contingencies: other miscellaneous expenses that are peculiar to your organization or community

These figures generally do not include the cost of a feasibility study that should be conducted prior to the campaign. See Exhibit 1–2 for sample forms for estimating a campaign budget.

The Phases of a Campaign

Most community-based campaigns can be conducted in fifteen to eighteen months from assembling the campaign planning committee to celebrating the campaign's success. This estimate does not include the many months of planning and preparation, nor does it include the feasibility study period. In fact, as discussed in chapter 4, one of the valuable elements of a feasibility study is a preliminary campaign timetable that will help establish calendar guidelines.

It is useful to think of the campaign's length in terms of its different parts. Most successful campaigns proceed in six distinct phases (see also Exhibit 1–3):

1. precampaign preparation
2. campaign planning
3. leadership-gift solicitation
4. advance-gift solicitation
5. general solicitation
6. cleanup and celebration

Precampaign Preparation

Before soliciting any gifts, an organization must spend ample time preparing for the campaign—building a strong and involved board, strengthening the development program, increasing the agency's visibility and reputation, conducting the strategic-planning process, and planning the project. The staff and

> *Capital campaigns are among the most cost-effective ways to raise money.*

Exhibit 1–2 Estimating Your Campaign Budget Using Standard Percentages

Campaign Size	Approximate Cost
Under $1 million	10%–12%
$1 million–$2 million	8%–10%
Over $2 million	5%–8%

_____ × _____ = $ _____
(Campaign Goal)   (% Cost)   (Estimated Campaign Cost)

Campaign Costs Broken Down by Expense Type

Personnel $_____
(campaign cost × 55%)
Office Expenses $_____
(campaign cost × 15%)
Materials and Events $_____
(campaign cost × 25%)
Contingencies $_____
(campaign cost × 5%)

Estimating Your Campaign Budget Using Itemized Expense Projections

Expense Type	Estimated from Percentages	Projected Itemized Expenses
Personnel		
Consultant		$_____
Campaign director		_____
Clerical support		_____
Benefits		_____
Personnel Expenses	$_____	$_____
Office Expenses		
Telephone		$_____
Computer hardware/software		_____
Copy, fax, etc.		_____
Postage		_____
Committee expenses		_____
Office Expenses	$_____	$_____
Materials and Events		
Letterhead/envelopes, etc.		$_____
Campaign brochure		_____
Presentation materials		_____
Direct-mail printing		_____
Cultivation meetings		_____
Campaign kickoff		_____
Celebration		_____
Materials and Events Expense	$_____	$_____
Campaign Expense	$_____	$_____
Contingencies (5%)	$_____	$_____
Total Campaign Expenses (Est. & Proj.)*	$_____	$_____

*These figures, arrived at in two different ways, will provide a cost range to help guide the budgeting process for campaign expenses. The expenses above do not include the cost of the feasibility study.

Exhibit 1–3 Phases of a Capital Campaign

Preparation	Planning	Leadership Gift Phase	Advance Gift Phase	General Phase	Clean Up Celebration
◆ Clarify mission and vision ◆ Define need for campaign ◆ Strengthen board ◆ Cultivate donors and volunteers ◆ Strengthen staff ◆ Select consultant ◆ Develop prospect lists	◆ Establish "kitchen cabinet" ◆ Conduct feasibility study ◆ Assemble campaign steering committee ◆ Develop case for support ◆ Outline campaign timetable ◆ Establish campaign policies ◆ Determine campaign goal ◆ Identify campaign leadership ◆ Review table of gifts ◆ Write proposal copy ◆ Establish campaign subcommittees ◆ Identify and enlist volunteers for soliciting lead gifts	◆ Review prospect list for leadership gifts ◆ Evaluate prospects ◆ Develop solicitation strategy for each gift ◆ Prepare proposals ◆ Train volunteers ◆ Solicit gifts ◆ Identify and enlist volunteers for soliciting family gifts	◆ Review prospect list for "family" gifts ◆ Evaluate prospects ◆ Develop solicitation strategy for each category of prospects ◆ Train volunteers ◆ Prepare proposals ◆ Solicit gifts ◆ Identify and enlist volunteers for general phase	◆ Review prospect list for general phase ◆ Prepare proposals ◆ Train volunteers ◆ Campaign kickoff ◆ Solicit gifts ◆ Phonathon ◆ Direct-mail campaign	◆ Solicitation follow-up ◆ Reporting to campaign volunteers ◆ Volunteer acknowledgment ◆ Extra thanks to donors ◆ Reinforce relationship with volunteers and donors

Optional Celebrations
Campaign kickoff
Goal-reaching party
Groundbreaking
Open house

Subcommittees

Building
Public Relations
Finance
Prospect Cultivation
Hospitality/Events

board may spend one, two, or even three years preparing an organization for the work ahead.

Campaign Planning

Once the preparations have been completed, the campaign planning begins. During this period, many organizations engage a consultant to conduct a feasibility study and assemble the campaign-planning committee. With the guidance and support of an experienced consultant and the campaign-planning committee, the staff will prepare the case for support, outline a preliminary campaign timetable, establish campaign policies, determine a preliminary dollar goal, identify campaign leadership, prepare a table of gifts showing the size and number of gifts needed to succeed, and design the campaign structure. Campaign planning is likely to take three to six months, depending on its success in recruiting campaign leadership and the campaign planning committee. This phase should result in a written document outlining the plan for the campaign. This document, though subject to revision as needed, will guide the staff and volunteers through the campaign.

Leadership Gift Solicitation

Once the campaign has been planned, the solicitation process begins. The first to be solicited are donors who have the potential to make the largest campaign gifts. These solicitations are usually planned individually to suit the situation, character, and timetable of each donor. Although there may be only 30 or 40 solicitations in this process, a campaign's fate rests on their success. Flexibility, patience, and persistence are the key words for this phase of a campaign. Every solicitation must bend to accommodate the timetables and realities of the lead donors. To ensure the needed flexibility, these solicitations are made prior to the public announcement of the campaign.

Advance Gift Solicitation

The advance-gift phase of a campaign encompasses the period during which both leadership gifts and "family gifts" are solicited. During this quiet period those people with the greatest giving potential and those closest to the organization are solicited. These will include board members, campaign leaders, campaign committee members, and active volunteers.

Together, the leadership and advance solicitations must raise 50 to 60 percent of the campaign goal so that when the campaign is announced publicly, the commitment of lead donors, the board, and the other people who are close to the organization will provide a strong example of generosity and commitment to the rest of the community.

Although in the best of all worlds, the advance-gift phase may be completed in two or three months, the length of these critical early solicitation periods is actually determined by the dollar amount raised rather than by a calendar date. For example, an organization might solicit leadership gifts for a campaign in June, hoping to be ready for a September kickoff, but then in August it may realize that several major gifts will not be confirmed until late October. Without these gifts, the campaign will have raised less than one quarter of its goal. A wise campaign director will postpone the kickoff until the next spring, when it is quite certain to have raised more than half the goal.

General Solicitation

Once one-half to two-thirds of the goal has been raised, the campaign is ready to enter the general solicitation phase. In many community-based campaigns, the public part of the solicitation process might be as short as six weeks or as lengthy as twelve months. The length of this phase depends on the campaign's design, and the design will depend on the staff and volunteer resources. Organizations with staff members who work full time on the campaign and with a sufficient number of volunteers willing to solicit donors will be able to organize and manage a broad solicitation process in a short time period. Those who must rely on part-time campaign development staff and a limited number of deeply committed campaign volunteers must extend the solicitation period, spreading the solicitation of various constituencies over a period of months.

When the personal solicitation has been completed, most campaigns finish the solicitation process with a combination of telephone and direct-mail solicitations. These generally occur in the final months of the general solicitation phase.

Follow-up

Most campaign veterans know that campaigns begin with a big bang and end with an entropic fizzle. They start in a flurry of well-organized energy and end in a mass of details that often takes several months of dedicated staff time to clean up. Often, long after the campaign has reached its goal, gifts still dribble in—sometimes in surprisingly large numbers.

A celebration during the cleanup period will bring the campaign to a public close. Long after the celebration, however, the staff is likely still to be tying up loose ends, thanking people, and making sure that the pledge payment system is functioning well. Indeed, since every pledge reminder is an excellent opportunity to communicate with donors, the campaign cleanup tasks will dovetail nicely with the ongoing development program.

Although campaign tasks fall into a very particular order that is critical to the campaign's success, there is great latitude as to the duration of each campaign phase. This permits a campaign design that fits the unique reality of a particular organization and its community of donors.

Timing Considerations

Campaign timetables can often be confusing. Because a campaign's phases will not run at the same time or for the same duration as either the pledge period or the period during which commitments made toward the campaign will count, it is important to clarify the meaning of a notion like that of the "three-year campaign."

Pledge Period

Most campaigns encourage donors to make financial commitments to be paid over a period of years. The pledge period is determined during the campaign planning process and is included in the written plan for the campaign. Although pledge periods for larger campaigns have been known to be as long as seven years, most campaigns today specify a three-year pledge period in their campaign materials but allow large gifts to be pledged over as many as five years.

Gift Counting Period

Campaign plans often specify the period during which gifts made to the organization will count toward a campaign. Some campaigns choose to count gifts that were received prior to the beginning of the solicitation period or even before the work of the campaign planning committee began. Prior to the campaign, an organization might, for example, receive a large, unsolicited challenge gift that provides the impetus for the campaign. The campaign plan will specify that this gift, and perhaps others received prior to the campaign itself, may be counted toward the goal. The period of time over which gifts count toward the campaign goal will make an important difference in how much money is raised and how high the goal is set.

Solicitation Period

The solicitation period also has a timetable of its own that is distinct from the gift-counting period and the pledge period. In most community-based campaigns gifts are solicited over six to twelve months.

So, perhaps, "How long will the campaign take?" isn't the right question. Instead, what will have to be determined are the answers to a host of questions that will define the campaign that works best for a specific organization.

- How long will it take us to become strong enough to undertake a campaign?
- How long do we need for campaign planning?
- How long do we anticipate for each phase of the campaign itself?
- How long will the leadership and advanced gift solicitation process take?
- When do we think we will be able to announce the public phase of the campaign?
- How long a pledge period will we allow?
- When will we begin counting gifts toward the goal?
- How much can our campaign staff handle at one time and what consequences will this have on the timing of the general phase of our campaign?
- When do we think we will be able to announce our success?
- Have we planned enough staff time for cleanup and follow-up throughout the pledge period?

The Campaign Plan

Just as one wouldn't take a road trip into unfamiliar territory without a map, an organization shouldn't begin a campaign without a plan. During the course of the campaign, the plan will be subject to numerous revisions, but in the beginning, it is important to have a basic idea of where the campaign is going and how it is going to get there. Certain elements should be part of the very first campaign plan. The consultant and the campaign planning committee will help expand and flesh the plan out, but an outline of the following areas will get the campaign planning process off to a good start:

> *Good planning lessens the risk inherent in capital campaigns.*

- preliminary campaign goal
- preliminary gift table
- prospect list and suggested gift amounts
- list of campaign committees and prospective campaign members
- preliminary campaign timetable
- preliminary campaign budget

A Time for Heroes

Capital campaigns are exercises in courage, faith, planning, and hard work. They provide opportunities to unite the energies and talents of a large group of people around the possibility of moving an organization forward so that it can accomplish more in the community. When they are well designed and executed, capital campaigns create heroes. The many individuals who have helped create that success—staff members, board members, donors, volunteers—share a part in the campaign's success. These people are amply rewarded by the knowledge that they have helped a worthy organization reach a new level of service.

In an era when people spend an ever greater percentage of their time in passive activities, and when many neighborhoods are no longer unifying forces in our society, capital campaigns help us rekindle the excitement and rewards that come from individual responsibility, effective collaboration, and shared goals.

Throughout this chapter are strewn what may be an intimidating collection of rules, guidelines, and requirements. Underlying all of this information, however, is the authors' strong belief that a relatively few people, if committed, astute, and hardworking, can make a major difference in the organizations that they serve and thereby create stronger communities.

Perceiving the world from a wonderfully broad perspective, the noted anthropologist Margaret Mead described this phenomenon in a way that the authors believe might serve as guidance and inspiration for anyone who is beginning the process of planning a capital campaign.

> Never doubt that a small group of thoughtful, committed citizens can change the world. Indeed, it's the only thing that ever has. (Mead, 1992)

Reference

Mead, Margaret. 1992. *The last word: A treasury of women's quotes.* Edited by Carolyn Warner. Englewood Cliffs, NJ: Prentice Hall.

Chapter 2
Capital Campaign Consultants

Chapter Outline

What Is a Campaign Consultant?

As an organization considers embarking on a capital campaign, it must evaluate whether to hire a consultant. A capital campaign consultant can bring to the campaign knowledge and expertise that can benefit and strengthen the organization's entire development program, yet the consultant's services can be a "big ticket" item in the campaign budget. Thus, to decide whether hiring a consultant is a wise investment, it is necessary to consider carefully the development department's current capabilities and how they can be enhanced by a consultant's services, as well as the size and complexity of the campaign. Whether or not a consultant is eventually engaged, it is worthwhile to interview a few, because, in the interview process, the consultants can provide useful information about running a capital campaign, the organization's readiness to undertake such a campaign, and indeed whether or not a consultant is necessary to the campaign's success.

This chapter looks at what a campaign consultant can and cannot bring to an organization and how to find, interview, and hire a consultant. It also considers instances where a consultant may not be the wisest use of the organization's resources and some other situations where a consultant might profitably be hired to assist only with specific tasks.

What Does a Campaign Consultant Do?

Consultants Bring Experience to the Campaign

A campaign consultant has experience designing and overseeing campaigns in a variety of organizational settings. While the campaign consulting business used to be dominated by large consulting firms, in recent years, small firms and individual practitioners have garnered a significant share of the market. A consultant may work alone, with a small number of associates, or in a large consulting firm. More important to the organization, however, is the consultant's combination of skills, style, areas of expertise, and personality traits. Whether associated with a large or small practice, a good consultant offers a depth and breadth of experience gained from many campaigns, an outside perspective from which to view problems, techni-

---

Practicing the Art of Diplomacy

We have a long-standing, well-respected board member—I'll call her Mary—who carries a lot of weight on the board. She was convinced that the bulk of the campaign money should be raised through special events—auctions, charity balls, and so forth. I knew that wasn't the way to go. It would be fine to incorporate a special event into the campaign, but to succeed, we would have to rely on gifts from individuals. Thank goodness for our consultant. She helped put Mary's ideas in a larger context, getting her to focus on the campaign kickoff while designing a larger campaign around it. In the end, Mary felt great about her role, but she might have caused some big problems had she gotten other board members to support her original idea. Fortunately, we had the consultant, who was able to redirect her energy. No one on our staff could have done that.

—Development Director

---

cal know-how, and the ability to impose a discipline from without that will help shape the campaign and keep it from wandering from its goals. Although it may be possible, and in some cases necessary, to conduct a campaign without a consultant, doing so will, in general, make the task much more difficult.

The best consultants are good teachers. They instruct the organization's fund-raising director and staff in how to apply their prior development knowledge to the campaign process. They help break down the campaign into manageable tasks. When the relationship works well, the consultant acts as a teammate who helps structure and design a campaign that makes sense for the organization. The consultant remains flexible throughout the campaign, helping the staff adjust the campaign's design as circumstances change, thus maximizing the chances for success. The consultant can impart confidence, stand firm in the face of conflicting opinions, and articulate credible reasons for designing and running a campaign in a particular way.

Capital campaign fund raising is not only a proven method of raising funds, but it is also a method that involves a very significant investment of time and energy. Therefore, it is important to involve someone on the team who has campaign experience and who knows how to apply that experience to the organization's particular situation. For example, an experienced consultant is keenly aware of the long-term consequences of decisions made early in the campaign. The campaign's direction is shaped by such early decisions—whom to involve and how to involve them, or when to act and when to hold back. Astute campaign decisions that are made early have far-reaching consequences and are more effective than massive last-minute corrective actions.

Experience also makes a difference when one of those niggling little questions comes up about campaign procedure, or protocol, or policy that just hasn't been considered before and that is seldom addressed in books or workshops. A consultant is likely to know the solution to a problem that might otherwise take hours for the staff to solve. And an experienced consultant is likely to be able to foresee long-term consequences of what may seem like inconsequential decisions.

Consultants Put Problems in Perspective

"Our campaign is stalled," wails the development director in frustration to the campaign consultant. "Contributions have fallen off, the volunteers are burned out,

and I'm just about ready to quit and move to Antarctica. We should have never gotten ourselves into this mess!"

"Relax," replies the consultant soothingly, "I've seen this happen in many campaigns. It's the nature of the beast. The middle is always tough, so let's take a deep breath, review what's really happening, and figure out how to pull the campaign out of the slump."

Now that the consultant has put the situation into a perspective that has been gained from other capital campaigns, the consultant and the development director can sit down together in relative calm and develop some workable strategies to get the campaign back on track. Together with the volunteers, they work to implement these strategies, and usually, the campaign regains its momentum. The development director is soon celebrating the campaign's success, and the longing for Antarctica melts away like the snows of yesteryear.

A skilled consultant will listen to problems, sympathize with frustrations, and then assist with finding solutions to those problems and focusing on specific tasks to get the campaign back on track.

Consultants Provide Technical Expertise

Good consultants are good coaches. They push their clients to continue improving their development skills. They teach new ways of doing the job and sometimes even new ways of thinking about fund raising. They are likely to have useful information about gift accounting, naming opportunities, and the solicitation process. Finally, as an outsider, the consultant can help the organization take a fresh look at its operation; thus breathing new life into stagnant systems. Consultants often leave an organization with a wealth of new insights and instincts, a stronger program, and enhanced skills.

Consultants Are Skilled Writers and Editors

In small organizations, key staff members commonly have a background in the agency's program area. Daycare directors, for example, often began as preschool teachers; hospice directors were often nurses; many library directors were formerly reference librarians. Writing may not be a strong suit for many agency directors, but good writing is important throughout a capital campaign, and a skilled consultant is able to provide help in this area. While the staff will provide the ideas, the organizational "language" and style, and the content, a consultant can help provide the shape for the many written pieces—the case for support, brochures, proposals, and appeal letters—that the organization will need in order to convey the campaign vision to others. The consultant can also help with ideas, language, style, and content.

Consultants Provide Gentle (and Not So Gentle) Nudges

Since consultants are only as good as their last campaigns, they have a strong interest in making every campaign that they undertake a success. Therefore, when the staff and volunteers begin to slip into complacency, feeling secure about progress to date and certain that the next $50,000 is just an ask away, the consultant will be relentless in asking whether Mrs. Smith–Jones has been contacted again, or whether Mr. Torquemada has been invited to the executive director's luncheon. The consultant will help focus and refocus attention on the campaign. In small organizations, the staff often continues to work on other projects during a campaign. A lack of single-minded focus can push the campaign onto the back burner, but there is nothing like an impending meeting with the consultant to generate time for campaign work. By something as simple as a meeting schedule the consultant can drive the campaign's progress.

Consultants Take Tough Stands

Consultants are outsiders, and as such they are able to take tough stands without flinching. Informed and empowered by their status as experts, they have both the experience and the understanding to shore up their opinions. So when, for example, a board member says, as he has so many times in the past, "I just don't think we should ask people for specific dollar amounts," the consultant can hold firm, with the knowledge gained from experience that asking for specific amounts, though annoying to some, raises more money than making non-specific requests. Sometimes it is just because the consultant is an outsider that the director or board members are able to accept ideas that they may for years have been unable to consider simply because they had been proposed from within the organization. Although it is often frustrating to see the consultant able to rush in where the development officer has been unable to tread, a wise development officer will use a consultant as a tool to help push through some of the development practices that the organization has resisted in the past.

As outsiders, consultants can sometimes broach subjects that are taboo within the organization.

Consultants Address the Issue of Board Giving

In many small, community-based organizations, any discussion of the subject of board giving is taboo. The executive director often feels as though it is not his or her place to talk to the board about their contributions; the board chair may not have the courage to deal with the issue directly; and the development director almost invariably examines patterns of board giving and despairs because getting board members to make contributions is certainly not *her* role.

As a board moves an organization into a capital campaign, the board members' roles as contributors loom larger and larger. As someone outside the organization's political intricacies, a consultant is able to address the issue of board giving directly. Consultants often help design and even execute a process that encourages the board to determine its own collective goal. By clarifying their key role in the campaign, the consultant helps refocus the board's attention on their responsibilities as donors and as leaders of the campaign.

Consultants Provide Emotional Support

The importance of hand-holding should not be discounted. During a capital campaign the stakes are high, and anxiety runs rampant. So, it can be an invaluable asset to have someone knowledgeable at hand—someone liked and with whom the staff feels comfortable, someone who can reassure when reassurance is needed.

What Can't a Consultant Do?

In spite of all the positive qualities and skills that the consultant brings to a campaign, the consultant is not, alas, superhuman. Many consultants complain of organizations that have impossible expectations of them. In reality, there are some things that consultants usually cannot accomplish.

Consultants Cannot Change a Leopard's Spots

If certain members of the board aren't willing to solicit gifts, a campaign consultant may not be able to change their minds. They may seem to gear themselves up a bit after a pep talk, but they will be back to their old ways before long. A campaign consultant, however, may be able to help the board understand the importance of personal solicitation and the board's role, which may in turn inspire the board to nominate "fund-raising types" when they next nominate new board members.

Consultants Will Not Lessen the Work Load

A campaign consultant is not a campaign manager. A consultant will offer suggestions on how to organize the work of the campaign, but the development director, the executive director, and the volunteers are the ones who must carry out the work. An organization's engaging a consultant might result in even more work. To perform effectively, the consultant must have a basic understanding of how the development office functions and who the organization's key players are. The consultant will need to know quite a bit of fundamental information about the organization. Consequently, to bring the consultant up to speed on the organization will require pulling together development records, donor files, and fund-raising analyses. One may be sure that the work load will not be lighter! And having come to understand the organization, the consultant may well make a number of suggestions that will result in even more work. The consultant may help find ways to learn more about po-

tential donors, to cultivate key community leaders, and to involve ad hoc committees, all of which may be great preparation for a campaign but are also enormously time consuming. The exception to this rule is the resident consultant. This type of consultant, discussed more fully later in this chapter, is placed in the organization and assumes responsibility for running the campaign.

Consultants Will Not Raise the Money

Fund-raising consultants are often mistakenly referred to as fund raisers. The truth is that the best fund raisers for an organization are the board members, volunteers, and the executive director. Prospective donors want to hear about the organization's future plans from the people who will be responsible for implementing that future. No one wants to talk to the consultant, who will be gone and forgotten when the campaign is over. Donors want to speak with those who are committed to the organization for the long term—those who themselves have made contributions and who are willing to put themselves on the line for the organization's cause.

An exception to this hands-off practice is a consultant who specializes in raising funds for churches. These are individuals of a particular faith who are trained to serve as solicitors for churches around the country. Although such a strategy may work in a congregation that is unified by a common faith and parlance, as a general practice it is not advisable to hire outsiders to solicit funds on the organization's behalf.

In some states it is actually illegal for registered consultants to solicit gifts on behalf of a client. In these states, the registration for fund raisers is more stringent than that for consultants and often requires that the fund raiser be bonded.

Finding a Consultant

Unlike attorneys, doctors, or accountants, who are subject to stringent professional standards, fund-raising consultants have no real accreditation process. While some consultants have moved into the field from development offices, where they may have earned Certified Fund-Raising Executive (CFRE) status, the CFRE designation does not provide an organization with a guarantee that the person in question is a qualified consultant. Similarly, while membership in a professional organization such as the American Association of Fund-raising Counsel (AAFRC) may indicate a certain professional commitment to consulting, it says nothing about the abilities of a consultant, nor does it ensure that a particular consultant is going to be suitable for a particular organization.

Fortunately, there are many fine campaign consultants across the country, and it should be possible to find

---

The Consultant with the Sympathetic Ear

In the middle of the campaign my energy began to flag. I was keenly aware of how important my certainty, my steady hand, and my cheerleading were to the volunteers. But I had no colleagues in-house I could really talk with about the stresses and strains of the campaign and really no one even to bounce ideas off. Fortunately, my consultant was able to fill that role. Sometimes I even called her in the evening just to have a chance to chew over what had happened and to get some reassurance. Her positive feedback and support really helped get me though the campaign in one piece psychologically.

—Campaign Director

a suitable one. However, those who have never worked with a fund-raising consultant may have no idea where to begin hunting for one.

What Kind of Consultant Is Being Sought?

Consultants have different working styles and personalities, and they have many different approaches to fund raising. It is important, therefore, to find a consultant who will be a good "fit" for the organization. The consultant will need to mesh well with the board, volunteers, and development director. Will the members of the organization respond well to someone who is highly aggressive and forceful, or will they work better with someone who takes a gentler approach? Are the board members and volunteers high-powered sophisticates or down-to-earth, no-nonsense folks? The consultant should match, or be able to adapt well to, the personality of the organization.

And what about the development director? Would he or she be better off working with someone who can act as a mentor, someone who will be patient in explaining the whys and wherefores of campaign planning and execution? Will the consultant tell the development director what to do, or will the two of them work collaboratively to explore alternatives? Will the development director be more comfortable with an informal style, or with tighter structures? These are all valid consulting styles, but not all of them work equally well in a given organization. Only through an understanding of the dynamics of the organization and how the different personalities in it function can one determine what type of consultant is to be sought.

Where Does One Look for a Consultant?

Most successful consultants obtain their clients through word-of-mouth marketing. Some advertise in places like *The Chronicle of Philanthropy*, but many competent consultants do not advertise at all. They rely on their former satisfied clients to spread the word. The best informational sources about consultants, therefore, are peers and colleagues in similar organizations. One should explore organizations that do the same type of work as one's own elsewhere in the country as well as organizations in the community that may not do similar work but are of similar size.

Although many consultants travel extensively and serve clients in a broad geographical area, there may be advantages to working with a consultant who knows the organization's community and is near at hand. A state's bureau on charitable organizations is another

> *The consultant should match, or be able to adapt well to, the personality of the organization.*

Finding the Perfect Match

I was feeling a little bit uncomfortable with the way our campaign had started. We really had no idea what we were doing. Through a string of events, I ended up talking to a neighbor at a Christmas party who had a son who worked for a big consulting firm. I drove up to meet the son. We had a three-hour breakfast meeting. He took a look at our plan and basically agreed that yes indeed, we had some problems and probably needed a consultant. At that point, we didn't even know that there were such things as fund-raising consultants.

The consultant felt we were an emergency case. Some people from his firm came up to meet us the next week, all dressed up in their business suits and white shirts. They convinced us that we needed some help, but somehow we didn't feel very comfortable with their Madison Avenue approach to fund raising. At that point we started asking around for a second opinion. We learned that a former university development director was out on her own doing consulting, and we spoke with her. She seemed to fit our organization, and we eventually hired her.

—Executive Director

source of information. If the state requires fund-raising consultants to complete an annual registration, the bureau will probably be able to provide a list of consultants. State registration does not imply endorsement, but it will give a preliminary source of names.

Generally, organizations that have experience with capital campaigns will be more than happy to share that experience. They will tell you whom they employed as a consultant and will offer an evaluation of their experience—they will undoubtedly have some good experiences to relate and some bad. It will be worthwhile to obtain the following information.

- What is the consultant's name, address, and telephone number?
- What was the organization's campaign goal and purpose?
- Was their campaign successful?
- Who recommended the consultant?
- What is the consultant's working style?
- Were there any problems? If so, how were they resolved?
- How did board members and volunteers react to the consultant?
- Did the consultant do what was expected?

- What were the consultant's strengths and weaknesses?
- Would they hire the consultant again?

It may also be useful to ask for recommendations from the more experienced fund raisers on the board or from local foundation executives who may have worked with consultants on other projects. Names of consultants can also be obtained from the local chapter of the National Society of Fund Raising Executives, the American Association of Fund-Raising Counsel, and the National Center for Non-Profit Boards. (See the reference list at the end of this chapter for address information.)

Selecting the Consultant

The organization's needs have been considered, some names have been pulled together, and possibilities have been discussed with key people in the organization. Now it is time to call the consultants who have been selected through the scouting process.

These conversations will provide a sense of the consultants' personalities and styles. The consultants will get a sense of the key person with whom they may be working, the organization's mission, the preliminary goal, and the organization's fund-raising history. They may offer to send some information about their services, a client list, and a brief summary of their background and qualifications. If they do not offer to send this information, it can certainly be requested.

Here are some points that should be kept in mind for this first conversation with prospective consultants:

- The devil is in the details. The small details of the very first conversation are likely to reveal as much about the consultant as any other part of the selection process. Who answered the phone? Was the consultant difficult to reach? Did the consultant return the call promptly? How tuned in was the consultant when first addressed? Did the consultant ask relevant questions? Did the consultant sound like someone worth meeting, someone with whom it would be worthwhile to work?

- What organizations has the consultant worked for? When an organization hires a consultant, it is counting on obtaining the benefit of that consultant's range of experience. Therefore, it is important to take a good look at their campaign experience. Although it is not particularly important that the consultant has worked on campaigns for organizations exactly like one's own, the consultant should be experienced in designing campaigns for organizations of similar size and geographical range. Because most consultants do not want to impose on their former clients more than necessary, they usually prefer that only those listed specifically as references be contacted. One should not hesitate, however, to contact an acquaintance who has worked with a particular consultant.

- Who in the consultant's organization actually works with the clients? In some large consulting firms, the principals seldom do the major work on small campaigns. Junior staff may, of course, be perfectly capable of providing the required assistance, but it is important to interview the individual who will serve as consultant should that firm be engaged. This isn't usually a problem in small shops, but when consultants work with associates, it is necessary to clarify just who will be assigned to the project.

- Trust instincts. If something is felt to be troubling about a consultant in the course of preliminary telephone conversations, that feeling should be taken into consideration, even if it is something that can't be clearly articulated. This individual is, after all, someone who might be a working partner for as long as two years, and those nagging warning signals have a way of growing into major irritations.

Preparing Material to Send to Consultants

Before calling consultants, an organization should assemble packets of material to send to each of the consultants who is being considered for an interview. The material might include annual reports, program descriptions, a copy of the organization's mission statement, and a brief description of the project that the organization is considering a campaign for. A complete information packet will provide the consultant with the material that they need to understand the organization's needs and will help them be more productive and specific by the time they arrive for the interview.

Reviewing Printed Material from Consultants

Material received from each of the consultants who is contacted should be dated. Although it is a minor consideration, and may have no bearing on how the consultant operates, in the selection process everything should be seen as an indicator. Material that arrives late might be a sign that the consultant is very busy or disorganized. Of course, material that arrives the next day may indicate a prompt and efficient work pattern, or it may signal that the consultant doesn't have enough work.

Careful attention to the details of how a consultant presents his or her firm will provide valuable clues about how they will perform.

In any case, it is worth noting every detail, because details may eventually fit into a pattern that develops as the selection process proceeds.

Printed material is also very telling in more obvious ways. The style and content of the cover letter can reveal much about the consultant. Did the consultant respond to what was actually said in the telephone conversation? Is the letter clearly and grammatically written? Is the text placed on the page so that it is visually appealing and easy to read? If the answer to any of these questions is "no," the proceed-with-caution light should be illuminated. If the consultant is sloppy and inattentive during the courtship, imagine what things will be like after the vows have been taken.

As the consultant's background information is reviewed, it is important to look closely at its style as well as its content. What is the consultant's apparent market? Is it smaller organizations or large universities? Did the consultant send an expensive, glossy, four-color brochure, or only a few poorly copied typewritten sheets? It may not be glossy, but is it classy? Is it pragmatic? Is it clear? Is it appealing? Does it speak to what the organization needs? If not, hiring that consultant may lead to a *liaison dangereux*.

As the development director, the executive director, and campaign chair begin to narrow down the list to three or four of the strongest candidates, Exhibit 2–1 might prove useful in deciding whom to interview.

Assembling a Selection Committee

After the field has been narrowed to three or four consultants, it is time to assemble a committee to help select the right consultant. The selection process is an excellent opportunity to educate key board members about capital campaigns. By taking part in the interview process, they will not only learn from the various consult-

ants' approaches, but they will also begin to acquire a sense of ownership in the campaign process even before it begins. And, even more important, when key board members have a voice in choosing the consultant, their endorsement gives the consultant considerable internal credibility right from the start.

Three or four key board members should join the executive director and development director for the interview process. Ideally, all of the interviews should be scheduled for a single day. Approximately forty-five minutes per consultant interview should suffice, with another fifteen minutes between interviews for discussion and breaks. The committee should be sure to arrive at least one-half hour prior to the arrival of the first consultant and plan on remaining at least one hour after the final interview has been completed. Thus, the team can work together to plan the flow of the interview process when it first gathers and, if possible, make its decision before the committee disbands.

Well in advance of the interview day, each committee member should be provided with a copy of the material about the consultants to be interviewed and encouraged to review it carefully. Exhibit 2–2 is a sample of such a form.

Interviewing the Consultant

Before the consultants are contacted to arrange the interviews, some time would be well spent reviewing the organization's needs, its expectations of the consultant, and how those needs and expectations might best be framed into questions. A list of questions might then be developed to guide the interviews. The questions should be varied enough to give a clear sense of how the consultant responds to different types of issues, though some questions might be quite specific while others are more open ended. The following questions are just a few among the many worth considering.

- What strengths do you bring to a campaign?
- What do you like best about campaigns?
- What led you to specialize in campaign consulting?
- What is your philosophy of capital campaign fund raising?
- How many campaigns have you counseled?
- What have been their goals?
- How would you describe your consulting style?
- What has been the most valuable lesson you have learned in your work?
- What is your usual fee for a campaign of this size?
- On what basis do you determine your fee and how do you handle billing?
- What other clients are you working with at this time, and how would you fit our project into your schedule?

Exhibit 2–1 Consultant Evaluation Form

The consultant:	YES	NO
❑ has worked primarily with community-based organizations	___	___
❑ has worked with organizations our size	___	___
❑ has worked on campaigns with similar dollar goals	___	___
❑ possesses a style that seems to fit the organization	___	___
❑ responded promptly	___	___
❑ sent clear and effective materials	___	___
❑ has several years experience working with similar campaigns	___	___

Exhibit 2–2 Consultant Rating Form

Name of Consulting Firm: _____

Name of Representative: _____

Name of Committee Member: _____

	Negative	Neutral	Positive
First Impressions			
Appearance			
Style			
Presentation			
Clarity			
Appeal			
Knowledge			
Experience			
Material			
Appearance			
Organization			
Writing Style			

	High	Moderate	Low
Cost			
Feasibility Study			
Campaigns			

General Comments:

Personal Ranking: _____

- What was your worst campaign experience and how did you cope with it?
- What is your least favorite part of the campaign process?
- How would you deal with a campaign in which the leadership gifts did not come in as planned? (See the Troubleshooting Guide in the Appendix for other difficulties that might be addressed.)

The committee should meet prior to the interviews, at which time question areas might be assigned to each committee member. In this way, every member of the interview committee will have an opportunity to interact directly with each consultant. Once again, close attention should be paid to the details of the consultants' behavior, for they are telltale signs about how the consultant would function while at work on the campaign. Are the consultants on time? Are they dressed in a style that fits your organization? Do they take the time to learn about each member of the committee? Do they seem well informed about the project? Do they speak in a manner that engages the attention of the committee? Do they mumble or speak too fast? Do they seem authentic to you? Do they treat each committee member, including staff, with respect?

It is crucial that the consultant be someone who can present him- or herself clearly and authoritatively before a formal group (the board, for example) and also be a friend, teacher, advisor, and collaborator for the campaign staff.

Following the interviews, but before any discussion, it might be a good idea for each committee member to write down the name of the consultant that they would most prefer. This encourages each person to do some independent thinking before being drawn into the vortex of committee politics. It often happens that the decision is clear, and everyone leans toward one person. Sometimes two or more candidates may seem equally appropriate. But occasionally the group is not sold on anyone or is sharply divided.

Soliciting Consultants' Proposals

Once the search has been limited to one, two, or perhaps three consultants, they should be invited to submit proposals for the work that has been outlined. To facilitate comparing proposals, it may be helpful to provide each consultant with a written description of the scope of the work to be addressed in the proposals. Consultants operate differently both in terms of fee structure and how they divide the work that is specified in their proposals. If more than one consultant is still in the running, these proposals should provide a simple way of helping to make the final decision. Each committee member should be sent copies of each proposal, and a committee meeting to make a final decision should be scheduled.

If, even after discussion, there is no clear consensus among the committee members to support one of the candidates, the committee would be well advised to take a step backward and reopen the consultant search. It is extremely important that the entire committee feel that they have selected the right consultant, and whatever is needed to make that happen should be done. There *really is* a suitable consultant out there somewhere.

Checking References

When the committee has developed a prioritized list of its top two or three candidates, it's time for a reference check. The consultants-elect should be able to provide a list of clients to call and it is well worth calling all of them. Occasionally, during the reference checks, red flags surface and should be heeded. Conversations with references can cover the standard due-diligence questions and also focus on suggestions about how to get the most out of the consultant who is selected. Other clients' experiences can be a great help in starting out on the right foot with the new consultant.

Hiring the Consultant

Once the decision has been made about hiring a consultant, the relationship will have to be clarified and solidified. This will require a written document that outlines the specifics of the working relationship between the consultant and the organization. Sometimes this is done by drafting a contract, but often a letter of agreement attached to the proposal provides what is needed more simply. No matter what kind of document is agreed on, it should answer the following seven questions.

1. How much will the agency pay the consultant?
2. What services will the consultant provide?
3. What will be the timetable for the consultant's work?
4. To whom will the consultant report?

5. How will the consultant report progress to the client? In what form and on what timetable?
6. Who will cover the cost of the consultant's expenses? What will they include, and will they add an administrative or service fee to the expenses before rebilling them?
7. Can either party cancel the contract? If so, what are the terms of cancellation?

The consultants will usually be able to prepare a contract or letter of agreement. Whether or not it is then sent to the organization's attorney for review, it most certainly should be carefully perused. In fact, it may be worth the time and effort to review it point by point with the consultant to make sure that both parties interpret the document in the same way. The contract or letter of agreement should be signed in duplicate by the consultant, the executive director of the agency, and the board chair.

Registration

Today, many states require that fund-raising consultants be registered with a bureau of charitable organizations. This agency's name varies from state to state. The consultant should be able to vouch for an up-to-date registration and should provide a registration number for the organization's files. In many states, a consultant must pay a fee and submit documentation annually on the firm's activity and staffing. Consultants are generally required to register in every state in which they have clients. This process can become costly and time consuming, and sometimes consultants who work in several states disregard the registration requirements.

Although state registration says absolutely nothing about the effectiveness or abilities of a consultant, it is a sound idea to work only with registered consultants. Problems in this area have an uncanny way of causing trouble when least expected. In some states, an organization that hires an unregistered consultant may be fined or otherwise reprimanded, and tangling with government bureaucracies can be costly and frustrating, even if an unregistered consultant has been hired unwittingly.

Information Flow and the Consultant

Consultants are outsiders. Their offices are remote from the organization, and they usually visit the clients only periodically. So, it is very important that consultants receive a steady flow of information from the organization. Shortly after hiring a consultant, an organization should add the consultant to the mailing list to receive all mail that routinely goes to external constituents as well as add the consultant to relevant internal distribution lists. These internal lists are likely to include board mailings and materials and development committee mailings.

Consultants and Fees

Ways of paying consultants fall roughly into three categories:

1. billing according to time
2. billing by the task
3. combination billing

Most consultants bill according to time, basing their fees on a daily rate. As of 1996, this rate can vary from $600 per day all the way up to $2,700 per day. The daily rate is generally determined by the market in which the consultant usually works. Larger institutions and larger cities generally support higher fees, and consultants who work in those areas tend to be at the upper end of the scale. These consultants also sometimes add a significant percentage of markup to their expense billings to cover the office expense of rebilling. Consultants who specialize in small clients and operate outside of the major metropolitan areas generally have lower fees.

A consultant might suggest a schedule of a certain number of days per month over a specified number of months, or perhaps a base number of days with an additional fee for any time spent in excess of the agreed-upon time. In negotiating with the consultant, it is necessary to understand how the number of days that are worked on a project is calculated. If the consultant must travel any distance, is the standard day rate to be paid for travel time?

Because it is difficult to predict the exact amount of time any long task will take, it may be advisable to encourage the consultant to agree to a maximum fee for the job. If the job takes longer than is covered in that fee, it would then require official approval for additional payment. The effect of this arrangement is to put pressure on the consultant to complete the task in a timely way and to protect the organization against unanticipated expenses. There is no one correct type of relationship, but it is necessary to understand exactly what type

---

The Woes of a Real-Life Consultant

I used to charge by the day until I realized how unpredictable my working effectiveness was. On the days when I could only stare at my computer and couldn't write a word of a client's report, I felt so guilty that I wouldn't charge them for that day. And then there would be times when I could write an entire report in one day. Unfortunately, my contracts with my clients didn't distinguish between the days when I was a dolt and those when I was a wizard! I never knew how many days to bill for, since I suspected that I needed the doltish days to get to the wizard state.

—Campaign Consultant

of relationship is being entered into, how much it will cost, and the scope of services to be received.

Some consultants prefer to bill by the task, determining in advance a flat fee for a specified amount of work. Usually consultants who use this arrangement determine the number of days that they think the work should take and then base their fee on that estimate. With a flat fee, it is known from the outset what the project will cost, and the consultant can focus on the work at hand rather than the number of hours or days. However, when the task is long and complex, like providing counsel for a capital campaign, it is often difficult to determine the correct fee up front, and few consultants are willing to take that risk. If a consultant is engaged to work this way, it will probably be necessary to make it clear that if, as the project progresses, the consultant has vastly miscalculated, then the fee can be renegotiated.

Some consultants prefer to combine various methods of billing, and there is no end to the number of permutations and combinations that might be considered in determining the fee: flat fees with add-ons for extensions; a daily rate with an agreed-upon number of days that the consultant will not exceed; a flat fee plus additional fees per interview (in the case of feasibility studies); and so on, ad infinitum. It is a point worth noting, then, that there is much room for creativity and exploration in the negotiation process.

Negotiations will proceed well if the needs of the organization and of the consultant are clearly understood. From the perspective of the organization, it is important to know ahead of time what the consultant is going to charge for his or her services so that there will be no financial surprises. On the other hand, because the timeliness of the consultant's work will depend in large part on the organization's ability to assemble committees, respond to draft documents, and gather information, the consultant would like to be protected from unnecessary project delays. In some sense the only product that consultants have to sell is their time, and no consultant is able to bill for all time worked. Thus, any consultant who has been in business for any length of time will want to be sure that he or she is paid appropriately for the actual time spent on a project.

The Scope of Consulting Services

Capital campaign consulting generally fits into two broad areas: feasibility studies and campaign counsel. Consultants vary on whether they prefer to contract for both at once or to cover the services in two separate contracts. The issues are colored by the importance of using the same consultant for both the feasibility study and the campaign itself. As will be discussed at length in chapter 4, the consultant who conducts the feasibility-study interviews obtains a great deal of confidential in-

---

Success in Spite of Themselves

A couple of years ago, I was called by an agency to see about providing campaign counsel. They had already had a feasibility study completed by a local consultant and had not found him to be a good fit. And indeed, when I reviewed his report, I understood why. This agency, often viewed as a left-wing organization, was very ecologically minded. And not only had the consultant relied excessively on the use of statistical analysis and multicolored photocopied charts to illustrate the results of a mere thirty interviews, but the entire report was triple spaced and printed only on one side. It was a job that could only be described as expensive, wasteful, and not particularly insightful. In a weak moment of exaggerated confidence, I agreed to become their campaign consultant. I spent the next two years trying to avoid the land mines I would have known about had I done the feasibility study myself. Now, I take a perverse pleasure in knowing that the campaign succeeded in spite of the inadequate feasibility study. But I rather suspect that I would have designed the campaign differently had I been the one to conduct the feasibility study.

—Campaign Consultant

---

formation through that process. Some of this information cannot be shared directly with the client, yet it will help shape a consultant's judgment about how the campaign should be designed. It is unwise, therefore, to change consultants in midstream.

On the other hand, because the information obtained during the feasibility study will help shape the campaign, it is very difficult to predict the scope and timetable for the campaign prior to the completion of the feasibility study. In general, therefore, it is recommended that the consultant be invited to submit two separate proposals, the first prior to the feasibility study and covering just those services, and the second outlining the campaign counseling services at the conclusion of the feasibility study.

How to Treat the Consultant

Once a consultant has been hired, it is development staff who are responsible for functioning in a way that draws the best out of that person. In fact, the way the

---

Consulting is a lonely job. Consultants appreciate getting feedback, being kept in the information loop, and being treated with warmth, openness, and honesty.

The Procrastinating Client

Last year I accepted a contract to conduct a feasibility study for a small social service organization. They decided to engage my services and sent the signed contract and first payment check the following month. But from then on my work with this client has been disheartening. After a delay of three months, they called to get dates for a preliminary meeting saying that they were anxious to get going as soon as possible. I gave them several dates for the meeting, but then I didn't hear from them for another two months—not a peep. In response to my calls they told me that they were still assembling the background material they needed for the meeting. Two more months passed before they called to say they had scheduled a meeting with some of their board members on a specific date two weeks later. I had another appointment for that date, but ever anxious to oblige, I juggled my schedule so that I could attend. The day before the meeting, they canceled, telling me that several board members could not attend. As of this writing, I am still waiting. Their material is buried in my files, and I am no longer eager to work for them.

—Campaign Consultant

consultant is treated, from beginning to end, will play a major role in the quality and effectiveness of the work that is provided. It is discouraging and enervating for a consultant to work for a lackadaisical client. If the client delays and postpones meetings or is ineffective with follow-through, even the most responsible and capable of consultants will have a hard time performing well. On the other hand, clients who follow through, operate efficiently, and behave in a clear, courteous, and businesslike way energize their consultants and are likely to get the same positive behavior in return.

Resident Consultants

Not many years ago, it was common practice for the large consulting firms to place a consultant in an organization for the campaign planning and solicitation period. The consultant would set up a full-time office (often with a secretary), conduct the feasibility study, and then proceed to serve not only as consultant, but also as campaign manager. Specifically, the consultant was responsible for spending a constant number of days per month at the organization, carrying out the campaign tasks directly by implementing and managing the campaign. This practice was widely used by large social-service agencies and one still occasionally encounters it today.

Traditionally, resident consultants were used because it was believed that an organization in the midst of a capital campaign needed the complete and undivided attention of one consultant. No one likes to think their needs are taking a back seat to someone else's, which is just the feeling that can arise if the on-demand consultant's time is divided among several clients. Organizations that engaged resident counsel did so as an alternative to hiring permanent staff. However, before a contract is signed with a resident consultant, it is important to consider carefully certain factors.

There are certain advantages to using an on-site consultant. The consultant will be focused on meeting short-term campaign goals, so things will necessarily happen at a fast pace. There will be full-time access to the consultant. The organization will receive a standard approach to the campaign, since most resident consultants are employed by firms that have their own established campaign plan that has worked with many organizations.

However, these advantages are often undermined by the relatively high fees that a resident counsel charges. Generally, the project fees are inflated by substantial expenses for travel, housing, and office space. Because most organizations are concerned with keeping costs down, the consultant may no longer be on-site at the campaign's end, when the majority of large gifts have already been raised. The organization is forced, therefore, to implement the final stages of the campaign on its own. And while staff may have had the opportunity to acquire some knowledge from the consultant, the consultant was probably not focused on sharing campaign strategy and skills with the staff while on site. As a result, the staff may have no idea about how to bring the campaign to a satisfactory conclusion. Typically, the resident consultant is a junior member of the consulting firm, and, while equipped with the firm's campaign plan and other resources, may lack the experience necessary to make sound judgment calls in situations that fall outside the scope of the plan.

Finally, and perhaps most critically, the resident consultant often focuses on an organization's ability to raise money to meet the campaign goal as quickly as possible rather than balancing immediacy with the organization's potential to build long-term and lasting relationships among donors and community leaders. Short-term resident counsel sometimes undermines this important long-term campaign outcome, and organizations may be better served by investing in permanent staff who can balance

Small, young organizations can seldom afford consultants but are often in the greatest need of them.

broader campaign objectives such as identifying new donors, building an organization's constituency, and raising its sites with the immediate needs of a capital campaign.

Deciding Not to Use a Consultant

Although there are many advantages to working with a campaign consultant, it usually doesn't make financial sense to hire a consultant for campaigns with goals of under $500,000. Because it takes as much of a consultant's time to help raise $500,000 as it does to help raise $3,000,000, consultants' fees become a disproportionate amount of the total campaign goal for small campaigns. No one likes to see a capital campaign in which the expenses exceed 20 percent of the funds raised, and consultants are wise not to encourage that practice.

What should be done, then, to get help for a campaign to raise $250,000? That's a great deal of money for a small organization to raise, even though most consultants will turn up their noses at it. And the process of raising $250,000 for a small organization may well be every bit as complex as it is for a larger organization to raise ten times that amount. Although there are no perfect solutions to these problems, there are some alternatives.

Self-Education

Although capital campaigns are complex processes, they aren't rocket science or brain surgery. They aren't even trigonometry. With a fair amount of common sense and a willingness to learn, it is possible for the develop-

ment director to lead the organization through a successful campaign.

This book is certainly a good starting place, and it should be read carefully. One should spend six months or a year learning from others who have been through campaigns. If the opportunity presents itself, the development director might become a volunteer for a larger campaign in the community. In short, one must submerge oneself in campaign information and experience. If the community is fortunate enough to have a good consultant based there, it might be possible to spend some time learning from him or her. Some consultants are happy to share their information and ideas at no charge so long as you don't begin to take their time and expertise for granted.

Finding Volunteers with Campaign Expertise

The self-designed education period is a good time to look for volunteers who have helped with other campaigns and who could become inspired by the organization's mission. Perhaps there are such individuals already assisting the organization. Perhaps a board member, a parent, or a program volunteer has had experience with a previous campaign. One must beware, however. Campaign volunteers often know only a narrow aspect of the campaign process. Solicitors may think of capital campaigns simply as getting five cards and making five calls. Those who have volunteered to organize a campaign kickoff may be certain that the kickoff party is *the* activity responsible for raising the bulk of the goal. And those who have helped develop campaign materials may be convinced that all that is really needed for a successful campaign is a good graphic designer.

It is only when one responsible individual has done a thorough job of self-education in the art of capital campaigns from a broader perspective that it will be possible for the entire process to be knowledgeably guided and for each volunteer to be used appropriately where he or she may have excellent prior experience.

Using Consultants Strategically

Even if a consultant can't be retained for the entire range of services, there are several times during the campaign planning process that a consultant's expertise and credibility will be invaluable.

The Feasibility Study

A feasibility study consists of personal interviews with members of the organization's constituency. It will give the organization an idea of where it stands with its donors. The information received will either provide encouragement to begin the campaign with the confidence that it can be successfully completed, or it will reveal that the campaign should be postponed until weak areas can be strengthened.

Since the results of the feasibility study will determine whether the campaign will proceed or be postponed, it is most important that the study be done properly. It must be done by someone whose opinion and advice will be respected and accepted by both the board and the community leaders. A consultant—as an objective observer—can provide that sort of credibility. Although engaging a consultant for the feasibility study will be costly, this will be money well spent.

Because the consultant will not be retained for ongoing campaign counsel, negotiations with the feasibility-study consultant should seek to include as much of a campaign plan as possible in the consultant's report. Although most consultants do include some campaign planning in the report, one might request that this section of the report be expanded.

Campaign Planning

It may even be desirable to extend the feasibility study contract through the campaign design and planning phase. Since part of that process is forming a powerful campaign planning committee, it can be an important confidence-building measure to have someone who can help guide the process of enlisting that committee and conducting the planning meetings. The best campaigns begin with a well-thought-out planning process, and the hands-on, seasoned experience of a campaign consult-

We Just Didn't Know Enough

Before I was hired as development director, my organization went through a strategic planning process. The decision was made to do a capital campaign to raise money for endowment and program initiatives. The organization hired an experienced "old-school" consultant to do a feasibility study. He told us that we might run into trouble raising money but that we needed to think big. So, the board decided to move forward.

I was hired after the decision to go into a campaign had been made. I had several years of development experience and had been on the periphery of a campaign in my last organization. I did some research on my own about campaigns and felt pretty comfortable handling the nuts and bolts of things that were bound to come up—gift tracking, prospecting, researching, training volunteers—but in retrospect, I realize that my organization and I were pretty naïve about what else a campaign entailed.

We talked about hiring a consultant and interviewed a few, but none seemed quite right for our organization. After discussing it, we decided that there wasn't anything scientific about capital campaigning and that we could do it ourselves.

To make a long story short, the campaign eventually ran out of steam. We ended the campaign far short of our goal. In retrospect, I can attribute the problems we had to two things. First, we didn't have enough information from our feasibility study to know how high to set our goal. Second, no one in our organization really understood capital campaign fund raising, and we hadn't hired a good consultant.

If we had hired an experienced consultant, perhaps we would have decided to delay the campaign, or perhaps we would have lowered our goal. Perhaps we would have changed the timetable or campaign structure. Capital campaigns can be very lonely, and I would have liked to have a consultant's expertise and support.

—Development Director

ant can help guide the campaign planning committee through the decision-making process.

Case for Support

The consultant might assist in providing advice in developing the case for support. A consultant's opinion and experience could help shape a document that will provide much of the language used in proposal letters, brochures, press releases, and speeches for the duration of the campaign. A local consultant may be willing to share his or her resource collection of good and bad examples without charging a fee. The case for support and the process that produces it are central to the success of the campaign, and money spent on a consultant at this stage may be money well spent.

Occasional Guidance

Finally, it may be possible to hire a consultant who will be available to the campaign for occasional guidance, advice, and encouragement on an as-needed basis. Perhaps an arrangement could be made between the development director and the consultant for a monthly meeting to bring the consultant up to date and discuss any questions and issues that have arisen. Perhaps the consultant could be placed on a small retainer that would make it possible to call for advice as the need arises.

Learning from Mistakes

When all is said and done, one hires a consultant to avoid making *their* past mistakes. There is nothing like experience to inform and educate. Because capital campaigns are such occasional events and so organization-

ally complex, very few people other than consultants have amassed enough mistakes to know what they are doing. And those directors and volunteers who have indeed made mistakes on one campaign or another may not have had enough opportunities to learn from their mistakes.

It is certainly possible to conduct a capital campaign without the benefit of a campaign consultant. In some cases, the sans-consultant route is the right route. For very small campaigns, young organizations, and organizations that benefit from the zeal and fervor of their founder, campaign consultants are often not appropriate. For many organizations, however, the right consultant will strengthen the organization's ability to conduct a successful campaign. Whatever the decision, there is much to be learned through the process of exploring the options.

References

American Association of Fund-raising Counsel, 25 West 43rd Street, Suite 820, New York, NY 10036; 212-354-5799

National Center for Non-Profit Boards, 200 L Street NW, Suite 510, Washington, DC 20036; 202-452-6262

National Society of Fund Raising Executives, 1101 King Street, Suite 700, Alexandria, VA 22314; 703-684-0410

Chapter 3
Why Give? Building the Case

Chapter Outline
- What Is a Case for Support?
- Developing a Credible Plan for Compelling Needs
- Writing the Case
- Once a Draft Has Been Completed . . .
- Checklist for an Effective Case

What Is a Case for Support?

When an organization decides to conduct a capital campaign, there is much work to be done before the first gift is solicited. One of the first tasks in preparing for a campaign is the process of developing a document that explains the project and its importance in the community. Such a statement is called the case for support.

The case for support lies at the heart of the campaign. Its words help persuade board members, volunteers, and donors to climb aboard the campaign train. It stirs them to action, moving them to support the campaign with their time and their dollars. And it reminds them why the organization is so important to their community. The case for support describes in simple and compelling terms those community needs that the organization hopes to address with the money it raises, and it presents a credible plan for satisfying those needs.

A preliminary draft of the case is presented to the organization's insiders and community leaders during the feasibility study, and their comments about it and about the organization will shape the direction of the campaign. The case for support helps recruit the campaign planning committee and steering committee as well as other volunteers, persuading them that they are signing on to an important and worthwhile venture. Volunteers use the case for support to devise talking points for

> *The case for support is not just one document. It is an evolving and emerging story about an organization and the project it is about to undertake.*

face-to-face solicitations. The case for support serves as a starting point for grant proposals, direct mail letters, and press releases and is the most important resource for drafting the text of the campaign brochure.

How can one document possibly serve so many purposes? Here is the secret: The case for support is not just one document. It is an evolving and emerging story about an organization and the new project it is about to undertake. As a campaign progresses, the case for support grows and develops, becoming stronger and more compelling as details of the project become available for inclusion.

The case begins as a draft document and progresses through many iterations, each becoming more polished and refined during the various stages of the campaign. The case might begin as a three- to five-page statement for use during the feasibility study. Afterward, when the feasibility study has borne out the practicality of the preliminary goal, when the steering committee has been formed, and as the organization begins to raise money toward its campaign goal, the case for support will be expanded to include the new information. Every time new information is added, the enhanced case for support will be all the more compelling in showing others that the campaign is likely to succeed.

The case is likely to take other forms as well. During the solicitation process it will become a spoken set of persuasive "arguments" to convince donors that they should support the organization. It will become a brochure. It may even become a video, a skit, or a direct-mail piece.

Even though some information in the case will change as it evolves, certain pieces of information remain the same. The case simply and succinctly explains to its readers how their gift will make a difference, not only to the organization but to the community as a whole. More specifically, the case ultimately presents the following information:

- the community or societal need that the organization addresses
- the organization's goals and programs

Recently I worked on a campaign to computerize a public library in the heart of Amish country. At the campaign kickoff the case for support was presented as a skit by a businessman who was serving on the campaign's steering committee. Wally was the head of a major business in the community, but he also just happened to be expert at speaking with an Amish accent.

As the skit opened, Amos (Wally dressed in black pants, oversized boots, and a black Amish hat) and his wife, who also dressed for the part, walked hesitantly into the public library. They were looking for reference material, and they clearly didn't know their way around very well. But they were embarrassed about informing the librarian just what it was exactly that they were researching. They indicated that they were looking for designs and specifications of—and here it became vague—a small structure. They didn't seem able to explain any better than that. The librarian thought she understood and tried to help them by consulting the microfiche catalog for information on sheds, barns, and garages. But none of those was quite what Amos and his wife were looking for. Finally Amos said, "No, no, we want to build a small building with a moon cut out of the door." Aha! At last the librarian understood, and she directed them to the library's reference material on the design, construction, and ventilation of outhouses. The audience understood how much easier a time the Amish couple would have had if the library had been automated and our friend Amos could simply have typed "outhouse" into the computer!

Without a doubt, Wally's presentation of the library's case for support was one of the most effective and memorable cases I have ever seen. People still chuckle about Wally's skit, but more importantly, they understood viscerally what library computerization was all about.

—Campaign Consultant

- the organization's past and present accomplishments
- the organization's role in the community
- the organization's products and services
- the organization's value to society
- the organization's future opportunities in light of the community's needs
- the organization's requirements for facilities
- the campaign goal

- the key people involved in raising the money
- a realistic plan of action to accomplish the goal

Because the case changes and expands as the campaign progresses, all of these elements will not be available in time for the early drafts. However, the first draft should include the first nine items listed above. Wise authors of case statements understand that with regard to the information they include in a first draft nothing is permanent except change. Their words will continue to evolve and improve as the case for support is shared with others and as new information becomes available. Therefore, every organization should invest in a rubber stamp with the word DRAFT in large letters and a red inkpad to go with it. A document that is stamped as a draft encourages input and comment from others, enabling them to contribute to the case.

The case for support explains the campaign's rationale and answers basic questions that would convince a reader that the project is important and feasible. Because it is used in many different forms throughout a campaign, the case should be seen as an evolving presentation of information and ideas rather than as a particular type of document.

All cases for support begin somewhere, however, and most begin as a brief written document. But beware! Simplicity is deceiving. The best cases do look as though they had been easily put together but only because many people put a great deal of time and effort into shaping them. The simplest case for support is usually the one that has been written and rewritten the most.

Just as important as the finished case is the process used to develop it. Since the case is written in a series of drafts, every draft gives people the opportunity to contribute their thoughts about the case and about the organization. A good case incorporates the ideas of many people into a coherent statement of values and possibilities for the organization; the case condenses and clarifies many ideas into a consistent and compelling story that underpins and strengthens the campaign. Paying attention to the ideas of others who care about the organization also builds ownership and encourages constituents to think about the organization perhaps more deeply than they have ever done before.

This chapter examines the elements of an effective case for support. It describes how to write an effective case and how to use the case to build ownership in a cam-

> *The case for support explains the campaign's rationale and answers basic questions that would convince a reader that the project is important and feasible.*

paign. This chapter also outlines some of the common pitfalls to be avoided in writing a case.

Developing a Credible Plan for Compelling Needs

The Declaration of Independence is a wonderful example of a case for support. Those who haven't read or heard it in a while should track down a copy and see for themselves. Granted, Thomas Jefferson wasn't trying to raise $1 million to refurbish and expand the assembly room in Independence Hall, but in writing the Declaration of Independence he incorporated many of the same elements one finds in an effective case for support.

The Declaration presented a problem that affected American society as a whole. Jefferson did not hesitate to list reasons for declaring independence. Indeed, the injuries committed against the colonies by King George III and the British Parliament clearly resonated with many of the colonists who read or heard the Declaration. The list of grievances describes the compelling need, and a compelling need is precisely what must be outlined in a case for support.

In the last paragraph of the Declaration of Independence Jefferson presents a plan of action—to break away from the mother country. It was a risky plan, yet those who pledged their allegiance to one another and to their new country believed that the goal was worth the risk. The plan conveys a sense of urgency while presenting a well-thought-out set of arguments designed to convince France to join with the colonists in their fight against England. Jefferson's style and tone urge the reader to action.

In terms of process, Jefferson himself was keenly aware of the problems that the colonies faced, and he was convinced of their need for independence. He wrote the first draft of the Declaration based on his own convictions. Then he submitted it to the committee of the whole for revisions. Through that process, every man in the Continental Congress who signed his name to the final document became a full owner of the Declaration and the ideas it represented.

Although Jefferson was not writing with the goal of a successful capital campaign in mind (the campaigns he engendered were political and military), if an organization can produce a document as compelling as the Declaration of Independence, its campaign will certainly be off to a good start.

The first draft of a case for support should include four distinct segments that inform the reader why the organization must embark on the campaign.

1. What needs will the campaign address? This question is a good starting place. An organization's needs are often clarified and amplified as it devel-

Blown Away by the Draft

I'll never forget my meeting with our campaign consultant as we began work on the preliminary case for support. We needed to send it out to the committee that was overseeing the feasibility study, and it was a rush job. I was full of anxiety, trying to get every word perfect. At one point the consultant turned to me and said, "Where's your draft stamp?"

"My what?" I replied.

"Your draft stamp," she insisted, "so we can stamp the copies of the case document we're preparing. If we don't leave opportunities for the members of the committee to add their ideas, they'll feel they've been presented with a *fait accompli,* and we will have lost a great chance to build ownership in this project."

"Oh, right, draft stamp," I said, taken aback. It then took me a few minutes to accept the fact that my words didn't have to be perfect. In fact, the more I tried to create the perfect document, the more likely it was that I would become defensive about any proposed changes during our committee meeting.

Well, the idea of presenting a document that was deliberately less than perfect was tremendously liberating. It just blew me away. The very next day I went out and bought a big, red draft stamp. And now, knowing that when I use it I'm indicating that I'd like others' opinions has freed me up. I still like to present fine prose, but I plan from now on to leave the door open for other people's suggestions.

—Public Relations Director, Hospice

ops a plan for the future. An organization might need a new building or a sophisticated computer system or improvements to its child-care center. Most needs addressed by a capital campaign are concrete and specific and will enable an organization to improve or increase its services.

2. Why would the organization's needs inspire someone to give? The organization's needs often spring from broader needs in the community, and it is those community needs that form the basis for a case for support. The needs of an organization are only compelling as they relate to the community it serves. For example, a donor is not likely to be excited by the fact that an organization needs a new office building. The new building becomes exciting to donors because of the good it will enable the organization to accomplish in the community. The case might describe the new adult literacy center inside the build-

ing, the increased numbers of patients who will be able to be treated in the new hospital wing, the greater efficiency of the staff, or any of the other consequences that the new building will have in improving life in the community. People give in order to make a difference to others, not to finance an organizational wish list.

3. Why is the organization's need important now? Organizational needs are usually fueled by changing circumstances in the community or among its constituents. To continue to provide good service, the organization must keep up with such changes. Perhaps its clientele is growing rapidly and the organization is running out of space, or perhaps it needs a new program to accommodate new needs that have surfaced. Whatever the specifics, the case for support must convey a sense of urgency.

   The case must be able to convince donors and the community not only of the project's importance but also of why it must be done now. Sometimes the answer to the "Why now?" question is simple: "Our building is being torn down." "We have long waiting lists of people we can no longer serve in our current space." "Our patient census has declined sharply because we can't perform the full range of services people require." All of these reasons contain the seeds of urgency. The strongest reasons for urgency are external—those based on community need.

4. How will the organization meet the need? It's fine to talk about meeting the needs of the community in a general fashion, but to convince anyone of the real need for funds, the case will have to tell the story of how the organization plans to address those needs. The plan must have its own logic, it must make financial sense, and it must resonate with the perceptions of both the organization and the community. The plan must describe the project crisply and clearly—size, shape, location, cost, timetable—so that, in a short time, the reader can grasp the gist of the project and understand that the organization has done its homework. Usually, the better the homework the clearer and more convincing is this part of the case.

To summarize, a case for support describes an organization's credible plan for meeting a compelling community need. But the best cases for support are more than stuffy documents; they are lively, interesting, fun

> *The best cases for support are more than stuffy documents; they are lively, interesting, fun to read, unpretentious, and moving.*

Using Humor to Engage the Reader

The Sciencenter in Ithaca, New York used humor to spice up one of the later versions of its case for support, seeding it with funny but relevant phony quotations like "The Sciencenter concept is *relatively* simple" (Albert Einstein) or "Combining science and fun is an *illuminating* idea" (Thomas Edison), or "You can't build a Sciencenter with *peanuts*" (George Washington Carver). Their tongue-in-cheek method made one want to read every word of the case.

---

to read, unpretentious, and moving. In the end, such seemingly peripheral characteristics count for as much as the actual content.

In drafting the case for support the following nine points should be kept in mind.

1. The case is an investment prospectus. Prior to investing in a company, a smart investor finds out as much as possible about the company. What are its mission and corporate vision? Where does it see itself going in the next few years? Who runs the company? What is its financial position?

   The case for support must also present a sound investment opportunity. The "investor" should be able to tell what an investment in the organization will accomplish for the community. And those proposed accomplishments must be framed in a way that is interesting and compelling to the investor.

2. The case answers basic questions about the organization. After reading the case, a prospect should understand what the organization does; when and why it was created; and, in the final versions, the names of the key people involved in the campaign. The case reflects the organization's mission and describes its priorities for the future.

3. The case must have broad implications for the community. The case must have broad, current, and universal appeal. It must stress societal opportunities, not merely discuss the organization's needs. It should state the value that will accrue to the community if the proposed program is carried out and how the community's quality of life will be enhanced.

4. The case must contain statements that are supportable and defensible. The case is not the place to exaggerate the organization's accomplishments or capabilities. Simple, straightforward language that presents the organization's strengths in a realistic and distinctive way will be more effective than overstated claims.

5. Successful cases are both rational and emotional. People give with their hearts as well as their heads. The case must appeal to both. While donors are touched by stories of people who have been impacted by problems in society, recent, highly publicized scandals in the nonprofit world have served to make donors much more aware of the issues of an organization's fiscal responsibilities, board governance, and accountability.

6. The case must be optimistic. Care should be taken not to overwhelm the reader with the magnitude of the problem, to the extent that the reader becomes sure that it cannot be fixed. The case should evoke a feeling of hope and promise.

7. The case should be brief. If one wants one's prospects to read the case for support, then it must be brief and well-written. It should be just long enough to cover the necessary information and inspire the reader, yet not so long that a casual reader will be put off by its length. If a reading of a draft of the case leads to eyes glazing over, then one may be sure that the case is too long and probably not well written.

8. The case should be easy to remember. The content of a good case is often translated into "talking points" for board members, campaign volunteers, and solicitors. The written document gives them confidence and information, but its real power is in solidifying the arguments for the project in a form that is easily broken down into three or four major points that solicitors can recall and use in conversation.

9. The case should move people to action. Just like the project discussed in the Declaration of Independence, the organization's project must happen *now*. The case is one of the many ways of inspiring action, and action is what will be needed if the campaign is to succeed.

Writing the Case

Who Should Write the Case?

Who should write the first draft of the case for support? Like many issues in campaign planning, there is no single correct answer. The case can be written by the development director, the executive director, the public-relations director (if the organization has one), the campaign consultant, or a freelance writer who specializes in development writing.

The case writer should have a good understanding of the institution's history. If the author is a staff person, much of the historical information will be readily available, either in memory or in the organization's files. However, staff members may be subject to political sensitivities within the organization, have a lack of objectivity about events in the organization's history, or be unable to step back and look at the organization with a fresh eye, thus limiting their effectiveness as writers of the case. If, on the other hand, a consultant writes the case for support, he or she will likely not be subject to such organizational pressures but will understandably need more time and assistance to learn about the organization.

A case is not written in a vacuum. The writer must be able to gather and process information from a wide variety of sources. These sources may include board minutes; annual reports; interviews with staff, key constituents, volunteers, and board members; and feature articles about the organization. The writer must be able to find the significant nuggets of information in these diverse sources and put them together to create a meaningful and persuasive document that engages the reader's heart and mind.

This may seem like a lot of work for what starts out as a short document. But even if the writer uses only a fraction of the accumulated material about the organization in putting together the case for support, the learning process will provide a feel for the case's audience, the style of language commonly used in the organization's materials, who the active participants have been, and the historical context in which the campaign is being planned. All of this background material will inform and improve decisions made throughout the campaign.

Finally, the writer must understand the purpose of a case for support. Writing such a document is different from writing a grant proposal, a press release, or an annual report. Whoever writes the case must understand these differences. The writer must know how the case will be used and have a thorough grasp of the elements that go into it.

It may be tempting to ask a board member or volunteer to draft the case for support, but here a word to the wise is in order. Writing a case for support can be a bruising task, and it is not wise to bruise an important volunteer. The willing volunteer may be happy to take on the task, but what if, as may well happen, the first draft is submitted and it's just plain bad? Then one is stuck either with an ineffective and poorly written case or with a bruised volunteer.

Board members and volunteers are wonderful sources for quotations, factual information, and general impressions about the organization, but unless one of them has particular expertise in this area, he or she should not be expected to take on the challenging responsibil-

> *Writing a case for support can be a bruising task, and it is not wise to bruise an important volunteer.*

ity of preparing the case for support. Furthermore, it is much easier for a board or group of volunteers to critique a document candidly and honestly if they know that one of their own was not involved in its creation.

Gathering Information

Before the writer actually begins writing the case, he or she will need some preliminary information. The executive director, development director, and the board fund-raising chair often sit down with the writer to clarify the campaign's goal, needs, plan, and benefits to the community to be sure that everyone shares a common understanding of the project.

The writer should know from the outset that the draft will be distributed to board members and other key volunteers for their input. Establishing agreement about the case's purpose and then making sure that the purpose and function of the case are communicated to the rest of the board will go a long way toward preventing misunderstandings during the critique and revision process.

The writer will need access to institutional documents that can provide background about the organization's history and growth and information about the important people in its life. Four types of documents that will probably be helpful to the writer are listed below.

1. Brochures. These can include fund-raising brochures, membership brochures (if the organization has a membership program), and general-information brochures. Such documents should give the writer a good overview of the organization's programs and services and prior fund-raising program as well as an understanding of how the organization views itself.

2. Annual reports. Like the brochures, annual reports will give the writer a good overview of the organization's programs and services as well as its mission statement and a listing of board members and staff. If for some reason the mission statement or a financial report is not included in the annual report, the writer should be provided with copies of this information.

3. Strategic plans. Since the motivation for conducting a campaign probably emerged from a strategic-planning process, the writer will need a copy of the strategic plan itself. Since the strategic plan provides the rationale for the campaign, it will be one of the most valuable documents for the preparation of the case for support.

4. Testimonials. Testimonials from individuals served by the organization are often very revealing. If the organization has done a good job of collecting them over the years they will give the writer a real sense of how people feel about the organization and the words they use to express those feelings.

All these documents should provide the writer with enough information to begin to understand and appreciate the organization. They will also serve as a good basis for beginning to prepare questions for interviews with the organization's insiders.

Involving Insiders

Drafting the case for support is an opportunity to engage key insiders in thinking through the reasons for the campaign. The discussions, the give and take, and the compilation of everyone's hopes and dreams for the organization can be exhilarating and can help build the necessary understanding and support for a successful campaign.

Who are these special insiders? They are the individuals who are most closely involved with an organization. Typically, they include representatives from the following categories:

- founders
- board members
- former board members
- volunteers
- donors
- professional staff
- constituents
- key community leaders

There are many ways to involve these insiders. Some organizations, stretched for time and energy, assemble an ad hoc committee to work with the case writer. Other organizations conduct a series of interviews with their insiders.

Using a Committee to Develop the Case

A committee can spend one or more sessions discussing key elements of the case for support and is then the first to review and comment on the initial draft. The committee should comprise from six to eight people representing a variety of the organization's constituencies. A moderator should be appointed, as well as a scribe to take notes of the discussion. Although the executive director may moderate the session, if there is a volunteer who would do a good job, then the director might be more valuable as a participant.

The moderator should be sure to solicit every participant's opinions and to encourage every viewpoint. A moderator's job is to manage discussion by keeping the group on task while ensuring that everyone participates and has a positive experience. It may be helpful to provide the moderator with an outline of responsibilities, which include:

- allowing the participants to introduce themselves
- reviewing the assigned tasks
- asking for a volunteer scribe to take notes
- reviewing the time available

- setting the ground rules for discussion
- focusing on people and process rather than content
- reflecting back to the group what you are hearing in order to clarify issues
- summarizing the results when the task is complete
- taking the time to make sure that consensus is reached
- assigning responsibilities for writing and distributing a draft

Moderators should ask the participants to be nonjudgmental—to listen first without immediately agreeing or disagreeing with another's point of view. They should encourage building on one another's ideas rather than each insisting on his or her own point of view. They should remain impartial. They should encourage the shy and contain the obstreperous. And they should summarize key points for the scribe.

To develop the concepts for a case for support through committee process, the moderator begins by describing the purpose of the case for support and the expectations of the committee. Then, each participant at the meeting should be asked to write down the three things that they find most compelling about the project and their three greatest worries or reservations. This task might be assigned prior to the committee meeting, but if every committee member is familiar with the project this may not be necessary. Using the committee's responses as a base, the moderator should guide a free-flowing and constructive conversation about the compelling arguments supporting the project and the underlying concerns that the case must address. By participating in the meeting, the writer will start to assemble a extraordinary collection of stories, opinions, and information on which to base a first draft.

The moderator should be prepared for the possibility that not everyone may agree about the campaign's purpose or about the organization's plan. It will not do to be afraid of potential conflict, which, if well managed, can often be a constructive force in developing the campaign.

Using Interviews to Develop the Case

In some organizations, instead of conducting meetings, the writer conducts a set of individual interviews with six to eight individuals familiar with different aspects of the organization and the community. During the interviews, the writer builds a set of impressions and opinions about the organization and how it has made a difference in people's lives. These stories can then be used to breathe life into the case.

The key to acquiring useful information from an interview is preparation. The first step in good preparation is to develop a list of open-ended questions based on a knowledge of the person being interviewed that will encourage a discussion of that individual's relationship to the organization and its impact on that person's life. A set of sample questions appears in Exhibit 3–1. The interviewer would do well to draw up a list of eight to ten standard questions that will work well for everyone and perhaps five to seven questions that have been developed specifically to address the interests of a particular individual.

Once these questions have been prepared, it is time to begin scheduling the interviews. First a letter to each individual should be drafted that will include the following information:

- background information on the campaign
- purpose of the case statement
- name of the person who will be doing the interview
- name of the person who will be contacting the individual and when they will be contacted

Those being interviewed will appreciate receiving, prior to the interview, a copy of the questions that they will be asked. People generally give better interviews when they have had the opportunity to think about the questions in advance and to organize their thoughts. A copy of the interview questions can be included with the letter.

The development office usually handles the administrative detail of gathering information for the case. They schedule committee meetings, send letters to interview subjects, and often even schedule the interviews. If a consultant or freelance writer is preparing the case for support, that individual may prefer to do the follow-up and scheduling in order to begin building the rapport that is necessary for a good interview.

Exhibit 3–1 Case Statement Interview Questions

1. How did you first become involved with the organization?
2. In your own words, describe the mission of the organization.
3. How has the organization's work affected you personally?
4. What contributions to the community does the organization make that are important to you?
5. What three words best describe the organization to you?
6. Why do you think this project is important to the community?
7. What is most compelling to you about the project?
8. What are your greatest concerns about the project?
9. What details would you like to see included about the project in the case for support?
10. What is the single most important reason that you believe someone would support the project?

Secrets of Conducting a Good Interview

A good interview doesn't just happen by itself. A good interviewer understands human nature. As a rule, people are happy to talk about themselves and will enjoy talking about themselves in relation to the organization. A good interviewer asks open-ended questions that put the individual at ease and encourage free discussion. A good interviewer is also sensitive to the possibility that the subject may feel awkward at first and therefore paces the interview to account for those first uncomfortable moments.

Good interviewing requires good listening. A good listener checks his ego at the door before starting the interview. He doesn't interrupt and patiently waits until the person being interviewed has had time to gather and express his thoughts in his own words.

A good interviewer also trusts his instincts. He may go into the interview with a set of prepared questions, but as a good listener, he will be guided by intuition to decide whether a tangent is worth pursuing. This sixth sense improves with time; the information that can be extracted from the last interview will probably be much better than that from the first interview.

There are also certain "mechanics" that go into making an interview a success. Being on time, dressing appropriately, having more pens and legal pads than could possibly be needed, and maintaining the discipline to take effective notes during the interview and to transcribe them soon after the interview has been completed will help set the proper tone for the interview. Some people like to record their interviews on tape. If one chooses to do this, it is absolutely necessary to obtain the express approval of the individual being interviewed. Others choose not to use a tape recorder because they believe that people will share their thoughts and feelings less openly if they know that they are being recorded.

While it is best to do as many interviews as possible in person, sometimes a personal interview isn't feasible and it will be necessary to conduct some telephone interviews. The same principles hold true as for face-to-face interviews, but in telephone interviews it will be necessary to be an even better listener to catch subtle differences in nuance and tone.

Sitting Down to Write the Case

Once the interviews or committee meetings have been completed, the material gathered, and all relevant information amassed, it is time to begin sifting through the reams of notes and information for those invaluable bits and pieces that are going to build an outstanding case.

The pages and pages of notes can seem overwhelming. How does one begin to impose order on chaos, rather than the other way around? Some writers take multitudinous notes and then condense the material into a well-organized and tight outline. Others review all the material in one sitting, then put it all aside and begin to write. Whatever process turns out to be the most satisfactory, it is important to remember that this document will be rewritten many times before the end of the campaign. And anyone who has ever written anything knows that the person who has the courage to do battle with a blank piece of paper deserves a medal.

For those who write best from an outline, a sample outline for the case has been included below. This outline may help in organizing one's thoughts into the four sections that generally work well in cases for support. It may be, however, that the muse will suggest a different organization for the case. As long as it covers all the

> *Good interviewing requires good listening. A good listener checks his ego at the door before starting the interview.*

necessary areas, has its own compelling logic, and reads well, any order is fine. Generally, however, the case document emerges more or less as follows:

1. The introduction to the project—a preliminary description of the project set in a context that describes community needs
2. The background for the project—information about the organization, including date of founding, mission, accomplishments, importance in the community, and growth
3. The project—a deeper look at the project: what, why, where, when, how, and how much
4. The project's benefits to the community—a summary of what the project will accomplish

Elements of Good Writing

Content aside, the case for support must be well written. In his book, *On Writing Well,* William Zinsser (1980, 5–6) defines good writing as having "an aliveness that keeps the reader reading from one paragraph to the next and it's not a question of gimmicks . . . it's a question of using the English language in a way that will achieve the greatest strength and the least clutter." A good writer is able to convey ideas clearly and simply, using the fewest words possible to communicate effectively in an interesting and readable way.

Mark Twain, one of America's greatest writers, once defined good writing in a single word: *rewriting.* Good writers relish the process of rewriting. They chew over their words, almost tasting their effectiveness. They celebrate every time they find a tighter, more succinct way to say something. Some even sleep with a pencil and paper by their beds just in case the perfect word comes to them in the middle of the night. As Strunk and White succinctly put the case for succinctness in their highly recommended book *The Elements of Style,* "Omit needless words" (1979, 23).

Alas, most of us are not great writers. We are not Mark Twain, nor are we Henry James or Edith Wharton. For us, writing is often a necessary chore. We agonize when we sit down at the computer or the notepad to begin a draft. Indeed, we may agonize over every sentence, running out for snacks, bathroom breaks, and anything else we can think of to keep us from the task. Even for the great majority of us nonwriter types, however, writing a good case for support should be within reach. While there are a number of excellent writing and editing resources available, the following four guidelines may prove a good place to start.

1. Employ the active rather than the passive voice. Which of the following sentences is more compelling?

An architect was recently engaged to develop a design for a new building. (passive)
The board recently engaged an architect to design a new building. (active)

In the second sentence the active voice vigorously grabs the reader's attention and forces the writer to identify the actor, or subject of the sentence. "An architect was engaged" doesn't tell you who did the engaging. Knowing that "the board engaged an architect . . ." gives the sentence additional clarity and force.

2. Avoid words with suffixes such as "-tion," "-ment," "-ize," and "-ility." These words are usually a sign of poor writing. Once the case for support has been completed, the author might circle every such word in the document. Getting rid of them won't be easy; nine times out of ten the entire sentence will have to be rewritten. However, the end result will be a crisper, cleaner, and more active sentence.

One might compare and contrast the following simple sentences to see what a difference active and targeted writing makes.

Not so good: "There is a need for community participation."
Good: "We want the community to participate."

Not so good: "The renovation of the former department store on First Street will be the focus of our campaign."
Good: "We will use the money we raise to renovate the former department store on First Street."

Not so good: "Provision of services will continue during construction."
Good: "We will continue to serve our clients while we renovate the building."

3. Find strong action verbs. Another telltale sign of poor writing can be found in the use of verbs. Good writers use active and specific verbs. They shy away from the many forms of the verb "to be," using instead verbs that are more descriptive and targeted. Rather than saying, for example, "There are ways to become a better writer," you might say, "You can improve your writing skills." Or, to use another example, consider how much stronger "He relishes his volunteer work" is than "He is an enthusiastic volunteer."

Below are several sentences that one may wish to rewrite just to get in the swing of becoming a good writer. There is no one correct way to rewrite any of these sentences, but all of them could be much improved. The authors have included their versions in Exhibit 3–3 at the end of the chapter to satisfy the curious.

- The reason he said no to our request was that he just gave a big donation to the symphony.
- There were a number of mistakes in our campaign assumptions.
- In the background section of the case statement, the history of the organization was described.
- While many of the people in our community thought our campaign was a good idea, there were many other people who thought that the organization wasn't ready.

4. Make sentences crisp and paragraphs short. The reader's eye tends to get overwhelmed when it must wade through long, dense, single-spaced paragraphs of text. One should make reading the case as easy as possible by using a simple style, employing short paragraphs, and never using two words where one will do. ("Omit needless words!") Short paragraphs and crisp writing are more important today than ever before. People read less, have less time to read, have less tolerance for the printed word, and have shorter attention spans. We are a nation of couch potatoes and headline readers. Readers should not be challenged to wade through murky blocks of turgid prose.

Simple Guidelines for Effective Layout

Good graphics are just as important in a case for support as is good writing. With good word-processing and desktop-publishing software it is possible to create a very satisfactory layout for the initial version of the case for support. It would be worthwhile to become familiar with six simple layout basics before preparing the first draft.

1. White space can be used effectively to show off text. Used effectively, white space frames the text. It can lead the eye, create drama and contrast, and emphasize key parts of the case.
2. An easy-to-read typeface makes the document, well, easy to read. For large blocks of text, a serif typeface works best. Serif type has small lines or feet, called serifs, at the tops and bottoms of the letters. Serif typefaces include Bodoni, Garamond, Palatino, Caslon, and Times, to name just a few. The typeface that is selected must carry the message, so fonts should be selected with care. Because of the ease with which typefaces can be changed in the word-processing program, it is easy to go overboard and employ a variety of type styles and sizes. Too many styles in one document—and that usually means more than one—are visually confusing and distract the reader from the message.
3. Bullets and headings organize the flow of the argument. Breaking up lengthy paragraphs with head-

ings and using bullets to denote items that would normally be included in paragraphs emphasize the writer's key points. Newspaper articles are often good examples of clarity and conciseness. The reporter will put only one idea in a paragraph; it is a style well worth emulating in writing the case for support.

4. Drawings and charts convey information and add variety. Sometimes it is a good idea to include simple charts or graphs to illustrate factual information about the organization. Some rapidly growing agencies will illustrate their growth history with bar graphs. More advanced versions of the case might well include an architect's rendering and floor plans of the new or renovated building. These drawings help make the project all the more real to readers.
5. Quotations add the human touch. People invariably read headings and quotations before they read text. Quotations can be used to restate the main points. They should be placed where they will catch the reader's attention: Rather than burying quotations within the text of the case, they should be placed at the top or the bottom or in the left-hand margin of the document so that they catch the eye at once. Extra-wide left margins can be used just for that purpose.
6. A graphic designer can spruce up the entire campaign. Spending some time talking with a graphic designer even at these early stages can pay enormous dividends. A professional will be able to start with a document that has already been prepared according to the guidelines discussed above and develop something even more readable and graphically pleasing. Graphic design is a complex and sophisticated specialty. Even with simple projects, the eye and know-how of a professional designer can make a terrific difference. If a designer is brought in early in the process, that person will have been able to develop a clear idea of the concept that the organization is trying to convey when the time comes for designing the campaign brochure.

Once a Draft Has Been Completed . . .

Gathering Opinions, Building Ownership

Throughout this chapter mention has been made of the importance of involving many of the organization's insiders in shaping the case. Not only will this help clarify the most compelling arguments for the project, but every time another individual contributes to the process that person learns more about the project and increases the stake in the project's success.

People should be involved strategically in an order and with a protocol that builds support. Because the draft of the case for support may well be the first document that sets forth in writing the specifics of a new project, the process of sharing it must be handled with care. In the early stages, the case is simply a working document that will help the committee and the board grasp and clarify a project that they may have been talking about for some time. The very first draft should, therefore, be shared only with the board.

After the executive director, the writer, and perhaps the case committee are satisfied with the first draft, it should be shown to the board chair and the development committee chair for their comments. Then, after their suggestions have been incorporated, it can be sent to the entire board. It should be sent with a cover memo from the executive director and/or board chair reminding everyone about the case's purpose and setting some guidelines for the board's critique. Establishing a framework for comments will simplify the job of gathering and incorporating suggestions. A sample of such guidelines is in Exhibit 3–2.

The first draft of the case often makes for lively discussion, and meeting time should be set aside for the board to ask questions and provide input. However, the meeting should not deteriorate into an occasion for writing by committee, and so care should be taken to focus the discussion on ideas and content rather than the specific choice of words and phrases. When a board member has a comment about word choice, it should be graciously noted but not discussed.

Sometimes it is hard to know whose opinions to incorporate and whose to leave out. Such decisions are influenced by politics and power as well as by the quality of the suggestions. When unsure whose suggestions to use and whose to leave out, it is helpful to remember that if the draft document captures the spirit and essence of the project, then each contributor will be happy to believe that he or she was among those who helped develop it. It is important to acknowledge and to thank everyone who provided input, whether or not their particular suggestions were actually incorporated into the text. Even the suggestions that were not used help determine the essence of the case.

Once the suggestions of the board have been incorporated, the case will be ready to use in the feasibility study. The feasibility study consultant will use this brief document of perhaps three or four pages during the study. The draft will inform those interviewed about the project and campaign plans and will also provide an opportunity for the consultant to gather input for later versions of the case for support.

Exhibit 3–2 Setting Guidelines for the Critique of the Case for Support: Sample Memo

MEMORANDUM

TO: Board of Trustees
FROM: Catherine Schwartz
RE: Review of Case for Support
DATE: May 20, 1996

Please review and critique the enclosed draft of the case for support and return it to me with your comments by June 15. I plan to use your comments to help fine-tune and polish our case. We will then send it to each of the people being interviewed in the feasibility study.

Please keep the following questions in mind as you read the case and let me know your suggestions about how we might make it more effective.

- Does it answer the basic questions about our organization?
- Does it clearly and completely describe the project we have embarked on?
- Does it frame the reason for this project in terms of our community rather than our immediate need?
- Does it appeal both rationally and emotionally?
- Does it inspire a sense of urgency?

Thanks in advance for your help! I look forward to receiving your suggestions.

Enclosed is a stamped return envelope.

Exhibit 3–3 Sentence Rewrites

Below are our versions of the sentences on page 40.

1. He turned down our request because he had just made a major gift to the symphony.
2. Our campaign assumptions contained numerous mistakes. *Or* Some of the things we assumed when planning our campaign were wrong.
3. The case statement's background section contained our organization's history. *Or* The background section of the case told our organization's story.
4. Many people supported the idea of a campaign but thought we weren't ready.

The Many Faces of the Case

As the case for support evolves, it begins to take on other forms. As it is used more frequently in solicitation activities, the case is translated into talking points for solicitors and into grant proposals, direct-mail letters, and press releases. If the organization chooses to do so, the case can also be presented in a video. When the campaign enters its public phase, the case will be presented graphically as a campaign brochure.

To develop the case step by step, follow these sixteen guidelines.

1. Review the purpose of the case for support.
2. Review the answers to the five *W*s: who, what, when, where, why.
3. Decide who will write the case.
4. Gather information.
5. Determine the best strategy for involving insiders.
6. Select the insiders to involve.
7. Enlist the insiders (either for the committee or for interviews).
8. Conduct the committee meetings or interviews.
9. Prepare the first draft of the case.
10. Review the text with the executive director.
11. Review the text with the case committee.
12. Revise according to committee input.
13. Meet with the graphic designer (optional).
14. Review and get input from the board.
15. Revise according to board input.
16. Distribute the new version to those who helped develop it.

Checklist for an Effective Case

An effective and compelling case arises out of the intense complexities of involving many people, and it crystallizes the intense simplicities that capture the essence and spirit of the project that the organization is about to undertake.

This chapter has discussed the process of developing a case for support. If the case for support is effective and the process used to develop it was successful, an organization should be able to respond affirmatively to each of the following four questions.

1. Have the board members and other insiders taken ownership of the case?
2. Does the case make a reader's heart beat faster? (with excitement, not anxiety!)
3. Does the case focus on the needs of the community rather than the needs of the organization?
4. Is the case a document that can be used and adapted as the campaign progresses?

If the answer to all of these questions is "yes," the case process has accomplished its goals and the organization now has a document out of which a successful campaign will grow.

References

Strunk, William, and E.B. White. 1979. *The elements of style.* 3d ed. New York: Macmillan.

Zinsser, William. 1980. *On writing well.* 2d ed. New York: Harper & Row.

The text of the Declaration of Independence is available on the World-Wide Web at: http://www.usia.gov/HTML/deceng.html.

Chapter 4
Can the Project Be Done? Conducting a Feasibility Study

Chapter Outline
- Dreams vs. Reality
- What Is a Feasibility Study?
- Do We Really Need a Feasibility Study?
- When Should a Feasibility Study Be Undertaken?
- What Will the Feasibility Study Evaluate?
- The Feasibility Study Process
- The Feasibility Study Consultant
- Enlisting a Feasibility Study Committee
- Overseeing the Interview Process
- The Feasibility Study Report
- Confidentiality
- Getting the Most out of the Feasibility Study
- A Feasibility Study Checklist

Dreams vs. Reality

Although fund-raising professionals tend to think of the feasibility study as belonging solely to the world of fund raising and development, professionals in many other fields also conduct such studies. An organization that is contemplating a feasibility study for a capital campaign may already have commissioned a feasibility study for the campaign's proposed project by a financial planner, land planner, architect, or land developer, thus there is often considerable confusion around the subject of such studies. The development officer and the campaign consultant may be bombarded with questions and comments from board members, and even staff, such as "I thought we had already done a feasibility study!" or "We need another feasibility study? What did all that money we paid to the developer go toward?"

The purpose of this chapter is to help the development staff and the organization's leadership understand the difference between a fund-raising feasibility study and other kinds of feasibility studies, to clarify what information a fund-raising feasibility study can and cannot provide, and to explain the mechanics of conducting a feasibility study.

What Is a Feasibility Study?

The purpose of all feasibility studies is to assist those who are planning a large project in evaluating the chances of the project's success before the project begins. Such studies provide an organized analysis of a project during its planning stages. This analysis allows the organization to determine what can realistically be accomplished in a campaign and indicates the most effective means of reaching those goals.

Feasibility studies are conducted by professionals in their fields, who gather data and examine and weigh the many factors that affect the outcome of the project. In particular, financial feasibility studies are likely to analyze market potential, population growth, demographic patterns, interest rates, income, expenses, and other elements that determine the financial feasibility of a project. Planning feasibility studies explore issues of zoning, land use, environmental restrictions, access roads, and other requirements and prohibitions that determine the development potential of a land parcel.

The Fund-Raising Feasibility Study Is Different

A fund-raising feasibility study will consider in detail an organization's potential to raise funds for a particular project through a capital campaign. A well-done feasibility study will help the organization make the right decisions about conducting a capital campaign before the planning for a project has progressed very far. Specifically, a fund-raising feasibility study:

- assesses how much money can probably be raised for a project
- outlines the most effective fund-raising strategy

> *A well-done feasibility study will help the organization make the right decisions about conducting a capital campaign before the planning for a project has progressed very far.*

- assesses the organization's readiness for a campaign
- makes recommendations for a realistic and appropriate campaign goal
- presents a preliminary campaign timetable
- provides a host of other insights about how the organization is viewed by insiders and community leaders

Sometimes these studies are referred to as precampaign-planning studies, and the two terms will be used interchangeably throughout this chapter. As this name perhaps more accurately implies, these studies do not directly answer the question, Can the organization raise money? Rather, they indicate what amount of money can most likely be raised, and they outline how the organization should prepare itself for carrying out the capital campaign. But a precampaign-planning study does much more than answer those questions. Such a study moves an organization forward by addressing more general issues. A study might highlight aspects of the organization that need to be strengthened and suggest concrete ways to address those issues. In other instances, a study may suggest alterations to the case for support that would be necessary to inspire contributors. A good study always provides important information to guide an organization to success, not only in its capital campaign but on into its future as well.

The Feasibility Study Helps Build Relationships

In addition to providing crucial information about a campaign's chances of success, feasibility studies are excellent ways to involve and cultivate donors and leaders for the campaign. The primary data that inform a feasibility study are gathered through a series of interviews conducted by the consultant. Through one-on-one personal interviews, major donors, primary staff members, and key volunteers have a very real and important opportunity to participate in the project's decision-making process. Indeed, to be singled out to be interviewed for a feasibility study is to be singled out as a leader—someone whose opinion is valued.

In many organizations, it is the feasibility study that constitutes the very first opportunity for individuals outside the immediate circle of the board to learn about and contribute to plans for advancing the cause of the organization.

Do We Really Need a Feasibility Study?

"All that unnecessary expense!" "It's just too much work!" "Why don't we just start asking people for money and see what happens?" "We already know how much we need." "Let's just *do it!*" Such comments are often heard from board members or from the executive director.

Below are listed three of the most common objections and fears that arise when it is suggested that a feasibility study ought to be commissioned.

1. "It is too much of a risk to solicit candid opinions about our organization." While this fear probably won't be directly articulated, it may very well be an unspoken one among board and staff. It is not pleasant to imagine an outside consultant poking about, talking to the organization's major donors and key volunteers, who might say things that cer-

---

The Feasibility Study That Saved Us from Ourselves

Before I joined my organization, the decision had already been made to start a new program and afterward raise money through a capital campaign to pay off the debt. This decision ended up a financial and philosophical disaster. In an attempt to salvage what we could, we sought advice from a campaign consultant. She told us very clearly that it is difficult to find funding after the fact. Donors often prefer to create something new, and so are not particularly interested in paying off debt.

Eventually we decided to raise money for a new building to bring all of our services to one location. It sounded like a great idea, especially as we were about to begin celebrating our twenty-fifth anniversary in the community. Our consultant conducted a feasibility study, and told us that we were not yet ready to undertake a capital campaign. He recommended that we devote a year to involving our major donor prospects more deeply in the life of the organization. That was not news we were pleased to hear.

Internally he also felt we weren't ready, citing problems between our board and our executive director, who was new in her job and who did not yet possess the full confidence of the board.

We accepted the results of the feasibility study. We did not go ahead with a campaign. During the following year we began our major donor work, and following a traumatic wrangle with the staff and board, the executive director resigned.

As it turned out, the feasibility study saved us from blundering into something for which we were not prepared and surely would have failed. Our entire agency would have been in trouble had we plunged ahead.

—Development Director

tain individuals would rather were left unsaid. The organization might learn some unpleasant things about itself that it would rather not know!

2. "If the study isn't positive, we may have to postpone our plan. And we have crucial needs, needs that can't wait." While it is not pleasant to contemplate the necessity of putting off attending to critical needs, it is much better to wait than to commit the organization to a campaign that is unlikely

to succeed. As exemplified in the story above, a feasibility study can help an organization pinpoint its weaknesses before committing itself to a campaign. Taking the time to prepare the organization thoroughly for the campaign is what spells the difference between failure and success.

3. "We were counting on the campaign to strengthen our development program. If the feasibility study says we can't move forward now, how can we generate the excitement that we need to advance our annual fund-raising program?" While it is true that one of the benefits of a successful campaign is a strengthened and renewed development program, this cannot be the primary purpose of a campaign. Moreover, a lackluster campaign will undermine, not strengthen, the development program. If the organization's fund-raising programs are weak, then before even considering a capital campaign it will be necessary to concentrate on building and strengthening relationships with donors, fine tuning record-keeping systems, and working with the board on basic fund-raising techniques.

We Need $250,000. Please Give.

A small private school was forced out the building it had occupied for many years. A college in the area offered land to the school and assistance if they could raise $250,000 to fund the project. The college was even able to locate an architect who was willing to donate a preliminary design. To raise the money, the school's board decided to hold their very first auction. The auction was held in the school's auditorium. Prominently displayed on the stage were drawings of the new building together with a list of rooms and the gifts needed to pay for them. The chairman of the board made an appeal from the stage, and then they waited for donations to come in. They have been waiting ever since.

The school's board learned several lessons from this auction, and they learned them, unfortunately, the hard way. They learned that it is impossible for a small organization to raise a quarter of a million dollars by bringing in 2,500 gifts averaging $100 each. They learned that their great need was not sufficient in and of itself to motivate people to make major gifts. They learned that if they wanted to raise major gifts they would have to make personal, targeted requests to individuals who already had an interest in the school. Finally, they learned that trying to raise money by the seat of their trousers without a credible plan simply would not work.

Although well intentioned, the board hadn't done its homework. (Not a good example for the students!) They understood their own needs—most of us are very familiar with our own needs—but they had no information about what their constituency might give to a campaign or what, for that matter, their constituency really thought about the planned relocation. There was no experienced fund raiser in the organization, and so, without background information and someone to guide them, they blundered ahead, souring their chances for a successful campaign.

Only when the fund-raising house is in order and fund-raising programs are stronger, will the organization be ready to risk a campaign. Although campaigns require risks and an optimistic viewpoint, foolhardy risks and naïve optimism are no help at all. And undertaking a capital campaign without a feasibility study is a giant step down the path of foolhardiness.

A good feasibility study will repay its expense. It will cultivate major donors; it will provide a way of assessing the probability of a successful campaign; it will give a sense of whether there is a strong group of supporters who are eager to help or whether the development staff is so far out in front that volunteer support will quickly evaporate. The feasibility study may or may not provide the answers hoped for, but whether the study recommends "full steam ahead," a lower goal or longer timetable, or even "Do not pass *go*, do not collect even two hundred dollars—yet" it will ultimately help the organization manage a successful campaign.

Not to have evaluated the probability of success for a capital campaign is to risk the future of the organization. Because a capital campaign is highly visible and involves a great many individuals who are important to the organization, it is vital that it succeed. A precampaign-planning study provides the information and the plan that are necessary to minimize the risk of a failure.

When Should a Feasibility Study Be Undertaken?

The timing of a feasibility study is critical. Studies are conducted after a major project has been conceived and a general project plan developed but before the plan is finalized. A feasibility study explores the primary constituency's reactions to a specific project and invites selected individuals to provide constructive input. All parties whose advice is desired should be consulted at this point, because once a project plan has been finalized, there is a very limited opportunity to alter it to reflect further suggestions.

Before a study is undertaken, therefore, the following aspects of the project should be known, at least in general terms.

- What project does the organization wish to accomplish with the money raised?
- How will this project be realized?
- When will it be completed?
- How much is it likely to cost?
- How will it be paid for?
- How much money does the organization anticipate raising through a campaign?
- Who are the key individuals on whom the success of the project depends (staff, architect, contractor, or other primary players if known)?

These questions are similar to those addressed in the case for support. Because people rarely give major gifts to organizations without knowing in some detail how their money will be spent, a clear idea of the project must be articulated before someone is hired to probe the reactions of the donor base. A donor might well evince small interest in making a large gift to fund an infant-care wing of a day-care center if that individual believes that a mother's place is at home with her preschoolers. That very same person, however, might give generously to fund a new wing to house an after-school program for elementary-school children. Therefore, a feasibility study cannot be successfully undertaken before a clear outline of the project has been developed.

It is also important to conduct the feasibility study fairly early in the planning process because it may be discovered that the organization's needs fail to match the donors' interests. It is far preferable to make such a discovery early than to launch a full-scale campaign for an enterprise that no one wants to support.

> *Studies are conducted after a major project has been conceived and a general plan developed but before the plan is finalized.*

They Told Us They Wanted a Nicer-Looking Library

The goal of our campaign was to automate sixteen libraries in the county-wide public library system. One of the things we learned from the feasibility study undertaken by our consultant was that many of our donors were quite eager to support the libraries, and moreover, they thought that the automation project was very important. However, they didn't think it was quite so important as improving the appearance of the main library. We knew that the library needed repairs, but we had thought that a renovation campaign was a campaign better left for another day.

As a result of the feasibility study we decided to fashion a case for support that combined the automation project with building improvements. We came up with a price tag of $2.1 million, which deflated our enthusiasm somewhat, since the feasibility study had concluded that we could probably raise no more than $1.5 million. The core committee met and discussed the money issue at length. We considered and considered again just what it would actually mean to try to raise such a large amount. The group finally decided that we could do it—that we should "go for it." And so we did.

Ultimately, we did raise the entire $2.1 million by our deadline—with four days to spare—but we really worked hard to make that happen.

—Executive Director

What Will the Feasibility Study Evaluate?

A thorough study will evaluate both the readiness of an organization to undertake a campaign and the readiness of a community of donors to support it. It should evaluate the following elements of the program and donor base:

- the organization's reputation with community leadership
- the effectiveness and reputation of the organization's chief executive
- the strength and giving potential of the board
- the willingness of the board to work on a campaign
- the size and giving record of the donor base
- the availability of volunteers to work on a campaign
- the potential for lead gifts
- the likelihood of recruiting an effective campaign chair

A study will also test the reaction of leaders and major donor prospects to the proposed project and campaign. It will help answer some of the following questions regarding the project:

- Is the proposed project perceived as important to the community?
- Does the project make sense?
- Are the plans appropriate for both the organization and the community?
- Does the project have a strong chance of succeeding?
- Are donors who have the ability to make major gifts likely to be major contributors to this particular project?
- How much money is the organization likely to be able to raise for this project?
- Who are the individuals whose participation and assistance will be most likely to make this project succeed?
- What are the best strategies and approaches for the campaign?
- Are there enough people willing to help with the campaign, and will they be dedicated enough to see the campaign through to completion?
- Is there sufficient staff to conduct a campaign properly?
- How much is the campaign likely to cost?
- What is a reasonable timetable for the campaign?
- What must the organization do to get ready for a campaign?

The Feasibility Study Process

Who Conducts the Study?

A feasibility study gives the organization a chance to take an objective look at itself and the project it has planned. To obtain truly objective information will require the assistance of an outside consultant. Although the organization's staff will be able to plan the project, an objective study cannot be accomplished with internal personnel, who are by definition simply too close to the organization.

Because of the close, ongoing ties with individuals in the community, it will be awkward for a staff member to ask certain questions that must, however, be posed, and it will also sometimes be difficult to hear what people are really trying to say.

In addition, an organization's staff is not likely to have the time it would take to conduct its own feasibility study. A feasibility study involves preparing questions, scheduling interviews, meeting with interview subjects, assembling and analyzing findings, and presenting the results to the organization's leadership. That can be a full-time, albeit temporary, two to four month job. At this point in preparing for a campaign, when there is already so much additional work, there is unlikely to be any qualified staff member with the time for such a demanding task.

Conducting a Feasibility Study

The feasibility study process falls into three categories: (1) preparing a preliminary case for support; (2) gathering information; and (3) preparing and presenting the report.

Preliminary case for support. Because feasibility studies solicit information, testing the potential of a specific

---

The Misinformed Director and the Misguided Feasibility Study

I had never worked for a nonprofit organization before, but I had considerable practical experience doing similar development work for other types of organizations. When this nonprofit advertised for a director, I thought, "This is something I'd like to do." They hired me, and, when I arrived on the scene, I was immediately handed a $2.6 million campaign goal, a goal that was based solely on the organization's needs.

In retrospect, I can't believe how naïve I was, but when I came in I was told by the board, "Don't worry, you won't have to do any fund raising yourself because we have a committee who will raise all the money. All you have to do is run the organization." Now, the board really believed this. They had engaged someone to head the campaign who was quite well known and well loved and who had raised a lot of money before. I thought we had it in the bag, and that all I would have to do was manage the building project. Well, that was mistake number one.

It also turned out that the "feasibility study" I had been shown was not a feasibility study at all, but rather something that one of the board members had written up about the project. It was really more of a modest first pass at a case statement than a feasibility study, but to the uninitiated it sounded pretty good.

When I finally realized that I couldn't just sit back and watch disaster strike, I brought someone on board to help us put together a business plan and to perform a real feasibility study. This feasibility study told us that we had a problem with name recognition in the community. The individuals interviewed could not conceive of a $2.6 million campaign for an organization that they had never donated to before. Facing a potential flop, we reconnoitered, reevaluated, and regrouped. We broke our campaign into phases, and now, having recovered from the first successful phase, we are gathering energy for the second.

—Executive Director

project, an organization must prepare a brief statement that clearly and convincingly describes the project that is to be evaluated. For the purposes of the feasibility study, the case for support is presented in draft or preliminary form. The case is usually three to five pages long, computer generated, simply presented, and copied. The preliminary case for support is sent to the people whose opinions are being sought through the interview process, giving them an opportunity to read and digest the information prior to the interview.

Gathering information. The primary method of gathering information for a feasibility study is through personal interviews. A typical feasibility study for a community-based organization should include personal interviews with community leaders, leaders of the organization, the organization's major donors, and other key constituents. Some feasibility studies also gather information from a broader cross-section of people in a community by sending surveys in the mail.

Interview questions are designed to solicit information in three areas: (1) the reputation of the organization, its programs, director and board; (2) the project being proposed; and (3) the potential for gifts and volunteer assistance to the capital campaign.

Preparing and presenting the report. After the material is assembled, a written report must be prepared. The feasibility-study report should summarize the process by which the material was gathered, synthesize and summarize the information gathered, and present clear recommendations about whether and how to proceed with a capital campaign.

It is a common (and wise) practice for consultants to share a draft of the report with the executive director and board chair before distributing it to the full board. This practice will help the consultant catch any errors that might have been made prior to a wider distribution of the report. It will also give the director and board chair the opportunity to reflect on the information contained in the report and to determine how and when the report should be presented to the committee and the rest of the board.

With a lengthy and complex report—which most feasibility study reports are—the committee members and the board should receive a copy of the report at least five days prior to the meeting at which the recommendations will be presented.

Because the material in the report is insider information, each copy of the report should be stamped CONFIDENTIAL before being distributed.

The Feasibility Study Consultant

Although chapter 2 describes in detail the process of selecting a campaign consultant, when it comes time to conduct a feasibility study, one develops a clearer idea of whom one does or does not want as a consultant. In many ways, the feasibility study consultant will serve as the organization's representative to the leadership of the community, lead donors, key volunteers, and any other individuals who are likely to be important to the organization.

The consultant is likely to hear all sorts of things—both good and bad—about the organization and its leadership. And the consultant will leave a distinct impression on the people interviewed—people important to the organization. The selection of the consultant is not to be taken lightly.

What Can Be Expected?

What can be expected from the feasibility study consultant? Lots! The organization has engaged an expert to guide it through a complex and sensitive process, and that is precisely what the consultant should do. In fact, by the time a contract has been signed, the consultant should have outlined the process and timetable of the study quite specifically. Answers should be obtained to the questions discussed below. To help put these questions and answers in perspective, each of the questions that might be put to the consultant will be discussed in some detail, for there is a wide range of styles and issues that determine whether the feasibility study, as proposed, is right for a particular organization.

Who Will Work with the Consultant?

Every consultant has his or her own way of organizing a feasibility study, but many experienced consultants encourage the involvement of key volunteers to oversee their work, thereby building internal ownership of the study. Experienced consultants understand that the purpose of the campaign is not only to raise money, but to build and strengthen relationships with the organization's donors. For these consultants, the process of organizing the feasibility study provides an excellent opportunity to involve key volunteers on an ad hoc feasibility study committee, thereby actively engaging key volunteers and donor prospects in the early phases of planning the campaign.

Who Will Draft the Preliminary Case for Support?

Will the development staff be completely responsible for the preliminary case for support, or will the consultant be involved in its development? The consultant's broad experience in capital campaigns can be employed to advantage in drafting an effective and compelling case for support. However, because the development staff knows and can articulate the organization's needs better than an outsider, the preliminary gathering of information and writing should be performed by staff.

How Will the Consultant Gather Information?

Most feasibility studies for community-based campaigns rely extensively on personal interviews. Occasionally, a consultant will suggest that only a very few interviews be conducted in person and that additional information be gathered by means of a telephone or mail survey. However, because people will often say things in person that they would not put on paper, the primary power of a feasibility study comes from personal interviews. The consultant who is selected should be willing to conduct enough interviews to cover all of the individuals who are most important to the organization as well as a good cross section of community leadership.

The number of interviews will vary, depending on the size of the organization and the size of the community. For an established agency in a community with a popu-

lation of 100,000 to 250,000, one might expect a consultant to conduct 30 to 40 interviews.

If a consultant from the area has been engaged, it is likely that the consultant will want to schedule the interviews to make the most effective use of available time and to be as flexible as possible in fitting the schedules of the interview subjects. But if the consultant will be coming in from out of town on specified days, then it will probably make more sense for the staff to be in charge of scheduling. Scheduling is always a complex and time-consuming task, but for someone not familiar with the area it can be particularly difficult.

It is important for the development staff to know who, from the consultant's agency, will actually conduct the interviews and to have the opportunity to meet that person. Because it is difficult for one person to conduct several dozen interviews and remain open and fresh, the interviews might be divided among two or three interviewers who can then compare impressions with one another to form a more accurate picture than that which is obtainable by a single interviewer.

When Will the Consultant Report?

Although consultants vary in their practices, some consultants give a verbal report to the oversight committee after completing approximately one-half of the interviews. In that way, the committee has a chance to learn firsthand about the interview process and how it is proceeding. Moreover, at this midway meeting, both the committee members and the consultant will be able to ask questions that may have arisen. In some cases this is also a good time to reconsider the interview list. If, for example, the consultant has had a high percentage of individuals who are unable or unwilling to be interviewed, or if the interview subjects have themselves suggested additional interview prospects, the committee may choose to add some names to the list.

What Sorts of Questions Will Be Asked?

The consultants can be expected to develop a series of interview questions to help guide the interviews. Consultants vary widely in their manner of conducting interviews. Some use detailed forms that can later be collated and scored numerically, thereby providing the basis for a statistical analysis of the interviews. Others use a simple outline to guide more general conversations and rely on extensive note taking to capture information.

Most consultants gather information in four areas—opinions about the organization, the project, the funding, and the leadership. Interviews often begin with the most general questions and move to the specifics of the subject's ability and willingness to help. Initial questions often establish the interviewee's relationship with the organization and determine his or her views of that organization, its board, its programs, and its staff. Then interviews elicit opinions about the proposed project—its importance in the community, its feasibility, and any reservations or concerns that the person might have. The interviews then explore the potential for raising funds and attracting volunteer leadership, including where major gifts might be sought and who in the community might be considered as a campaign leader. And finally, the interviews should probe the giving potential of the subject and his or her willingness to help with the campaign.

In general, one is well advised to beware of statistical analyses with a small interview sample. Among those interviewed are certain to be a few individuals whose responses are absolutely crucial in determining the goals, timetable, and probability of success for the campaign. In a sample of 25 or 30 interviews, the importance of those few opinions that carry significantly more weight than the others will be lost in an analysis that accords equal weight to all responses. Therefore, although it may be interesting to see an objective statistical report on the response to each interview question, this type of reporting does not provide the judgments that are really needed.

What Will Be in the Report?

Feasibility study reports vary as widely as styles of consulting. Some consultants produce lavish, lengthy reports printed on elegant paper. Others prefer a simpler, more straightforward approach. Although there is no single acceptable format for the report, its style should reflect the requirements of the organization. It would not do, for example, for the consultant to submit a seventy-page, triple-spaced report copied on only one side of a page to an organization whose primary mission was to save trees. On the other hand, an exclusive private school with a wealthy, high-powered board might not take seriously a report without a cover and an elegant format.

More important than the style is that the report be well written with no errors in spelling, grammar, and punctuation. (It is amazing how many reports are littered with such lapses.) The information should be clearly and simply presented. It should be prefaced with an executive summary for those who don't have the time or patience to read a long report. It should contain a summary of the interview findings, conclusions reached, recommendations as to how the organization should proceed, and a list of people interviewed.

The report of the feasibility study should include conclusions and recommendations on the following topics:

- the reputation of the organization
- the effectiveness and validity of the case for support
- the readiness of the volunteer and staff leadership to accept major roles in the campaign

- the willingness of key volunteers to make leadership campaign pledges
- the readiness of other major donors to support a campaign
- the conditions external to the organizations that are likely to affect the campaign
- an outline of how to proceed, along with a preliminary timetable

Although not all consultants are willing to offer an estimate of how much money they believe can be raised if their advice is followed, such a recommendation (often in the form of a dollar range) should be part of every feasibility study report. This issue should be discussed with the consultant before a contract is signed.

How Will the Report Be Distributed?

Organization leaders should discuss with a consultant how they plan to present the report to the organization at large. Will the executive director have the opportunity to review a draft prior to its broader distribution? Who will be responsible for duplicating and distributing the report? Will the consultant be available to present the findings at a board meeting in person? Once again, consultants vary in their practices. While there is perhaps no one way to accomplish this, the organization should discuss the consultant's process beforehand.

How Long Will the Feasibility Study Take?

The feasibility study should take anywhere from six weeks to four months, depending on the size and scope of the study. From the consultant's point of view, the key issues in scheduling a feasibility study are the client's ability to enlist a committee to oversee the process and the difficulty in scheduling interviews. If the interviews require considerable travel (which is unusual for a community-based organization), the interviews will be more difficult to schedule. If the study takes place during the summer or over the holiday season, interviews may take longer to schedule because people are harder to reach and have less free time. A good consultant should be able to predict with reasonable accuracy the length of time the study will take. The consultant, however, has no control over the scheduling of committee and board meetings. These should be planned well in advance so that the organization itself is not responsible for delaying the process.

How Much Will the Study Cost?

The authors have polled a few of their colleagues regarding feasibility study costs and although we can't give you a specific number, for a small- to medium-sized organization, conducting a feasibility study with 25–30 interviews, the fee can range anywhere from $8,000 to $25,000, with most falling in the $10,000 to $14,000 range.

Enlisting a Feasibility Study Committee

After the consultant has been hired and the organization's leadership has become familiar with the scope and purpose of the study, it is time for the organization to ready itself for the feasibility study to begin.

All fund raising is based on involving people in meaningful ways in the life of the organization. The organization's staff and leadership should seize every opportunity to make such meaningful experiences happen, and a feasibility study is just such an opportunity. To this end, a meeting of the executive director, the development director, the consultant, and the board chair should be called to determine who should be invited to serve on an ad hoc committee to oversee the progress of the feasibility study. The individuals who take part in this way will have a bird's-eye view of the emerging project. They will become familiar with the goals of the organization. They will come to understand the importance and excitement of the new project. They will actually have the chance to put in their two cents' worth (or perhaps even more) about the case for support. In essence, those involved in this process are very likely to become thoroughly engaged in planning for the organization's growth.

Because this will be a working committee, it should consist of approximately eight members. Thus, if five or six members can make it to a meeting, adding in the development director and the consultant, a group will result that is a good size for serious discussion. The group might include two or three of the strongest board members, a few of the most generous donor prospects, and also a few individuals who are emotionally committed to the organization and capable of clear and effective thinking. Ideally, the committee should be a mix of those already passionate about the organization and those who have financial or leadership potential and whose greater involvement would be especially beneficial.

The committee will probably wish to meet about four times over a period of two or three months. It will be charged with assisting and overseeing the work of the consultant on the feasibility study. When the study is completed, the work of the committee is completed.

The development director must be very clear with the volunteers as to what is expected of them: what their time commitment will be and when their job will be finished. Clarity about expectations from the beginning offers the best chance of ending the process with happy and satisfied volunteers.

> *A feasibility study is an excellent opportunity to involve people in the life of an organization.*

Thoughts about Volunteer Management

Volunteers will be far more likely to agree to do five well-defined, time-limited tasks, sequentially, than to sign on for one long, amorphous job. Volunteer involvement might be thought of as a series of links in a chain. Each link can be opened and closed, much like a loose-leaf binder ring. The task of involving volunteers is to define each link so that it is not too big and can be accomplished successfully. People are invited to help link by link, their success highlighted and recognized after each link. Those volunteers who worked well and were excited by their work in a particular link may be invited back to assist with the next link, but they are neither expected nor required to do so.

By knowing that they have only signed on for the short haul, not only are volunteers likely to be more willing to help, but since they have been offered only a limited engagement, the director can pick and choose whom to invite to help with the next stage of the project. It becomes possible to let some volunteers go and then bring new ones into the process without offending anyone. Committees become better and better as the collection of tried-and-true volunteers grows.

From a volunteer's perspective, it is much more attractive to sign on for a small task and then to sign on again if things went well. The volunteer is employed effectively and is amply recognized but doesn't feel saddled with a heavy burden. By the way, according to this theory, boards without term limits are not good for an organization. They are frozen links that tend to create organizations that stagnate and spoil.

This pattern of volunteer involvement can be used throughout a capital campaign. The first link may have been the committee to help choose the consultant. Perhaps the second link will be the feasibility study committee.

The Work of the Committee

The feasibility study committee has multiple tasks and these must be carefully explained to potential committee members before they are asked to serve.

Review the case for support. The committee members can be an excellent sounding board for the case for support, primarily because they will bring a variety of viewpoints to the task. If the case is unclear, or the explanation of the needs seems not to make sense, they will articulate these concerns. The input from these individuals will provide another opportunity to refine the case so that it is clear and precise before it is presented to campaign prospects.

Develop the list of people to be interviewed. Since the members of the committee are peers and colleagues of those who will be interviewed for the feasibility study, they will be able to offer suggestions as to who can provide the best information, whose opinions are really going to matter, and which people are likely to be the most influential and helpful during the course of the campaign.

Review the questions that the consultant intends to ask during the interviews. While the consultant is primarily responsible for developing the interview questions, the committee members may offer others or perhaps suggest different ways of phrasing a particular question. Because they know both the organization and many of the individuals who will be interviewed, they may have some interesting and useful insights into the effectiveness of particular questions in eliciting information.

Help draft a letter to be sent to all interview prospects prior to scheduling the interviews. It is customary and appropriate to send a letter to each individual on the interview list requesting an interview. This letter is usually sent by the organization and is signed by either the executive director or the chairman of the board. The letter explains that the organization has hired a consulting firm to conduct a feasibility study to evaluate the potential of raising funds for a specific project. It lets them know that they are among a small group of community or organization leaders who have been selected to be interviewed and requests that they make time to meet with the consultants. A copy of the preliminary case for support is sent along with the letter so that the person may choose to read about the project prior to the interview. A sample letter is included in Exhibit 4–1.

Meet with the consultant for an update sometime around the midpoint of the interview process to assess progress and make course corrections if needed. Staying in contact with the consultant during the study is very important. The feasibility study's course should be flexible, and certain adjustments may be needed. Making adjustments is not a sign of bad planning; rather, it implies that the oversight committee is paying proper attention to what is going on.

Review a draft of the report. Once the feasibility study is complete, the committee will receive a draft of the report before it is sent on to the board. This gives both the committee members and the consultant the opportunity to review and discuss the report's recommendations while they are still in draft form. If the oversight committee has had a chance to review the report, and then accepts it and recommends its findings to the board, there is a good chance that the board, too, will accept it.

Exhibit 4–1 Sample Letter for Interview Prospects

Date

x
x
x

Dear _____:

Organization X is rapidly outgrowing its facilities. To meet the growing demand for our services, we are exploring the possibility of building a larger facility.

To help us in our planning, we have engaged the firm of Jones, Jones, and Jones to conduct a series of confidential interviews with those persons whose opinions we believe would be most valuable in assessing our proposed plans. I hope you will be willing to share your thoughts about Organization X with Jones or her associate Jones.

Within the next few days, Mary Smith from our staff will contact you to schedule the interview. The interview should take no more than forty-five minutes. Your comments during the interview will be held in strictest confidence, and you will not be solicited during this meeting.

Thank you very much for helping us make sure that our plans for Organization X will reflect the needs and ideas of our supporters and our community.

Sincerely,

_____

P.S. Enclosed is a preliminary description of our plans.

Overseeing the Interview Process

During the interview process, the consultants will be spending considerable time in the community, speaking face-to-face with board members, major donor prospects, and key volunteers. If the consultants are good interviewers, they will do more listening than talking. But they will also find opportunities during the interviews to speak about the strength and effectiveness of the organization. They will try to engage each individual they interview in a discussion that brings out that person's specific interests, hopes, and concerns about the organization and the project.

In some cases, the consultants may have to rely on telephone interviews. Occasionally, someone on the interview list is not available in person or is residing in another state or even another country for a few months, and it is too costly or time consuming for the consultant to travel to that location. When necessary, telephone interviews are better than no interviews. Over the telephone, however, the interviewer can rarely build the kind of personal rapport that leads to the deeper understanding one hopes for from these interviews.

Most consultants prepare a preliminary table of gifts to take to each interview that shows how many gifts of specific sizes will be needed to make up the campaign goal. For a campaign of $1 million, for example, the table might show the requirement of one gift of $150,000, two gifts of $100,000, four gifts of $50,000, and so on. The interviewer will probably ask for an indication of the level on the table at which the individual might envision making a gift. Through this process, combined with other information gathered from the interviews, the consultant will be able to develop a reasonably accurate sense of the potential for leadership gifts for the project.

The Interview Process Can Be Stressful

The interview process often raises the level of anxiety within the organization. In fact, the entire feasibility study process makes some directors and development directors very nervous. After all, their major donors and volunteer leaders are being asked to give their candid opinions about them, and those opinions will be reported back to the full board!

To help alleviate some of this anxiety, the staff should stay in close touch with the consultants. The consultants may not be able to report everything they are hearing in the course of their interviews, but they will be able to dispel most of the horror stories that an overactive imagination may be concocting.

During this period, the community grapevine begins to become active as well. Soon after the consultants begin receiving information about the organization, the organization will begin to receive information about the consultants. The chairman of the board may call to re-

During a feasibility study interview period, the community grapevine will probably become active as the community leaders who have been interviewed begin talking about the project.

port about his interview. A long-time volunteer who had recently been inactive may call the development director to schedule lunch in order to find out the latest and to gossip about the interview process. It won't take long before the grapevine begins to present a fairly clear picture about the interview process. Now it is time for the consultants to be nervous! All comments thus received should be listened to carefully. If for any reason there are a number of comments that ring alarm bells about the consultant, the feasibility study committee and the consultant should be summoned to discuss the problem and suggest remedies. There will be further discussion on how to handle this type of problem in the troubleshooting guide in the Appendix.

Thanking the Interview Participants

Immediately after completing an interview, the consultants should send a personal thank-you note to the individual they have interviewed. The official thank you from the organization is usually sent after the report has been written, so that the thank-you letter can include information about the outcome of the study. The consultant should assist in reviewing the list of interview subjects to decide to whom to send a full copy of the report and to whom just a summary.

At the conclusion of the interview process, there will usually be a few individuals who could not be reached. Perhaps they were out of town, or perhaps they simply were unwilling to be interviewed. Together with the consultant, the organization should decide how to reach closure with each of these individuals. In some cases, a letter of regret will be the appropriate response. In others, it may be desirable for a member of the organization to meet with that person in place of the consultant. In all cases, however, once the initial letter has been sent, the contact must be closed appropriately.

The Feasibility-Study Report

Although many who have been through feasibility studies a number of times have come to understand that the process is at least as important as the product, it is quite natural for a first-timer to see the written report as the centerpiece of the study. As mentioned before, studies vary greatly in both style and content. Some consultants belong to the "heavier is better" school—a leftover attitude from high school and college. They figure that the client is paying a large sum for a report, and so the client may feel cheated if the report does not, through sheer heft, provide a sense that it is worth the money spent on it. It is not uncommon to see studies that run one hundred pages or more, with fancy dividers, charts, and graphs, and printed on heavy stock that further increases the weight of the report. Other consultants prefer reports that have distilled the essence of what they have learned.

But whether one prefers the heavy or light variety, every responsible report should include the following elements:

- Appearance. The report should feature an attractive, professional-looking title page and cover.
- Executive summary. An executive summary of one to two pages encapsulates the primary findings and recommendations of the report.
- Table of contents. There should be a table of contents with page numbers to facilitate locating information.
- Content. There should be sections in the body of the report that briefly describe the process used to conduct the study, a description and analysis of findings from the interviews, conclusions drawn from the findings, and specific recommendations about how the organization should proceed.
- Appendices. There should be an appendix of names of all those interviewed, as well as appendices that collect all the relevant information and material used to conduct the study. This will include a list of committee members, the case for support, the interview questions, the table of gifts, and any other relevant documentation.
- Quotations. Some consultants include a section of selected quotations from the interviews. These are often organized by topic and are presented without attribution. Although not necessary, a selection of well-chosen quotations gives those who read the study an understanding of the range of opinions heard during a set of interviews.
- Other report elements. Consultants sometimes employ charts to illustrate graphically the distribution of the interview subjects' responses to the various questions. Although, as has been discussed earlier, these illustrations can be an effective way to present information, in the world of capital campaigns, not all men and women are created equal, not all opinions are equally important, and a neutral statistical analysis might actually be misleading.

The report should be written in prose that is clear, concise, and effective. Some consultants attempt to inflate their style through the use of passive verbs, but this only serves to make their writing turgid and dense. One can get an idea of the consultant's writing style by looking at one's accumulated correspondence. Many consultants do not have editorial assistance, so the style in their letters is likely to be what will appear in the report.

The consultant should be encouraged to submit a draft of the report to the development director, executive director, and the board chair to read before it is shown to anyone else. This will provide a chance for these individuals to digest the material, to discuss any problematic areas with the consultant, and to catch any inconsistencies or errors that may have occurred. Once the report has been distributed to a larger group, it will be more difficult for the consultant to make changes without jeopardizing the credibility of individuals within the organization.

Once these three have had a look at the report, the next draft should be distributed to the feasibility study committee for their consideration before being presented to the board. A meeting of the committee should be called, and the report should be sent to the committee members several days before that meeting to give them sufficient time to read it. And as always, it should be stamped DRAFT in large, preferably red, letters on the front cover. The consultant should be encouraged to present the report as a draft at this meeting and to solicit advice and suggestions for its improvement. It should not have a fancy cover or any other "bells and whistles" at this stage so that in its provisional appearance it will encourage the committee members to be free with their suggestions. Such an exchange will lead to a better report and will solidify the committee's support for the final version.

Once the report has been accepted by the committee, copies should be sent to every board member. Each copy should be attractively bound and be professional in appearance. These reports should be sent with a cover letter requesting the members to read the report and to be prepared to discuss it at the next meeting when the consultant presents his or her findings. Sometimes these reports are presented to the board as part of a longer meeting that covers other issues. Sometimes, if the report includes controversial or difficult material, the report is presented at a special meeting of the board. The consultant should make a verbal presentation of the report and then ask the board to accept the report.

Confidentiality

Most consultants begin each interview with a statement that the content of the interview will be held in confidence and that the material that has been gathered will not be attributed to any particular individual. This promise of anonymity frees the individuals who are being interviewed to express opinions that they might otherwise withhold if they knew that their thoughts would be reported back directly. People often use the interview process as an opportunity to pass constructive sugges-

> *When the feasibility study process works well, it encourages individuals to express their thoughts and ideas freely, sometimes closing a communications gap that may have been hidden before the study.*

tions to the organization anonymously and sometimes even to vent their frustrations about the organization's direction or operation.

Because many people feel uncomfortable expressing criticism openly, opinions are often left unstated if they go against what is perceived as the consensus. There are more hidden opinions around a board table than there are those that are openly expressed. A feasibility study provides a voice to some of these undercurrents in a fashion that can lead to constructive debate.

Unless specific approval from an individual has been obtained, the consultant will be very careful not to attribute to a specific individual the ideas and opinions that have been gathered in the study. Members of the organization, on the other hand, will be very curious about who said what. When the process works well, and sensitive issues are put on the table, some individuals may have more courage to express their thoughts and ideas directly, closing a communications gap that appeared not even to have existed prior to the study.

The consultant should not be asked to reveal specific information that cannot be shared. The interview forms will remain with the consultant—not with the organization, and the consultant's reputation rests on his or her ability to respect each interview subject's right to confidentiality.

Getting the Most out of the Feasibility Study

Once the study is complete, there will be an excellent opportunity to build on the relationships that were strengthened during the study. This chance should not be allowed to slip away. Key board members and donor prospects should be telephoned. They should be invited to lunch; their opinions should be sought. They should be involved in the next steps outlined in the study. Feasibility studies usually raise a host of far-reaching issues around which people can rally. Using such opportunities to draw people closer to the organization is the wellspring of effective fund raising.

A Feasibility Study Checklist

1. Are the function and purpose of a fund-raising feasibility study understood?
2. Can that understanding be articulated to board members, staff, and volunteers?
3. Has a consultant been hired who can conduct the feasibility study?
4. Has a preliminary case for support been drafted?
5. Is the consultant's role in conducting the feasibility study well understood?
6. Has a list of prospects for the feasibility study committee been drawn up?
7. Have materials for the feasibility study committee been prepared?
8. Is it clear what the committee's function will be?
9. Has the committee drafted the letter requesting a feasibility study interview?
10. Has it been made clear to the consultant that the organization's leadership expects to see the first draft of the report?
11. Is the confidentiality aspect of the feasibility study well understood?
12. Does the report make clear, timely, and specific recommendations?
13. Is the report being distributed so as to build understanding and ownership in the project?
14. Have interview participants been thanked and informed of the results of the study?
15. Have committee members been thanked?

Chapter 5
Who's Who? A Guide to Prospect Research

Chapter Outline
- Knowing What's Right
- Whither the Search?
- Where Not to Look . . . and Where to Look
- Building a Prospect List Through the Research Process
- Capturing Information
- Filling in the Details with Secondary Sources
- Knowing Right from Wrong
- Patience and Practice

Knowing What's Right

Campaigns succeed when the right prospects are asked for the right gifts by the right solicitors at the right time. To succeed, campaign managers must make many judgments about each solicitation. Who are the right prospects? What is the most appropriate gift for a particular donor? Who would be the right person to ask for that gift? To know the right answers to each of these questions requires information—lots of information. This chapter will attempt to demystify the area of fund raising known in large organizations as "prospect research" and will suggest simple, commonsense ways to gather, store, and make effective use of information about donors in ways that will benefit both donor and organization.

Whither the Search?

Prospect research is the process of gathering information about potential donors to determine as nearly as possible a prospective donor's giving potential, institutional interest, readiness to contribute, and the person or persons who are best suited to cultivate and solicit the donor. Ideally, a development officer would like to obtain in-depth information about every potential donor in order to make the very best judgments about each of them. In reality, however, there will be time and energy for gathering information about only a relatively small number of individuals. To use that time most efficiently, the development officer must work strategically,

focusing on those individuals who are most likely to be helpful in making the campaign successful.

The Search for Money

Unquestionably, money is a key ingredient in the success of a campaign. Where, then, does one find people with money? Who has given generously to the organization? Who has given consistently? Who in the community are the holders of wealth? Who has a reputation for a philanthropic spirit?

For the campaign to succeed, the organization must find enough such people—both those who have a prior history of giving to the organization and those who have a generous giving history in the community.

Some people give . . . and some don't. Giving patterns are rooted deeply in the human psyche. Some people develop the philanthropic spirit in their churches or synagogues, others from their families, and some just seem to have been born with generous natures. Although there are examples of individuals who become donors in a rush of inspiration, most giving runs in predictable patterns. There are those who give small gifts to many organizations, and others who give a few large gifts. Some give often, others never give. Whatever a donor's pattern, however, it is a pattern not generally amenable to change, and so one should not conclude that every wealthy person can be converted into a donor. A donor not only must possess some financial resources but also a philanthropic mind and spirit.

The Search for Power

In the search for prospects, one typically looks for individuals with the resources to make a substantial gift.

> *Most giving runs in predictable patterns. Some people give small gifts to many organizations, some give a few large gifts, some give often, and some never give.*

Often overlooked in the process is the value of searching out individuals with influence. For a successful campaign, it is important that organizations recruit not only people with the ability to give, but also those who have the power to encourage others to give.

Power is often defined as control or influence over others. In a campaign, however, power is also energy—the energy that accomplishes miracles, that turns a crisis into an opportunity, a quandary into a challenge, and caution into commitment. Power is acquired in many different ways. Some attain it through their positions, others because they have money. Some have it because of the circles in which they move. Still others owe their power to their excellent reputations.

When looking for people with power, organizations must seek some combination of influence, affluence, and charisma. Ideally, such people should be already committed to the organization or have a reasonable chance of becoming committed.

An organization's power base usually lies in no more than twenty-five people. In the case of a large organization, these may be people who can donate millions of dollars or who can attract major, national figures to the cause. In small organizations the power list may include top donors who can give no more than $10,000. In either case, however, assembling a list of twenty-five names and learning as much as possible about those individuals will help the development staff assess its most important resource—a tool already at hand—the power of committed individuals.

The Search for Commitment

The process of researching, estimating, and analyzing the financial resources of prospective donors can become such an all-consuming task that one might easily forget that it takes more than money to make a major donor.

A major donor must not only have money but must also be inclined to part with it. Having the *inclination* to give is at least as important as having the *resources* to give. People with passion, inclination, and zeal can often find ways of giving that are remarkably effective even if their financial resources are limited. Sometimes they are willing to solicit wealthy friends or relatives to make deferred gifts or gifts of property, or perhaps to make large gifts pledged over several years. And sometimes, people who appear to have few resources actually possess great wealth.

While stories like this do not occur with great frequency, its lesson is that those who are committed to an organization are far more valuable than wealthy people with no inclination to give. Committed donors, even those without apparent major resources, breathe life into campaigns, drawing in other people with their energy, enthusiasm, and generosity. Conversely, small gifts from uncommitted

wealthy individuals can lower expectations and take the wind out of a campaign before it even gets started.

Although it is helpful to know who has resources, it is far more useful to identify those who are seriously inclined to support the organization's mission—those with passion and with the willingness to stretch generously for the organization's sake.

Where Not to Look . . . and Where to Look

Knowing Where Not to Look

Those new to prospect research often see it as the great panacea for fund-raising woes. "If we only look through enough books and scan enough on-line resources," they assure themselves, "we'll find enough prospects to make raising money a breeze." They imagine that corporations, foundations, or even individuals somewhere "out there" are just waiting to be identified and asked to support a worthy cause. The overwhelming number of advertisements for corporate, foundation, and individual directories does little to disabuse the dreamers of this notion.

But think again! Virtually all gifts, whether from individuals, corporations, or foundations, come from persons who have a relationship with the organizations in which they show interest and who have a stake in the projects they fund. Although corporate and foundation fund raising may seem formal and impersonal, even in those organizations, decisions are made by individuals—men and women who are driven by many of the very

> *Virtually all gifts, whether from individuals, corporations, or foundations, come from persons who have a relationship with the organizations in which they show interest and who have a stake in the projects they fund.*

same considerations that drive donors everywhere when they decide to make a gift. Whether or not they are giving away their own money or someone else's money, people give to credible causes that they support and believe in and to people in whom they have confidence.

In the search for prospects, time is usually not well spent attempting to ask for money from wealthy individuals who have no affiliation with or reason to be interested in the organization.

Finding Money, Power, and Commitment Close to Home

An organization's very best, most generous, and most likely contributors are either individuals, businesses, or foundations that staff and volunteers are already aware of.

A well-established annual fund program that includes some personal solicitation, telephone fund raising, direct-mail solicitations, and special events will already have a solid base of donors. These donors are the best starting place in the search for those who will be most likely to give generously to the campaign. Although they will vary in their resources, commitment, and generosity to an organization, among them will be the staunchest donors and volunteers. Somewhere in the organization's current or former donor lists are the people who will make the campaign a success by giving money and by raising money on the organization's behalf.

Finding those golden nuggets requires a transformation of the unwieldy and ill-defined list of cold, bloodless names into portraits of flesh-and-blood human beings. Evaluating attentively the lists of prospects to arrive at the most likely names and then moving beyond the basic, impersonal facts to learn about each donor will enable an organization to determine the right gift, the right time, and the right solicitor for that donor.

Building a Prospect List Through the Research Process

The Search for Insiders

A good way to begin the research process is by assembling a list of the organization's insiders—a list drawn from founders, current board members, former board members, major donors, volunteers, and staff members. This list may hold up to two- or three-hundred names, depending on the organization's size and age. The development officer may already be familiar enough with the list to be able to identify the names of its ten most powerful individuals without even looking at it.

The next step is to learn what information is already on file about these individuals. A complete profile will include giving history, biographical information, a history of involvement with the organization, press clip-

pings, as well as anecdotal information about their families, educations, religious affiliations, interests, and their patterns of giving to other organizations.

A few surprises may surface with the information. There may be considerably more, or less, information in the files than one had assumed. Some surprising facts, hitherto unknown or perhaps long forgotten, about a particular individual may rise to the surface. Long-buried documents may be unearthed, identifying some of the organization's early founders or other individuals connected to the organization whose names have been lost.

The Past Paved the Way for a Gift

In preparation for a capital campaign, the development director of a private girls' school was delving through her files in search of information on the school's donors. She happened upon a dog-eared manuscript that turned out to be a copy of a speech presented by a long-retired headmaster at the dedication of a new library. By way of making some point or other—perhaps it was the relationship of love of learning to just plain old love—the headmaster recounted how Annie Day, a student at the academy almost a century earlier, had met John Frank, the son of the school's headmaster. The two young people fell in love, and, in 1871, they were married. We may assume that they lived happily ever after. Thirty years had passed since the dedication of the library, and during that time, the entire staff of the school had changed. There was no institutional memory of this love story, and it was just by chance that this speech had found its way into the development director's hands, for, as is usual with old files, those records had been consigned to the oblivion of deep storage.

Yet perhaps it was not entirely chance. The development director's well-honed instincts had directed her to that old filing cabinet in the dusty storeroom. Blessed with a historian's curiosity, she was intrigued by the story of Annie Day and John Frank, and she was aware of the Frank Foundation. Was there a connection? Indeed there was! That scrap of information about Annie Day led to a rekindling of the relationship that had lain dormant for more than thirty years between the school and the Frank Foundation, whose director was the great-grandson of John and Annie. That relationship grew and developed and eventually resulted in a leadership gift to the campaign.

The Search for Previous Donors

Although it may seem a monumental task, an organization must look carefully at its previous donor list. If well maintained, lists of names, addresses, and donation histories can reveal much about the strength of previous donors' commitment to the organization.

In her excellent set of videos, *Grassroots Fundraising Series* (1995), Kim Klein emphasizes that the real purpose of fund raising is not to raise money, but to acquire donors. The reason behind acquiring donors, of course, is to raise money, but the process of cultivating and acquiring donors and asking them again and again actually develops and cements a donor's relationship to the organization.

Many donors, says Klein, begin their relationship with an organization by making a small impulsive gift. By the time they have given several small gifts, they have begun to see the organization's cause as their cause. They pay more attention to the material that they receive from the organization, they become better informed about its mission, and they are more likely to champion the cause when speaking to their friends and acquaintances. If they are pleased with the material that they receive and the ways in which their commitment is acknowledged, they may begin to give larger gifts, thoughtfully rather than impulsively. Someone who gives gifts of $25 to many organizations may not give much thought to those gifts. But that same person, when asked to give $250 or $2,500, is probably going to consider the matter with some care. And when a donor makes a gift that stretches him or her to a new level, that is a signal that for some reason the donor has attained a higher degree of commitment to the organization.

Giving is a sign of commitment, and it is a source of commitment. Donors who give again and again and who increase their gifts over time gradually embrace an or-

> *A pattern of repeated gifts, though they may be small, by a donor who has been helped by the organization may well signal a good prospect for a larger gift.*

ganization more fully—they are the donors who make campaigns succeed. Figure 5–1 illustrates this continuum of commitment.

An examination of donor records of organizations that have asked for gifts early and often is likely to yield many individuals who have moved through the pattern described above. These donors often begin as casual acquaintances and impulse givers and move all the way through the sequence until they become thoughtful supporters, and finally committed donors. A healthy group of committed donors—the fruit of years of hard work on annual giving programs—prepares an organization well for a capital campaign.

But what if an organization lacks a strong annual giving program? In today's fund-raising climate, the organizations that don't do a good job of asking, or don't ask often enough, or don't invite their donors to increase their gifts, are likely to have flat donor patterns and only a small group of thoughtful supporters or committed donors. Organizations with immature or inactive annual giving programs will have some catching up to do, and they may wish to delay a capital campaign until they can broaden their donor base and move donors up on the commitment continuum. Whether an organization begins the process now or in two or three years, the prospect of planning for a capital campaign will provide the impetus and the opportunity to examine, analyze, and strengthen the donor base.

One Impulse Gift $	Repeated Gifts $$	Increased Gifts $$$	Gifts + Involvement $$$$
Casual Acquaintance	Concerned Friend	Thoughtful Supporter	Committed Donor
One or Two Low-Level Gifts	Regular Pattern of Giving over an Extended Period	Increase in Dollar Amount + Gifts to Special Projects	Larger Gifts + Personal Involvement

Lowest commitment / Lowest dollars → Greatest commitment / Highest dollars

Figure 5–1 The Commitment Continuum

Types of Donors

The best campaign donors are those with the greatest commitment. Founders, current board members, former board members, major donors, volunteers, and staff are the most obvious place to look. These are the people who, because of their proximity to and involvement with the organization, have had the opportunity to see first-hand how it accomplishes its mission, whom it serves, and how well it serves them.

More difficult to spot at first glance are the good donor prospects among the many who have given numerous small gifts to an organization over the years. Sometimes those prospects are individuals who have been served, or whose families have been served, by the organization. A pattern of repeated gifts, though they may be small, by a donor who has been helped by the organization may well signal a good prospect for a larger gift.

These grateful donors also often make good helpers. Just as most people don't make financial contributions unless asked, most don't volunteer unless invited to do so. Many thoughtful supporters are ready to become volunteers—they just haven't been asked to help.

A capital campaign provides many opportunities to invite people to help. And because capital campaigns often boost an organization from one level of operation to another, helping an organization during these growth spurts builds enthusiasm and energy among its constituents far beyond what is possible in business-as-usual times. By inviting donors to help and helpers to give, an organization expands its base, strengthening the commitment of people who had previously been only marginally involved. A committed donor who is asked to help and is treated well as a volunteer is likely to become even more generous and committed—and those are the people who make generous gifts to capital campaigns.

Most donor lists have a large group of people who fall into the "casual acquaintance" or "concerned friend" category. This group includes individuals who have given again and again but whose donor records don't stand out in any other way. They have not been volunteers. Their giving has not made any notable leaps. They have not been served by the organization. Because there are often many donors of this sort, identifying the good prospects among them can be daunting. Rather than sorting through them one by one, an organization might design a way to encourage them to identify themselves. This might be done with a mail or phone survey that invites each person to respond with information that would help the staff better understand their commitment and interest in the organization.

The Search in Less Obvious Places

Often overlooked in the search for insiders are those who have been important to the organization in the past but who have slipped into obscurity. Those who work for an institution that has a long history should consider going on a plaque walk. This involves their taking a clipboard and walking the halls and grounds of the agency looking for plaques and portraits. Any names that appear on old plaques should be recorded, and likewise the names of individuals in the portraits. This can be an enjoyable process for those with a taste for amateur sleuthing or historical research. Although much of it may lead nowhere, the chances are good that something of interest or importance will turn up. There may, perhaps, be family names that also appear among those of the current insiders. Names, dates, locations of plaques, and any other information that seems significant should be written down. It may sometimes be helpful to take the plaque walk with a friend—someone to play Watson to your Holmes. Good-humored speculation about who these people were and what they did often sparks ideas that lead to important results. Those whose names are commemorated on plaques were most likely very important at some point to the life of the institution, and descendants are often interested to learn about the important roles their forefathers and foremothers may have played and are pleased that someone has taken the time and effort to contact them.

Looking to Others: Prospect Screening

One of the very best ways of gathering information about prospective donors is to ask their peers and colleagues to tell what they know. Most people know more about their friends, colleagues, and acquaintances than they would ever readily admit to. Although people seldom talk about their own wealth, they are very astute about recognizing signs of it in others. They notice neighborhoods, houses, cars, manners, interests, style, clothing, jewelry, travel, schools attended by children, and charitable causes supported, to name just a few. All of these are clues to power, wealth, and commitment. It is information that does not come in books, nor does it appear on lists. It comes through observation and conversations with other people.

Once information in the files has been organized into usable form, it is time for others to be invited into the research process. In fund-raising circles, this process is called prospect screening. Small groups of individuals who are likely to know one another are invited to meetings to review lists and to discuss other individuals they are likely to know. Not only is a great amount of information gathered about the target prospects, but the process is an excellent opportunity to involve people in the early stages of the campaign, thereby bringing them closer to the organization.

The process begins with a trial screening meeting to give the staff an opportunity to learn about the screening process. It involves six to eight people who are already committed to the organization and who will be able to share information about prospects. It is often helpful to include a couple of people who are familiar with fund raising and prospect research to break the ice and lead the way.

The campaign chair, if this individual has already been selected, should invite these people to a meeting to help the organization learn more about a group of prospects. (If the campaign chair has not yet been chosen, the board chair, fund-raising chair, or executive director can issue the invitations.) Screeners should be told that the organization is in the early stages of preparing for the campaign and that it needs help identifying those individuals who might be good workers, good leaders, and good donors for the campaign. The meeting might last one to two hours, depending on the size of the group and the number of names they will review.

The session will require a facilitator who understands the purpose of the session, who can keep things moving, who can keep attention focused on the task at hand, and who has a relationship with at least a few of the others who will be attending. A good facilitator can make the difference between an excellent screening session and a mediocre one, so this person should be chosen with care. Depending on his or her particular strengths and skills, the facilitator might be the board chair, the development chair, or the executive director. The development director should be on hand to take notes of what was said and by whom.

Such a group can review approximately forty to fifty names in an hour. For the meeting to be effective, the individuals to be discussed must be those likely to be known to the screeners. For example, board members might review lists of donors and former board members, major donors might look at major-donor prospect lists, staff members at staff lists, and so forth.

Although there are many ways to conduct meetings of this sort, the best information is often developed through discussion. To stimulate discussion, staff members should give each screener a profile of each prospect, which should present the existing information about the prospect without divulging sensitive or privileged information. For example, it is appropriate to share how many gifts someone has made to an organization over a period of time, and whether those gifts were small, medium, or large according to the ranges that the organization has set. But it is not appropriate to divulge specific dollar amounts. To avoid discomfort, the names of those who have been invited to attend the meeting should not be included in the material that is distributed to the screeners.

The sessions should focus on two questions: (1) What is the prospect's *ability* to make a financial contribution to a campaign? and (2) What is this prospect's *inclination* to make a gift?

In the answers to these two questions lies a wide range of information about each prospect. Because people are often uncomfortable discussing dollars, salaries, and other specific aspects of wealth, it is useful to establish a code to sort the prospects from highest ability to lowest ability and from highest inclination to lowest inclination. It is easier, for example, for a volunteer to say, "Mr. Croesus's ability to give is probably a 5" (on a scale of 1 to 5) than to say, "I would estimate that Clyde Croesus makes upwards of $300,000 a year." For the purposes of this meeting, relative rather than absolute assessments are to be sought.

The words *ability* and *inclination*, together with the scale, can be posted in large letters on the wall in front of the meeting room:

ABILITY TO GIVE:	1	2	3	4	5
	Lowest			Highest	
INCLINATION TO GIVE:	A	B	C	D	E
	Lowest			Highest	

The prospect lists given to the screeners should include a place for the screener's name at the top of the first page and a place to indicate ability and inclination ratings for each prospect. See Exhibit 5–1 for an example.

The facilitator should go through the list and, allowing time for discussion about each prospect, collect and gather information to arrive at *ability* and *inclination* ratings for each name. The scribe should capture as much anecdotal information as possible, such as children, schools, divorces, marriages, interests and hobbies, religious activities, reliability, apparent wealth, and so on. The screeners should write their own names at the top of their lists before turning them in, so that it will be clear who is to be contacted for additional information.

In many cases, prospect screening is a volunteer's first exposure to the campaign. A high standard of organization and excellence should be set for this initial meeting, which should be well run and fun. This is a clear-cut, task-oriented meeting, and a simple and clear agenda should be prepared. The meeting should start and end on time. If the group is diverse, time should be allotted for personal introductions. Instructions should be clear, simple, and effective.

After the first screening meeting is over, the meeting organizer should take time to think about the many things that have been learned, not only from the forms that the participants filled out but also from the notes that were taken about the prospects. In addition, through careful attention to the dynamics of the meeting much valuable

Exhibit 5–1 Sample Prospect Screening Form

Screener's Name _____		Today's Date _____

Mr. and Mrs. John Simons 448 South Smithson Street Clarkson, PA Comments:	First Gift: 1991 Most Recent: 12/95 No. Gifts: 5 Total $: 635 Board '97	Ability (1–5) _____ Inclination (A–E) _____
Ms. Sandy Gasten 22 Green Hills Greenhills, PA Comments:	First Gift: 1994 Most Recent: 4/95 No. Gifts: 2 Total $: 2,000 Member	Ability (1–5) _____ Inclination (A–E) _____
Mr. Sam Smithgall 2239 Glenellen Lane Clarkson, PA Comments:	First Gift: 1987 Most Recent: 7/94 No. Gifts: 14 Total $: 8,300 Former board '94	Ability (1–5) _____ Inclination (A–E) _____
Mrs. Judy Kaiser 445 South Street Greenhills, PA Comments:	First Gift: 1990 Most Recent: 3/96 No. Gifts: 12 Total $: 3,000 Volunteer	Ability (1–5) _____ Inclination (A–E) _____

information will have been acquired about those who attended the meeting. Here are some issues to consider:

- Who promised to attend but didn't?
- Who arrived late?
- Who was disruptive?
- Who was wonderfully helpful?
- Whose opinions seemed to carry the most weight? (This is the person to whom everyone listens, not necessarily the one with the loudest voice!)
- Who was comfortable talking about money?
- Who was uncomfortable talking about money?
- Who asked good questions?
- Who kept getting the group off the task? And who kept pulling them back?
- Who was the most enthusiastic?
- Who radiated energy? Who sapped it?

> *By being alert and perceptive in observing others, one can learn an incredible amount, and be able to define tasks for individuals that they are likely to accomplish successfully. Sharp powers of observation will help make informed judgments, and well-informed judgments about people lead to successful campaigns.*

Through thoughtful reflection on the behavior of each participant in the meeting, the development officer will begin to determine whom to invite again for assistance, and whom to thank graciously and let go.

In addition to learning a great deal about the screeners themselves during the meeting, campaign leadership has also learned about the prospects. As soon as possible after the meeting, the staff must collate that information into a clear and manageable format. It is always the best prospects who are being sought—those with the greatest ability and inclination, power and connections, credibility and energy. Once the information has been gathered, campaign leadership is ready to select those prospects who will most likely be the best campaign volunteers and donors. These individuals, along with the best from the trial screening group, will be poised to help expand the research effort.

With the knowledge gained from the trial prospect-screening session, the development staff can fine-tune the prospect-research process. To gather enough information on all the prospects, staff may have to hold many screening meetings. Each meeting provides an early opportunity to talk with insiders about the campaign that is being planned; it gives valuable information about these individuals as volunteers and provides excellent material about prospects. The following twelve guidelines will help in perfecting the technique.

1. Groups should be small—not more than six to eight persons per session. The larger the group, the more inhibited is the conversation.

2. If the organization is large and small groups are not feasible, then each large group of volunteers should be divided into smaller subgroups.

3. Volunteers who are likely to know the individuals on the lists under review should be invited. People tend to know people who live in the same area, who have children of similar ages, who worship together, or who are of similar social status.

4. A group should not be given more to accomplish than it can manage in the allotted time period.

5. Careful notes should be taken about the volunteers immediately after each meeting. Campaigns are long and memories are short.

6. Thank-you notes should be sent to the volunteers after each meeting.

7. At each meeting, the participants should be asked for names of individuals whom they know who might be helpful to the campaign.

8. The volunteers should be told clearly just what is being asked of them, and they should be provided with material that will make their task easy.

9. Careful attention must be given to how each meeting begins. The first few minutes should be used to establish the tone for the entire meeting. If the meeting begins too formally, the participants may feel reluctant to take part. If it is possible to engage everyone early, each participant will be more likely to contribute with enthusiasm to the meeting.

10. Seats should be arranged so as to increase participation and decrease any sense of hierarchy. Classroom-style seating is the worst. A large round table is the best. A large square one will do just fine.

11. Informality is greatly to be encouraged. The purpose of these meetings is to gather information, and people give information when they feel comfortable. Everything possible should be done to help the participants feel safe, cared for, and comfortable.

12. Meetings should be scheduled at different times of day to accommodate different schedules.

Looking to Community Leadership

All communities have a core group of individuals, corporations, or foundations whose names carry special weight and who often make or influence gifts to most of the community's major campaigns. These individuals have served on boards and campaign steering committees before. They know what that responsibility entails, and when they agree to help, they will usually understand that their commitment to the campaign includes a generous gift. Once associated with a project, these community leaders can be good sources of information. They will be excellent advocates for the organization's cause and the campaign's very best solicitors as well.

These individuals or organizations may or may not have a relationship with the agency that is planning a campaign, but as the campaign planning stage moves ahead, the organization must identify and cultivate them so as to increase the chance that they will assist and support the campaign. A sizable gift from a lead person or institution in the community early in the campaign will not only make a good financial start, but will also lend credibility to the entire campaign. Identifying and cultivating these individuals and organizations is, therefore, extremely important.

If the organization completed a feasibility study prior to embarking on the campaign, it may have included a good number of these leaders among those who were interviewed. The feasibility study may also have identified other individuals who are perceived as leaders. The organization should now take the time to identify, research, and cultivate those community leaders before it develops its campaign structure.

If the organization is based in a large city with many diverse sectors and power bases, identifying the community power structure within that larger environment is a complex undertaking. In essence, an organization must look for individuals and organizations whose names bring credibility, whose interests dovetail with the organization's mission, and with whom it may find a common point of contact.

The search for community leaders may occur on many levels at once. Here are seven approaches worth trying.

1. The most powerful board members should be asked for the names of the most powerful people whom they know whose interests might overlap with those of the organization.

2. Major donors should be asked to assist in identifying and cultivating individuals.

3. Local newspapers and other publications probably contain clues about potential donors.

4. Programs from the symphony, theater, and other organizations that publish their donor lists are sources of valuable information. Of particular interest would be overlaps with people whose names surface around the organization's cause.

5. One's colleagues should be asked for the names of their acquaintances, who, in their opinion, really make things happen.

6. Annual reports of agencies with related missions should be collected and studied. Eventually, certain names will begin to pop up again and again. Those are the people who are being sought.

7. It would probably be worthwhile for the development director or executive director to join the chamber of commerce or other community organizations in order to meet the heads of some of the large businesses and foundations in the community. Perhaps they will be willing to help, and in any case, people in positions of power know other powerful people.

Throughout the research process, the list of prospects will expand. Volunteers and staff members will gather information on each prospect that will facilitate educated judgments about how best to approach each prospect.

Capturing Information

Setting Up a Prospect Information System

Prospect research can yield thousands, even hundreds of thousands, of pieces of information. This information is useless if it is not stored accurately and in a manner that permits easy retrieval. The time and resources that have been committed to gathering information on a potential donor will have been wasted if that information is inaccurate, or later becomes inaccessible or incomprehensible.

What makes an effective information system? First, it must hold the right information. Research will uncover all sorts of data, some of it relevant, some of it not. Sometimes it will uncover information that may be sensitive. Items about family discord, sexual behavior or preference, drug or alcohol addiction, financial scandal, or other closet skeletons might well be important information that would affect the manner in which the prospect is solicited, but this information does not belong in open files.

To determine whether information is relevant, the following eight questions should be considered.

1. Does the information help to understand the donor's social group?
2. Does it give an indication of wealth?
3. Does it help to understand the donor's interests?
4. Does it add information about any relationship to the organization?
5. Does it help to assess what sort and how big a gift the prospect might make?
6. Does it provide information about family?
7. Does it provide clues as to how the prospective donor might wish to be treated?
8. Does it give information about giving patterns?

Information that helps in any of these ways is relevant, but when considering whether to include such information in the file, one should ask (1) Can this information be shared with a solicitor without violating the prospect's privacy? and (2) Is this information that one would feel comfortable sharing directly with the prospect?

If the answers to these two questions are "yes," then the information can be included. If, however, the information is important to the solicitation but has the potential of being hurtful or damaging, then it should not be included in the general file.

Organizing information in an easily accessible way is sometimes the most difficult part of prospect research, but the time spent to set up a system that is easy to use and that permits accurate storage and efficient retrieval of all necessary data, will be saved many times over in the long run.

A form that is prepared in advance for prospect research can be very helpful in gathering and maintaining information. Most likely three distinct prospect research forms will be required—one for individuals, one for corporations, and one for foundations. Samples are included in Appendix 5–A.

While there are software packages specifically developed for fund raisers, such forms can be created in any database program. Basic information can be maintained on the computer, with backup information on major donor prospects in the paper files. Computer files can be updated easily. A clean paper copy for the paper files should be produced each time records are updated so that a fresh, up-to-date copy will be available whenever a staff member or solicitor may need it. Wise development directors back up all computer files frequently. Electronic data is compact and convenient, but thousands

---

The Attorney Who Writes Children's Books

One day during a casual conversation with a board member, the director of a public library discovered that her friend, a successful attorney in town, had just published a children's book. Now, an interest in books ought to translate into an interest in libraries, and, more particularly, an interest in children's books ought to translate into an interest in the children's section of the library, whose renovation just happened to be the subject of the library's campaign. The director and the board member invited the attorney to lunch. Over lunch, the attorney informed them that although he had never been a donor to the library, he was exceedingly unhappy with the poor condition of the children's section and was very interested in helping raise money for the project. He indicated that he had a great many important contacts in the community that he was willing to cultivate on behalf of the project. He became an excellent solicitor (no pun intended) and made a generous gift to the campaign.

of data records can disappear in an instant when a hard drive crashes.

Simple Systems

Like a mother's work, donor research is never done. Information accumulates bit by bit over the years. Much valuable information is lost because it is not captured as it comes in. The development officer may have a conversation with a board member, for example, in which it is learned that a donor has just remarried, or moved, or changed jobs. Perhaps someone's sole remaining parent has recently passed away. All of these scraps of information are important, but all too often they go unrecorded.

The development officer is responsible for making sure that notes about any contact that takes place between the staff and a donor are added to the file. A steady stream of notes adds a wealth of information that may later prove important. Sadly, such information is often lost in the press of other tasks.

A workable system for gathering and storing such bits of information should be instituted. It does not have to be complex. A file folder or even a shoe box might do the job quite well. Every time a salient fact about someone is acquired, the name of the individual concerned and the relevant information should be written down and placed in the research file. When the file is full, or once a month, or on whatever schedule is appropriate, the information should be logged into the database or hard-copy file. Over time, this process will give the development director a wonderful sense of familiarity with the donor list. Those individuals will gradually begin to seem less like one-dimensional bits and bytes and more like real people.

Some donors, however, require a considerable amount of research. It is time-consuming and labor-intensive work, and most smaller nonprofit organizations do not employ a full-time prospect researcher. Therefore, the development officer should make a list of the top twenty-five donor prospects and gather information on those individuals or organizations in a particularly disciplined way. When the first group of twenty-five is completed, the development officer can select another ten prospects and then ten more. Slowly, over time, a significant and impressive file of donor information on the best prospects will have been fashioned that will aid the organization in its preparations for a campaign, and indeed in its entire fund-raising effort.

Filling in the Details with Secondary Sources

Most small nonprofit organizations have few resources for acquiring prospect-research tools. A research library is expensive, as are most on-line subscription services. The development staff can begin to supplement and verify its

---

The Major Donor and the Overdue Book

Imagine how embarrassing it was for the solicitor who went to ask a donor for a major gift for the library only to find her fuming, "As for the library, you should hear about my experience! I was receiving a barrage of overdue notices for a book I had returned months ago. I telephoned the library to try to clear the matter up, and I was treated extremely rudely by a staff member." This woman had eventually discussed the issue with the director of the library, who succeeded in smoothing her ruffled feathers. But the director had failed to make note of the incident in the development files, and the unfortunate solicitor was completely unprepared for the onslaught she received about library employees' lack of consideration. This tale has a happy ending, however. The donor recovered her good humor about the situation, and the solicitation was successful. Nonetheless, the solicitor was rightly distressed by having been placed in a most awkward situation by a lack of information. Information can prevent catastrophe.

---

prospect information by getting to know a full-time prospect researcher. Most colleges, hospitals, and other large not-for-profit organizations have a full-time employee whose sole responsibility is prospect research. Such individuals are pros at acquiring information. They often have extensive research libraries in their offices that they are sometimes willing to share. But more importantly, they can provide advice about whom to ask and where to go for many kinds of information. Every community is different, so it is especially worthwhile to explore the local resources with a professional in one's own community.

Joining the Association of Professional Researchers for Advancement, formerly the American Prospect Research Association, is another option for novice researchers. This professional association provides numerous resources for researchers in organizations of all sizes. It has local chapters in many cities and holds an annual conference.

In many communities, the local public library is an excellent resource. Today, most libraries have on-line reference services, and reference librarians can help track down information about individuals, corporations, and foundations. The librarian at the local newspaper office may also be a gold mine of information about individuals in the community. These reference people are well worth knowing, and if possible they should be engaged in the organization's cause.

A new and growing area in prospect research is the use of electronic media. With a desktop computer and modem it is possible to access a vast array of research information without leaving the office. Through a commercial Internet service such as America Online, Compuserve, Prodigy, GEnie, or Delphi, to name but a few, one can access "prspct-l," a forum for prospect researchers. To sign on, one sends an e-mail message to listserv@uci.edu. The body of the message should read as follows: subscribe prspct-l <your name>. Subscribers to this list receive e-mail from prospect researchers from all over the world and are able to ask questions of professionals in the field. Although subscribing may result in an unwanted deluge of electronic mail, the forum can provide an excellent opportunity to become familiar with the field of prospect research and the use of the internet to access information.

In addition to prspct-l, the internet can be used to access information from a wide variety of sources. There are Internet White and Yellow Pages, Corporate Financial Online, PR Newswire, the Thomas Register of American Companies, the Directory of Funding Agencies, and many other such services, many of which are free of charge.

Hunting for information on the Internet can be daunting, because much of the information about prospective donors is currently unindexed and undigested. Focus the search by querying other prospect researchers as to which Web sites and databases are particularly helpful.

It may prove useful to develop a systematic list of places to check for information. A vast number of resources contain precisely the information being sought. The challenge is to discover which sources have the desired information about a particular prospect.

Many development directors who work in smaller, community-based organizations will find that their best information comes through conversations at screening meetings, informal discussions during social events, and one-on-one conversations. Most communities are small, and residents of small communities know remarkably much about other peoples' business.

To learn more about community leadership as well as the organization's donors, a good development director must play an active role in the community. By joining and becoming active in service organizations, reading the newspaper attentively, listening for information that might indicate excess income, and being particularly aware of discussions about vacation houses, art collec-

tions, exotic travel, antiques, or other such indicators, astute listeners can often recognize the signs of high levels of disposable income. As calculating as it may seem, development staff may want especially to look for those whose children have finished college or whose parents have recently passed away, since such individuals are frequently in a strong financial position and are just beginning to explore ways of using newly available resources. With these simple techniques and a good system for recording information, an organization will be able to assemble a remarkable amount of usable material about its best donor prospects.

A Cautionary Word

Word travels fast in small communities. It is not a good idea to poke around into other people's business in a way that donors may find offensive. The smaller the community, the more attention must be paid to not stepping over the line of propriety. People don't like to know that someone else is digging into matters that they consider private. For example, a prospect is not likely to look favorably on the local homeless shelter if his sister-in-law who works at the courthouse calls him one evening to tell him that the director of the shelter was trying to find out how much he paid for his house.

Researching Individuals

As mentioned above, a development officer can find out about a prospect in many ways—by listening to the prospect talk about himself, by listening to what others have to say about him, or by consulting secondary sources, such as newspaper articles and biographical references like *Who's Who*. There are benefits and drawbacks to each method of research, yet each is important, since information that is gathered one way might confirm or enhance information that is gathered another way. For example, if a volunteer mentions that she knows that a prospect is "some kind of dairy farmer," but doesn't know anything more about him, the staff can check various individual and corporate references. In doing so, the development officer might discover that instead of being just a dairy farmer, the prospect owns and operates one of the largest dairies in the state and has assets of well over $4 million.

When researching individuals, the goal is to provide answers to the following four questions.

1. What is the prospect's financial capacity?
2. What are the prospect's philanthropic interests?
3. How well does the prospect know the organization?
4. Who is the right person to ask the prospect for a gift?

Several secondary sources are available that provide information to researchers on financial capacity and philanthropic interests. A development officer may want to check the following four sources.

1. Salary lists. To get an estimate of the prospect's salary, one should look first into *The American Almanac of Jobs and Salaries,* which is updated yearly. Another source is the company's proxy statement, which lists the compensation of its top officers. Finally, checking periodicals such as *Business Week* or taking a quick glance at the *Reader's Guide to Periodical Literature* or the *Business Periodical Index* will provide a wide range of articles on the subject of salary.

2. Stock holdings. While knowing a prospect's salary is helpful, it doesn't begin to give a complete financial picture. Most major donors will not make their gifts out of their salaries; typically, it will be financially more advantageous to them to make a gift of an appreciated asset such as stock.

   There are several ways to find information about a prospect's stock ownership. Securities and Exchange Commission (SEC) reports are a good place to start. If the individual is a director or officer of a corporation registered with the SEC, there are ways of ascertaining his or her stock holdings in that corporation. The SEC has proxy statements and a monthly publication available at a nominal charge to help in a search.

   The SEC registers all corporations with 500 or more stockholders and at least $1 million in assets, as well as those listed on one of the U.S. stock exchanges. Stockholdings of the corporation's officers and directors are listed in its proxy statements. Frequently, the individual's salary and other compensation are also listed, as well as directorships held in other corporations. Some proxy statements also list director's trusteeships of educational and other nonprofit institutions. Proxy statements can be obtained from the corporation itself or from the SEC.

   The Official Summary of Security Transactions and Holdings is a monthly publication of the SEC that lists all stock transactions of directors and officers for a given month, including the number of shares bought or sold, the price traded at, and the total shares held at the month's end. One should check back at least one full year through this publication when researching corporate directors and officers. Unfortunately, directors and officers are listed by company, so, in order to obtain a complete picture of an individual, a researcher will have to know each

individual's company affiliation and look each one up separately. Many public and university libraries subscribe to this publication, and can be ordered from the Superintendent of Documents.

3. Real-estate holdings and other sources of income. County office buildings can be a useful source of information. The assessor's office can provide information about the value of the prospect's home and other personal property (automobiles, for instance) that is taxed. One should inquire as to how often assessment takes place and what percentage of the market value of the home the assessed value represents. This information is also available from the company Lusk and Sons, which compiles the information from assessors' offices. For a subscription fee, they can provide a set of microfiches with the assessed value of every property in the county, though the local library might well subscribe to this service. Checking the Lusk microfiches is a method that avoids the possibility of running into the prospect's sister-in-law at the county assessor's office.

4. Courthouse records. The county courthouse can also be a good resource. If a person's wealth is inherited, the county courthouse's probate records can be checked for a list of assets. Sometimes, depending on the circumstances, such records may be closed to the public, but it's worth a try. If the prospect has been divorced or involved in a civil suit, those records can be checked as well. Divorce records often contain financial statements. Civil cases often include information on assets and potential liabilities. These, too, may be closed, but this source of information is worth looking into.

To locate information on a prospect's philanthropic interests, researchers may want to check the newspapers and local magazines. The indexes of these publications should be checked to learn whether the prospect's name appears. Newspapers and magazines often profile community leaders, and such articles may indicate hobbies and interests. Annual reports and donor lists from other organizations also provide information. Acquiring donor lists from other organizations that have been

> *In community-based campaigns that rely on community leaders for major gifts, community resources are likely to be the best source of information.*

published in annual reports, playbills, or programs can sometimes give a good indication of the prospects' interests as well as the the degree of financial commitment.

Researchers will need to keep in mind that unless a prospect is fabulously wealthy, his or her name is not likely to appear in directories of wealthy individuals. In community-based campaigns that rely on community leaders for major gifts, community resources are likely to be the best source of information.

Researching Corporations

Corporations are often easier to research than are individuals. Many corporations publish giving guidelines, so it is worth a call to the corporation to get the most recent version. Many companies also send press releases following a major-grant award, so when one is requesting giving guidelines, one should also request to be added to the company's press list. While many of these press releases won't be directly applicable to a fund-raising effort, a quick scan will provide an update on the company.

Most smaller companies, however, don't have formal giving programs. In these companies, grant activities might be handled by the communications department, the personnel office, or even the president's office. When calling a smaller company for information, one should ask the receptionist who handles corporate giving. The receptionist may even be willing to share valuable information about how decisions are really made. The person in charge of corporate giving should be tracked down and asked for information about the company's giving priorities, schedule, and contributions budget.

To get a well-rounded picture of the company's history, current health, and outlook for the future several sources are worth checking.

Standard and Poors Register of Corporations, Directors, and Executives is a basic resource that includes sales figures, number of employees, products, address and telephone numbers, and names of the company's officers and board of directors. It also includes a corporate family tree listing the company's subsidiaries.

Dun and Bradstreet Corporate Reporting Services is a service whose reports provide a summary that includes a financial strength rating, the date the company was founded, its net worth, number of employees, brief history, and the company's condition and outlook. It will also list recent "special events" in the company's history and details on ownership.

Corporate Foundation Profiles is a reference book that gives in-depth analyses of the largest corporate foundations, including the types of organizations that they typically fund and the size and purpose of the grants.

Locating information on publicly held companies is fairly straightforward. It is not so easy to find information about privately held companies. A good place to

start in such a quest is *Ward's Business Directory of Major U.S. Private Companies*. This volume includes an address and telephone listing for the company, sales figures, and a list of officers.

Community libraries often keep files on local companies. If these don't prove fruitful, one may want to check the company's articles of organization, which are the papers a company must file with the state when it incorporates. This document will provide the following information:

- the names and addresses of the company's officers and directors
- the purpose of the organization
- the amount and kind (common or preferred) of stock authorized
- the beginning and end of the fiscal year and the date of the annual meeting of the principals
- the amount of stock subscribed for each incorporator

Unfortunately, this information isn't uniformly required by each state. Sometimes the same information can be gleaned from a Dun and Bradstreet report, although such information may not always be on file for private companies.

Researching Foundations

Local charitable foundations or foundations specifically interested in their communities are another source of funds. First, a list of likely foundation prospects should be compiled. What were the organization's previous foundation grants? Who has funded it in the past? Are those foundations likely to be interested in a particular component of the capital campaign? If so, they should be put on the research list and their most recent giving guidelines should be requested.

Additional sources of foundation funding can be located in the state foundation directory, which gives brief descriptions of each foundation, including its giving priorities, gift recipients from previous years with the amount of the gift, names of trustees, and the name and address of the foundation's contact person. These listings are most useful if the researcher knows the donor list well enough to be able to recognize the name of a foundation board member as someone who has given to the organization. As with most fund raising, grants are made by people to people, and the ability to bring in a foundation grant has at least as much to do with the contacts that the organization has within the foundation as it does with the importance and credibility of its project. Special attention should be given to ascertaining who serves on which boards.

If the project will serve people primarily within a limited region, it is a waste of time researching foundations outside of the area, unless there is a compelling reason to do so. With the exception of the Kresge Foundation in Michigan, no other major foundation regularly funds building projects outside its own locality. If, however, the brother of the organization's board chair is married to a trustee of a major foundation elsewhere in the country and she invites the organization to submit a proposal, then that is another matter entirely.

If the project will provide services far beyond the local region, then it may be worthwhile to spend some time with *The Foundation Directory*, published every two years by the Foundation Center (see Appendix 5–B). This is a basic foundation research resource that should be a staple of the development research effort. It includes geographical listings of foundations whose assets exceed $2 million or whose annual grants exceed $200,000. Each entry contains information on the foundation's assets, grants awarded, contact person, interests, types of support, giving restrictions, board meeting dates, publications offered, foundation trustees, and information regarding proposal submission requirements. It includes several helpful indexes as well.

Another source of information about a foundation is its "990-PF," the form that every tax-exempt organization must file with the Internal Revenue Service. The 990-PFs can be found at the Foundation Center or at one of its library centers. The 990-PF forms are on microfiche, and much of the information will be helpful, depending on how detailed the foundation reports its grant activities. The 990-PF will report the foundation's geographic concentrations, assets, project interests, types of support, size of grants, diversity of grants made, and a list of its direc-

> If those involved with the organization observe that other people's confidences are respected and that information is used constructively, they will be willing participants in the research effort.

tors. Some foundations are much more forthcoming than others about their grant-making activities; many will provide more information than you will ever need, and others provide only the bare minimum.

A more descriptive (and sometimes easier to read) source of information are a foundation's giving guidelines and annual report. In particular, the chairman's and/or chief executive's letter at the front of the report gives a development officer a feel for the foundation's priorities and future directions, as well as for the foundation's "corporate language" and style that can be used when writing a proposal.

Knowing Right from Wrong

Before beginning prospect research and placing calls to board members or other volunteers to gather prospect information, the development officer must understand thoroughly the roles and responsibilities of a researcher. A development officer is not an investigative journalist, although some of the techniques are similar. Nor is the role that of government prosecutor, hunting for information on financial misbehavior that might lead to an indictment. The development officer is not a gossip columnist, sniffing out information of an embarrassing nature that could give the organization clandestine power. The development officer is, rather, a responsible professional, who, while collecting and analyzing information, always keeps the prospect's sensibilities in mind.

A development officer must use good judgment about whether to include certain information about a donor in the files and not only because the donor may ask to see the file someday. An effective development director and researcher respects every prospect. Insensitive or thoughtless treatment can be hurtful and damaging. When deciding whether or not to use a particular piece of information, a development professional must look at it from a prospect's point of view. Would the researcher want similar information included about himself in an organization's files? If a researcher empathizes with and respects the individuality of every prospect, the donor records will paint an effective yet sensitive portrait of each person.

The development professional is responsible for creating a climate of trust and security in the organization. By example—when and how information about donors is shared—the development officer will establish an atmosphere in which volunteers will know what types of information it is appropriate to share. If those involved

The Prospect Researcher's Dilemma

A young man attended a local college to which his father was a major donor. Unfortunately, not only was he a poor student, he also frequently found himself in trouble for drinking and cutting classes. When the prospect researcher was updating the donor's file for a solicitor, she added the information that his son attended the school but did not include any reference to the boy's difficulties. Instead, she prepared a private note about the student's problems for the solicitor and sent it along with the donor's file. She did not keep a copy or a record of the memo, reasoning that it would be helpful for the solicitor to know of the son's difficulties before he visited the father, but that in the long run such information, if kept in the files, might someday serve to mar the reputation of the father or the son.

with the organization observe that other people's confidences are respected and that information is used constructively, they will be willing contributors to the research effort. If, however, they hear that the development officer is broadcasting confidential information or gossiping about a prospect's problems, they will begin quietly to withhold information and gradually become less involved.

Patience and Practice

After several years of patiently pursuing a prospective donor, a CEO received a seven-figure gift and a lovely small plaque from the donor. That's right, the donor gave the plaque to the CEO! The plaque stated, "Patience is not a virtue, patience is a practice" (The Thompson Letter, 1989).

Prospect research requires both patience and practice. By assembling piece after piece of information about its donors, an organization will know enough to enlist the right person to solicit the right gift at just the right time.

References

Association of Professional Researchers for Advancement, 414 Plaza Drive, Suite 209, Westmont, IL 60559; 708-655-0177.

Kleim, Kim. 1995. *Grassroots fundraising series.* The Headwater Fund. Videocassette. (612) 879-0602.

Superintendent of Documents, P.O. Box 371954, Pittsburgh, PA 15250-7954, (202) 512-1800.

Thompson Letter, The. 1989. The Thompson Group, Nashua, NH.

Appendix 5–A
Sample Prospect Research Forms

Confidential Individual Prospect Information Sheet

Date Researched _____ Code _____

Updated _____ Solicitor/Organization Contact _____

Prospect's Name _____

Primary Home Address _____ Dates at This Address _____

_____

Primary Home Telephone _____

Secondary Home Address _____ Dates at This Address _____

_____

Secondary Home Telephone _____

Business Address _____

_____

_____

Business Telephone _____ Business Fax _____

Title _____

Personal

Birthdate _____

Spouse's Name _____ Anniversary _____

Children's Names & Ages _____

_____

_____

Other Affiliations (clubs, board memberships, etc.) _____

Education _____

Giving Information

Gift potential _____

Amount and date of largest gift to organization _____

Amount and date of last gift to organization _____

Lifetime giving to organization _____

Special interests _____

_____

Other Philanthropic Interests _____

Indications of Wealth _____

Cultivation Information

Recent Contacts (include date of contact, who made the contact, and result of contact) _____

_____

Additional Information _____

_____

_____

Foundation Profile

Date Researched _____ Code _____

Updated _____ Solicitor/Organization Contact _____

Foundation Name _____

Contact Person and Title _____

Address _____

_____

Telephone Number _____ Fax Number _____

Brief Description of Foundation _____

_____

_____

_____

Financial Data for Past Three Years

Year _____

Assets _____ Grants _____ Average grant amount _____

Year _____

Assets _____ Grants _____ Average grant amount _____

Year _____

Assets _____ Grants _____ Average grant amount _____

Interests _____

_____

_____

_____

Restrictions _____

_____

_____

_____

Officers/Directors _____

_____

_____

_____

Application Information _____

_____

Sample Grants to Other Organizations
(include dollar amount, purpose, institution, geographic location) _____

_____

_____

_____

Corporate Profile

Date Researched _____ Code _____

Updated _____ Solicitor/Organization Contact _____

Company Name _____

Contact and Title _____

Address _____

_____

Telephone Number _____ Fax Number _____

Type of Business _____

_____

_____

_____

Address of Headquarters (if different from above) _____

_____

Financial Data

Year Ending _____

Revenues _____

Net Income _____

No. of Employees _____

Senior Officers/Directors _____

_____

_____

Corporate Giving Program _____

_____

_____

Previous Contacts with Organization _____

_____

_____

Previous Giving _____

_____

_____

Additional Comments _____

_____

_____

_____

_____

_____

_____

Appendix 5-B
Prospect Research Bibliography

In addition to the references source listed in chapter 5, we've included the following research sources below.

The publications below, in addition to other helpful resources, are available from The Foundation Center, 79 Fifth Avenue, New York, NY 10003-3076. 800-424-9836:

The Foundation Directory, 1996 Edition.
Guide to U.S. Foundations, Their Trustees, Officers, and Donors
National Directory of Corporate Giving, 4th Edition
Corporate Foundation Profiles, 9th Edition
The Foundation 1000, 1995/1996 Edition
New York State Foundations, 4th Edition
Directory of Missouri Grantmakers, 1st Edition
Guide to Greater Washington D.C. Grantmakers
Southeastern Foundations
Grant Guides; series lists grants awarded by foundations in various subject areas
Foundation Grants Index, 1996 Edition

Foundation Center World Wide Web Site (http://fdncenter.org): Includes information on philanthropy, fund-raising research, and Foundation Center libraries.

The publications below are available from the Taft Group, 835 Penobscot Building, Detroit, MI 48226, 800-877-8238; fax: 313-961-6083:

America's New Foundations 1995
Foundation Reporter 1995
Fund Raisers Guide to Human Service Funding 1995
Major Donors 1995
Owners and Officers of Private Companies 1995
Who's Wealthy in America

Other helpful publications that can either be purchased or found at local libraries include:

American Almanac of Jobs and Salaries, by John W. Wright. (New York: Avon, 1993)
Chronicle of Philanthropy Newsletter, 1255 23rd Street, NW, Suite 700, Washington, DC 20077, 202-466-1025.
Directory of Corporate Affiliations "Who Owns Whom" (Wilmette, IL: National Register Pub. Co., 1991)
Dun and Bradstreet Million Dollar Directory (New York: Dun and Bradstreet, 1993)
Social Register
State foundation directories
Files at local libraries that pertain to local businesses, organizations, and people

Note: While these resources may be helpful, don't forget that the best way to gather information on the prospects in your community is to talk to other people who know the prospect. By broadening your network of people, you will learn far more about a prospect than any reference book will tell you.

Chapter 6
Building the Campaign Team

Chapter Outline
- Seeing the Big Picture
- The Campaign Planning Committee
- The Campaign and the Board of Directors
- Campaign Leadership
- Campaign Structure
- Setting the Stage for Highly Effective Volunteers
- Celebrate Every Effort and Every Success

Seeing the Big Picture

Board members, staff, and other community leaders have usually been involved in the capital campaign from its inception. They may have participated in a planning retreat, helped develop a vision statement or case for support, participated in a feasibility study, or worked with a site selection committee. In fact, it is not uncommon for board members to have spent many years doggedly pursuing a goal like the renovation of the organization's building. However, when the time and conditions for a campaign finally arrive, even volunteers who have pushed hard to move their organization ahead usually know little about the campaign process and about their roles in that process.

Even those who have previous campaign experience are often unaware of all it takes to plan and implement a successful campaign. They often remember only their own specific tasks and are oblivious to the monumental edifice of staff and volunteer hours; the mountains of paperwork that flow through the development office; the thousands of telephone hours spent following up with volunteers and donors; or the myriad meetings to develop strategy for solicitations, encourage volunteers, and track results. Most see only the concrete manifestations of the campaign—the campaign brochure, the kickoff party, and the index cards that tell them whom they are to solicit—and seldom reflect on the underlying structure that guides the campaign process.

This chapter is a guide to building an effective campaign team by involving, educating, and empowering the board, the campaign chair, and the many committee volunteers throughout the campaign process. It includes a wide spectrum of information, from complex issues like the role of the board of directors in the campaign process, to simple but important fundamentals about enlisting the help of volunteers. This chapter explores the building blocks of which campaigns are constructed.

The Campaign Planning Committee

Function of the Planning Committee

Assembling the committee that will plan the campaign is the first concrete step in the campaign process. This campaign planning committee is charged with the weighty task of developing a specific, reasonable, clear, and sound plan for the campaign. The plan will include decisions on many of the critical issues that affect a campaign's success, such as the campaign goal, timetable, volunteer structure, and policies on gift accounting and donor recognition. Although chapter 7 discusses each of these important aspects of campaign planning in detail, this chapter will outline the human aspects of assembling the committee—whom to involve, how to involve them, and how to treat them once they are on board.

In planning a campaign, an organization must begin by assembling a group of the most powerful, most wealthy, most wise, and most influential volunteers it has the power to recruit. These people will set the tone and standard for the entire campaign. Their involvement lends credibility to the campaign from the start, making it easier to attract both donors and volunteers throughout the campaign process.

> *Assembling the committee that will plan the campaign is the first concrete step in the campaign process.*

Optimum Planning Committee Size

The size and membership of the campaign planning committee will vary from organization to organization. Large, well-established organizations with big, powerful boards of directors might enlist a subcommittee of the board to plan the campaign. Smaller institutions with working boards often begin by enlisting their key board members and then adding powerful individuals from the broader community.

Planning committees vary in size roughly from twelve to twenty. The smaller size is easier to work with and encourages greater individual participation. A larger group allows for broader representation and enables an organization to expand its power base in the community. The best strategy is often to assemble a planning committee that combines board members and community leaders.

Defining Committee Tasks

Because the planning committee often involves individuals with varying levels of commitment to the organization, the planning committee's tasks are tightly defined and of limited duration. Those invited to serve on a campaign planning committee are asked to attend three or four meetings, bring their experience and wisdom to the task of designing the campaign, and lend their names to the campaign.

Over the course of its meetings, the committee will develop recommendations for the campaign that will be submitted to the board of directors for approval. After the campaign planning process is complete, most, if not all, of the committee members will be invited to help implement the campaign. For small organizations without "power" boards, it is wise, however, to break the commitment into manageable pieces rather than inviting the participants at the outset to help with the entire campaign. Someone with limited commitment to an organization is more likely to agree to attend three meetings and help plan a campaign than to agree to serve on a campaign committee that will meet for two years and be responsible for the success of the entire campaign.

The relationship of the committee members to the organization will determine the design of the planning committee. Those with a deep commitment to an organization will probably be willing to give more time and energy than those with only a passing connection. The duration and responsibilities of the campaign planning committee must therefore be designed to reflect what its members are likely to be willing to do. Those with a great commitment and long familiarity with the organization—current board members, former board members, and founders—may be willing to assume ongoing responsibilities for the campaign. If, however, to strengthen its power base an organization must reach beyond those individuals with a strong vested interest in its mission

and operation, the planning committee should be designed to require a shorter commitment.

Choosing the Planning Committee

Choosing and enlisting the members of the planning committee is one of the most important steps in a campaign. One wants to be able to identify and enlist the very best people for the job. On this committee, then, should be people who themselves have the potential to be major donors, people whose names would bring credibility to the campaign, people who are knowledgeable about the organization and committed to it, and people who represent various aspects of the organization's constituencies.

It is easier and less time-consuming for the executive director and board chair to select and recruit the people to serve on the campaign planning committee, but it is more effective to assemble a small group of powerful people for the task. Although this process takes time, for many small and midsized organizations, effective process is the key to successful campaigns. The very first campaign committee, therefore, should be a small ad hoc group of the influential people who will help determine the membership of the campaign planning committee.

This crucial group of decision makers, let's call them the "invited co-conspirators," will attend one meeting to review names and discuss the composition of the campaign planning committee. Their knowledge of the community, their judgments about people, and their willingness to help enlist others often determine the actual outcome of the campaign.

The size of this ad hoc group should be no larger than six. Larger groups seldom muster the requisite conspiratorial zest, and that zest adds energy and enthusiasm to the campaign process. Each committee member should have significant power and influence in his or her own right and should bring specific knowledge about a segment of the organization or the community. The group might, for example, include an industry leader, a major donor, the head of a large foundation, a well-respected board member, someone who has played a leadership role in other campaigns, and the executive director. The spheres of influence of the members should in aggregate cover all the relevant power bases in the community.

Recruiting the Invited Co-conspirators

Because one begins capital campaigns by enlisting the most powerful individuals, the enlisting process should be

> *Most people would be pleased to be asked to join the very inner circle if they believe that those who will be sitting with them are worthy of their company.*

conceived just as carefully and strategically as that of soliciting major gifts. Depending on the organization and the specific personalities, the board chair and/or the executive director are probably the best choices for this task.

Most people would be pleased to be asked join the very inner circle if they believe that those who will be sitting with them are worthy of their company. So, to increase the chances of positive response, it is a good idea to begin by enlisting the most powerful individual possible and then use that person's acceptance as an inducement to others.

Although all of these people will probably join the campaign planning committee, one begins by inviting them to only one meeting. For powerful people who have not had deep involvement with the organization, this first meeting may help induce them to serve on the larger committee when asked at a later time. At that meeting, the group should determine a prioritized list of planning committee prospects and determine the strategy for enlisting each of them. If the ideal planning committee has from fifteen to eighteen members, this list will need to have up to twenty-five names to allow for the few people who decline.

The campaign planning committee should comprise approximately twelve to eighteen people. These individuals should be the most powerful and influential group that the organization is able to assemble. The committee should include key members of the board of directors, community leaders, major-gift prospects, and a representative sampling of the relevant subgroups of the organization's constituencies. Organizations that serve more than one geographic area should be sure that the committee includes at least one person from each of the most important regions. The sample form below has been designed to help evaluate the composition of the planning committee.

Organizations whose services or alumni are geographically dispersed may have to organize minicampaigns in several different regions. In that case the campaign planning committee will include representatives from each constituency (alumni, parents, etc.) and from each major region.

Recruiting the Campaign Planning Committee

The process of recruiting the members of the campaign planning committee will emerge from the co-conspirators' meeting. If that meeting is successful, it will determine not only who should be invited to serve on the planning committee, but also who is best suited to proffer each invitation. One begins by enlisting the most powerful and respected members and then moving down through the power hierarchy. If the most important individuals are unavailable, perhaps on vacation or out of the country, it is usually worth delaying the process in order to involve them first.

Before enlisting the members of the planning committee, the dates and times of its meetings should be determined. The meetings should be planned to begin four to six weeks after all invitations have been extended. The longer the intervening period, the better the response rate will be.

Because there will likely be several individuals enlisting people to serve on the planning committee, all of the relevant information about the purpose of the meetings, the dates and times, and the specific responsibilities of each committee member should be written in a clear, easy-to-read document to be distributed to each of those helping to assemble the committee. Exhibit 6–1 is a sample campaign planning committee recruitment worksheet.

Recruiting "Rights"

It is just as important to find the right time and place for asking someone to agree to serve on a committee as it is for asking that person to make a gift to a campaign. Although an affirmative answer to such a question asked in a public setting can encourage others to sign on, should the answer be negative, those others may reconsider their commitment. In general, therefore, these invitations should be offered in a private setting where frank discussion can take place and the person being enlisted can accept or decline without broader consequences. It is not wise to put the person being asked on the spot. If the person feels awkward about saying no, it could lead them to feel that they are being coerced into helping. In the long run, this will lead to resentment.

The Dangers of Public Enlistment

As we were finishing up a meeting of the feasibility-study committee, our consultant mentioned that the next step in the campaign would be to assemble a campaign planning committee. I made the mistake of saying in an off-hand way that I hoped everyone would sign on to the planning committee. Much to my amazement, Joan, one of the members who runs a large local foundation, said immediately that she would not be willing to help! My heart sank as a much-too-quiet pause settled on the group. Bless her heart, Joan realized what she had done and went on to say that she wished she could serve, but she thought it would be a conflict of interest given her position with the foundation. The dangerous moment passed but somehow the spirit of the group waned. Never again will I casually ask a group of people if they would be willing to help!

—President, Foundation Board

Exhibit 6–1 Campaign Planning Committee

Recruitment Worksheet

Date _____

Primary Name	Alternate	Code*	Enlister	Yes/No
1.				
2.				
3.				
4.				
5.				
6.				
7.				
8.				

*These codes should indicate this person would fill on the committee. They might include indicators such as **B** (board member), **LD** (lead donor), **BS** (business), **PF** (patient family), etc.

Effective volunteers lead to successful campaigns. If a campaign is built on these simple truths about people, it is sure to succeed.

- People like to feel that they are part of a group.
- People want to keep "good" company.
- People want to be part of a successful venture.
- People want to make a real difference in their worlds.
- People like to give advice.
- People feel good when their knowledge and skills are recognized.
- People need to know they are special.
- People know more than they will admit about power and money.
- People feel most comfortable with people of similar status and power.
- People are more likely to say "yes" to people of similar status and power.
- People like to be insiders.

The Campaign and the Board of Directors

The Potential for Conflict

Because campaigns have their own committee structures that overlap with but do not encompass the entire board and because campaign committees often have more resources and community power than the board, the relationship between the board and the campaign steering committee often becomes strained. Social-serv-

ice agencies in particular have difficulties in this area. Their boards are usually structured as nonfund-raising boards, some of whose members do not have the ability to make significant financial contributions or are not among the powerful players in the community. However, even though the campaign committee may be more visible and better heeled, the board of directors continues to be responsible for the organization's health and well-being.

Most board members of smaller organizations have never been involved in a capital campaign. Because they are legally responsible for the health of the organization, they are often wary, curious, and excited as their organization plans a capital campaign. The better the board understands the campaign process and the more each member is involved, the more effective it will be in guiding the organization through the campaign period.

Particularly if a board is not a fund-raising board it is likely to have many misconceptions about the campaign, the campaign committees, and the campaign chair. It is not uncommon, for example, for a board to believe that hiring a campaign consultant absolves it from doing any of the work. Conversely, if the campaign leadership and committees are more powerful and wealthier than the board, then board members may feel powerless to carry out their legitimate responsibilities.

Usually, boards of smaller organizations represent a broad mixture of various strengths and capabilities. The task of involving a board in the design and execution of a campaign is that of determining what each board member is capable of doing well and finding a campaign assignment that fits that person's skills and position. All too often, executive directors feel stymied by a board that seems unwilling to participate in the campaign. Yet in most cases, board inaction is not due to a lack of commitment on the part of the board, but is rather the result of a failure to match the skills of board members to the appropriate campaign tasks and not adequately engaging these important individuals in the campaign process.

Getting the Board Involved

From the perspective of a board member who has neither extensive financial resources nor moneyed contacts it is both perplexing and demeaning to be expected to raise leadership gifts. Even the most willing board members are likely to become disenchanted if they are assigned tasks that they have little hope of completing successfully. Campaigns require work of many kinds, from soliciting leadership gifts to stuffing envelopes, from delivering public addresses about the organization to speaking about it at dinner parties or with friends, from hosting a cultivation dinner at the country club to preparing refreshments for a more intimate cultivation meeting. In this panoply of tasks, there can most certainly be found an appropriate task for every board member, a task that will make each of them feel that they have an important part to play in the success of the campaign.

There are four principal techniques of keeping the board engaged and informed throughout the campaign.

First, educate the board. Every available opportunity should be taken to educate the board about campaigns. The consultant can be invited to a special meeting with the board to describe the process, philosophy, and practice of capital campaigns. Individuals from the community who have just finished comparable campaigns can be invited to share their experiences with the board. Opportunities can be provided at every board meeting for discussing the campaign. The campaign chair, if he or she is not a board member, can be invited to speak with the board. The chairs of the various campaign committees can be invited to educate the board about their particular segments of the campaign.

Educating the board is not a one-time affair. Campaigns extend over a long period of time. They go through many phases. They evolve as they proceed. The

In most cases, board inaction is not due to a lack of commitment on the part of the board, but is rather the result of a failure to match the skills of board members to the appropriate campaign tasks.

board should be privy to the growth and progress of the campaign and not only through monthly reports of how much money has been raised. The executive director and the board chair should design an ongoing campaign curriculum for the board, to explain to them what is going on at every stage in the campaign and to maintain their interest and involvement.

Second, know the board. In order to involve every board member, an executive director should become familiar with each member's interests, capabilities, and skills. Many organizations already know their board members well and have only to set about developing the best strategy for involving each board member. Some directors, however, know little about their board members' interests and abilities. While preparing for a campaign, therefore, the director or board chair should gather as much information as possible about each of these individuals in order to determine how that person might most effectively assist the campaign.

Third, identify campaign roles for board members. Board members should be involved in every aspect of the campaign. Not only does this provide a role for every type of person on the board, but it provides an initial group of committed and informed volunteers to begin filling some of the many volunteer positions in the campaign.

The board chair, development chair, and other key board members should serve on the most important campaign committees. One of these board members should be responsible for communicating with the rest of the board about the campaign, and should do so at regular board meetings.

One should beware of the temptation to generalize about board responsibilities. All too often one hears statements such as, "It's up to the board to raise the money," or "The board is not contributing enough to the campaign," or "The board is not lifting a finger to help the campaign." Although there may be some merit in generalizing about a board's culture or behavior, such sweeping generalizations are not going to be helpful in motivating individual board members to action. The key to involving a board in a capital campaign is to develop a strategic plan for engaging each member in the way most appropriate to that individual's abilities and temperament and then provide sufficient opportunity to each board member to learn, to share information with others, and to celebrate successes.

Fourth, remember the chain of command. The board of directors shoulders the responsibility for the organization. The board, then, has the responsibility of approving or denying the campaign plan that is outlined by the campaign planning committee. The plan developed by this committee should be drafted as a set of recommendations to be presented to the board of directors for their approval. The board should not be seen by the campaign planning committee as an obstacle to the success of the campaign but as the commanders-in-chief to whom the planning committee presents proposals for the campaign ahead.

Board Giving

Even though most boards of smaller organizations are not fund-raising boards, every board nonetheless has a financial responsibility to the campaign. Board giving is often an indicator of success for foundations or others who regularly give to campaigns. Major foundations regularly ask what percent of the board members made a financial contribution to the campaign and the cumulative amount of money raised from the board. It is particularly important, then, that the board understand that they have an obligation to support the campaign financially. However, board members should not be placed in the untenable position of being expected to give more than they can. Perhaps Karl Marx was writing about board giving when he penned those famous words, "from each according to his ability. . . ."

From early in the campaign planning period, the board should be encouraged to discuss openly and fully the issue of board giving. The board should engage as a group in determining goals for percent participation and the amount of money that the board will collectively give. If possible, boards should try to get every board member to make a gift to the campaign. In some cases, this is not easy; however, the results are often worth the effort.

Developing Goals for Board Giving

Contrary to common belief, the appropriate level of board giving to a capital campaign is not a specific percentage of the campaign goal. Although one often hears consultants and others say that the board must give at least 30 percent of the campaign goal, such generalizations are appropriate only for boards who were recruited in part because of their financial strength.

Many social-service organizations quite appropriately build strong and effective boards that include very few people with significant wealth. These organizations are often more interested in having boards that will play a hands-on role in conducting the work of the organization. They look for board members who represent different constituencies and ethnic groups. Unlike people of significant means, who are often asked to work on campaign after campaign and who are experienced donors, most mid-level board members are new to the capital-campaign process and are inexperienced as major donors.

For these mid-level boards, the subject of board giving is particularly uncomfortable. They are told again and again of the importance of board giving, yet they are intimately acquainted with the limitations of their own re-

sources. And many of them have never considered making a charitable contribution of more than $250 or $500.

To further complicate the situation, many boards have had disagreements or even outright strife over their role in the annual giving program. Indeed, the issue of the boards' capital-campaign gifts sometimes sits atop troubled waters.

The topic of board giving might be compared to a large and dangerous monster hiding under the living room rug. There is clearly a large lump right in the middle of the floor, and that lump makes people uncomfortable and also diminishes the usefulness of the living room. Everyone knows that the monster is there but is afraid that lifting the rug will unleash something much worse than a lumpy carpet. A campaign is a good time to look under the rug.

Small-Group Rating Session

The executive director should ask two or three of the most senior board members to rate each board member's perceived ability and inclination to give. The same process that is outlined in chapter 5 will work quite well. Any lead-donor prospects should be included in this rating committee. The names of the committee members should also appear on the rating sheet, so that each person will rate him- or herself as well as everyone else.

The Campaign Chair Who Got Every Board Member to Give

Early in our campaign, the board met to determine their giving goals. After lots of talk, the board resolved that their giving goals would be 100% board participation and $120,000. I did my job and solicited every board member. Most of them gave promptly and generously, contributing more than the $120,000 they had committed to, but one board member didn't come through. As the campaign moved toward the kickoff I was determined to get this guy to give, so I wrote him a letter indicating that I would make a special gift to the campaign over and above what I had already given to match any gift he would make. The next week I happened to run into him. Though he looked a bit sheepish, he clearly was torn between not wanting to part with his hard-earned money and wanting to hold my feet to the fire by making me give more than I had bargained for. As I suspected, his inclination to be a nongiver swayed his gift more than his desire for revenge. He did give a gift. It was small, but with that gift we got our 100% participation.

—Campaign Chair

Exhibit 6–2 Board Rating Example

Sample Giving Capacity Rating Codes

Code	Estimated Giving Capacity*
1	$500–$4,999
2	$5,000–$9,999
3	$10,000–$24,999
4	$24,000–$49,999
5	$50,000 and up

estimated giving capacity over three years

Interest Level Rating Codes

Code	Estimated Inclination to Give
A	Clearly enthusiastic; strongly inclined to give
B	Active and enthusiastic
C	Moderately active and interested
D	Minimal interest
E	Disenchanted; no perceived inclination

Sample List of Board Members

Name	Board Term	Giving History*	Interest	Ability
Joe Brown	1994–2000	15 gifts/$$$$$		
Jeff Solomon	1996–2002	4 gifts/$$$		
Sally Smith	1995–2001	22 gifts/$$$$		
Mike Stutz	1993–1999	6 gifts/$$		
Barbara Northrup	1955–(emeritus)	many/$$		
Peggy Manes	1997–2003	2 gifts/$$$$$		

Giving history is often shown according to the total number of gifts an individual has made to the organization and the relative gift range.

For a typical social service organization planning a capital campaign to raise $2,000,000, the board rating material might look like Exhibit 6–2.

Each board member reviews the list privately, filling in the codes for interest and ability. Each person should write his or her name at the top of the form. This can be done in a group or individually but because the information and the process are somewhat sensitive, the board members should not take the lists out of the office.

A staff member should assemble the rated lists and collate the information into one master list with all the codes listed next to each name.

The list might look something like Exhibit 6–3.

The development director and board chair review the collective ratings—paying close attention to the self-ratings (indicated in boldface in Exhibit 6–3)—and make a judgment about the most likely gift range for each board member, thereby arriving at a list something like Exhibit 6–4.

Their judgments are guided by the information given on the rating sheets and also by any other information that the development director may have about each person's actual intention or ability to give. Often, when examining rating sheets, one learns a great deal about each of the persons doing the rating. Those who consistently rate others low are likely themselves to be low givers. Those who rate high are likely to give more.

Once each person on the board has been assigned a giving range, the low-end and high-end amounts should be separately totaled to arrive at a cumulative dollar range. For an entire board this range might be, for example, $125,000–$250,000.

Self-Rating at a Board Meeting

The subject of a board campaign goal should be placed on the board's meeting agenda. At that meeting, each board member should be asked to rate him- or herself. Index cards should be distributed showing giving ranges within which each board member might choose to give. The cards might look like this:

Estimated Campaign Pledge over Three Years
$100–$499
$500–$2,999
$3,000–$4,999
$5,000–$9,999
$10,000–$24,999
$25,000 and up

Exhibit 6–3 Collated Ratings

Name	Board Term	Giving History	Collective Ratings
Joe Brown	1994–2000	15 gifts/$$$$	A3, B4, **A4,** A2, B5, A4
Jeff Solomon	1996–2002	4 gifts/$$$	C2, **B3,** C4, C4, C3, B5
Sally Smith	1995–2001	22 gifts/$$$$	A3, A1, A2, B3, A3, **A2**
Mike Stutz	1993–1999	6 gifts/$$	**B3,** C2, C3, B3, C2, B2
Barbara Northrup	1955–(emeritus)	many/$$	A2, A5, A4, A2, A2, **A3**
Peggy Manes	1997–2003	2 gifts/$$$$	C5, B4, B3, C4, C4, **A4**

Each board member should be asked to indicate which giving category reflects the gift he or she would consider making to the campaign over a three-year period. They should be asked to fold their cards without signing them. The cards should be collected and the giving ranges tallied. Estimated ranges for any missing board members should then be added to arrive at a board-giving range.

This range should be reported back to the board during the same meeting, and it should be compared to the range arrived at through the earlier rating process. It is helpful to post these two ranges on a large sheet of newsprint where everyone on the board can see them. Often the two ranges are quite close, but it is not unusual for the board to rate itself higher than had the smaller group.

This information now can serve as the basis for a discussion of the board's giving goal. The board chair should conduct an open discussion about where in the range the board would like to set its giving goal. Sometimes boards aim high, sometimes they are more conservative. No matter what the results of the discussion, it is important that the board arrive at a consensual goal through a participatory process.

At the conclusion of the discussion, the chair should request a motion that specifies a dollar goal for the board. Some boards also resolve to obtain the financial participation of every board member. If, as occasionally happens, someone on the board is unwilling to make a financial gift, such a resolution is not realistically attainable. Usually, however, a hesitant board member can be brought around through private conversations with the board chair who might remind him or her that even a small gift would send a strong statement if it established unanimous board commitment.

Campaign Leadership

Characteristics of a Campaign Leader

Whoever assumes the role or roles of a campaign leader guides by both word and deed. Campaign leaders are often the primary motivators and solicitors for the campaign. The campaign leader is often the individual to whom the other committee members will look for acknowledgment and approval.

In most books on fund raising and capital campaigns, one reads about the salient characteristics of campaign chairs, and indeed these considerations are of great importance. Good campaign leaders really are responsible, trustworthy, generous, wealthy, and committed. These characteristics arise from an expansive definition of leadership that will be useful to examine here briefly.

"Leadership," states Max DePree in his book *Leadership Jazz* (1992, 7), "is not a position but a job. It's hard and exciting and good work. It's also a serious meddling in other people's lives." And so it is with the leaders of capital campaigns. They undertake a job that is challenging, inspiring, and demanding. They extend themselves and reach out to others. They sail on the highs and anguish through the lows.

Campaign leaders often have many of the following campaign-specific qualifications.

First, campaign leaders lend credibility to the campaign. In every community there are individuals whose involvement carries with it the understanding that the project will succeed. "Oh," exclaim prospective volunteers and donors, "so-and-so is involved. The effort is bound to be a success." These individuals have earned reputations as winners. They work hard to ensure that any project in which they are involved will succeed. They motivate others to extend themselves. They commit their own resources to the projects that they undertake, and they ask others to join them. They go above and beyond their job descriptions to make certain that they and the campaign succeed.

Second, campaign leaders are capable of making leadership gifts. Campaign leaders lead best by example. Sometimes the campaign chair will be able to make the largest gift to the campaign. In other cases, this may not be possible. However, every effective campaign leader must make a gift that is generous within the context of his or her resources. Although a true leader will understand this without being told, the importance of the

> *Whoever assumes the role or roles of a campaign leader guides by both word and deed.*

Exhibit 6–4 Gift Range

Name	Board Term	Giving History	Potential Giving Range
Joe Brown	1994–2000	15 gifts/$$$$	$10,000–$25,000
Jeff Solomon	1996–2002	4 gifts/$$$	$ 5,000–$10,000
Sally Smith	1995–2001	22 gifts/$$$$	$ 1,500–$ 5,000
Mike Stutz	1993–1999	6 gifts/$$	$ 1,500–$ 5,000
Barbara Northrup	1955–(emeritus)	many/$$	$ 2,500–$ 5,000
Peggy Manes	1997–2003	2 gifts/$$$$$	$10,000–$25,000

chair's gift should be discussed before a particular individual is asked to serve in a leadership capacity. A wealthy chair who gives a small gift or a chair of modest means who doesn't give at all is probably worse than no chair at all.

Third, campaign leaders devote time and energy to the campaign. The ideal campaign chair should have enough time to work on the campaign. The chair's jobs are varied and demanding. The chair cultivates and solicits lead donors, attends and leads campaign meetings, and is an advocate for the campaign at public events and in the media. When recruiting campaign leadership, the organization should be specific and candid about the amount of time required of the chair so that there are no unpleasant surprises for the chair or for the organization once the campaign is in full swing. One should beware of the prospective chair who offers to contribute a name and a major gift but who has no time to

work. That person might be better placed as honorary chair of the campaign, or as cochair together with someone who may have a lesser name but more time.

Finally, campaign chairs motivate other volunteers. As a volunteer, a campaign chair can relate to other volunteers and motivate them in a way that staff members cannot. Campaign chairs motivate others by example, by praise, or by a candid observation about what the volunteer is—or is not—doing.

The Team Approach to Campaign Leadership

The past decade has seen many changes in volunteer patterns. Most people in the not-for-profit sector understand all too well the challenges of relying on volunteers in a society where women work outside the home, corporations are "right-sizing," and the older generation of experienced campaign leaders feels burned out. Because of many structural changes in our culture, it is more and more difficult to find that one person who embodies everything one would wish for in a campaign chair. Many organizations, therefore, have been forced to explore other leadership configurations that spread the burdens and opportunities of leadership among two, three, or even four people. With the right combination of people and effective organization and communication, this team approach to campaign leadership can work very well. In some cases, the combined skills, gifts, and influence of a leadership team can be far greater than that of a single individidual.

The simplest configuration for campaign leadership is that of one campaign chair who has all the characteristics and conditions needed to make him or her an ideal chair—money, time, commitment, energy, knowledge of the cause, leadership characteristics, name, reputation, integrity, and an established history with the organization. If there is one person who is an obvious choice, this clear-cut leadership model is ideal in that it avoids the pitfalls of more complicated structures.

Sometimes a person who has only some of the qualities required for the job may nonetheless be a good candidate for campaign chair. In many communities, the older generation of leaders seems to be tiring of chairing campaigns and is concerned that the next generation is not stepping

The Chairwoman Who Was Too Busy

The non-profit that I was working for during the campaign had asked a busy public figure to serve as its campaign chair. She was wealthy and had a well-known and respected name among most of our constituents—in fact, many of our prospects were honored to know that they might have the opportunity to meet this woman. Unfortunately, because of her busy schedule she simply didn't have enough time to meet with people. She believed in the organization's work one hundred and ten percent—she made one of the largest gifts to the campaign and was willing to solicit and cultivate prospects when she had the time. But all too often she just didn't have the time. In retrospect, we would have been better off using her as an honorary chair and bringing her in for the really big solicitations and finding somebody else who might have had less stature but who had the time to do more of the day-to-day work.

—Development Director

forward or being trained effectively to take their places. Occasionally, one has a chance to capitalize on this concern by recruiting a younger campaign chair with the explicit help of an older power figure in the community. Although the older person need not take on the visible aspects of campaign leadership, that individual might be willing to help ensure the success of the campaign by working behind the scenes, reaping the satisfaction of passing the leadership torch to someone of the new generation with strong prospects as a community leader.

Often, however, no one person surfaces as the clear and obvious choice. Many individuals have some but not all of the characteristics required of a campaign chair. One person may have resources and reputation but little time. Or someone may have reputation, time, and even money, but poor leadership skills. The many permutations of these qualities are as numerous as campaigns and their potential leaders. Creating two chairs, or co-chairs, enables an organization to combine the skills and characteristics of two people into a workable leadership partnership. The key to successful co-chairing is enlisting two individuals who respect and approve of each other and then carefully defining the role and responsibilities for each. In particular, it is important to establish clear lines of responsibility and communication so that everyone involved (board chair, executive director, and each co-chair) understands who will be expected to do what and how information will be communicated.

Sometimes it is advisable to assemble an even bigger leadership team. In some cases, having a team of three co-chairs can be an effective strategy. This might be the case when the leaders of a community decide to lock arms on behalf of a high-risk but important community organization. When several well-known community leaders come together publicly to share the leadership of a campaign, their visibility makes a powerful impression. This approach was used in the extreme by the Commonwealth Partnership in Pennsylvania, which was composed of twelve well-known private colleges and universities across the state. When this organization prepared large foundation proposals, they often accompanied the proposals with a cover letter signed by all twelve college and university presidents. The process of getting all twelve signatures was cumbersome, but those twelve signatures carried enormous weight and could not be lightly ignored. In the same way, a campaign can sometimes benefit from a larger, more powerful leadership team.

It should be kept in mind, however, that too many cooks can indeed turn soup into swill. In general, the larger and more complex the leadership team, the stronger the role the staff must play in guiding, communicating, and managing the process. There are many ways to configure the responsibilities of campaign leadership, and the best configuration is the result of clear, thorough discussion among the board chair, the director, and those being recruited for leadership positions.

Responsibilities of the Campaign Leadership

The first responsibility of a campaign chair is his or her gift to the campaign. It is not uncommon to hear stories such as that of the campaign chair who didn't understand that he was expected to contribute a major gift to the campaign until after he had agreed to take the chairmanship. Gradually he became aware that the director expected him to make the lead gift, but his business was having difficulties and he was not able to do so. His financial discomfort continued throughout the campaign and compromised his effectiveness as a chair. Even more often, one finds that although both the organization and the proposed campaign chair understand in a general way that the campaign chair is expected to give a major gift, neither side is comfortable discussing the specific amount of the gift that the candidate should give and so the matter is let slide. So, for example, the board chair and executive director may have in mind that a fitting campaign chair gift might be $30,000, while the candidate for chairmanship might think that $5,000 is a big gift. Expectations should be discussed before the fact, not after.

It is imperative that the candidate's intention to give to the campaign be discussed. The table of gifts and campaign goals should be reviewed with the candidate. If the candidate is a person of wealth, his or her gift should

There are eight dos and four don'ts for comunicating with multiple chairs.

Do:

1. Communicate directly with all of them
2. Include all of their names in the salutation of correspondence to them all
3. Keep them all as informed as possible
4. Maintain personal contact with all of them throughout the campaign
5. Give each of them opportunities to play a public role
6. Highlight them all in printed material
7. Define specific roles for each of them
8. Find the patience and discipline to celebrate each of their accomplishments

Don't:

1. Respond to a question from one by communicating with another
2. Send correspondence meant for all of them to one person with copies to the others
3. Gossip about one of them with the others
4. Pit one against the others

be among the top ten. If, however, the candidate does not have financial resources but brings other important qualities to the task, then the gift should be a gift that is impressive but realisitic for someone of that person's means.

The second responsibility of a campaign chair is his or her public visibility. The campaign chairs are the most visible people in the campaign, and they should fully understand the opportunities and responsibilities associated with this public image. Their names will appear on campaign materials. Their signatures will be used for all proposals and requests for funds. Their names and statements about the organization and the campaign will appear in press releases. They will be expected to give speeches at campaign events. And in their workplace and the community, they will be expected to represent the organization and the campaign in a responsible and constructive way.

People often recognize the potential for status and visibility that comes with a position of leadership, but they are less likely to understand the burdens and high risk that also come with the job. Clear and thoughtful discussion of the responsibilities of being a public figure prior to an individual's agreement to become chair will create an understanding of just what is being taken on, so that the person who eventually does become chair will walk into the task with open eyes. Although such a frank discussion may discourage the candidate from accepting, if the candidate accepts the position with a full understanding of the expectations, risks, and rewards, that individual is likely to give a better performance in this demanding role.

The third responsibility of a campaign chair is his or her time. Just how much time will be required of the campaign leader? This, too, is an important consideration for a campaign chair, and figuring out the correct answer results from a blending of the campaign's needs and the volunteer's availability. Some campaign chairs turn the campaign into a full-time job. They attend every volunteer meeting; they work on the campaign at home at night; they are on the telephone at all hours recruiting people, following up on solicitations, and driving the staff. Others focus on the specific tasks that they know they alone can accomplish. Both of these models can work well. Trouble arises, however, when an organization thinks it is getting the first model and what the volunteer has in mind is the second! Once again, a thor-

ough conversation about expectations before the fact will lay the foundation for a good relationship!

The fourth responsibility of a campaign chair is soliciting gifts. The campaign's leaders play an important role in soliciting gifts. At a minimum, they are responsible for soliciting the other volunteers who assume key positions in the campaign. Because all volunteers must make their own gifts before soliciting others, the structure and timing of these solicitations is important to the success of the campaign. The campaign leaders should understand that they will be expected to make their own contributions to the campaign early and that they will be responsible for soliciting those volunteers who assume committee and division leadership. All too often in the campaign process, these solicitations are not taken care of, on the vague assumption that the campaign volunteers will make their own gifts without being asked. If the campaign leaders understand and carry out their roles in this task early in the campaign, the entire campaign is likely to flow more smoothly.

Campaign leaders usually also solicit other major donors. Some campaign leaders solicit only a few key gifts for a campaign, others take on single-handedly the task of soliciting most of the major-donor prospects. Either of these patterns will work as long as expectations are clear. The early solicitation process also provides the added benefit of enabling campaign leaders to hone their solicitation skills on individuals already committed to the campaign, thus preparing them to solicit other major donors. Solicitation skills get better with practice, and people who are already committed are often helpful in finding the right words and building confidence in the process.

The final responsibility of a campaign chair is attending meetings. Campaign leaders chair campaign steering committee meetings and preside over public events. Once again, there are many effective ways to define these tasks. The right techniques for a specific campaign will depend on the character, desires, and abilities of both the staff and the leaders. Many campaigns are largely staff driven. Staff members prepare the agenda, schedule the meetings, and instruct the campaign leaders on their roles. In others, however, the campaign leaders will want to participate more fully in the design and planning. To work well, the leadership and staff must complement one another. Advanced discussion of roles and expectations will help all parties determine whether they can create an effective team.

Job Descriptions for Campaign Leadership

Written job descriptions help clarify the expectations of campaign leaders. A job description for a volunteer campaign leader, however, might serve better as an agenda for in-depth discussion than as a prescription for the role. The most effective approach to recruiting campaign leadership demands flexibility, comfort with collaborative exploration, a thorough understanding of the fundamental responsibilities of campaign leadership, and a healthy dose of creativity.

Conversations with prospective campaign leaders should be more like collaborative discussions about out how to build a successful campaign than like job interviews. That said, the job description may look something like Exhibit 6–5.

Questions to Guide the Recruitment Discussion

A set of questions, prepared in advance, will help guide the discussion into and through areas that might be uncomfortable for both parties. The questions might include the following:

- How much input into the campaign process will the chair want to have?
- How much time does the chair anticipate being able to devote to the campaign?
- What is the chair's leadership style?
- With what roles is the chair comfortable and what roles would be better avoided?
- What would the chair like to take away from his or her leadership experience?
- In what range does the chair anticipate making a gift to the campaign?

Exhibit 6–5 What We Need from Campaign Leadership

1. **The leaders of a campaign must be willing to:**
   ✔ make a generous and early financial commitment
   ✔ be the public persona for the campaign in person, print, and the media
   ✔ help enlist volunteers to serve in key campaign positions
   ✔ solicit other campaign volunteers and major donor prospects
   ✔ attend and chair regular steering committee meetings throughout the campaign
   ✔ attend campaign kickoff, cultivation, and celebration events
2. **Campaign leaders might also:**
   ✔ participate in frequent strategy sessions to guide the campaign and solicitation process
   ✔ attend solicitor training meetings to help encourage and motivate volunteers
   ✔ help rate prospects
   ✔ review and edit proposals, letters, and other campaign material
   ✔ make behind-the-scenes contacts to help motivate donors
   ✔ speak about the organization and campaign in various public forums

Assembling an Information Packet

Although in most cases the prospective campaign leaders will already be familiar with the organization, it is reassuring for a leadership candidate to be presented with a simple, well-organized package of background information about the organization and the campaign. The contents of the package will vary depending on when in the campaign planning process the campaign leadership is enlisted. If the leadership is enlisted early, before the campaign planning committee has been recruited, then the package will include a mission statement, the feasibility study report, the preliminary table of gifts used in the feasibility study, the preliminary case for support, a preliminary timetable for the campaign, and a list of those who have already become involved in campaign planning.

If, as sometimes happens, the recruitment takes place after the campaign planning meetings, the package might also include the documents that were developed through that process—a chart showing the structure of the campaign, a discussion of campaign policies, the campaign goal and table of gifts, and the names of the people who served on the campaign planning committee. It would be unusual to recruit campaign leaders who were not invited to serve on the planning committee, but every once in a while due to scheduling conflicts this happens.

The Recruitment Process

The board chair and executive director are usually the people who decide who will be recruited to serve as the campaign leader. The process of recruiting the campaign chair is usually preceded with many informal conversations about leadership with board members and others who have been involved in preparing for the campaign. From these discussions, the names of one or more people are likely to surface as potential chairs.

The recruitment process itself takes place when the executive director and board chair select the most likely candidate for campaign chair. Usually, this is the most influential and generous person who is committed to the organization's cause. The board chair and the executive director explore the various leadership options. If they determine that the most likely candidate would indeed make an excellent chair, they set up a meeting to recruit that person. If they deem that the team approach would work better, they set up a meeting to explore the options with the lead candidate. No matter which strategy is the best for a specific campaign, the board chair and director should do ample homework before the meeting.

In the recruitment process, attention to detail is critical. Many experienced leaders have learned to generalize from brief encounters. They are astute observers and good listeners. Although they are unlikely to comment openly about a poorly planned meeting or sloppily organized material, such indicators are likely to figure into such a person's decision about whether or not to accept a leadership position.

Every detail of a meeting for recruiting campaign leadership is important. Such meetings should be planned and considered with care. Printed material should be well written, well organized, and attractive. The meeting should be designed to promote serious, professional discussion and exploration—it should not come across as a social occasion, with the leadership question thrown in casually at an opportune moment.

Recruitment meetings should be models of an organization's best behavior. They need not be fancy or formal, but they should be well thought out. Materials should be prepared in advance. The following simple guidelines will increase the chances of a recruitment meeting's success.

First, there should be no surprises for the candidate. When presented with the invitation to the meeting, the candidate for a leadership position should be informed that he or she will be asked to chair or cochair the campaign. If possible, material should be sent to the candidate in advance. In that way, the person will have a chance to consider the matter beforehand, clarify any questions, and be prepared to discuss the offer seriously.

Second, roles should be assigned before the meeting. Recruitment meetings are often called by the board chair and the executive director. Prior to the meeting, these persons should determine the roles each will play at the meeting. Who will review the background information and materials? Who will pose the leadership questions? Who will keep track of the time? If these questions are decided ahead of time, the meeting is likely to progress in a clear and straightforward manner.

Third, there should be no beating about the bush. While some small talk is usually necessary to put everyone at ease, as soon as everyone has settled down, the topic of the meeting should be broached clearly and directly. It is a common pitfall to delay asking the critical question for fear of an early rejection. If, however, a candidate has agreed to attend a meeting to discuss becoming campaign chair, he or she is certainly willing to consider the issue seriously and is not likely to decline the offer in the first five minutes. The fact that the candidate has taken the time to come to the meeting is a strong indicator that the individual is likely to accept. As much of the meeting time as possible should be used to discuss and explore the many issues and requirements of leadership. One should not give in to the temptation to delay the discussion.

Fourth, financial expectations should be discussed. An early and straightforward discussion of the candidate's gift to the campaign will avoid ambiguity and ill will later.

Finally, follow-up steps should be determined. If at that meeting the candidate agrees to serve, the discussion should proceed immediately to outlining the next campaigns steps. If the proposed chair needs time to consider, a date and time for a decision should be agreed on.

When to Enlist the Campaign Leadership

In some campaigns it is obvious from the very beginning who will chair the campaign. Sometimes one person has driven a project, is capable, and is willing to lead the campaign. Even in such cases, however, a structured discussion about the role of the campaign chair will help clarify expectations, provide an official opportunity for that person to be invited to serve as the chair, and allow for consideration of others who might serve on a leadership team. The board chair and/or executive director are responsible for setting up the recruitment meeting, and if possible, this meeting should occur before the campaign planning meetings.

In many campaigns, the choice of campaign leadership is less obvious. Often, by the time an organization is prepared to proceed with a campaign, many people have agreed to help and several people may be seen as leadership candidates but no one person is a clear choice or clearly willing to take on the task. In such cases, the recruitment of the campaign planning committee provides an excellent opportunity to prepare someone for the job of campaign chair. The small co-conspiratorial group convened to determine the membership of the campaign planning committee might well be used to identify and engage the campaign leadership. Although these co-conspirators have no official role, by taking responsibility for selecting and enlisting the campaign planners they are in fact acting as campaign leaders. Astute observation of each of these individuals will often provide clues that will lead to wise decisions about campaign leadership. If so, the leadership recruitment might occur between the co-conspirators' meetings and the planning committee meetings.

In more difficult cases, the optimal configuration of campaign leadership may not reveal itself until later in the process. If the leadership is in place prior to the planning meetings, that person will chair those meetings. If not, someone else, often the board chair, must be recruited for that task.

The longer one waits to decide who will chair a campaign, the more unspoken anxiety will permeate the campaign organization. An organization is ill served, how-

> *You honor a person with an invitation to serve as the chair of a campaign. A recruitment meeting should be thought of as a discussion about opportunities for mutual gain.*

ever, if it hurries to nail down the campaign leadership without striving for the very best and strongest leaders it can get.

Campaign Structure

The Structure of the Campaign

The structure of a capital campaign varies from organization to organization and will be discussed in detail in the next chapter. Every campaign, however, will include a planning committee, a steering committee—which is sometimes referred to as the campaign cabinet—task-oriented committees, and solicitation divisions. Campaigns for organizations that encompass more than one geographic region may include a regional structure as well that covers each region in which the organization has a constituency.

The Campaign Steering Committee

Campaigns are protracted efforts. They often last as long as a year and a half, two years, or even longer. Different groups of people are more or less active during various phases of the campaign. Although many campaigns are actually midwifed by a small group that usually includes the campaign chair, development director, executive director, and perhaps a campaign director or consultant, a larger committee should meet periodically to oversee the campaign's progress and report on it to the board.

This group, often referred to as the steering committee or campaign cabinet, is composed of the various committee chairs and division leaders in addition to the campaign leadership team, the board chair, and the executive director and other appropriate staff members. The steering committee usually meets monthly, although during some phases of the campaign they may meet more or less often.

The steering committee serves as the communications hub, enabling those heading up one or another piece of the campaign to learn what is going on in other areas. During steering committee meetings each member has an opportunity to review the activity in his or her committee or division, and the campaign chair is able to discuss progress toward the campaign goal.

The steering committee also guides the course of the campaign. Its members evaluate the campaign's progress and are brought up to date on the solicitation of lead gifts. Using this information as a guide, the committee determines the timing of the campaign kickoff and makes a recommendation to the board for the level of the public goal before the general solicitation materials are printed.

Task-Oriented Committees

Every campaign has at least two committees that have been established to accomplish particular tasks. The most common of these are the public relations and materials committee and the events committee. Some campaigns also include a cultivation or outreach committee and a prospect rating committee. In other organizations these functions are handled largely by staff without the benefit of a committee.

The public relations/materials committee coordinates with the public relations staff to support the campaign effort in three areas.

1. Solicitation of materials. This committee works in conjunction with a graphic designer or advertising (or marketing) firm to oversee the development of the solicitation materials. Solicitation materials include the campaign brochure, pledge cards, and any other solicitation pieces used during the campaign. These materials are discussed in detail in chapter 11.
2. Media coverage. The committee explores ways to increase media coverage of the organization during the first phase of the campaign and oversees media coverage of public campaign events such as the kickoff event, groundbreaking ceremony, and the celebration when the goal has been reached.
3. Internal communication. The committee works with the staff to determine how best to inform the many campaign insiders about the progress of the campaign.

Campaigns are punctuated by events, some large, some small. The campaign events committee helps plan and implement these events. Often the events committee provides an ideal opportunity for those who are uncomfortable with soliciting gifts to be involved in the campaign in an important and visible way. Event planning is time consuming and requires great attention to detail. A strong events committee expands volunteer opportunities in the campaign and thereby adds energy, expertise, and enthusiasm to an important part of the campaign.

Solicitation Divisions

The core of every campaign is the organization of solicitors and prospects so the most appropriate volunteer will solicit the most likely prospects. Solicitation divisions are organized groups of volunteers who are enlisted to solicit selected groups of prospects. Sometimes the divisions are organized according to giving level. The leadership-gift division, for example, might be responsible for soliciting all prospects considered capable of making a gift of $25,000 or more. In other cases, the divisions are organized by other categories—geographic region, business affiliation, relationship to the organization (grateful former patients, for example, or former board members, or staff members, and so forth).

Large divisions might be divided into sections and these into teams for ease of communication and contact.

Smaller divisions may consist of four or five individuals who select their prospects from a narrow universe of prospects. In any case, the goal of every solicitation division is to put the right solicitor together with the right donor to ask for the right gift at the right time.

Recruiting Committee Chairs and Division Leaders

Each committee and division is headed by a volunteer or team of volunteers who help recruit workers and generally play a leadership role in its respective committee or division. Those who have worked on campaigns before know from experience that the success of any committee or division is often shaped by the effectiveness of the volunteer leaders. Although the staff can often perform the bulk of the behind-the-scenes work, the behavior and leadership of the volunteers sets the tone of each committee and division. In those unfortunate instances when a volunteer division leader does not function well, the entire division is likely to be compromised, but when a campaign is fortunate to recruit an excellent volunteer to head up a division, that division is likely to raise a sum well above its goal.

Good leaders of campaign divisions and committees are hard workers and are good at following through. They must be willing to make a significant gift to the campaign. They must be willing and able to recruit other effective campaign workers. But most of all, they must be individuals who do what they say they will do, and do it in a timely manner.

The most difficult campaign volunteers are those who agree to do a task and then put it off . . . and off . . . and off. Not only do such volunteers fail to carry out their appointed tasks, they won't step aside so the task can be assigned to someone else. They block every path and cause frustration that leads to inaction. Before a volunteer leader is recruited for a committee or a division, that individual's track record on other committees should be investigated. A few timely questions in the right places can keep an entire division from getting bogged down with a leader who doesn't follow through.

Unlike job descriptions for campaign chairs, which are customized to fit the will and abilities of the candidates, job descriptions for committee and division chairs are quite standard and straightforward. They are, therefore, easier to prepare and the tasks and timetables clearer to specify.

When recruiting a volunteer to chair a campaign committee or division, the job description should include at least the following information:

- purpose of the committee or division
- time and duration of the leader's role
- approximate number of meetings to be attended
- specific tasks to be accomplished
- financial responsibility to the campaign

> *The success of any committee or division is often shaped by the effectiveness of the volunteer leaders.*

A job description for a committee chair might look something like Exhibit 6–6.

Exhibit 6–7 is a sample job description for the chair of a division that solicited businesses and local foundations for a community-based hospice.

Often the process of developing the job descriptions for committee chairs helps staff members clarify their own thinking about roles, timing, and responsibilities. Job descriptions should be as specific as possible without being overwhelming. They should be clear, businesslike, and easy to read. In these days of desktop publishing and user-friendly graphics packages, every organization can produce simple and attractive documents that convey just the right message in a clear and convincing way. Bold face, italics, indentation, and section headings can be used to enhance job descriptions, agendas, and simple memos.

Campaign consultants are often able to help develop job descriptions for the volunteers. Because they have experience in other campaigns, they can help clarify the tasks, project the likely duration of a committee's work, and even help explain the process to prospective volunteer leaders.

Setting the Stage for Highly Effective Volunteers

Ten Suggestions for Enlisting Volunteers the Right Way

1. Always invite people to do things that they are likely to be able to do successfully.
2. Enlist the most powerful and important people first.
3. Provide long horizons between asking someone to do something and the actual task.
4. Assign a person of similar class, wealth, and position to help enlist a particular candidate.
5. Prepare a list of clearly written expectations before asking anyone to do anything.
6. Define the end or exit of every volunteer project before recruiting people for the beginning of it.
7. Break all volunteer activities into small, manageable links that join together to create a longer chain. Then ask volunteers to help link by link.
8. Let "no" be an acceptable answer.
9. Celebrate all successes, no matter how small.
10. Don't forget to tell them that it's likely to be fun.

Exhibit 6–6 Sample Committee Chair Job Description

Job Description
Special Events Committee Chairperson

Committee Goals: To assemble a committee of capable and knowledgeable individuals to assist the museum in planning special events for the campaign. These will include the campaign kickoff event, two cultivation gatherings prior to the public phase of the campaign, and a campaign celebration at the conclusion of the campaign.

Tentative Timetable:

Cultivation events:	December 1997 and March 1998
Campaign kickoff:	June 1998
Campaign celebration:	March 1999

Responsibilities of the Chairperson:
- ✔ Help identify and enlist six to eight individuals to serve on the special events committee
- ✔ Conduct committee meetings to plan each event
- ✔ Assist with the work of the committee
- ✔ Serve on the campaign steering committee, which will meet monthly throughout the campaign
- ✔ Serve as advocate for the campaign

Staff Support: The staff will work with the chair of this committee to maintain effective communication and follow-through for all aspects of the committee's work. The committee will also meet with the campaign consultant as needed.

Exhibit 6–7 Sample Division Chair Job Description

Job Description
Business/Foundation Division Chairperson

Division Goals: To identify, cultivate, and solicit business and business-related foundations that may be able and willing to make contributions of between $1,200 and $30,000 to the Hospice campaign. The financial goal of this division is $220,000.

Primary Time Period: July through December 1998

Responsibilities of the Chairperson:
- ✔ Help identify and enlist eight to ten individuals to serve on a business-division committee
- ✔ Solicit business-division committee members
- ✔ Conduct two division meetings to organize the business-solicitation process
- ✔ Attend and chair two meetings for business-division solicitors
- ✔ Serve as advocate for the campaign and committee
- ✔ Serve on the steering committee, which will meet monthly throughout the campaign
- ✔ Make a gift to the campaign

Staff Support: The staff of hospice will work with the chair of this committee to organize the business division, provide lists and solicitation material, maintain effective communication and follow-through for all aspects of the committee's work. The campaign consultant will conduct a solicitor training session for the business-division solicitors.

Planning Meetings to Achieve the Best Results

Fund raising is high-risk behavior. Many people find the very mention of money distasteful and are uncomfortable with the process of asking others for it. When creating a campaign structure, one therefore works to build safe environments that foster confidence and that support volunteers in what for many is an uncomfortable task.

Although much is known about the psychology of groups, development directors and campaign directors seldom step back from the press of immediate tasks to reflect on the principles that guide the behavior of the groups that they assemble to build a campaign.

The way people feel within a group setting has an enormous effect on their confidence, openness, effectiveness, and success. Comfort and trust set the stage for successful solicitation.

People feel more comfortable when they: (1) feel that they are an accepted and valued part of the larger group, (2) believe that the other members of the group share responsibility with them, (3) have faith that the group will be able to achieve the goal successfully, and (4) understand what is expected of them and have confidence that they know how to do it.

Without question, people function better when they feel safe. They participate more, they are willing to take risks, they have more fun, and they have more confidence in themselves. Successful campaign directors should thus pay careful attention to creating safe and supportive environments for their staff and volunteers.

The pattern of real participation is often established very early in a meeting. The first sixty seconds should model the desired behavior for the rest of the meeting. If the purpose of the meeting is to engage the participants in active dialogue, the beginning of the meeting should be structured to provide everyone with a brief opportunity to speak.

Simple Strategies for Successful Meetings

- Initial meetings should be planned with ample time for informal discussion in order to give people a chance to get acquainted.
- Strategic choices need to be made about seating—seats should be assigned if that would help people feel comfortable or the choice can be left up to the participants if all the members of a group know one another.

> *Fund raising is high-risk behavior. When creating a campaign structure, one therefore works to build safe environments that foster confidence.*

- The seating arrangement should be one that puts the participants at their ease.
- People should be invited thoughtfully to share their ideas in a meeting. The process of engaging the participants should be designed as carefully as the agenda.
- The leader should begin every meeting by modeling the kind of behavior that is appropriate to the task at hand.
- Meetings should be designed to enable every member to speak early in the life of the group.
- Goals, tasks, responsibilities, and timetables should be clarified early in a meeting.
- Training meetings should actively involve people, letting them try out their skills in a controlled environment.

Becoming a Furniture Mover

The arrangement of tables and chairs can have a profound effect on the outcome of a meeting. To stimulate discussion, participants should be seated at a round or square table. These configurations diminish the supremacy of the leader and create groups in which everyone feels equally valued. Even at a square table, however, different seats have more or less power. In general, the seats in the center of each side of the table are the most dominant locations. From these seats one has the best sight lines and can both see and be seen by everyone else. Therefore, if people sit in a large square or wide rectangular configuration, one might place the people of greatest importance in the center seats.

To discourage real participation (and there are times when one might wish to do just that), group members should be seated in rows facing forward with the leaders placed in the front. This minimizes opportunities for people to respond to one another and virtually eliminates the participants' ability to gauge the response of other members of the group by observing body language or facial expressions.

Involving the committee members in the process of rearranging tables and chairs is an excellent way to get them to participate in those first sixty seconds.

Although it is not always possible to control all the variables that make people feel safe, careful planning and attention to every aspect of a meeting will pay large dividends. Even experienced organizers of meetings and those experienced in working with volunteers would do well to review the following twenty-five questions prior to every meeting.

Preparation
1. Do the participants know exactly where to go and how to get there?
2. Do they know where to park?

3. Will someone be at the meeting place well before the meeting begins?
4. How will the tables and chairs be arranged to further the ends of the meeting?
5. Should this arranging be done ahead of time or should it be done by the group?

Arrival

6. Who will greet the participants?
7. Where will they be greeted?
8. Will the participants know one another?
9. What's a good way to break the ice?
10. Should the participants wear name tags?
11. Is the lettering on name tags large enough to be read across the table?
12. Should the participants have assigned seats or should they select their own seats?
13. Should there be refreshments? If so, are they located in a place that will encourage conversation?
14. What printed material is needed and who will prepare it?
15. Is the room equipped with the necessary equipment (flip charts, markers, tape, etc.)?

The Meeting Itself

16. How will printed material be distributed? Before the meeting? On the table at each participant's place as the meeting starts? Distributed during the meeting? Or distributed afterward?
17. Who will call the meeting to order?
18. How soon after the meeting starts will every person have had an opportunity to participate?
19. Who will make sure that the meeting stays on schedule?
20. Whose job will it be to help every participant's opinion be heard?
21. Whose job will it be to make sure that the environment remains comfortable?
22. Who will wrap up the meeting by summarizing what has been accomplished?

Aftermath

23. What follow-up will occur after the meeting and who will attend to it?
24. Who will follow up with a disgruntled participant?

> *People who work on campaigns must constantly remember to recognize, acknowledge, and applaud every accomplishment and every little step forward.*

25. Who will debrief key participants to solidify their roles?

Celebrate Every Effort and Every Success

Campaigns are times to celebrate. Those who work on campaigns care about a cause. They dream of making an organization stronger, and they find in themselves the power and will to stretch in extraordinary ways to make a difference in their communities or their organizations. There is thus daily cause for celebration.

No matter how successful they are in the end, campaigns are fraught with frustrations and disappointments. For every person who agrees to help, two or three or perhaps more will decide not to. For every gift that is made, several prospects will decline to give. For every volunteer who does a great job, there will be two who do a mediocre job and one who does no job at all.

People who work on campaigns must constantly remember to recognize, acknowledge, and applaud every accomplishment and every little step forward, because those celebrations are what keeps the morale of the troops alive.

References

DePree, Max. 1992. *Leadership jazz.* New York: Currency Doubleday.

Grace, Kay Sprinkel. 1991. Managing for results. In *Achieving excellence in fund raising.* Edited by H.A. Rosso and Associates. San Francisco, CA: Jossey-Bass Publishers.

Hall, Holly. 1984. How to avoid pitfalls in picking the chair of a capital campaign. *The Chronicle of Philanthropy,* 8 March, 40–42.

Marx, Karl. 1875. The critique of the Gotha program. In *The Marx-Engels reader.* Edited by Robert C. Tucker, 1972. New York: W.W. Norton and Co.

Chapter 7
Planning the Campaign

Chapter Outline

- The Importance of Campaign Planning
- The Planning Process
- The Case for Support
- Determining the Campaign Goal
- Developing the Table of Gifts
- Campaign Structures That Work
- Deciding What to Count and How Much It's Worth
- The Capital Campaign and Annual Giving
- Projecting a Realistic Campaign Timetable
- Determining How Gifts Will Be Solicited
- A Plan for Recognizing Donors
- Gift Accounting and Reporting

The Importance of Campaign Planning

Successful campaigns are carefully planned. They have clear goals, structure, policies, timetables, and practices that have been determined and agreed upon in advance. The process of developing a campaign plan educates and engages the volunteers. A carefully developed, realistic campaign plan enables volunteers to understand their particular roles and to see how their efforts fit into the larger campaign. The planning process gives the campaign leadership an opportunity to explore various options for campaign design and to shape the campaign so that it is appropriate for their organization and their community. A thorough campaign plan provides information and material that will answer questions that are likely to arise during the campaign itself. Through the planning process, staff and volunteers acquire an understanding of how the campaign will unfold, a sense of commitment to its goals, and confidence that the campaign will succeed.

The Planning Process

After many months or even years of preparing for a campaign, an organization finally begins the campaign by assembling a team of influential individuals to explore, develop, and embrace a campaign plan. As discussed in chapter 6, the campaign planning committee serves as the architect of the campaign. It draws together those who have the power, influence, and resources to make a campaign successful, and it engages them in shaping the campaign. If well executed, the planning process is an opportunity to educate staff and volunteers in capital campaign fund raising, to demystify the campaign process, and to present a clear and comprehensible picture of the campaign.

Responsibilities of the Campaign Planning Committee

The planning committee is responsible for developing a set of recommendations that will form the basis of a planning document for guiding the campaign. The resulting planning document will be presented to the board of directors for discussion and approval.

That document should include the following:

- a statement of campaign objectives and a case for supporting those objectives
- a recommended preliminary dollar goal for the campaign and a table of gifts showing the number and size of gifts needed to reach the goal
- policies covering questions of campaign accounting, duration, goals, methods of solicitation, commemorative gifts, giving levels, and constituencies to be solicited
- a proposed campaign organization chart with committee structures, responsibilities, and reporting relationships
- a procedure for identifying and evaluating prospective donors
- a campaign timetable

Together, these elements constitute a campaign plan. Although some elements of the plan might be altered as the campaign proceeds, the shape, structure, and policies set forth at the start will guide the campaign from beginning to end.

When individuals are enlisted to serve on the planning committee, they are usually not asked to sign on for the duration of the campaign. However, many of those who participate in developing the plan will be invited to participate in the various committees that prepare for and implement the campaign.

This opportunity for disengagement from the campaign enables the campaign leadership to evaluate each participant's performance and to make a judgment as to whether and how that individual should be involved further. It also gives planning-committee members a chance to evaluate their interest in becoming more involved with the campaign. This strategy enables those who have only a passing acquaintance with an organization to take a closer look at the way the organization functions. If they are pleased with what they see, they are more likely to agree to help with the campaign itself than they would have been had they been asked to do the same tasks prior to the planning process.

Number of Meetings and Topics

It usually takes the campaign planning committee three to four meetings to accomplish its tasks. Ideally, these meetings are conducted weekly over three to four weeks. This timetable is tight enough to create a sense of urgency and accomplishment but provides enough time between meetings for research and reflection. When the members of the committee all come from the same community, they will often have many conversations among themselves between meetings, a practice that can increase their sense of ownership and heighten the excitement.

When planning committee members are scattered across the country and must travel long distances to get together, the planning process will have to be scheduled so as to minimize travel and increase the chances that everyone will attend. In this case, the meetings might be scheduled as a two- or even three-day retreat. The retreat format may create a sense of momentum and camaraderie, though it is expensive and requires extensive planning.

When scheduled as three meetings, the planning process might be covered as follows:

At the first planning meeting there should be:

- a charge to the committee
- a presentation of the organization: past, present, and future
- a capital campaign primer

The first meeting of any new group sets the stage for the tasks ahead. People want to see who else is there. They begin to feel out their position in the group and explore the limits of safety. This meeting not only establishes the collection of individuals as a group, but also helps create and strengthen the connections between the individuals and the organization.

Because the best planning meetings are participatory work sessions, the meeting should begin with an ice-

---

A Limited Involvement Yielded Big Returns

My father-in-law is the CEO of a major company in our town. When I was involved in helping our local Planned Parenthood move into a capital campaign, I asked him to serve on the campaign-planning committee. I knew he was very busy and was sure that he wouldn't be able to give us much time, but I also knew that his name and clout in the community would really help our campaign. He had never met the organization's director, had never been to the Planned Parenthood offices, and had little more than a passing acquaintance with what we did. I suppose he agreed to come to the three planning meetings only because I asked him. He actually only showed up for two of the three meetings. He participated in the discussion and really helped plan the campaign. He allowed us to use his name on the letterhead. And when it came time to solicit lead gifts not only did his foundation make a really generous gift, but he helped me leverage another big gift from a foundation we had never thought would contribute at all!

—Former Development Director, Planned Parenthood

---

breaker to reveal existing connections between the individuals and the organization. Inviting each person to give a brief personal introduction to the group and share a story about his or her connection with the organization often proves revealing. For example, at the first meeting to plan a campaign for a hospice, several group members discussed worries about their aging parents. One woman spoke about the death of her husband, and one man discussed the hospice care his daughter had received. These personal stories bonded the group around the mission of hospice and created an early sense of intimacy and familiarity that got the group off to an excellent start.

At a first meeting of a new group, everyone in the group wonders why they were chosen and what they will be expected to do. Anxieties are often lingering just under the surface, and these anxieties extend to even the most experienced participant. When these lurking questions are addressed and put to rest, one can quite palpably feel the group begin to relax. At this meeting, the chair should candidly address the process that has led up to the selection of the committee, highlighting its importance and indicating the care with which each member was chosen.

The first meeting must also give everyone enough information about the organization to allow for effective participation in the planning process. Because each member comes to the process with varying degrees of involvement with the organization, the first meeting must level the playing field by synthesizing relevant background information. Simple reports about the organization's mission, history, programs, and staffing might be combined with an operating budget, annual report, and other printed material to paint a clear and lively portrait of the institution. Those already knowledgeable about the organization will get a refresher course, and newcomers will begin to make the organization their own.

The description of the organization and its past, present, and future should include a description of the needs that will be addressed by the campaign. Although a full presentation of the project will start off the next meeting, a thorough understanding of the needs of the campaign now will provide the proper focus for the remainder of the planning process.

Opportunities for questions are extremely important during the first meeting. Sometimes a few planted questions can pave the way for relaxed discussion and participation.

Finally, the first meeting should set the stage for the discussions that will begin during the second meeting. Although most people are familiar with the expression "capital campaign," very few outside of the fund-raising world have more than a vague notion of what those words really mean. To provide a context for campaign planning, the consultant or development director should describe the principles of capital campaigns and the relationship of the campaign to the organization.

At the second planning meeting there should be:

- a case for support
- a campaign goal

The second planning meeting intensifies committee participation through a discussion of the case for support and a determination of the campaign goal. A discussion of the case for supporting the project provides opportunities for participants to articulate the reasons why they would support the project and to confront their own reservations. The determination of the campaign goal quantifies what it will take to make the project a reality. Together, these two elements of a campaign plan create a justification and a structure for the campaign, and, through the process of discussing and agreeing on them, the committee increases its commitment to the project.

An in-depth discussion of these elements of the campaign plan appears later in the chapter.

At the third planning meeting there should be:

- a table of gifts
- a campaign structure
- a campaign timetable
- a campaign policy

> *People remember more of what they say during a meeting than of what anyone else says. When someone has participated actively in a meeting, they leave that meeting with a stronger sense of ownership.*

By the third meeting, the committee should have embraced the project and be ready to review and explore the nuts and bolts of the campaign. These more technical aspects of campaign planning elaborate a picture of how the money will be raised, where it will come from, and how long it will take to raise it. They also establish principles of accounting and donor recognition that will inform the entire campaign. Determining in advance the guiding principles of the campaign keeps an organization from making later ad hoc decisions that can be detrimental to the campaign.

Written Materials

Materials that will inform the work of each meeting should be prepared for each committee member and presented to them during or before the meetings. In addition, a summary of the decisions reached at each meeting should be distributed at the next meeting; thus providing a written record of the planning process. These should be clearly and attractively presented. Three-ring notebooks with tabbed sections work well since material can be added at each meeting. Committee members will appreciate dividers that separate the material into sections, making the different pieces easy to find. At the conclusion of the final meeting, a summary of the committee's final decisions should be sent to each committee member. These decisions, once they are presented to and approved by the board, constitute the campaign plan.

Role of the Consultant

If an organization has hired a consultant to help with the campaign, that person will be very important during the planning process. The consultant brings to the planning table experience and knowledge from many other campaigns and not only helps plan and prepare for the meetings but also serves as a source of expert information during committee discussions.

The Case for Support

The feasibility study is usually the first application of the case for support. Often, however, time elapses between the feasibility study and the campaign planning process. Projects grow and evolve. The case developed for the feasibility study is likely to contain some information that is still pertinent but that requires updating, revision, and even some rethinking. The campaign planning process is an excellent opportunity to present, review, and revise the case for support. During the second planning committee meeting, the director or some other appropriate staff member should make an oral presentation of the case for support. The information that is presented should cover the following five questions:

1. How will the project serve the community?
2. Where will it be located?
3. What will it look like?
4. How much will it cost?
5. When will it be built or developed?

It is relatively easy to present large quantities of information about an organization and a project. It is far more challenging to distill that information down to its essentials and to present it in a clear and compelling manner. A good presentation enables the listeners to absorb just what they need to know without requiring them to wade through extraneous information. Charts, slides, models, or drawings (although they need not be fancy) can be effectively combined with a brief spoken presentation.

A presentation of the case for support opens the way for active discussion. Every project has positive and negative aspects, and the planning committee should explore both sides of the issue—honing the case for supporting the project and understanding and responding to potential barriers to wholehearted support. Exploring both the positives and the negatives will enable committee members to resolve their own objections, thereby aligning themselves more securely with the project and preparing themselves and the organization to address such issues as they arise.

Because people are often uneasy about expressing their ideas (and particularly their concerns) in a group, the planning process should be designed in such a way that it gives every participant explicit license to contribute. The index-card technique is a good way to give permission to share one's views: Two index cards are distributed to each member of the committee, who are then asked to take five minutes to write down the three things that they find most compelling about the project on one card and their three biggest concerns on the other. Then each person is invited to share what they've written while a staff person records the pros on one flip chart and the cons on another. Usually the result will be perhaps four or five pros and two or three cons that most have listed and a wide assortment of other comments both for and against. The responses common to most of the committee help clarify the most compelling arguments in support of a project and the most troublesome of its negative aspects. The committee can then summarize the positives and develop responses to the negatives, not only to satisfy itself of the project's ultimate

The single biggest factor in ensuring success is determining the right campaign goal.

worth but also so that it can be prepared to allay the anxieties of other potential supporters.

The material that is gathered from the discussion of the case for support will form an excellent basis for reshaping and refining the written case for support, which can then be distributed at the next meeting.

Determining the Campaign Goal

Every campaign should succeed. Unlike a military campaign, whose goals, strategy, and timetable are usually set by exigencies beyond the power of the campaign generals, by the time a capital campaign is set in motion, the goals, strategy, and timetable should have been arranged so as to ensure success. The single biggest factor in ensuring success is determining the right campaign goal. Embedded in the campaign goal are the answers to these five questions:

1. What does the organization need to enhance its effectiveness in the community?
2. How much money is it feasible to raise from the constituency or community?
3. What will count toward the campaign goal?

Engaging the Planning Committee

We had had a somewhat lackluster first planning committee meeting. We covered the necessary material but no one seemed to get really engaged. There seemed to be no passion. We had set the second meeting aside for the discussion of the case for support, and I was worried that we would have a whole hour and a half for discussion and no one would participate. Wow! Was I wrong. We began the meeting by asking each person there to tell us their personal reasons for supporting the home, and before we got through three people, I knew we had a winner. Perhaps we were fortunate or perhaps it was in the meeting design, but from the very first person on, everyone spoke from their hearts. They spoke of their religious beliefs and convictions. They spoke of their parents who lived in the home. They spoke of their own fears of growing old. By the end of that meeting not only were we all clear about the case for supporting the home, but the group had bonded around the project.

—Development Director, Home for the Aged

4. How committed and courageous is the campaign committee?
5. How long can the campaign wait before publicly announcing an official goal?

The answer to each of these questions affects the campaign goal.

What is needed? Most capital campaigns are based on specific and well-defined organizational needs. The organization has defined a particular need and has presented a convincing rationale for meeting that need in its case for support. Whether the need is a complex of projects and programs or something as concrete as a new building, the scope of the project, and consequently the dollar figure attached to it, must be commensurate with the needs of the organization and the community it serves.

What is feasible? It may or may not be feasible to raise all the money that an organization needs for the project it has planned. Therefore, the fund-raising realities of the community, the reputation of the organization, and its readiness to solicit major gifts must be taken into account when setting the goal. If the organization's needs are higher than the amount that can be raised as projected in the feasibility study, the organization will have to develop a plan to finance the difference.

What will count? Although many people never stop to think about it, the campaign goal is determined in part by what is counted toward it. If, for example, an organization chooses to count a $250,000 bequest that will be applied to the project but that was received during the year before the campaign, the goal may be higher than if the bequest is not counted. Or if an organization includes three years of annual giving in the campaign goal, the goal (and scope of the campaign) will be different than if annual giving is not counted.

Who is committed? The courage and commitment of the campaign-planning committee is an important element in determining the campaign goal. Although needs, feasibility, and counting are key factors in determining the goal, the courage, commitment, and enthusiasm of the campaign planning committee, though it defies quantitative measurement, can raise or lower the goal. Some planning committees decide to set a "stretch goal" and shoot for an amount well beyond that recommended by the consultant. Others choose a more conservative approach. Committee discussion of the campaign goal, particularly if it is accompanied by gift tables for various goals, gives each member of the committee an opportunity to consider quietly his or her individual gift. Often, potential lead donors on the committee understand where their gifts will fit in the giving pattern and guide the determination of the campaign goal according to the gifts that they have in mind.

When will the official goal be announced? A common practice to safeguard an organization's reputation is to determine a working goal for the campaign. This is a temporary, or provisional, goal used during the quiet phase of the campaign. It is not published in campaign material and appears only in material that is designed to be viewed by a select audience. Then, after the results of the quiet-gift phase become clear but before the campaign is made public, the campaign steering committee reviews the goal. If the advance-gift solicitations have proven disappointing, it might lower the public goal. If, on the other hand, the early phase has gone better than anticipated it might raise it somewhat.

Developing the Table of Gifts

The table of gifts, or giving pyramid as it is sometimes called, is the road map for a campaign. Based on standardized giving patterns and tempered by the realities of the specific organization, a sample table of gifts for a specific campaign appears in Exhibit 7–1.

In this table, the lead gift constitutes 15 percent of the campaign goal, and just under one-half of the campaign total will come from the ten largest gifts. Tables of gifts vary depending on the organization and campaign for which they are developed. A small, young organization with a limited but wealthy donor base might, for example, use a table of gifts for a million-dollar campaign such as the one in Exhibit 7–2.

In this table of gifts, half of the goal comes from just five gifts, and the total goal will be reached with 100-plus gifts.

For a broad-based, mature organization with thousands of annual donors and no history of major gift fund raising the pattern of giving might be more accurately projected with the table in Exhibit 7–3.

Approximately one-half of the campaign goal for this organization will come from 41 donors.

Although the patterns of these three campaigns vary somewhat, they all require lead gifts of between 10 and 25 percent of the campaign goal and call for more donors as the size of the average gift declines.

Often a campaign consultant will help design the table of gifts. However, the process of exploring different combinations is an excellent exercise to focus the attention of the leadership of an organization. An early informal meeting to devise a suitable table of gifts will force those involved in the planning process to begin thinking in specific terms about which particular donors are likely to give at the various levels.

Once an appropriate table of gifts for a campaign has been created, it can then be used as a tool to help design the campaign itself. It is a straightforward matter to estimate from the table of gifts how many prospects the campaign will have to solicit. Knowing how many so-

Exhibit 7–1 Gifts Needed to Raise $1,000,000

Number of Gifts	Amount of Each Gift	Amount from Level	Cumulative Amount	Cumulative Percent of Total
1	$150,000	$150,000	$150,000	15%
1	75,000	175,000	225,000	22%
2	50,000	100,000	325,000	32%
6	25,000	150,000	475,000	47%
10	10,000	100,000	575,000	57%
20	5,000	100,000	675,000	67%
40	2,500	100,000	775,000	77%
80	1,000	80,000	855,000	87%
160	500	80,000	935,000	93%
many	under $500	65,000	1,000,000	100%

Number of Gifts: 320+

licitations will be needed will then make it possible to determine the number of solicitors and solicitation teams. Developing a table of gifts that fits the organization is critical to the design of a successful campaign.

In all of this, remember: Don't lower the lead gift! Although tables of gifts should be designed to fit the realities of each organization, it is difficult if not impossible to conduct a successful campaign with a lead gift that comprises less than 10 percent of the campaign goal. If a lead gift of at least that amount is not in the offing, the organization should either put off the campaign while it develops a major-gifts program to cultivate the lead gift, or lower the goal to a more appropriate level. Trying to run a capital campaign without a lead gift is not likely to broaden the bottom—it is more likely just to lop off the top.

Estimating the Number of Prospects Required for Each Gift

Using the table of gifts as a guide, an organization can explore the number of prospects it has for each gift and compare that number to the number of prospects that are needed. Opinions vary on how many prospects are needed for each gift. Some people estimate more conservatively that it will take five prospects to get one gift. Others use a three-to-one ratio. Generally, however, an estimate of three to five prospects for every gift will be in the right ballpark.

By looking more carefully at the prospect-to-gift ratio it is possible to fine-tune the numbers somewhat more precisely by differentiating among prospects with respect to the closeness of their relationship with the organization. One can divide the broad field of prospects into three categories, *prospects*, *suspects*, and *fliers*. The in-

Exhibit 7–2 Gifts Needed to Raise $1,000,000 (for a small young organization with a wealthy donor base)

Number of Gifts	Amount of Each Gift	Amount from Level	Cumulative Amount	Cumulative Percent of Total
1	$250,000	$250,000	$250,000	25%
1	100,000	100,000	350,000	35%
3	50,000	150,000	500,000	50%
8	25,000	200,000	700,000	70%
12	10,000	120,000	820,000	82%
24	2,500	60,000	880,000	88%
40	1,000	40,000	920,000	93%
60	500	30,000	950,000	95%
many	under $500	$50,000	1,000,000	100%

Number of Gifts: 100+

Exhibit 7–3 Gifts Needed to Raise $1,000,000 (for a mature organization with a broad donor base)

Number of Gifts	Amount of Each Gift	Amount from Level	Cumulative Amount	Cumulative Percent of Total
1	$100,000	$100,000	$100,000	10%
1	50,000	50,000	150,000	15%
4	25,000	100,000	250,000	25%
10	10,000	100,000	350,000	35%
25	5,000	125,000	475,000	47%
60	2,500	150,000	625,000	62%
150	1,000	150,000	775,000	77%
300	500	150,000	925,000	92%
many	under $500	$75,000	1,000,000	100%

Number of Gifts: 551+

dividuals in each of these categories have different types of relationships with the organization, making them more or less ready to make a generous campaign gift. The prospect-to-gift ratio varies from category to category.

- Prospects are individuals and foundations or business decision makers
  — who have a strong and committed relationship with the institution
  — about whom there is substantial information regarding their area of interest, ability to give, and inclination to give
  Gift ratio: Two prospects per gift
- Suspects are individuals and foundations or business decision makers
  — who have been identified as potential donors
  — who have some relationship with the institution
  — about whom there is limited information regarding their ability and/or inclination to give
  Gift ratio: Four suspects per gift
- Fliers are individuals and foundations or business decision makers
  — who have been identified as prospective donors
  — who have no relationship with the institution
  — about whom there is little information regarding their ability or inclination to give
  Gift ratio: Twenty fliers per gift

Although it may be cumbersome to use these categories when calculating the necessary number of prospects, it is nonetheless instructive, particularly when determining how many prospects will be required at the top of the giving pyramid.

With the help of the table of gifts, one can estimate approximately how many individuals must be solicited to make a campaign successful by evaluating how many real prospects and suspects an organization has and estimating the appropriate multiplier for each giving category. Because the chances of getting a gift from a flier is relatively low, it is wise to focus attention on prospects and suspects and consider any gifts from fliers to be unexpected windfalls.

An informal rating of an organization's donor lists by someone familiar with the organization and the community might lead to a reasonably accurate estimate of the number of solicitations that will be needed in the campaign. The goal is to review the donor lists, looking for prospects and suspects at each giving level. The prospect whose gift one is reasonably sure of should be given a multiplier of 2. Those who are likely to give to the campaign but whose giving level is less well-defined might be categorized as suspects for a particular gift. So, for example, if an organization has two prospects and five suspects for gifts of $50,000, it has an excellent chance of raising two gifts of $50,000 each by soliciting those seven individuals.

In practice, the further down on the gift pyramid, the more difficult it is to estimate the prospects and suspects accurately. Below the $10,000 level, for a campaign to raise $1 million, one might just as well use the ratio of four prospects per gift.

A table of gifts used to estimate the number of solicitations might look like the one found in Exhibit 7–4.

Trying to run a capital campaign without a lead gift is not likely to broaden the bottom— it is more likely to lop off the top.

Exhibit 7–4 Gifts Needed to Raise $1,000,000

Amount of Each Gift	Number of Gifts in Category	Number of Prospects/Suspects	Number of Solicitations
$150,000	1	2p/0s	2
75,000	1	2p/0s	2
50,000	2	2p/4s	6
25,000	6	6p/12s	18
10,000	10	8p/24s	32
5,000	20	80	80
2,500	40	160	160
1,000	80	360	360
500	160	640	640

Total Personal Solicitations: 1,300

It is reasonable to assume that the gifts below $500 will come from a combination of solicitations at a higher level that actually came in at a lower level together with telephone and direct mail rather than personal solicitation.

Calculating the Number of Solicitors for the Campaign

Once the number of personal solicitations that are required for the campaign has been determined, it is a simple calculation to determine the number of solicitors. On average, one person will be willing and able to make approximately four solicitations. Dividing 1,300 solicitations by 4, therefore, shows that the campaign will need 325 solicitors.

Of course, the real world is far messier than these numbers would indicate. Some will make ten or more solicitations. Others will agree to do five but will actually only do one or two. Some will agree to do only one or two.

Making things even more complicated is what might be referred to as the "cascade phenomenon." Donors solicited for a specific amount often decide to give at a lower level. If one were to construct a list of who gave what and compare it to the original prospect-to-suspect rating, one would see that the pattern of gifts really winds up looking rather like a waterfall, with donors tumbling down from one giving category to another, landing in just the right place for them and replacing people who were solicited in that category but who have also tumbled to the next lower level.

> *Successful campaigns solicit leadership gifts very early in the campaign. These are the gifts that set the pace of the campaign.*

Even though this way of looking at campaigns is more fluid than precise, it has proven to be very useful in focusing attention quite specifically on the real tasks of the campaign—the solicitations.

Campaign Structures That Work

Having determined the number of solicitations and solicitors needed for a campaign, it is possible now to develop a campaign structure that organizes the solicitations into specific areas. Once again, there are many ways to categorize solicitation groups and a wide variety of terms used in the fund-raising world to describe them.

Soliciting from the Top Down

All successful campaigns are organized so that the top donors, those from whom approximately one-third to one-half of the campaign goal will come, are solicited first.

Campaigns are organized by the size of the gifts to be solicited. A basic structure divides the giving levels into three categories: "leadership gifts," "major gifts," and "general gifts." These levels are illustrated in Exhibit 7–5.

Successful campaigns solicit leadership gifts very early in the campaign. These are the gifts that set the pace of the campaign. They determine the standard of giving and establish the campaign's chances of success. The leadership-gift division assembles the organization's most powerful solicitors and donors around the task of raising these largest gifts. In the example in Exhibit 7–5, approximately seven solicitors will ask approximately twenty-eight prospects for the top ten gifts. If successful, these solicitors will be responsible for raising nearly one-half of the campaign goal.

This division is sometimes called the "pacesetter gift division" or "strategic gift division."

Exhibit 7–5 Top-Down Soliciting

Leadership Gifts

Amount of Gift	Number of Gifts	Number of Prospects	Number of Solicitors	Amount Solicited in Gift Range	Percent of Total
$150,000	1	2		$150,000	
$75,000	1	2		$75,000	
$50,000	2	6		$100,000	
$25,000	6	18		$150,000	
Totals	10	28	7	$475,000	47%

Major Gifts

Amount of Gift	Number of Gifts	Number of Prospects	Number of Solicitors	Amount Solicited in Gift Range	Percent of Total
$10,000	10	32		$100,000	
$5,000	20	80		$100,000	
$2,500	40	160		$100,000	
Totals	70	272	68	$300,000	30%

General Gifts

Amount of Gift	Number of Gifts	Number of Prospects	Number of Solicitors	Amount Solicited in Gift Range	Percent of Total
$1,000	80	360		$80,000	
$500	160	640		$80,000	
Totals	70	1,000	260	$160,000	16%

Below the leadership gifts, but still extremely important are the major gifts. These gifts constitute approximately one-third of the campaign goal and must be solicited in person. They are usually solicited after the public campaign has begun.

The general-gift solicitations require the largest number of solicitors and bring in the smallest amount of money. Nonetheless, this portion of the campaign involves a great many individuals in the cause and builds a base for continued giving.

Soliciting from the Inside Out

The size of the gifts is not the only factor determining the campaign structure. Successful campaigns build enthusiasm and attract volunteers to the cause by beginning the solicitation process from the inside, soliciting those who are closest to the organization, and proceeding outward to those less involved.

Although campaigns carry out this process in different ways, one way is to organize a family division that is responsible for soliciting gifts from those insiders not already being solicited by the leadership division.

The family division is likely to be responsible for soliciting the board, former board members, founders, key volunteers, former staff, and anyone else close to the organization. In general, solicitation of current staff is handled separately because of the sensitivities that often complicate that process.

The family division is organized during the quiet phase of the campaign, before the campaign becomes public.

Family-division solicitors are likely to solicit in both the major gifts and general gifts categories. The family division solicits the following groups:

- board
- former board
- founders
- former staff
- campaign planning committee
- active volunteers
- other insiders

In some cases, of course, the insiders are able to make leadership gifts, and the family division does not solicit these large gifts. They are assigned to the solicitors of the leadership-gift division. In smaller organizations, it is more likely that many of the board members, founders, former board members, and other insiders do not have the resources to make large gifts even if they stretch well beyond their normal giving.

Together, gifts solicited by the leadership-gift division and the family division are referred to as *advance gifts*. The term refers to the fact that these gifts are solicited in advance of the campaign kickoff. The money raised by these two divisions is often called a "nucleus fund." As it grows, this fund serves as a magnet for the larger number of remaining, more broadly based gifts.

The top donors to a campaign are comforted by the many donors that give lower-level gifts, while the lower-level donors are comforted by the leadership gifts. Very few donors, no matter what the extent of their wealth,

want to feel totally responsible for the success and ongoing stability of a campaign or an organization. A broad base of donors gives the lead donors confidence that they alone are not responsible and that they are contributing to a cause with a broad base of support.

Lower-level donors, on the other hand, know that by themselves they cannot make a campaign successful. And no one chooses to be part of a failing venture. So for lower-level donors the lead donors are necessary to reassure them that the campaign will succeed. Furthermore, the fact that those with money to spare are putting money into the organization signals to the lower-level donors that the campaign is a good investment for them.

Because the best solicitations usually combine people of like minds, wealth, and position, solicitation divisions are often organized according to categories that best sort the constituency. Business people often succeed best by soliciting other business people; doctors solicit doctors; religious leaders solicit other religious leaders; residents of a particular neighborhood solicit their neighbors. Although it is sometimes difficult to determine the best categories around which to build the divisions, in many organizations the division categories will be obvious.

The solicitation divisions of a typical campaign for a social-service organization might be structured as in Figure 7–1.

The division categories should, of course, reflect the constituencies of the particular organization.

Campaign structures include more than solicitation teams. Volunteers often assist with many of the specific

Figure 7–1 Sample Campaign Structure

tasks that are necessary to a campaign. Task-oriented committees within the campaign structure help define the role of nonsolicitor volunteers and clarify their role in the larger campaign. Common task-oriented campaign committees are the special events committee and the public relations committee. Some campaigns have a separate cultivation committee and a committee for prospect rating and evaluation as well.

The special events committee is responsible for helping organize the various events that punctuate a capital campaign. The most common of these are the campaign kickoff, the groundbreaking (for building campaigns), and the final celebration of success. Occasionally, the special events committee will organize other spirit-building events as well.

The public relations committee helps develop a public relations and media plan for the campaign. They work cooperatively with the staff person in charge of public relations for the organization during noncampaign times. The public relations committee also oversees the design and production of the solicitation and communication materials used in the campaign. These materials will be discussed in detail in chapter 11.

A cultivation committee can work wonders for a campaign by organizing an ongoing series of small events—luncheons, small presentations, tours of the facility, or other nonfund-raising encounters with prospective donors. In an ideal world, all of the cultivation will have been completed prior to the campaign, but in reality, most organizations have only scratched the surface of this process, and some have never even thought about developing an organized cultivation process.

Prospect screening and evaluation is an integral part of any campaign. Sometimes these tasks are organized within each division, and sometimes they are organized separately by staff members who recruit volunteers to review lists. For small organizations with limited staff time it may be preferable to incorporate the screening process into the early divisional meetings, thus engaging the solicitors in rating and evaluating the set of prospects they will be soliciting.

With a proliferating series of divisions and committees and a campaign planning committee that vanishes after three meetings, one might ask: Who actually oversees the campaign? The campaign steering committee is composed of the chairs of each division and committee plus the campaign chair or chairs.

> *Organizations run into difficulty when they neglect to clarify counting guidelines in advance of the campaign.*

Eating Your Way to Success

The executive director of an organization was floored by the suggestion that he schedule at least one informal luncheon every week at his center with a couple of major donor prospects. He simply had never thought that getting to know the donors was part of his job. In fact, he was quite sure that major donor prospects would have no interest at all in getting acquainted with him. Although getting him to try it was like pulling teeth, little by little he became more comfortable with the process and just maybe he'll incorporate this practice as part of his regular schedule. If he does, his next campaign is likely to go way over its goal.

The steering committee should include one or more board members and should report regularly to the board of directors on the campaign's progress.

Deciding What to Count and How Much It's Worth

When to Start Counting

Although it seems obvious on the surface that campaign counting should begin once gifts resulting from campaign solicitation begin coming in, in some cases a campaign may wish to count gifts made prior to the campaign. Occasionally, for example, a fund has been built over the years to help plan a new facility. When the campaign is planned, it may be appropriate to count that fund toward the campaign goal. Or an organization might receive a challenge grant to stimulate fund raising for a new project. If an organization decides ahead of time to do so, it is appropriate to count that challenge grant in the campaign goal. Organizations run into difficulty when they neglect to clarify these guidelines in advance of the campaign.

What to Count

Gifts made to further the purposes of the campaign, in general, will be counted toward the campaign goal if they are made with the intention of being used for the campaign objectives. This rules out gifts that might come in during the campaign period but that are designated to fund an unrelated project. For example, an organization might be conducting a building campaign to renovate their headquarters and a donor might decide to give a major gift to the organization to open an off-site satellite office. This gift, because it was not made with the intention of helping to renovate the headquarters building, would not be counted toward the campaign goal.

Sometimes an organization may receive a gift that was not specifically intended to further the campaign goals and did not result from a campaign solicitation. If such a gift was not specifically designated for another purpose, the board of directors may elect to assign the gift to the campaign and thereby count it toward the campaign goal.

Most campaigns count pledges that are committed for a multiyear period. The pledge period varies, generally from three to five years. Most commonly, a three-year pledge period is encouraged while pledges of up to five years are accepted at the donor's request.

How to Value Gifts

Many kinds of gifts may be contributed to an organization. To avoid confusion or the appearance of impropriety, the campaign planning committee should adopt a written set of policies outlining just how gifts of each sort will be valued. In an effort to standardize reporting practices by college and university development offices, the Council for Advancement and Support of Education (CASE) in conjunction with the National Association of College and University Business Officers (NACUBO) has developed a set of norms for fund-raising practices. These standards, *Management Reporting Standards for Educational Institutions*, are revised periodically and are available from CASE and NACUBO. The following summary addresses the kinds of gifts most often received through a capital campaign.

Gifts of cash and checks are clear and straightforward. They are counted toward the campaign on the day they are received, at face value.

Campaign gifts are often made in multiyear installments. The total pledge amount may be counted toward a campaign when a signed and dated pledge form has been received that indicates the total amount of the pledge and the anticipated payment schedule.

Gifts of securities are often given to campaigns. These gifts should be valued by the organization at market value on the date of their transfer. The value is established by averaging the high and low prices on that day. This amount may differ from the amount actually realized from the sale of the security, but neither gains nor losses nor brokerage fees should alter the counted value of the gift. Most organizations adopt a policy of selling securities as soon as possible and within a specified number of days after they are transferred. Securities may be held by the organization for a longer period only if instructed in writing by the donor. Most organizations cover the cost of the brokerage fees.

Gifts of readily salable or usable real estate, art, equipment, and other gifts in kind are usually credited to the goals of the campaign at the full fair-market value as determined by a mutually agreed upon independent expert appraiser. Small gifts worth $5,000 or less may be valued by the donor without a qualified appraisal. Donors must provide a qualified written appraisal for gifts of property exceeding $5,000. The donor is responsible for obtaining the appraisal because it is the donor who is responsible for reporting the value of the contribution to the Internal Revenue Service. The donor must include the appraisal with the required Form 8283, which the organization must sign if it receives property appraised at more than $5,000. In signing the form, the organization verifies that it received the property and agrees to file From 8282 if it sells or disposes of the property.

Note that the donor must have the property appraised by a bona fide appraiser. In general, that will include neither the donor himself nor the receiving organization.

Many organizations safeguard themselves against receiving unwished-for gifts of real and personal property by adopting an official policy that requires the board to review and accept gifts of real and personal property worth $5,000 or more. Policies of this sort are especially important for gifts of real estate, which sometimes bring major hidden liabilities to an organization.

In-kind gifts to a campaign are common. A graphic designer might contribute the design of the campaign material, a printer might donate the printing, a builder might even contribute a new roof. All gifts of this sort are counted at their full fair-market value as established by the donor and agreed upon by the organization.

Crediting gifts of life insurance can be tricky. Is the policy paid up and if not, will the donor or the organization be responsible for making payments? There are also different values for a policy—the cash-surrender value, the premium amount, and the amount that the donor can claim as an income-tax deduction. In general, when a donor makes a gift of life insurance to a campaign and names the organization as both beneficiary and irrevocable owner, the organization counts only the face value of the policy toward the campaign goal. However, Debra Ashton, in her excellent manual *The Complete Guide to Planned Giving*, describes four other options for crediting gifts of life insurance (1991, 133):

1. Credit for the cash-surrender value of a nonpaid-up policy.
2. Credit for the cash-surrender value of a fully paid-up policy.
3. Credit for the amount of premiums paid directly to the organization (on the theory that the payment creates a capital asset).
4. Credit for premiums paid directly to the insurance company by the donor if the donor sends evidence of payment, usually in the form of a canceled check.

See also *Planned Giving Essentials: A Step by Step Guide to Success,* by Richard D. Barrett and Molly E. Ware, also in this series.

Unless a capital campaign has an endowment component, deferred gifts are usually not applied to the campaign. On occasion, however, an organization will receive payment from a bequest during the campaign period. In these cases, the board of directors should have authority to determine whether those funds should be applied toward the campaign goal. Such decisions should be made on an individual basis.

Campaigns that have an endowment component will need to develop guidelines for counting deferred gifts. In developing crediting guidelines for life-income gifts such as charitable-remainder trusts, pooled-income funds, and gift annuities, the organization will need to think carefully about the implications of each crediting decision.

Charitable-remainder trusts, pooled-income funds, and gift annuities may be credited at fair-market value. In cases where a portion of the principal will be returned to a beneficiary, the remainder interest only may be credited. An exception to this rule is that some organizations choose to establish a minimum age base of 70 or 75 and credit gifts of donors who meet the age requirement at full-market value.

Charitable-lead trusts are encountered infrequently. This is an arrangement whereby a donor makes a gift that provides the organization with an income for a specified number of years. At the end of the income period, the balance reverts to the donor or the donor's beneficiaries. Only the annual income that is received from such a trust may be included in the gift totals.

Crediting bequests that are received for the endowment portion of the campaign can be complicated because bequests are revocable and because the value of a bequest is sometimes difficult to determine, particularly if the bequest is a percentage of the donor's estate rather than a specific amount. Many organizations take the position that a bequest intention does not entitle the donor to a gift credit. Instead, they recognize bequest donors through a separate bequest society or giving club.

Other organizations have chosen to develop a type of compromise that gives donors beyond a certain age, usually 70 or older, full credit for their bequest intentions, contingent upon receiving a statement from the donor indicating the exact amount of the bequest. This amount is then entered into the organization's record-keeping system as a pledge.

Because of their nature, bequests can be difficult to deal with during a campaign, and it may be less complicated administratively for an organization not to count

> *It is common for annual giving to increase during a campaign period as a result of increased prospect cultivation, organizational visibility, and donor commitment.*

bequest intentions at all as part of the campaign. If it decides to do so, however, it will need to establish strict guidelines within which bequests are to be counted.

The Capital Campaign and Annual Giving

There are few topics in capital-campaign planning that cause more consternation than that of the relationship between the capital campaign and the annual giving program. Volunteers who help with the annual campaign are often quite anxious about the potential effect of the capital campaign on annual giving returns even before the campaign has been planned. However, their fears of falling annual-giving revenues during campaign years are rarely confirmed. In fact, it is more common for annual giving to increase during a campaign period as a result of increased prospect cultivation, organizational visibility, and donor commitment.

There are two general approaches to handling the relationship between the capital campaign and annual giving.

Fold the Annual Campaign into the Capital Campaign

Because it might be confusing and burdensome to both staff and donors to ask for two types of contributions during the same period, some organizations include the annual appeal in the capital campaign during the first year. In effect, they increase the campaign goal to include the funds that would normally be included in the annual campaign.

During the first year when capital-campaign funds are being solicited, the organization does not conduct a separate annual appeal but designates a specified amount from capital-campaign revenues to cover annual operating expenses during the three years of the campaign period. Once the capital-campaign solicitations have been completed, the organization reinstates the annual solicitation. Those who have made three-year pledges are not solicited again during the following two years, but those who have not given during the capital campaign are solicited together with new prospects when the annual campaign recommences.

For this model to be effective, the campaign-planning committee must determine specific dollar amounts that the campaign will designate for annual operating expenses during each of the three years and then increase the campaign goal and broaden the campaign's objectives appropriately.

Maintain the Annual Giving Program Alongside the Capital Campaign

It is often possible and may even be preferable to continue the annual-giving program right through the capital campaign. This practice works best when the capital campaign will fund a project that is clearly distinct from the organization's ongoing operations. So, for example, while a college or university might blur the lines between the annual campaign's goals and those of the capital campaign by including endowed chairs in the campaign, a small organization would likely make a clear distinction between a campaign to build a new building and the annual support of its ongoing operations.

When the campaign's goals are clearly distinct from operational expenses, many donors will see the logic in making a special campaign pledge to boost the organization to a new level while at the same time continuing their steady support to the organization's operations by maintaining or even increasing their gift to the annual campaign.

One common strategy for organizations that have decided to continue the annual solicitation process through the campaign period is "double mention, double ask." With this approach, donors are solicited separately for the annual and capital campaigns. The campaigns are timed to provide breathing room between the solicitations, but each solicitation mentions the other campaign so that donors are not surprised when they are asked to give again at a later time and people who have given as a result of the earlier solicitation are acknowledged for that gift while being solicited again.

For more information about annual giving, see *Donor Focused Strategies for Annual Giving,* by Karla A. Williams, also in this series.

Projecting a Realistic Campaign Timetable

A campaign plan should, of course, include a realistic month-by-month timetable that clarifies the flow of work and provides benchmarks for the staff and the campaign leadership. The timetable must take many factors into consideration. Among them are:

- **Project dates.** Critical project dates such as the architectural-design schedule, zoning-approval schedule, and groundbreaking will figure importantly in the timetable. Sometimes the very nature of the project drives the campaign schedule. If, for example, money is being raised to rebuild a playhouse that had collapsed under the weight of a major snowfall, the internal exigencies of the project—opening night on June 17—will be the incentive for a quick and intense campaign.
- **Staff availability.** The campaign schedule must reflect the amount of staff time and support available for the campaign. A campaign that will be run by a development-staff member dedicated only to the campaign process can proceed more quickly than a campaign run by someone with other ongoing development responsibilities.

- **Geography.** The geography of the organization's volunteer base will also affect the timetable. When volunteers are far-flung and the campaign requires regional organization, such factors will most likely increase the length of the campaign. When volunteers are within a small geographic region and form a well-defined constituency—a church congregation, for example—the timetable might be shorter.
- **Weather.** Different climatic areas have different ideal solicitation periods. Communities where the winter is cold and snowy might choose to schedule the campaign so that the volunteer-intensive solicitation period takes place during the summer, when roads are clear and people of means have returned from their winter homes in warmer climes. In other communities the summer may prove difficult for solicitation if many families are away on vacation during the long school holiday.
- **Volunteer schedules.** The period between Thanksgiving and Christmas presents special challenges. Although the year's end continues to be a principal time for giving as people are reflecting on the Lord's bounty in November and have gift giving on their minds anyway in December, as well as examining the tax consequences of their financial year, it is an extremely challenging time for recruiting volunteers.

The Phases of a Campaign

Campaigns are punctuated by three major events that mark the beginning, middle, and end of the campaign. These events determine and are determined by the sequencing of many other aspects of the campaign.

- **The campaign planning committee.** The campaign begins with the planning process. Once the planning committee has been assembled, there is no turning back, and a clear and timely sequence of events must unfold from that point if the campaign is to build momentum and retain the effective participation of the campaign planners and leaders.
- **The campaign kickoff.** The campaign kickoff marks the second critical point. Although campaigns are not closely guarded secrets before the official beginning, the kickoff commences the public phase of the campaign. The campaign kickoff occurs after at least 40 percent of the campaign goal has been raised through advance-gift solicitations. It takes place after the volunteer solicitors have been recruited for the general phase of the campaign but before they begin soliciting gifts. The kickoff is an opportunity to build spirit, obtain media attention, announce the public goal and progress to date, and prepare the ground for the broad-based solicitation phase.

- **The campaign celebration.** Although campaigns always begin with clear definition and focus, they can easily lose their focus in a myriad of details that must be attended to, often over a period of many months. To make the most of the campaign and to bring it to a fitting conclusion, a celebration that draws a campaign to a public close should definitely be on the agenda. Such a celebration bonds the leadership and volunteers to the organization even as it provides closure for their campaign responsibilities.

Presenting the Campaign Timetable

Because people absorb information in different ways, it is usually wise to present the campaign timetable in two ways—a timeline and a month-by-month schedule. A timeline illustrates graphically the duration of each major task of the campaign process with a bar on a chart, and is easily prepared with desktop publishing software. This format clearly shows the timing of the campaign kickoff in relation to the quiet phase of the campaign and enables volunteers to get a quick overview of the shape and timing of the campaign. Figure 7–2 shows a sample timeline schedule.

> *To safeguard against a sense of failure, it is possible to present alternative timetables.*

A month-by-month schedule lists the tasks to be accomplished during each month. Using this format, the campaign can be outlined quite specifically, including much more detail than a bar-graph timeline. The month-by-month schedule is also easier to use, adapt, and alter as the campaign proceeds. Exhibit 7–6 shows a sample month-by-month schedule.

Presenting Timetable Alternatives

It is sometimes difficult to predict accurately the schedule on which leadership gifts might be committed to a campaign. To safeguard against a sense of failure, it is possible to present alternative timetables contingent on the actual timing of the advance-gift phase of the campaign. One schedule might, for example, project a fall kickoff, with perhaps only four months for the advance-gift phase. An alternative schedule projecting a spring kickoff might be presented at the same time, providing a

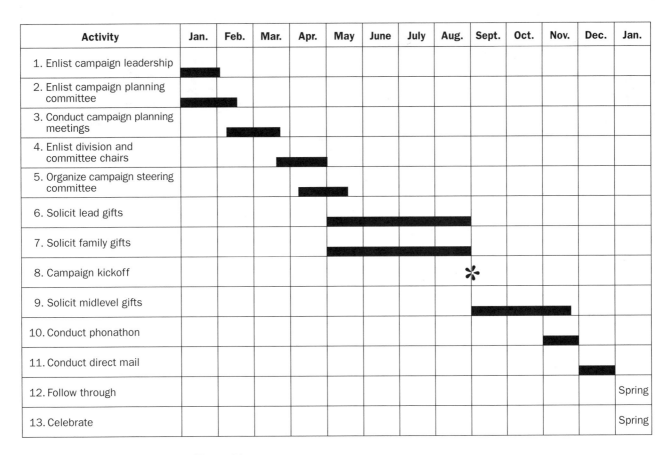

Activity	Jan.	Feb.	Mar.	Apr.	May	June	July	Aug.	Sept.	Oct.	Nov.	Dec.	Jan.
1. Enlist campaign leadership	▬												
2. Enlist campaign planning committee	▬	▬											
3. Conduct campaign planning meetings		▬	▬										
4. Enlist division and committee chairs				▬									
5. Organize campaign steering committee				▬	▬								
6. Solicit lead gifts					▬	▬	▬	▬					
7. Solicit family gifts					▬	▬	▬	▬					
8. Campaign kickoff								✳					
9. Solicit midlevel gifts									▬	▬	▬		
10. Conduct phonathon											▬		
11. Conduct direct mail												▬	
12. Follow through													Spring
13. Celebrate													Spring

Figure 7–2 Capital Campaign Timetable

Exhibit 7-6 Sample Campaign Schedule

January	☐ Enlist campaign planning committee	☐ Complete campaign materials
	☐ Organize lead-gift prospect lists	☐ Complete campaign-kickoff
	☐ Prepare campaign-planning materials	preparations
	☐ Identify and enlist campaign chairs	☐ Plan media approach for campaign
February	☐ Conduct campaign-planning committee	kickoff
	meetings	☐ Complete enlisting volunteers for
	☐ Conduct prospect-rating sessions	midlevel solicitations
March	☐ Complete campaign plan	**September** ☐ Conduct campaign kickoff
	☐ Present campaign plan to board	☐ Begin soliciting midlevel gifts
	☐ Organize lead-gift division	☐ Follow through on unfinished lead-gift
	☐ Enlist leadership for committees and	and family solicitations
	divisions	☐ Campaign newsletter #1
	☐ Rate lead-gift prospects	**October** ☐ Continue soliciting midlevel gifts
	☐ Prepare solicitation material for lead-gift	☐ Begin to plan phonathon
	solicitations	☐ Plan direct-mail campaign
April	☐ Organize campaign steering committee	**November** ☐ Follow through with all unresolved lead-
	☐ Begin soliciting lead gifts	gift and family solicitations
	☐ Organize family-gift division	☐ Continue midlevel solicitations
May	☐ Continue soliciting lead gifts	☐ Campaign newsletter #2
	☐ Begin soliciting family gifts	**December** ☐ Conduct phonathon
	☐ Organize special-events committee	☐ Plan campaign celebration
	☐ Organize PR/materials committee	☐ Follow through with midlevel
June	☐ Continue soliciting lead gifts	solicitations
	☐ Begin to plan campaign kickoff	**January** ☐ Conduct direct-mail campaign
	☐ Begin work on campaign brochure and	☐ Follow through with donors and
	materials	volunteers
July	☐ Begin to organize midlevel gift divisions	☐ Continue work on campaign celebration
	☐ Continue work on campaign kickoff	☐ Campaign newsletter #3
	☐ Continue work on campaign materials	**February** ☐ Review and plan donor recognition
	☐ Continue lead-gift and family	☐ Follow through with donors and
	solicitations	volunteers
August	☐ Complete lead-gift and family	☐ Celebrate success!
	solicitations	**March** ☐ Final campaign newsletter

fallback position if the gift level is not high enough by the fall to warrant a public kickoff. Although this strategy may lessen the pressure to do what needs to be done for a fall kickoff, it might provide a necessary safeguard for an organization without a strong history of major-gift fund raising.

Determining How Gifts Will Be Solicited

Although chapters 8 and 9 cover the solicitation process in some detail, the campaign plan should describe general guidelines about how gifts will be solicited. Reviewing this process with the campaign planning committee prepares them for the solicitation process and prevents possible misconceptions. And misconceptions on this topic abound.

The great majority of funds raised for a capital campaign are raised through personal solicitations. Indeed, the ideal campaign is a campaign in which every prospect is visited in person and invited to make a campaign gift. Of course, the real world requires us to compro-

mise. Most organizations have limited staff time and a limited cadre of volunteers who are willing to solicit gifts. To establish an effective limit on the solicitation process, an organization should determine a dollar amount below which a prospect will not be solicited in person. This amount will vary from campaign to campaign depending on the campaign goal, the number of volunteers, and the amount of time. For many small-to-midsized organizations, individuals will be solicited only for gifts and pledges of at least $1,000.

The campaign plan should also clarify two important aspects of the solicitation process.

- Solicitations should be preceded or accompanied by written proposals sent to the prospect.
- When being solicited, prospects should be asked to consider a gift of a specific amount or in a specific dollar range.

In every campaign involving inexperienced campaign volunteers, solicitors usually find themselves uncomfortable with the thought of asking prospects to consider a gift of a specific amount. A thorough discussion of this subject in the campaign planning committee will help those serving on this committee to understand the wisdom of this approach and become comfortable with this process before solicitation efforts begin.

The campaign plan should also clarify whether and how lower level prospects will be solicited. Although some campaigns are designed to include only personal solicitations, with the lower level donors left for the annual campaign, many community-based capital campaigns solicit lower level donors through telephone solicitation and direct mail, thus providing an opportunity for everyone, no matter what their resources or giving history, to make a campaign gift.

A Plan for Recognizing Donors

Although it often seems remote during the campaign planning process, a clear plan for recognizing donors should be in place before the first gift is solicited. Donor recognition will be discussed more fully in chapter 12, but the following three elements should be part of every campaign plan.

Giving Levels and Categories

Donors to most campaigns are distinguished and recognized according to the size of their gifts. Giving categories should be established that are appropriate for the campaign. Each category should have a designated dollar range and should be named in a manner that is appropriate for the campaign. Some organizations use such standard terminology as *founder*, *patron*, and *contributor*. Others take a more whimsical approach, with names that reflect the organization or the project. For example, an orchestra might offer the categories *maestro, concertmaster, principal tuba,* and so on. Donor recognition categories for a capital campaign should be different from those used for the annual giving campaign.

Donor Listing Practices

Typically, donors to a capital campaign are listed publicly in a number of ways, unless they request anonymity. The campaign plan should clarify whether and how public recognition will indicate the various giving levels. Many organizations elect to list donors alphabetically within broad giving levels. Generally these listings are organized to highlight leadership donors, beginning with giving categories high enough so that the number of donors in the top range is small. Subsequent catego-

ries include larger number of donors. For example, a donor listing might look something like Exhibit 7–7.

Some organizations list donors alphabetically within giving categories but elect not to include the specific dollar amounts on wall plaques. Instead, they include them in programs or other campaign reports.

For reasons that stem from an organization's culture, some organizations do not sort donors according to giving levels, but rather by donor type—individuals, businesses, and foundations—and then alphabetically within each type. Still others prefer not to categorize donors at all and list them all alphabetically. For example, some religious organizations do not wish to highlight the social or class differences among the members of their congregations.

Controversial organizations must tread carefully when they publicly list the names of their donors, taking care to give them the opportunity to remain anonymous or not to have their giving level publicized in any way.

Strictly from a fund-raising perspective, listing according to donor category provides a strong motivation for people to give more than they might if their gift was not going to be made public. However, fund raising is only one aspect of the health and life of an organization and decisions about donor listings and recognition must be made in such a way as to build constructive long-term relationships between the donors and the organization.

The campaign planning process provides an excellent opportunity to discuss some of these issues and help clarify them early in the campaign, thereby avoiding confusion when or after the gifts have been solicited.

Exhibit 7–7 Donor List

Founders ($250,000+)
Mr. and Mrs. Andrew Abelsmith
Mrs. Woodrow R. Blatsworthy

Master Builders ($100,000–$249,999)
Ms. Ellen Catting
Donald L. Cohen, Esq.
Samuel Wiffen
Mr. and Mrs. Robert W. Worthing

Builders ($25,000–$99,999)
Mrs. Thomas Esbenshade
Jessica Farthing
The Howing Foundation
Barbara and Benjamin Trestler
Mr. Chester Smith, III
Mrs. Trevor Training
Mr. and Mrs. Harvey Ulright

> *If those who volunteer to serve on a capital-campaign planning committee are the campaign's heart, then a well-conceived campaign plan is its brain.*

Donor Plaques and Other Donor Listings

The campaign plan should also clarify the public posting of donor names. Most important in this area is a determination of who will be listed on permanent donor plaques. If, as is usual, donors will be recognized by giving level, the campaign plan should specify the lowest giving level that will be recognized on a permanent plaque. A campaign plan might also spell out the various print media in which donor lists might appear and the policy to guide the staff so that they know which names they may or may not publish. In general, major donors must explicitly consent to having their names used in public media.

Although the campaign plan need not spell out the specifics of naming opportunities and commemorative techniques, it should indicate whether or not plaques that recognize donors or commemorate other individuals will be part of the donor recognition program. See chapter 12 for more detailed information about donor recognition.

Gift Accounting and Reporting

Finally, the campaign plan describes the roles and responsibilities for gift accounting and reporting. In most organizations, the burden of this responsibility falls to the development and bookkeeping staffs. In some small organizations, however, even these tasks are performed by volunteers. The campaign plan clarifies just who will tally gifts, keep giving records, and handle billing for pledge payments.

Checks and Balances

In these days of growing cynicism about the honesty of large nonprofit organizations, it is vital that an organization be completely above board and accountable when it comes to gift accounting and reporting. Whenever possible, someone on staff should tally gifts and send acknowledgments and their tally should always be corroborated by someone else in the finance/bookkeeping department. For reasons of accountability, a staff person is always a better choice than a volunteer.

If the organization does not already conduct an audit each year, the campaign is a good excuse for beginning that practice. Financial audits not only ensure accountability, they also provide a thorough review of the organization's accounting practices—and an audit is a good learning experience as well.

Reports on campaign progress are a vital part of building and sustaining campaign momentum. The campaign plan should determine who is responsible for this process and in what forms and with what frequency campaign reporting will take place. Often the organization's staff will produce monthly reports throughout the quiet phase of the campaign for the campaign planning committee members and the campaign steering committee. Once the campaign becomes public, the public relations committee may develop several issues of a campaign newsletter. Although the details of the reporting process need not be spelled out in a campaign plan, the plan should assign responsibilities for regular reporting and develop expectations about frequency and type of communication.

If those who volunteer to serve on a capital-campaign planning committee are the campaign's heart, then a well-conceived campaign plan is its brain. The plan outlines all the critical aspects of the campaign and provides a document that guides the many staff members and volunteers through a complex and demanding process. Without a clear and comprehensible plan, both staff and volunteers are likely to flounder in a sea of ad hoc decision making.

References

Ashton, Debra. 1991. *The complete guide to planned giving: Everything you need to know to compete successfully for major gifts.* 2d ed. Boston: JLA Publications.

Dove, Kent. 1988. *Conducting a successful capital campaign: A comprehensive guide for nonprofit organizations.* San Francisco: Jossey-Bass Publishers.

Management Reporting Standards for Educational Institutions. Revised February, 1996, Council for Advancement and Support of Education. Available from CASE by calling 1-800-554-8536.

Chapter 8

Asking for Major Gifts: Person to Person

Chapter Outline
- Motivation: The Key to Successful Solicitation
- Lead Gift Solicitation
- An Overview of the Solicitation Process
- Asking People for Money—Face to Face
- Solicitor Training
- Special Techniques for Soliciting Corporations and Foundations

Motivation: The Key to Successful Solicitation

What Motivates People?

People who have a deep understanding of what motivates other people hold important keys to success. Good supervisors motivate workers to be productive. Successful politicians motivate citizens to vote for them and convince their colleagues to support their legislative initiatives. Parents motivate children to behave in appropriate ways. For successful fund raising, campaign leaders and workers must motivate people to give. It is no wonder, then, that theories, articles, and books on human motivation abound. Human motivation is a complex phenomenon—it varies from culture to culture and from epoch to epoch. But as with many complex subjects, some simple principles of human motivation resonate with the truths of human nature within a particular culture.

To become grounded in the subject of human motivation, it may be helpful to spend a few minutes writing down the reasons why one does anything. It is an enlightening exercise to write down a number of sentences beginning with the phrase "I do the things I do because . . ."

Different people may find different words to express the same concepts, or rank them differently in importance, but the authors have found in asking their friends and colleagues to perform this simple exercise that the reasons people give for doing what they do share common roots.

Some of the most common responses heard are:

- I do the things I do because they make me happy.
- I do the things I do because they make other people happy.
- I do the things I do because I want what will result from doing them.
- I do the things I do because I will suffer if I don't do them.
- I do the things I do because someone asks me to do them.
- I do the things I do because I want to impress other people.
- I do the things I do because I feel guilty if I don't do them.
- I do the things I do because doing them will make me feel better.
- I do the things I do because I want to make my community a better place.
- I do the things I do because I want to fit in.
- I do the things I do because they are the right things to do.
- I do the things I do because I am compelled to do them.
- I do the things I do because no one else is doing them.
- I do the things I do because life is short.

This simple but provocative exercise provides useful clues as to what motivates people. These motivations appear generally to fall into three categories.

1. **Pleasure.** We do the things we do because we enjoy doing them.
2. **Consequences.** We do the things we do because of the results that they will accomplish.
3. **Duty.** We do the things we do because we feel that we should do them.

Of course, many things that people do are motivated by a complex of causes, and one dominant reason for doing things often masks other reasons. It appears, however, that people do most of what they do for some combination of these three reasons: because they enjoy doing them, because they want what will result from the action, or because they feel a sense of duty. Successful campaigns are organized to capitalize on all three of these primary motivators.

Successful campaigns give people pleasure. People enjoy giving. They feel good about what their money will accomplish and about having done their duty.

Successful campaigns accomplish specific goals or consequences that will move an organization to a new level. Through a campaign, donors help an organization reach its goals for the benefit of the community. Often they also are able to achieve personal goals such as a display or acquisition of influence or status.

Successful campaigns involve the people who feel a duty to the organization, to give something back to the community. Campaigns often depend on this sense of duty to keep volunteers and donors engaged even during the inevitable frustrating campaign periods.

Why People Give

Individual donors make gifts for a variety of reasons. Solicitors who understand what motivates their prospects are able to highlight aspects of the project that the prospect will find most appealing. In their book *The Seven Faces of Philanthropy* (1994), Russ Alan Prince and Karen Maru File outline seven common donor personalities.

1. **Altruists** contribute out of generosity and empathy. They believe that philanthropy is a moral imperative that gives life a sense of purpose.
2. **Communitarians** give primarily to improve their community.
3. **Devout** individuals support nonprofits for religious reasons and feel that giving is a moral obligation.
4. **Dynasts** give because they are expected to. Giving is deeply imbedded in their family tradition and often plays an important role in family relationships.
5. **Investors** see their contributions as investments and look for the return on investment both for their communities and for their bottom line.
6. **Repayers** give out of a feeling of loyalty and obligation. They believe that they should give back to the communities and institutions that have contributed to their lives.
7. **Socialites** believe that giving provides entry into a desirable social circle.

Each of these donor profiles is familiar to most fund raisers. If they take the time to ask their donors why they give, they are likely to receive the following sorts of answers:

- "I really believe in what your organization is doing and would like to help."
- "I've been very fortunate in my life and it's time to give something back."
- "I asked Joe for a gift for the symphony and he gave, so when he told me about your group and asked me for a gift, I felt I had to give something."
- "My accountant told me a gift of this size would be a smart move this year."
- "When I get old, I hope your organization is still around and strong so that it will be able to help me and my family."
- "I so enjoy being a volunteer there. It's a big part of my life."
- "I get such a feeling of accomplishment. When we first began, it was just a little organization in a backroom office and now it serves the whole county."
- "I've just always given to that cause. We're like old friends."

Why Does a Donor Give to a Specific Cause?

With the proliferation of nonprofit groups and the growing sophistication of fund-raising techniques, every donor must choose among many organizations to support. Although some support a broad range of groups, even these donors must be selective. Here is how people weed the field.

First, people give to organizations whose mission appeals to them. While a savvy donor takes into account the organization's leadership, financial health, mission, and impact on the community it serves, that which tips the giving scale for many donors is their own interest in the organization's work. Their interest may stem from their background, hobbies, family circumstances, or moral and religious values. Even the wealthiest donors are not likely to be motivated to make a gift unless they are interested in the organization or at least sympathetic to its work.

Second, people give to organizations with which they have been involved. Volunteering for an organization gives donors a first-hand glimpse of how the organization is run. They learn about its strengths, its weaknesses, and its needs. Donors often have only a passing interest in an organization when they first become involved. Perhaps they are drawn in by a friend. But as they become more involved, their level of commitment grows.

> *When an individual has developed a relationship with individuals in an organization, that organization tends to rise to the top of their list of charities.*

Christmas in May

My second development job was with a small theater company. The theater relied heavily on volunteers to help with all kinds of things, from ushering to typing to fund raising. A retired doctor who had previously contributed small amounts to the theater helped in my office. We used a cumbersome and time-consuming system for donor renewals. Each month, someone had to look through a file of about 300 index cards to locate everyone who had made a gift in that month the previous year and then pull the cards and print out the letters on a memory typewriter, manually inserting the amount of the previous year's gift in each letter. Once I asked the volunteer to pull the index cards. The next month I asked him to pull them again. After several months he said, "This would be much easier if all this information were on a computer." I heartily agreed, but explained that our operating budget was already stretched rather thin. The next week when he came in, he put a big box on my desk and said, "Merry Christmas. The laser printer is still in my trunk." Inside the box was a new computer.

—Development Director

Third, people give because they feel a kinship with others in an organization. Donors must choose what they will support from among many worthwhile causes. When an individual has developed a relationship with individuals in an organization, that organization tends to rise to the top of their list of charities. Personal relationships help donors feel that they are "part of the family." Personal contact fosters a sense of trust between the prospect and the organization and enables staff and volunteers to get a clearer idea of the prospect's interests and personal history.

Fourth, people give because they have been touched by an organization's work. Many gifts are made by donors because the organization's work has touched them deeply. Organizations exist to meet community needs, and by doing so they affect the lives of many people.

Organizations that do good work benefit from a ripple effect in their communities. It is not uncommon for someone to become involved in an organization or make a contribution because they know someone else whose life was touched by that organization's work.

Fifth, people give to support a project that they care about. People give to organizations through which they can make a difference in the world. Donors want to know

that through their gifts an organization is going to address issues, solve problems, grasp opportunities, or create works of art that they could not create themselves. Such organizations provide the means through which many donors are able to live out their dreams.

Sixth, people give because they are asked to give. Many people are aware of causes to which they would like to give, but unless they are asked to give they are unlikely to do so. Whether from inertia, embarrassment, or the lack of knowledge and time, people must often be invited to participate in something, either financially or as a volunteer, before they become sufficiently motivated to do so.

Finally, people will give because they are asked to give by someone they know. It is harder to turn down someone you know and respect. The very fact that that person is willing to ask for money adds credibility and weight to the request and increases the psychological value of the gift.

Why People Volunteer to Solicit Gifts

Understanding donor motivation is only half the picture in a capital campaign. The picture is completed by understanding why people volunteer to solicit others. In a society in which the discussion of money is generally off-limits, it is remarkable that anyone at all volunteers to solicit contributions. The solicitation process is extremely uncomfortable for many people, since it asks them to go against many cultural taboos related to money.

Why, then, do people volunteer to solicit gifts? Think back to the three primary motivational categories—pleasure, consequences, and duty. Since most people do not find it pleasurable to ask others for money, those who volunteer to solicit gifts are likely to be acting either because of the consequences of the process or because they feel that it is their duty to help.

Just Like Family

One of our former board members, a retired financial officer of a large corporation, moved to an independent-care facility in the next state to be closer to his brother. Our executive director visited him several times a year and kept him informed about what was going on in our organization. Our director genuinely liked this individual and benefited from his advice and wisdom. He was not specifically cultivating him as a potential donor, but when we began our campaign, this former board member made the lead gift of $500,000 because, as he put it, "You are like family to me."

—Development Director

Volunteers who agree to solicit gifts usually do so for one or more of the following reasons:

- They strongly support the goals of the campaign.
- They are asked to volunteer by someone they can't refuse.
- They want an opportunity to interact with other volunteers or with those whom they plan to solicit.
- They are active volunteers in the organization and feel that it is their duty to help.

Some people do in fact find pleasure in fund raising. Volunteers whose solicitations have resulted in generous gifts often acquire a taste for fund raising. These seasoned solicitors enjoy the challenge and revel in the rewards. Fortunate are the organizations that have many seasoned and successful solicitors behind their cause. Not only are these solicitors likely to continue to be successful, but they also inspire others and help train those who do not yet delight in the task.

Lead Gift Solicitation

The do-or-die portion of every campaign is the solicitation of the ten to twenty largest gifts. The solicitation process of each of these gifts requires careful, individualized, strategic thinking. Some experts recommend that staff retain full control of the process by assigning solicitors to prospects based on information that is gathered during prospect rating and screening sessions. Others recommend that the campaign chair and a small subgroup of the steering committee be responsible for matching prospects and donors.

Soliciting the lead donors is one of the primary responsibilities of the campaign chairs. In many cases, the chairs have been selected specifically because of their knowledge of the people who have the potential to make lead gifts to the campaign and their potential influence on these individuals to make a generous gift. Often, of course, the lead gifts will be made by the chairs themselves.

Soliciting the Campaign Chairs

In any case, every lead gift should be specifically solicited. Every lead gift donor should be treated with respect and care. And every lead gift solicitor should be in frequent touch with the development staff so that they can provide encouragement, information about the prospect, and up-to-date reports about the status of the other lead-gift solicitations.

The very first gifts to be solicited should be those of the campaign chairs. If, as has been suggested, a discussion of each chair's gift was a part of the recruitment process, this subject may already have been broached. However, in many cases the initial discussion was rather general in nature and may not have resulted in a signed pledge form or letter of intent. Solidifying the chairs' gifts, then, is often the initial step in the solicitation process. This should be done either by the chairman of the board, the executive director, or a combination of the two.

Those who solicit the chairs should treat this encounter with the utmost respect and importance. The chair should be solicited at a meeting that has been set up specifically to discuss his or her gift. The solicitors should prepare for the meeting thoroughly and bring a table of gifts, a blank letter of intent, and the list of naming opportunities. If both the board chair and the executive director plan to solicit the gift, they should discuss their respective roles before the meeting. Often in such cases, the chairman of the board will run the meeting and solicit the gift while the director is on hand to provide specific information about the project, the organization, and the campaign.

Before the meeting, these two should discuss the gift and determine the amount that they wish to ask the campaign chair to consider. Also before the meeting, both the board chair and the director should discuss and make their own gifts. Although these may not be lead gifts, they should make financial commitments to the campaign that are at the upper levels of their financial ability.

In many cases, the campaign chair may arrive at the meeting with a specific gift in mind. Sometimes, the chair may even arrive with a signed letter of intent. It is important, however, to discuss the gift in detail. How does the chair wish his or her gift to be acknowledged? Does the chair wish to name a room or a space? How and when will the gift be paid?

Not only will the early discussion of all of these issues get the campaign off to an effective start but doing so will clear the air of some of the uncomfortable tensions that often poison a campaign.

If, as is common today, the campaign has more than one chair, the chair solicitation process should begin by soliciting the chair who is likely to be able to make the largest gift. That person then helps solicit the other chairs. Each chair should be solicited in a private meeting, in a clear and intentional fashion, and early in the campaign.

Soliciting Other Lead Gifts

If the campaign chairs have been well selected and properly solicited, then the campaign will already have some momentum by the time the other lead gifts are solicited. Indeed, the process of soliciting these early gifts builds a lead gift team to solicit the remaining lead gifts.

Many campaigns will have no more than twenty-five prospects for the top ten gifts. Often, the best way to develop a strategy for soliciting each of these gifts is by establishing a small committee of leadership donors. This leadership gift committee may meet weekly in the early stages of the campaign to review each prospect and determine the best way to solicit that individual. For each prospect, the committee will discuss questions in the following eight categories.

1. Who should solicit the gift?
   - With whom is the prospect friendly?
   - Who, if anyone, has recently been solicited by the prospect for another cause?
   - Whom does the prospect trust and respect?
   - Who among the group of possible solicitors is an effective solicitor?
   - Should more than one person solicit the gift?
2. What giving level should the prospect be invited to consider?
   - Has the prospect him- or herself indicated a giving range?
   - What has the prospect given to other, comparable projects?
   - What is the prospect's relationship and giving history with this organization?

- What is known of the prospect's financial resources?
- Where is the prospect likely to place him- or herself in a table of gifts?

3. What is the best solicitation approach?
   - Is there a specific aspect of the project that might appeal to the prospect?
   - Is the prospect likely to want to be seen as a leader?
   - Is the prospect likely to prefer to remain anonymous?

4. Should the solicitor suggest a specific naming opportunity?
   - Has the prospect named rooms in other projects?
   - Are there one or two rooms that might particularly interest the prospect?

5. When should the person be solicited?
   - When will the prospect be in town?
   - At what time might the prospect generally prefer to meet?
   - Would it be possible and advisable to try to reach the prospect even though he or she is in Florida, for example?

6. How should the solicitation meeting be conducted?
   - Should the prospect's spouse or partner be included in the solicitation meeting?
   - Is the prospect likely to prefer a longer, more social meeting, or is the prospect likely to prefer a shorter, more businesslike meeting?
   - Where should the meeting take place?

7. What materials should be used to solicit the prospect?
   - What aspects of the project should the solicitation proposal stress?
   - Who should sign the proposal letter?
   - Should the proposal be sent ahead of time?

8. What are the action steps?
   - Who will call to set up the appointment?
   - Who will prepare the packet of materials?
   - Who will report to the staff on progress?

Sometimes the answers to these questions are clear, and the entire discussion about a particular prospect may take no more than ten minutes. In other cases, after hours of discussion, no clear approach emerges. In the latter case, although it is tempting simply to assign the solici-

> *Resist the temptation to assume that campaign leaders will on their own make their gifts generously and early. Find the courage to solicit the campaign chair to get the campaign off to a rolling start.*

One by One

Our group of lead gift solicitors was very small. In fact, it consisted of just me, our executive director, and one other volunteer. Our lead gift prospect list was long, and the more we worked, the longer it seemed to get! Somehow I just couldn't enlist others to help very much. Occasionally, when I knew just the right person to solicit a gift, I'd ask them to help, and sometimes they did, but by and large the two of us volunteers seemed to be the best solicitors for just about every prospect. In fact, we raised virtually all the leadership gifts for the campaign. I'm not sure to this day (the campaign concluded successfully almost a year ago) whether we really were the best people for the job or whether I was just afraid to give up control.

—Campaign Chairman

tation to someone just to have done with it, it is often a better strategy to hold off until more information can be gathered.

Soliciting the Lead Gifts in the Right Order

The sequence of soliciting lead gifts should be determined both by the size of the gift and the chances of its success. If at all possible, prospects who are capable of making the largest gifts and who are seen to be most likely to make those gifts should be solicited first. Then come the lead gift prospects for whom the solicitation strategy seems the clearest and most certain. Last come the prospects toward whom no one seems to know the best approach.

Ken Wyman, in his excellent manual *Face to Face: How to Get Bigger Donations from Very Generous People* (1993, 69), establishes a numerical system for prioritizing prospects, presented in Exhibit 8–1. Although in the lead-gift process most of the decisions are best made through discussion among peers, Wyman provides a quantifiable approach to prospect sequencing.

Materials for Soliciting Lead Gifts

Each lead gift solicitor should be acquainted with the material that might be used in soliciting lead gifts. Although a packet of materials should be selected and organized for each lead gift prospect, the materials that might be included are listed below.

- proposal letter
- case for support
- drawings and/or plans
- project schedule
- project budget

Exhibit 8-1 Major Gift Prospects: Who to Ask First

Prospect's Name _____

Criteria	Points	Score
Prospect gave to us previously	100	
Prospect is rated to give a very large gift	35	
Prospect's gift will be easy to get	35	
Prospect's decision will influence others by example	35	
Prospect is or was on our board	25	
Prospect is known to make big gifts to other nonprofit organizations	25	
Prospect is or was a volunteer with us	20	
Prospect is or was a participant and we have stayed in touch	15	
Prospect is on the board of one or more other nonprofit groups	15	
We have a personal contact	15	
Prospect knows about and is interested in us	15	
Prospect is religious	10	
Prospect apparently has money to give	10	
Prospect is interested in our issue but apparently doesn't know about us	7	
Prospect has been given awards for community service	5	
Prospect has a high profile in the community	5	
Prospect is conservative (no matter how he/she votes)	5	
Prospect is over 55 years of age	5	
Prospect is in a professional or managerial occupation	5	
Prospect is an active volunteer with other groups	5	
Prospect is university educated	3	
Prospect is still married to first spouse	3	
Prospect has children	2	
Total Score (maximum 400 points)	400	

Source: Reprinted with permission from K. Wyman, *Face to Face: How to Get Bigger Donations from Very Generous People*, written for the Canadian federal government's Voluntary Action Program, available through Ken Wyman & Associates, 64B Shuter Street, Suite 200, Toronto, ON, Canada M5B 1B1, © 1993.

- table of gifts
- list of naming opportunities
- location and drawing of plaque (if available)
- categories of giving
- brochures or other printed material about the organization
- summary of the organization's accomplishments
- list of the organization's board of directors
- list of the campaign leadership and steering committee

- operating budget
- most recent audited financial statement

In addition to the material that might be selected to send or present to each lead gift prospect, every lead gift solicitor will need additional information to facilitate the task of solicitation. Packets for lead gift solicitors should include the following items:

- updated lists of the prospect's solicitation assignments

- letters of intent or pledge forms
- copies of proposals sent to their prospects
- solicitation call report forms for each prospect plus some extras (See Exhibit 8–8)
- thank-you note cards and envelopes
- campaign letterhead and envelopes
- an information sheet on each prospect to be solicited
- names and telephone numbers (home and business) of co-chairs, board chair, executive director, and development director or campaign director

Building Confidence by Sharing Lead Gift Progress

Because each lead gift helps to set the pace for the campaign, strategic sharing of information is of vital importance. The lead gift solicitors are true campaign insiders. They are extremely aware that the burden of the campaign rests on their shoulders. Every new lead gift that is committed to the campaign inspires and motivates other lead gift prospects as well as their solicitors, and thus, prompt and effective communication during this phase of the campaign is extremely important. The executive director, campaign chair, and development director must work as a team to make certain that information about each new lead gift is shared with the other lead gift solicitors.

Early in the lead gift process, every lead gift meeting should include an up-to-date accounting of campaign progress. Since lead gifts are large gifts, it doesn't take very many of them before the campaign has made significant progress. It is also often helpful for lead gift solicitors to be updated regularly on gifts in progress. A sample lead gift update is presented in Exhibit 8–2.

Exhibit 8–2 Sample Lead Gift Progress Report

Lead Gift Progress Report
January 5, 1996–January 19, 1996

Gift Report
Campaign goal	$1,000,000
Lead gift goal	$475,000
Total gifts pledged as of January 5, 1996	$75,000
Gifts pledged since January 5, 1996	$50,000
Gifts pledged as of January 19, 1996	$125,000

Activity Report

Solicitations assigned	15
Solicitation meeting has taken place, gift made	3
No progress reported	5
Solicitation meeting set up but not completed	3
Solicitation meeting has taken place, decision pending	2
Solicitation meeting has taken place, gift refused	2

Think Magnets

Once when I was a child my father brought home a magnet and a jar of iron filings. We sprinkled the iron filings on a sheet of paper and then, placing the magnet under the paper and moving it about, we were able to attract the iron filings and direct their course over the paper. To my child's mind it seemed like magic. The power of lead gifts is like the power of the magic magnet. These gifts draw people in and attract other gifts, directing the course of the campaign ahead in ways far more significant than the dollars they represent.

—Campaign Consultant

This sort of report, regularly updated for the lead gift meetings, shows campaign progress quite clearly and motivates the solicitors to show activity on the solicitations to which they have been assigned.

Training Lead Gift Solicitors

Lead gift solicitors are usually a mixed group. Some have worked on campaign after campaign and are excellent solicitors. Others, though experienced solicitors, have adopted solicitation strategies that are ineffective. Still others have little solicitation experience. The task of the development director or campaign manager is to design an approach to solicitor training that will highlight the excellent solicitors in the group, reeducate those who are experienced but ineffective, and encourage and train those who are new to the field.

Because the lead gift solicitors comprise a small group, solicitor training can actively involve the solicitors. The training might effectively incorporate role playing and active discussion of specific prospects. This sort of participatory training actually helps solicitors find and practice the words and phrases to use with their prospects. They will have a chance to think through responses to objections that their prospects might raise, and they will be able to experiment with different strategies for soliciting the gift.

Although this chapter covers solicitor training in detail later, a few guidelines might be helpful to lead gift solicitors.

- The more the prospect knows about the project, the more the prospect should be thought of as a partner in the process of determining the best gift for him and the organization.
- An excellent lead gift solicitor listens for what the prospect wants to accomplish through the gift and then works with the prospect and the organization to accomplish those goals.

- Lead gift solicitors are tenacious and creative.
- Lead gift solicitations often require multiple meetings.
- Lead gift solicitors must not become discouraged from soliciting others by a "no" answer from one prospect.
- Lead gift solicitors often maintain contact with their prospects even after the prospects have made their gifts.

An Overview of the Solicitation Process

Although the meeting between the solicitor and the donor is the core of the matter, in reality, this encounter is embedded in a much larger organizational framework that has been established to increase the chances of that encounter's success. This section describes the various preparations and activities that support and surround the solicitation. To make matters specific, the major gift solicitation process for a small, community-based, social service organization will be described. The pattern may be adapted to any division in any campaign.

To provide the essential planning information, the table of gifts that was developed in chapter 7 will be used in Exhibit 8–3.

Identifying Qualified Prospects

In the process of planning for the campaign, the organization has conducted several screening sessions to learn more about its prospects and to determine the appropriate request level for each. In preparation for the major-gift division, the staff has reviewed the database and has iden

Exhibit 8–3 Table of Gifts

Leadership Gifts

Amount of Gift	Number of Gifts	Number of Prospects	Number of Solicitors	Amount Solicited in Gift Range	Percent of Total
$150,000	1	2		$150,000	
$75,000	1	2		$75,000	
$50,000	2	6		$100,000	
$25,000	6	18		$150,000	
Totals	10	28	7	$475,000	47%

Major Gifts

Amount of Gift	Number of Gifts	Number of Prospects	Number of Solicitors	Amount Solicited in Gift Range	Percent of Total
$10,000	10	32		$100,000	
$5,000	20	80		$100,000	
$2,500	40	160		$100,000	
Totals	70	272	68	$300,000	30%

General Gifts

Amount of Gift	Number of Gifts	Number of Prospects	Number of Solicitors	Amount Solicited in Gift Range	Percent of Total
$1,000	80	360		$80,000	
$500	160	640		$80,000	
Totals	70	1,000	260	$160,000	16%

tified approximately 400 donors who might reasonably be invited to consider a gift in this range. This judgment has been based on the ratings of inclination and ability by other volunteers, staff evaluations, patterns of prior giving, and the prospects' history with the organization.

Designing the Division

The organization knows from the table of gifts developed in the campaign plan that it will take approximately 70 gifts of between $2,500 and $10,000 to raise $300,000. It also knows that each gift will require approximately four solicitations and that consequently this division will need 272 solicitations. If every volunteer is capable of making five solicitations, this division will require 54 volunteer solicitors (272 ÷ 5).

To organize the division into manageable segments, the division should be divided into teams of six solicitors, one of whom will be designated team captain. The division in this example might well be divided into two sections and each section into five teams of one team captain and five solicitors. Each section will comprise thirty volunteers (in addition to the section leader or division chair) and will be responsible for up to 150 solicitations. While this structure in theory provides 300 solicitations, or 28 more than necessary, in practice, the actual numbers of volunteers will fall somewhat short of the goal because some team captains may not be able to find enough solicitors to fill their teams and some solicitors probably won't follow through. And, if for some reason everyone is successful in their recruiting, the organization will only benefit from the additional solicitors. This structure is illustrated in Figure 8–1.

Enlisting the Volunteers

Enlisting volunteers for the division proceeds from the top down. The campaign chair enlists the division chair. The division chair enlists the section chair. Section chairs enlist the team captains, and team captains enlist the volunteers. It is important to coordinate the selection of volunteers so that one volunteer is not recruited by several team captains. The simplest way to avoid overlap is to invite all the team captains to a meeting to discuss and clarify their role in the campaign. They will be invited to review lists of prospective solicitors and to place their names next to those whom they would like to recruit. Beyond the initial selection, the names of potential recruits should, if possible, be cleared through the development staff before they are contacted. Although it is sometimes helpful to define the teams according to their town or neighborhood, thereby reducing the potential for overlap, team captains usually prefer to recruit their friends and acquaintances, and patterns of friendship no longer commonly reflect neighborhood or community boundaries.

Soliciting the Solicitors

Every volunteer solicitor should be solicited before that solicitor solicits others. Although many campaigns assume that solicitors will make their gifts without being solicited, this is rarely the case, and this phase of the solicitation process is most effectively accomplished by organizing a clear and explicit schedule by which every volunteer is solicited by the person who recruited him or her. Not only does this address the issue of solicitor giving in a straightforward manner, as it should, but it gives every volunteer

Team captains solicit team members. Solicitors each visit five prospects. Each team will be responsible for approximately 30 solicitations.

Figure 8–1 Sample Major Gift Division Structure

an opportunity to practice the solicitation process with a fellow solicitor. If handled properly, each of these solicitations can be not only a fund-raising call but also a chance to talk about the solicitation process—about what worked and what didn't. This method eases the tension for both volunteers. In some cases, the section leaders and team captains have their own solicitor-training session. This prepares them to be good solicitors and good coaches for the solicitors they have recruited. In other cases, they are trained alongside their fellow solicitors.

Matching Prospects with Solicitors

With four hundred qualified prospects and roughly fifty-six solicitors, one needs a simple mechanism for pairing each solicitor with the five most suitable prospects. In the lead-gift solicitation process, solicitation strategies are determined prospect by prospect. With the larger numbers of prospects and solicitors in the major-gifts division, such an approach is not feasible.

The following prospect-selection strategy accomplishes the task in a way that:

- pairs each solicitor with the most likely prospects
- avoids duplication
- highlights the prospects who are most likely to make a gift
- provides feedback to the staff about who is soliciting whom

The prospect-selection meeting is the selection process that takes place at a meeting of all of the volunteer solicitors. The meeting should take approximately one and one-half hours and should be convened in a room large enough to seat all the volunteers classroom style, with a speakers' table and/or podium at the front and several long tables around the perimeter of the room for displaying prospect cards.

For some solicitors, the prospect-selection meeting will be the first opportunity that they have to become familiar with the campaign in an official setting. Many of them are likely to know the organization from previous contact, and all of them will have had conversations with their team captains or section leaders, though many will have only a passing understanding of the goals of the campaign and what is expected of them. The prospect-selection meeting provides an opportunity to inform and instruct the volunteers.

A typical agenda for the meeting might be organized as follows:

1. welcome and review of the meeting agenda and contents of packets (campaign chair)
2. mission and accomplishments of the organization (executive director)
3. summary of campaign goals (campaign co-chair or other)
4. description of division goals and the solicitation process (division chair)
5. instructions for selecting prospects and reminder of the next meeting (staff)
6. prospect selection (group)

Questions and discussion should be encouraged throughout the meeting.

Prospect cards should be prepared well in advance of the meeting by the staff. Each card contains the prospect's name, address, phone numbers, and a code that indicates the prospect's level of prior giving and relationship to the organization. The ideal system uses duplicate cards attached by a perforated edge. A sample is given in Figure 8–2.

The 3 × 5 cards that are used for tractor-feed printers work well. They are perforated and can be pulled apart in sets of two. Because most computer programs will not print duplicate information in the correct order, organizations often print two sets of mailing labels with the appropriate information and affix them to the cards. The cards should be kept in alphabetical order unless there is a particular reason to do otherwise. Every solicitor will thus be able to find the cards of specific prospects or institutions whom they have decided in advance that they wish to solicit.

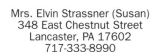

Mrs. Elvin Strassner (Susan)
348 East Chestnut Street
Lancaster, PA 17602
717-333-8990

$$$$ Former board member, volunteer

- -

Mrs. Elvin Strassner (Susan)
348 East Chestnut Street
Lancaster, PA 17602
717-333-8990

$$$$ Former board member, volunteer

Figure 8–2 Sample Prospect Card

Sometimes prospects whose names have surfaced in the lead-gift-rating sessions are for one reason or another not solicited in that division. These cards might then be included with those that have been identified for the major-gifts division. These special cards and any others that have been deemed particularly important should be identified with a special mark. One might, for example, place a gold star on each half of such priority-prospect cards.

The cards should be set out on the tables around the room prior to the start of the meeting. They should be arranged alphabetically, and large signs showing the alphabetic categories of each table should be displayed on the wall above each table or on the tables themselves.

Information packets should also be prepared prior to the meeting for each solicitor. Simple pocket folders work well. Some organizations invest in folders specially printed with the campaign name and logo, while others put campaign mailing labels on the outside of the folders. As in most details of small campaigns, presentations need not be extravagant or glossy to be effective.

Material in the folder should include:

- the meeting agenda
- background information about the organization and the project being funded
- a description of the role of the volunteer in the campaign
- information about the volunteer's team: names and phone numbers of teammates, team captain, and coordinating staff member (a diagram of the campaign showing divisions, sections, and teams is helpful)
- a list of key dates for the division
- a copy of the proposal letter to be used in the solicitation process

Prospects are selected at the conclusion of the meeting when volunteers are requested to pick five prospect cards from among the cards laid out on the tables. If possible, solicitors should give special priority to the cards with stars but nonetheless should select individuals whom they know or with whom they share a contact. After selecting their cards, they should print their first and last names on the front of each half of the cards. They may take one half of the card home for reference and should return the other half to a staff member before leaving.

Contacting absentee volunteers is ideally done by the team captains. They will ask those on their teams who were not present to meet with them to review the packets with the team leader and to select their prospects. If the team captain is unable to do this, a staff member will have to pick up the loose ends.

Assigning leftover prospect cards should wait until the first round of solicitation has been completed. To give the volunteers a wide enough selection so that they will be likely to find prospects whom they know, it is ideal to have more than five times as many qualified prospects as solicitors. This means, however, that some prospect cards will remain after the selection process is complete. Although solicitors should be encouraged to select starred cards first, if there are any leftover starred cards, they should be assigned in a second round to the most successful solicitors. Other remaining cards might be added to the prospects for another division or added to the list of phone solicitation or direct mail prospects.

Preparing Proposal Letters

Every solicitation should be preceded by a written proposal letter. This letter should be no more than two pages long. It should be personalized for the specific prospect and should be signed by the campaign chair or leadership team. The proposal letter includes four important elements.

1. a summary of the case for the project
2. a statement that a specific volunteer will be calling to set up an appointment
3. a request that the prospect meet with that volunteer
4. a request that the prospect consider making a gift of a specified dollar amount or within a specified range

The letters should be signed by the campaign chair. People are often confused about this strategy, wondering why the letters don't come from the solicitor. That the proposal letters are signed by the chair serves as an indication that the request for support comes from the campaign rather than from the volunteer solicitor. Through this strategy, the prospect is asked to support the goals of the campaign rather than to give based on his friendship with the volunteer. This approach also removes the burden of stating the actual amount of the request from the shoulders of the volunteers, many of whom feel uncomfortable doing so. Because the letters will be sent over the signature of the campaign chair, the salutation must match the chair's relationship with each prospect.

The proposal letters also motivate the volunteer solicitors to complete their calls. If solicitor Cecily knows that the campaign chair, a person of influence in the community, has sent a letter to Mr. Ernest Worthing informing him that a Ms. Cecily Bracknell will be calling him to set up an appointment, chances are good that Cecily will follow through.

Exhibit 8–4 is a sample proposal letter that was created for a fictitious organization. Much of the language in this letter was developed for the case for support and then adapted for many campaign communications. The letter should be short, easy to read, and nonbureaucratic. It should get to the point in the first paragraph and draw

Exhibit 8–4 Sample Proposal Letter

Dear Jennifer and Steve:

Salutation is appropriate for Sam Smith, the campaign chair, who signed this letter. He knows them well.

Letter begins with a reminder of what an important resource the library is

The County Library is one of the busiest places in downtown Lancaster. Every year, more than 400,000 people come to the library to borrow books, get information, study, do research, or just browse.

Highlights benefits of project to library users

This year the Lancaster County Library is getting ready to computerize its collections. Instead of struggling with the old microfiche system, you'll be able to find any book easily and accurately by typing key words into a computer. Every book and resource in the library will be coded, and scanners at the check-out desk will enable you to check out books easily and quickly.

With the next system, all sixteen county libraries will be linked to one computer system so that you will be able to get up-to-date information about whether a particular resource is anywhere in the library system, where it is, and whether or not it has been checked out. The library staff will be able to tell you what books you already have checked out and when the book you are waiting for is due back in. In short, the library will be able to serve you and your family better.

Positions the project as a public/private partnership. This is important for libraries!

To make this a reality, we need your help. Our County commissioners and many other generous individuals and corporations have already pledged more than $1 million toward the $1.8 million it will take to complete this project. We are now asking each of our library donors to consider making a special gift to help raise the remaining $800,000 before the end of the year.

States total goal

Highlight amount left to raise

Although we have no way of knowing whether or how much you would like to contribute to the campaign, we hope you will consider making a pledge of between $500 and $1,000 per year for up to three years. If you are in a position to consider a gift of more than that, we would, of course, be thrilled. If on the other hand, a gift of that size does not fit your situation, we will be truly grateful for whatever contribution you feel is appropriate.

Mentions pledge period

Gently requests a gift in a specific range

Sets up expectation that Barbara will call

Within a few days, Barbara Johansen will call to set up an appointment to talk with you about this project. I hope that you will take the time to meet with her and consider a generous contribution to the Open Sesame Campaign.

Indicates Sam's commitment

The health of our public library reflects the values of our community. Please join me in helping to make sure that our county library remains strong well into the next century.

Puts request in larger context

With sincere appreciation,

Sam Smith
Campaign Chair

P.S. The enclosed brochure will give you a more complete picture of the project. This brochure was contributed as a campaign gift by a generous area designer and printer.

Often in small campaigns, people are uneasy about spending money to raise money

the reader inexorably through to the end. After reading the letter, the prospect should know what the project is about, who will call, what the call will be about, and what size gift the organization is asking him to consider.

Timing is crucial. Proposal letters must be prepared between the prospect-selection meeting and the solicitor-training meeting. The cards that are collected at the conclusion of the prospect-selection meeting provide the staff with the name of the solicitor—the final piece of information that they need to prepare the solicitation letters. The staff

prepares drafts of the letter for each prospect prior to the solicitation-training meeting. The drafts of the letters to their prospects are given to each solicitor at the training meeting so they have a chance to review them for content and accuracy before they are sent. This helps the solicitors to become familiar with the contents of the letters, allows them to review (and occasionally alter) the amount of the gift being requested, and increases the chances of catching any errors in spelling or grammar that may have sneaked by the in-house error sleuths.

Training the Solicitors

The solicitor-training meeting marks the beginning of the actual solicitation process, and all volunteers in the division are expected to attend. At that meeting they not only learn how to solicit a gift but they also receive copies of the proposal letters that have been prepared as well as all other material that they will need to solicit their prospects.

This meeting usually lasts about two hours. It should be held in a room large enough to accommodate all of the solicitors, staff, and other speakers in a seating format that encourages participation. Ideally, the solicitors from each team should sit at a round table with their team captains. A refreshment table should be located in an area where people can mingle, and a speakers' table or podium should be at the front of the room.

For this meeting, each solicitor should receive a prepared name tag from a table by the door. Depending on the time of day, simple but attractive refreshments give people a chance to relax and break the ice as everyone arrives.

Information packets for team members should be given to each team captain to distribute at the table. Extra information from the last meeting should be on hand for those who forgot their packets.

The agenda for this second solicitors' meeting might be as follows:

- welcome and introductions (campaign chair or board chair)
- review of purpose of meeting (campaign chair)
- review of campaign goals and progress to date (campaign co-chair)
- review of division goals, structure, process, and timetable (division chair)
- distribution and review of drafts of proposal letters (team captains and solicitors)
- solicitation training (consultant)
- distribution of other material (staff)

By reviewing the draft of the proposal letter before it is sent, the volunteer is able to make adjustments. Any volunteer who on reviewing the draft letters to his or her prospects finds an error in the letter should be instructed to mark the error or any other suggested changes directly on the letters and return them to the staff. Or if a volunteer disagrees with the amount of the gift that has been suggested in the proposal and believes that a higher (or lower) amount would be more appropriate, that too should be noted.

The staff will make all corrections, have the final letters signed, and send final copies to the solicitors at the same time that the letters are sent to the prospects. Solicitors should be instructed to begin calling their prospects to set up appointments when they receive copies of the final proposal letters in the mail.

Some campaign managers prepare simple spiral-bound handbooks for their volunteer solicitors. The handbook might have a nice cover with the campaign name and logo. This handbook format helps solicitors keep the information that they will need in a well-organized, easy-to-use format. A volunteer handbook might include the following:

- statement of campaign objectives
- campaign goal and table of gifts
- rules of thumb for soliciting a gift
- guide to a successful solicitation
- answers to tough questions
- ways to give to the campaign
- relationship between annual giving and the campaign
- gift crediting guidelines
- donor recognition opportunities
- names and telephone numbers of staff resource people

Maintaining Contact during the Solicitation Period

Volunteers are usually expected to complete their solicitations in four to six weeks. The division structure establishes a clear pattern for communicating with volunteers during the solicitation period, and effective team captains call each of their solicitors every week to check on their progress and to see whether they need help or advice.

It is also helpful to schedule two or three informal reporting meetings for team captains, section leaders, and the division chair. These meetings might be organized as drop-in meetings during a specified afternoon or evening in which people stop by with their updates, signed pledge forms, and questions. These meetings are most effective if they are scheduled for one hour every week during the solicitation period. They provide an opportunity for team captains to hear what is happening in other teams, for the section leaders and staff to track progress, and for the staff to provide assistance and advice as needed.

Throughout the solicitation period and often well beyond, solicitors must be informed when someone whom they have solicited sends in a gift. Although solicitors are strongly encouraged to keep control of the pledge

> *Have mercy on those in your group who are not among the eagle-eyed! Names on name tags should be at least one inch high and written in fat, dark, legible type so that one doesn't have to invade another's personal space to read his or her name.*

form until it has been signed, in practice many solicitors are unable to stand firm on this dictum and are likely to leave a pledge form with their prospect. When pledge forms are sent to the office, someone on the staff must be responsible not only for acknowledging and thanking the donor and recording the gift but also for informing the solicitor that the gift was received.

As the solicitation period procedes, the staff might prepare brief, written progress updates reporting on how many calls have been made and how much has been raised by the division to date. These serve as reminders and motivate solicitors to complete their visits.

The solicitation process has a way of beginning with a bang and ending with a whimper. The organization should make every effort to highlight the timetable and to encourage the solicitors to complete their calls by the end of the solicitation period.

Completing Unfinished Solicitation

At the end of every solicitation period there is an untidy group of unfinished calls. Some volunteers could not reach one or another of their prospects. Some volunteers just didn't follow through. Some prospects asked for time to consider and then the volunteer didn't get back to them. Sometimes a prospect will make a verbal commitment to the solicitor but not sign a pledge form. Occasionally, a pledge form is returned with an amount different from that reported by the solicitor. No matter how you look at it, cleaning up unfinished calls is time-consuming and messy.

The first stage of the cleanup falls to the team captains. They review their lists of prospects and get in touch with their solicitors to determine the best strategy for completing each call. Sometimes the team captains themselves complete an unfinished call. Sometimes, however, this process gets passed to the staff member in charge of the division. The staff member, through phone calls, personal visits, or letters, wraps up the process, bringing any open solicitations to a close.

Reporting Success, Thanking Solicitors, and Acknowledging Donors

No solicitation process is really complete until everyone knows the final tally; the solicitors are thanked by the campaign chair, the section leader, and the team captain; and every donor has been thanked by the solicitor, the campaign chair, and the director of the organization. Coordinating this entire process is usually the responsibility of the development staff.

Summarizing the Process and Meetings

There is a great deal to keep in mind in organizing a solicitation division. The outline of meetings and tasks in Exhibit 8–5 may help to crystallize the process. This outline may be effectively adapted to any division in any campaign. Following the list of tasks in order from beginning to end will help ensure that the right solicitor solicits the right donor for the right gift.

Job Descriptions for Division Leaders, Team Captains, and Solicitors

Although the structure and timing of each piece of a campaign is extremely important, a campaign must also recruit effective division leaders, team captains, and solicitors if it is to succeed. Entire teams and even divisions have failed to raise as much money as they otherwise might have because one solicitor in a lead position did not follow through, became dissatisfied and slacked off, or was perhaps diligent but nonetheless ineffective.

One way of avoiding such misfortune is to specify the role of these leaders in advance so that they know what will be expected of them before they agree to take the job.

Simple job descriptions outlining the tasks as clearly and specifically as possible often provide the necessary focus, enabling a volunteer to look realistically at other commitments in light of the campaign calendar. Although some volunteers may turn down the job once they know what is involved, those who agree to help will know just what they are getting into and so will be more likely to do the job well.

Job descriptions for division leaders, team captains, and solicitors should include information about the purpose of their part of the campaign, the number of meetings that they will be expected to attend, the tasks for which they will be responsible, and the projected timetable and duration of their involvement.

Exhibits 8–6 and 8–7 are sample job descriptions that may be adapted for other divisions and other campaigns.

Asking People for Money—Face to Face

Solicitation of gifts falls into four distinct phases.

1. setting up the appointment
2. preparing to make the solicitation
3. soliciting the gift
4. following through

Each phase presents its own set of challenges and requires discipline and attention to detail. Although solicitors focus most often on the actual solicitation of the gift, successful solicitors pay attention to all four stages.

Setting Up the Appointment

Once the proposal letter has been received by the prospect, it is up to the solicitor to call the prospect to set up the meeting. For many volunteer solicitors, the phone call is the most difficult part of the process. The telephone becomes an enemy. The phone call provides the very first opportunity to be rejected. The specter of such early and

Exhibit 8–5 Outline of the Solicitation Process

Task	Responsible Persons
❏ Enlist division chair (DC)	Staff and campaign chair
❏ Rate prospects	Staff and volunteers
❏ Design division structure	Staff, consultant, division chair
❏ Enlist section leaders (SL) or team captains (TC)	Division chair
❏ Schedule division meetings	DC and Section leaders
1. Solicitor training meeting for DC/SLs/TCs	
2. Prospect selection meeting	
3. General solicitor training meeting	
4. Report meetings for DC/SLs/TCs	
❏ Enlist team captains	SLs
❏ Enlist solicitors	Team captains
❏ Plan prospect selection meeting	DC, SLs, and staff
1. Plan agenda	
2. Prepare prospect cards	
3. Assemble packets for solicitors	
4. Prepare speakers	
5. Prepare room	
6. Send reminder notice	
❏ Conduct prospect selection meeting	All
❏ Prepare proposal letters	Staff
❏ Plan solicitor training meeting	DC, SLs, and staff
1. Plan agenda	
2. Arrange for room set-up and refreshments	
3. Send reminder notices	
4. Prepare speakers	
5. Enlist consultant as trainer	
6. Organize campaign material for solicitors	
❏ Conduct solicitor training meeting	All
❏ Prepare and send final proposal letters	Staff
❏ Solicit campaign volunteers	DC, SLs, and TCs
❏ Solicit proposals	Solicitors
❏ Track solicitation progress	SLs, TCs, and staff
❏ Conduct report meetings	SLs, TCs, and staff
❏ Close all open-ended solicitations	SLs, TCs, and staff
❏ Thank volunteers	TCs, campaign chair, and staff
❏ Thank donors	Solicitors, campaign chair, and executive director
❏ Report success	Staff

summary rejection is at least as bad as the fear of any rejection that might come later. Indeed, many volunteers are so afraid of the initial phone contact that they sabotage the process and aren't even conscious of what they are doing. Take, for example, the volunteer who calls a prospect every day at exactly the same time though receiving no answer to any call. Or the volunteer who calls the prospect's work number in the evening. Or the volunteer who learns that it is a wrong number but somehow fails to take the initiative to get the right number. An anxious volunteer is perfectly capable of feeling justified in believing that every reasonable effort has been made but that the prospect just couldn't be reached.

More courageous solicitors overcome their initial panic and contact their prospects on the phone. Effective phone callers practice four strategies that make their calls successful.

1. The caller assumes that the donor will say yes.
2. The caller hears only what is actually said and neither embellishes nor reads into the conversation negative connotations stemming from the solicitor's own anxiety.
3. The caller always listens attentively and validates whatever the prospect says.
4. The caller keeps the initiative, suggesting dates and times for a meeting or asking for a better time to call back.

Read more on setting up the call in "Setting Up the Major Gift Meeting" (Klein, 1990).

Exhibit 8–6 Responsibilities of a Team Captain for a Business Division

---

Goal of the Business Division
The Business Division of the Day Care Center Campaign is charged with raising $250,000 by soliciting 140 identified area businesses.

Description of Tasks
Prospect Type: Area Financial Institutions
The task of the financial instituion team within the business division is to:
- ◆ review and evaluate the list of 28 currently identified financial institutions
- ◆ add financial institutions that may have been left off the list but may be deemed good prospects
- ◆ enlist people to solicit the financial institutions (approximately one solicitor per five institutions)
- ◆ solicit the financial institutions

Requirements
1. Attend one meeting of team captains to review and evaluate prospect lists.
2. Enlist team members (solicitors), each of whom will visit five prospects.
3. Attend one meeting with team members to learn about the project and select prospect cards.
4. Attend one solicitor training meeting.
5. Solicit team members.
6. Maintain contact with team members during the solicitation period.
7. Attend two report sessions during the solicitation period.
8. Complete unfinished solicitations.
9. Attend wrap-up meeting of the business division.
10. Make a financial contribution to the campaign.

Anticipated Timing and Duration of Business Division: March 1, 1996–May 30, 1996

Effective phone callers also know that it is not the end of the world if a prospect says no. Indeed, the expectation is that it takes two to five or more prospects to bring in a single gift, and experienced solicitors know that their personal worth does not ride on the success of each and every solicitation.

The telephone can be a trap. Successful solicitors phone only to make the appointment, and they do not let themselves be drawn into discussing the contribution over the phone. They hold out instead for a face-to-face meeting that will be set up specifically for the purpose of discussing the project. Lunch is generally not a great time to solicit someone. If the solicitation must be combined with a social call, the solicitor should meet early to get the business accomplished first and only afterward go for lunch or dinner.

Preparation

Gather information. Once the meeting date has been set, a solicitor will benefit by doing some homework before meeting the prospect. Solicitors should gather as much information as possible about the person being solicited. Often a few informal conversations with friends will provide valuable information to add to that provided by the organization. Before making the call, the solicitor should review all available information. What values are important to the prospect? How do those values relate to the project? What specific factors in the prospect's life are likely to provide a bridge to the project?

Check the amount. Because most solicitations are preceded by a proposal letter suggesting that the prospect consider a gift of a specific amount, the solicitor should review the letter to make sure that the dollar amount that has been suggested remains clearly in mind.

Review personal commitment. Successful solicitors make their gifts to a campaign before they solicit anyone else. They understand their own reasons for supporting the campaign and are willing and ready to share them with the prospect. Often, personal stories are the most compelling parts of the solicitation process. Not only do they reveal something about the solicitor that helps bridge the distance between the solicitor and the prospect but such a story might also reflect a specific aspect of the project in a new light.

Practice making the case. It is helpful to practice stating the case for the project before meeting with the prospect. Spouses, friends, or staff members make good audiences. It is not uncommon for someone to try stating the case three, four, or even more times before it becomes comfortable. Gradually, through practice, one learns what can be omitted and what is critical to the solicitation.

Exhibit 8–7 Sample Solicitor Tasks

Responsibilities of a Solicitor
1. Attend one meeting on March 20 from 4:00–5:30 P.M. to obtain background information and select prospect cards.
2. Attend a meeting on April 10 from 4:00–6:00 P.M. to review proposal letters and become a trained solicitor.
3. Solicit five prospects between April 15, 1996 and June 1, 1996.
4. Report results of solicitations to team captains during the solicitation period.
5. Deliver completed pledge cards to the team captain or to the development director by June 15.
6. Make a financial contribution to the campaign.

The Solicitation Meeting

Provide time for the dust to settle. Solicitation meetings often begin with general conversation about issues of common interest. This provides a period during which both parties can absorb information about the other person and the setting before bringing their attention to the task at hand. A solicitation call is not a social visit, however, and the solicitor is responsible for turning the conversation in due course to business.

Ask questions and listen. Without a doubt, asking questions and listening actively are the two most important skills of an effective solicitor. Before making a presentation on behalf of the organization and asking for the gift, effective solicitors draw out their prospects by asking open-ended questions that invite the prospect to express his or her values, opinions, hopes, and concerns. During this period, the solicitor turns the conversation to the project and then asks the prospect about his or her involvement, attitudes, and feelings about the organization or the project. Often prospects will articulate the reasons for their interest, thus laying the groundwork for discussing their contribution. During this discussion, the solicitor will also have an opportunity to answer any questions that the prospect may have about the organization and the project.

Make the case. Often, the questioning and listening process leads quite naturally to the case for making a gift to the project. In the best instances, the prospect

will make the case himself and the solicitor will have only to follow up by asking for the gift and organizing the details. In other instances, the prospect will not know enough about the project and will want to learn more. The solicitor then has an opportunity to summarize the specifics of the project and the campaign. This should take no more than ten minutes.

Ask for the gift. Although the gift has in a sense already been requested in the proposal letter, the solicitor is responsible for restating the request. The dollar amount or range in the letter is a starting point for the discussion. The prospect may of course choose to give more or less. The solicitor might say something like, "I know you have received a letter from the campaign chair asking you to consider a gift of $10,000. Would you consider making a gift of that amount?"

After making the request, seasoned solicitors know not to say anything more until the prospect responds. It is tempting to continue speaking, but no matter how long the response takes, it is the donor's place to respond, not the solicitor's to interrupt.

Once again, active listening is all-important. The solicitor must listen carefully to the donor's response and hear accurately what he or she is really saying. It is not unusual for an inexperienced solicitor to be so anxious about the response that he or she hears a negative answer no matter what the prospect has really said.

When the prospect does respond, the solicitor must acknowledge the response positively and constructively. If the prospect says yes, the solicitor must express thanks appropriately and explore ways of finalizing the gift. If the prospect says no, the solicitor might suggest a different gift level or an alternative way of helping the campaign. If the prospect delays the decision, the solicitor must maintain the initiative and follow up again and again if necessary until the donor has either made a gift or has said no.

It is not unusual for the solicitation process to require several contacts between the donor and the solicitor. Solicitors should always remember that their job is to help the donor make a decision about the gift level. Both yes and no are appropriate answers, and solicitors have accomplished their goals when the donor's intentions are resolved either way.

The solicitor must determine how to proceed further before closing the solicitation meeting. If the solicitor receives a signed pledge form during the meeting, the donor should be informed exactly how the organization will follow up. If the prospect postpones a decision, the solicitor should specify a date and time when the donor will be contacted for a decision.

Follow Through

As soon as possible after each solicitation visit, the solicitor should write a thank-you note to the prospect, whether or not a contribution was made, and complete a solicitation call report form for the development office, informing them of the results of the call. Most campaigns provide the solicitors with report forms to help them capture the most important information. See the sample report form in Exhibit 8–8.

Other Considerations

Soliciting in teams often strengthens the solicitation process. Sometimes a staff member who is intimately familiar with the specifics of the project will join a volunteer who has a strong relationship with the donor. Together, they are likely to be able to make a stronger statement than either of them could individually.

This team approach must be planned carefully in advance. The timing and strategy of the meeting should be well considered. Who will cover what material? Who will ask for the gift? Who will ask questions? Who will present the project? And who will close the meeting and determine the follow-up steps? If these issues are explored and discussed ahead of time, and if each person actually stays with the agenda, the team approach can be excellent, and it often reduces the intimacy and intensity of

> *Effective thank-you notes say something that is authentic and that relates specifically to the encounter with the prospect.*

the interaction, thereby lowering the solicitors' anxieties. Care should be taken, however, that the soliciting team not gang up on the prospect. The prospect must be an active participant in the solicitation process, and the solicitors *must* leave room for the prospect to express his or her thoughts and ideas. If the prospect's role is brushed aside in favor of the choreography of the soliciting team, this approach will weaken rather than strengthen the request.

A good location for the solicitation meeting is often at the organization, where it should be preceded with a tour or a demonstration of some sort. The solicitation meeting itself should take place in a quiet and private meeting room. If the organization does not have an appropriate conference room or if such a room is not available at the right time, a tour or demonstration might be scheduled independently from the solicitation meeting.

If an on-site meeting is not possible, then other suitable options would be either a neutral location like a quiet club or the prospect's office or home. Although the latter may provide clues to the prospect's family and interests, it can be a problematic venue if the meeting is frequently interrupted by secretaries, telephone calls, or children. In the final analysis, the best place for a solicitation meeting will depend on what works best for the prospect and what best matches his or her style.

Solicitor Training

Soliciting gifts takes courage. Development directors should develop a sympathetic understanding of the fears that swirl around the gift solicitation process. Understanding and acknowledging the discomfort that is involved and celebrating the extraordinary courage that solicitation requires encourages solicitors far more effectively than simply telling them not to be afraid.

While effective solicitor training does not eradicate fears, it does prepare solicitors to solicit gifts in spite of their anxieties. Training sessions provide a safe environment in which solicitors are able to learn and to practice their art. Because most people learn best when they participate actively in the learning process, the best solicitor training provides every solicitor with opportunities to find the right words and to practice the solicitation process. By practicing in a safe environment, volunteers begin to find the words, phrases, and approaches that ring true for them, and as that happens, they develop the confidence to help them overcome their fears.

Exhibit 8–8 Sample Call Report Form

Solicitor's Call Report Form

Prospect name: _____

Contact: Phone call _____ Date _____

Meeting 1 _____ Date _____

Meeting 2 _____ Date _____

Prospect's attitude toward hospice: _____

_____

_____

Prospect's attitude toward the center: _____

_____

_____

Amount suggested: _____ Amount committed: _____

Type of gift: check_____ stock_____ other _____

Payment preference: number of years_____ payments/year _____

Other areas for involvement: _____

_____

Next steps: _____

_____

Solicitor's name: _____ **Date:** _____

Send, phone, or fax to: Susan Jones, Hospice of Aspen County
P.O. Box 555, Anywhere, PA 17606-5179
Telephone 717-555-1234   Fax 717-555-4321

Before describing effective approaches to solicitor training, a reminder of just what it is that solicitors fear may be helpful.

Fear of Fund Raising

It is rare to find a person who is not afraid to ask others for money. Even those who solicit gifts year after year have to resist the natural anxiety that comes from putting oneself on the line.

Although it doesn't make the fear disappear, an understanding and acceptance of the many facets of these fears helps one to act in spite of or even because of that fear. In soliciting gifts, there is much that is enlightening to learn about oneself that transfers to many other endeavors in life.

Perhaps the most common fear is that of personal rejection. People confuse the word *no* with the phrase, "I don't like you." Most people find it hard to separate a request on behalf of an organization from a request for personal approval. And to be fair, a prospect's sense of

guilt at not giving can sometimes be projected onto the solicitor himself.

Many solicitors are afraid that they don't know enough about the project and the organization to do a good job. They worry that they will present the case incorrectly or unconvincingly, that they will not know the answers to questions that the prospect raises, and that they will respond in a way that loses the gift. Soliciting is indeed a heavy burden, and although it seldom requires as much learning as the solicitor might fear, it is easy to understand the concerns of volunteers who are only occasionally involved in the solicitation process.

Most people are afraid to fail—we tie our self-esteem to success. And as has been discussed earlier in this book, capital campaigns are designed to incorporate a great deal of failure. With only one gift expected from four solicitations, three of those four solicitations *should* fail! Of course such a lighthearted attitude toward failure may be fine in the campaign planning phase, but those who solicit those three prospects who decide not to give are often left feeling as though they have contributed to the failure of the project rather than to its success.

In soliciting gifts, volunteers must not only put forward the general case for the organization and the project, but they are actually required to ask their prospects for specific amounts of money. For those who grew up in a society in which discussion of money is considered much more personal than a discussion of, say, sex, it is no wonder that the solicitor fears embarrassment.

The experience of soliciting is not unlike that of attending a concert that one has particularly enjoyed and being the first to rise during the applause. The potential embarrassment of not being joined in a standing ovation keeps many a concertgoer from rising early no matter how much they liked the concert. The act of initiating a standing ovation is implicitly an invitation to others to join you in supporting the performer. And if they don't join in, then the inference is that they disapprove of your sentiment and of the action you took.

Asking for money requires similar courage. One takes a stand on behalf of an organization and through the solicitation process invites others to do the same. This public commitment on behalf of a specific project can be especially difficult if one has lingering reservations about the project—and it is a rare project indeed about which one has no reservations!

Solicitor-Training Workshops

Solicitor training is a small but important aspect of capital campaigns, and as with many parts of this complex process, there are many ways to train solicitors. Usually the solicitor training is designed by the consultant and/or the development staff, whose approach reflects their specific style as well as the logistical realities of assembling the solicitors at one place and one time. For community-based organizations, logistics are relatively simple, and the solicitors can be expected to attend a training workshop lasting two to three hours. If the solicitors are traveling across the country, however, they will be likely to attend the workshops only if the workshops are embedded in a larger schedule of events.

The workshops will also vary depending on the number of participants. If volunteer training is done division by division or even section by section, each training workshop may have no more than fifteen or twenty participants. Although that is an ideal size, it is possible to design an effective workshop for fifty or more people.

Consultants have varying opinions about the style and length of the training process. Some believe that volunteer training is best and most simply accomplished by a lecture-style motivational presentation delivered at the campaign kickoff. Others believe that every volunteer solicitor should attend a workshop of two to three hours that both presents the necessary information and actively engages the volunteers. Although each approach has been used successfully, the latter is probably better.

A Solicitation Workshop That Works

The solicitation workshop outlined here is designed for eighteen people. It should be moderated by the consultant or development director and should include people who have extensive solicitation experience and also those who can illustrate issues that may arise with real-life stories and examples.

Duration: two hours

Room Arrangements: one large oval or rectangular table to seat everyone, one flip chart at the front of the room, and enough space to form six seating clusters of three chairs each.

Meeting Agenda: The specifics of the agenda will vary from group to group and project to project, but the following agenda may be adapted and expanded to fit any training workshop.

- welcome and thank you
- introductions
- objectives of the meeting
- presentation on how to solicit gifts
- finding one's own words
- practicing the solicitation process
- objections and responses
- key points to remember
- next steps

1. Welcome and Thank You (5 minutes)

The very beginning of any meeting has an import far beyond the brief time allotted to it. The opener sets the stage. It makes volunteers feel warm and welcome or anxious and put off. Even a simple, "Hello" and "Thank you for coming" from the campaign chair should be planned to convey excitement and urgency as well as to highlight the importance of the volunteers in completing the campaign.

2. Introductions (15 minutes)

Many of the solicitors who are attending the training session will not know one another. A simple introductory exercise can ease the initial tension and help the solicitors get acquainted. The participants should be asked to introduce themselves by giving their names, perhaps telling a little-known fact about themselves, or relating one positive fund-raising experience that they have had.

An amiable and confident volunteer should be selected and asked to begin the introductions. The process then continues around the table. (Selecting a specific person to begin the introduction process and providing the order of participation works best early in a meeting. Later on in a meeting one might choose a less directive strategy.)

3. Objectives of the Meeting (5 minutes)

The objectives of the training meeting will include:

- helping each volunteer understand how to solicit gifts
- helping solicitors find and practice their own solicitation styles and words
- identifying likely objections and appropriate responses
- clarifying the next steps for the solicitors

If the solicitor training is being conducted in the context of a larger process, both the agenda and the objectives will have to be expanded to accommodate the additional campaign tasks.

4. Presentation on How to Solicit Gifts (20 minutes)

The consultant and/or the development staff will present material on the solicitation process. Everyone organizes this information somewhat differently and uses different handouts. However, a discussion of the following elements is essential.

- understanding why donors give
- setting up the meeting
- preparing for the meeting
- conducting the meeting
- handling objections
- defining success
- following up

5. Finding One's Own Words (15 minutes)

This part of the meeting begins the participatory section of the training. While everyone is sitting around the table, one index card is distributed to each volunteer, who is asked to take five minutes to write down two or three sentences that best describe his or her own reasons for supporting the project. After the five minutes are up, invite people to volunteer their reasons while the facilitator writes them down on the flip chart. This process will give the group a look at the many reasons others have for supporting the project, while clarifying and putting words to their own reasons. The newsprint sheets are then taped to the wall where they will remain visible during the role-playing exercises.

6. Practicing the Solicitation Process (30 minutes)

The solicitors are divided into six groups of three each. It is often simplest for the participants to move away from the table to form clusters of chairs. Each group should assign the roles of a solicitor, a prospect, and an observer. The prospect may assume whatever identity he or she chooses, including his or her own. Each solicitor is given five minutes to solicit the prospect. At the conclusion of each five-minute period the observer comments on the process, highlighting what worked and

suggesting other approaches if there were difficulties. This process is repeated three times so that everyone has had the opportunity to play all three roles.

7. Handling Objections (15 minutes)

The full group reassembles around the table and each group is asked to name the objections to making a gift that arose from their solicitation process. Then the full group reviews appropriate responses to each of the most commonly encountered objections. The facilitator captures the objections and responses on the flip chart.

8. Key Points to Remember (10 minutes)

Following the participatory exercises, the consultant or facilitator summarizes the solicitation process by presenting a simple and clear list of key points to remember. These are usually prepared in advance both on newsprint at the front of the room and on handouts for the volunteers to take away.

9. Next Steps (5 minutes)

The training usually concludes by reminding the volunteers of what they should do next, reviewing the solicitation timetable, and answering any questions.

Although it may be preferable to divide a large group into two or more sessions, the workshop that is outlined above can be adapted quite simply for a larger group. For an expanded session to accommodate fifty or more people, it is necessary to redesign the room arrangement, allow approximately an extra half hour, and streamline the participatory processes so that people share their ideas with subgroups rather than the entire group.

The best arrangement to accommodate a large number of people is a room large enough for round tables with seating for six persons at each. The participants are asked to seat themselves at the tables as they enter the room. The facilitator stands in front of the room, and chairs are placed around the tables so that everyone has a view of the facilitator. The meeting proceeds in the same order as with the smaller group, but all of the participatory portions—the introductions, the index-card exercise, and the role-playing—are centered around each table. For the section of the meeting that is devoted to identifying objections, each table is asked to come up with two or three objections that occurred the most frequently during the role-playing and to share them with the entire group.

Misconceptions about Participatory Training

Although all the studies highlight active participation as a vital component of effective adult training, some people worry that their board members or volunteers will resist the process. However, experience has shown that well-designed role-playing exercises actually energize even the crustiest of volunteers. Again and again, people who have taken part in effective participatory training sessions return from their solicitation calls grateful that they had the opportunity to try out their solicitation techniques in advance.

Special Techniques for Soliciting Corporations and Foundations

Soliciting foundations and corporations is similar in many ways to the process of soliciting individuals. They do, however, require some special attention.

Foundations

In a campaign, development staff will be responsible for securing funding from two types of foundations. Most common for community-based organizations, however, are the foundations that support only local projects. Raising money from this type of foundation is similar to raising money from individuals. In both cases, decisions are made by people who live and work in the community, who may recognize the need that the organization is addressing through the campaign, and who may have first-hand knowledge and experience with the organization. Just as with soliciting gifts from individuals, personal contacts with the donors are invaluable in these settings. These foundations include community foundations and family foundations.

Community foundations support only local needs. Their funding comes primarily from bequests and memorial funds, though they may conduct annual fund drives as well. Grants given by these organizations are usually determined by committee. The foundations often have specific funding guidelines, application forms, and submission deadlines.

Family foundations often support local needs as well. Compared to the large national foundations, they have little bureaucracy, and the trustees are usually members of the family.

To approach these organizations successfully requires research about the funding patterns and guidelines of each as well as an understanding of the contacts and links that exist between the organization and the foundation. Volunteers are often helpful in unearthing information about these foundations that will help the staff develop the best strategy for approaching each.

Staff members should request a copy of the funder's current guidelines, proposal-submission requirements, and a list of recently awarded grants if they are available. If, as is often the case with small family foundations, there is no published information, either a staff member or a volunteer should contact someone at the foundation, present a brief explanation of the project, and ask whether their foundation would be interested

in receiving a proposal. In most cases, the foundation contact will provide clear and appropriate instructions.

Corporations

Some local corporations also require a special approach. Many corporations give to organizations that serve their employees and in which their employees are involved. Organizations that think ahead often invite key corporate employees to serve on their boards well in advance of a campaign. Sometimes an organization will involve an employee of the corporation on the campaign planning committee. It will also help an organization to receive funding from a corporation if it can document the number of employees who have benefited from its services.

Securing corporate contributions depends on knowing who makes the funding decisions. There are several ways to obtain such information. Some corporations publish giving guidelines that provide a clear outline of the decision-making process and a list of corporate officers who are involved in the decisions. In some cases, however, this information is not accurate or up-to-date. Wise organizations develop personal contacts with the management of the corporation and use those contacts to learn the realities of how funding in that organization is decided.

Organizations are often disappointed to learn that corporations with manufacturing plants in their community are not likely to be generous supporters. Unless an organization is headquartered in a community, funding for a substantial gift is likely to be funneled through the plant manager, who selects the projects that he or she will support and then submits them to corporate headquarters. The plant manager is often the gatekeeper for gifts, but often has little say over decisions made at headquarters.

Submit a Proposal

Rarely will a foundation or corporation make a grant without receiving a written proposal from the organization. In its simplest form, a proposal outlines the project, gives the funder background information on the organization and why it is engaged in the campaign, describes how a gift from the funder will enable the organization to serve its constituency better, provides a budget, and describes who is in charge of implementing the project. In essence, a proposal is a carefully tailored adaptation of the case for support.

A prospective funder will want one of two types of proposals. Many small foundations and corporations require only a two- to three-page letter containing a description of the project. While having to write two to three pages may at first glance seem much easier than having to write ten or twelve, it is often a more difficult task, since a great deal of information must be condensed effectively and compellingly into a small amount of space. A development officer must bring to bear all of his or her writing and editing talent on the project, since two to three pages means exactly that and no more.

Other corporations or foundations may want to see a full proposal, which may include many of the following nine components.

1. A brief executive summary describing the request and the case for supporting the project
2. Information about the organization's history, background, mission, and services
3. The reason for the request
4. The project's impact on the community
5. A plan for evaluating the effectiveness of the project
6. A project budget and timetable
7. A listing of the key personnel who are involved in the project and a summary of their qualifications
8. The most recent audited financial statement
9. A copy of the IRS letter granting the organization its 501(c)(3) status

If an organization has done an effective job of preparing its case for support, preparing a proposal should not be difficult. If the organization has hired a campaign consultant, the consultant may be helpful in reviewing and critiquing the proposal.

Solicit the Gift

Some foundations and corporations welcome the opportunity to meet with volunteers and staff members who represent the organization to learn more about the project and to discuss a potential contribution. Others prefer that all communication be handled in writing. The organization should apprise itself of the preferred approach in each case.

Follow Up

Response procedures vary from funder to funder. Some corporations encourage applicants to follow up their proposals with meetings and phone calls; others prefer that applicants not contact them. Whatever the preferred procedure, a development officer must be prepared to provide additional information to the funder if asked for it, to arrange for particular individuals to attend a meeting if it is requested, and to be persistent in following up with a funder who has not responded in a timely manner.

If funds are granted, the development director also has the responsibility of making sure that the funder is thanked promptly and appropriately. Some funders prefer that their names not appear on any lists, while others want it plastered over everything. Representatives from the foundation or corporation should receive institutional newsletters, invitations to special events, and most importantly, once the grant period is over, a report on how the grant has been used and its impact on the community. This is one of the most important ways to build a strong relationship between the funder and the organization—funders appreciate knowing how their money has been spent.

If the funder denies the request for a donation, an organization should make the effort to find out why. The volunteer can talk "off the record" with the foundation or corporate contact, or the development officer might call the funder and politely and tactfully ask why it was turned down and inquire about whether the organization might submit another request in the future.

The success of a campaign rests on its ability to secure major gifts. While the concept of major-gift fund raising can be daunting to those who have never dreamed of asking another person for a large gift, understanding the motivation behind the donor and the solicitor can help an organization use its volunteers in highly effective and successful ways. Armed with a broad understanding of the organization's mission, the campaign's purpose, and the elements of the solicitation process, solicitors can feel confident about their own ability to ask successfully for a major gift. Indeed, as a solicitor becomes empowered by affirmative responses and learns from the negative ones, he or she may even grow to believe that having the opportunity to share a commitment to an organization with another person and then asking for a gift to support its work may be one of the most personally rewarding, and perhaps even enjoyable, of experiences.

For more information on corporate and foundation fund raising, see *Corporate and Foundation Fund Raising: A Complete Guide from the Inside*, by Eugene Scanlan, another book in this series.

References

Klein, Kim. 1990. Setting up the major gift meeting. *Grass Roots Fund-raising Journal* 9 (June): 1–6.
Prince, Russ Alan, and Karen Maru File. 1994. *The Seven Faces of Philanthropy*. San Francisco: Jossey-Bass.
Wyman, Ken. 1993. *Face to Face: How to Get Bigger Donations from Very Generous People*. Written for the Canadian federal government's Voluntary Action Program, available through Ken Wyman & Associates, 64B Shuter Street, Suite 200, Toronto, ON, Canada, M5B 1B1; 416-363-2926.

Chapter 9

Telephone and Direct Mail in the Capital Campaign

Chapter Outline

- Raising Money through Telephone Solicitation
- Organizing the Volunteer Phonathon
- Direct Mail and the Capital Campaign
- Simple Reminders about Direct Mail

In this chapter, we return to the table of gifts, the campaign's road map. While chapter 8 considered gifts at the upper levels, in this chapter we address the solicitation mechanisms often used to raise money from the lower levels of campaign giving. Using as a model one of the example campaigns described in chapters 7 and 8 with a goal of $1,000,000, we will explore the best ways of soliciting donors capable of giving $500 or less to the campaign. As that table of gifts (reproduced in Exhibit 9–1) shows, the campaign will require 300 gifts of $500 and a great many gifts of under $500 to raise the $225,000 needed from this giving category.

An organization's ability to muster volunteers for personal solicitation will determine how many prospects will be personally solicited in the course of the campaign. Whatever that number, the remaining people on the prospect list who were not solicited face-to-face must be given an opportunity to make a campaign gift. Ideally, for this campaign to raise $1,000,000, all gifts of $1,000 or more will be solicited face-to-face. This leaves another 500 to 700 gifts of smaller amounts to be solicited in other, less personal ways.

The last two rows represent the lower-level gifts that will most likely be solicited by telephone and mail. This chapter reviews effective strategies and techniques for raising money for capital campaigns through these less personal, but important, techniques.

Raising Money through Telephone Solicitation

After the personalized proposal letter has been followed by a face-to-face solicitation—the most personal and effective approach to solicitation—telephone solicitation is the next best way to solicit lower-end donors.

Although some people find telephone solicitation intrusive, if organized correctly, telephone solicitations can provide an extremely effective and rewarding way to reach donors who would otherwise be relegated to the mail.

Carol Blanton's article, "The Pitfalls and the Promise of Telephone Fundraising" (1994), describes the results of a test that was conducted by the Nature Conservancy of California to measure the effectiveness of telephone fund raising against the response rate of a two-letter direct-mail appeal. The results show telephone fund raising to have ten times the response rate and less than half the cost of the direct-mail appeal! Although this test was carried out in the context of an annual giving program, it is consistent with results that the authors have seen in phonathons conducted to solicit lower-level gifts for capital campaigns. Through telephone solicitation, an organization can significantly increase the returns from a group of donors, both in the number of gifts and the amount per gift.

While it would be wonderful if a trained volunteer could personally solicit every prospective donor, the large number of prospects usually makes such an approach impractical. Various combinations of mail and telephone solicitation produce results that directly correlate to the extent of the personal relationship developed between the solicitor and the prospect. Yielding the highest returns, of course, are personal solicitations preceded by a personalized proposal letter. The next most effective approach is a proposal letter in conjunction with a telephone call from someone who is known and well respected by the prospect. Less effective is just a phone call from a friend, and so on down the effectiveness ladder. The following list shows the order of effectiveness of various types of solicitation combinations.

- proposal plus face-to-face solicitation from a respected friend or acquaintance
- face-to-face solicitation from a stranger
- phone solicitation by respected friend or acquaintance
- phone solicitation by stranger

Exhibit 9–1 Gifts Needed to Raise $1,000,000 (for a mature organization with a broad donor base)

Number of Gifts	Amount of Each Gift	Amount from Level	Cumulative Amount	Cumulative Percent of Total
1	$100,000	$100,000	$100,000	10%
1	50,000	50,000	150,000	15%
4	25,000	100,000	250,000	25%
10	10,000	100,000	350,000	35%
25	5,000	125,000	475,000	47%
60	2,500	150,000	625,000	62%
150	1,000	150,000	775,000	77%
300	500	150,000	925,000	92%
many	under $500	$75,000	1,000,000	100%

Number of Gifts: 551+

- mailed appeal with personal note from friend or acquaintance
- mailed appeal with no note

Telephone Solicitation and the Capital Campaign

Many organizations regularly raise money through direct-mail solicitations, but they resist telephone solicitation. Not only is organizing telephone solicitation more demanding than assembling a mail campaign, but many people are so bombarded by telephone sales calls that board members and staff hate to burden their donors with yet another dinnertime phone call. However, prospects do make contributions as a result of telephone solicitations, particularly if they feel that their opinions are being heard and their questions are being answered by knowledgeable and informed volunteers.

Telephone fund raising serves an important function in a capital campaign. It provides an opportunity for the organization to make personal contact with the most likely remaining prospects who weren't solicited earlier in the campaign. Since the phonathon takes place near the end of the campaign's public phase, most of the organization's prospects have read about and heard about the campaign through the newspapers, on television, or from friends. Since they have been donors to the organization in the past, these people may actually be waiting to be solicited. Telephone fund raising gives these donors the opportunity to speak directly with someone who represents the organization to learn more about the campaign, ask questions, and make a campaign gift.

Volunteers vs. Paid Solicitors

Telephone solicitation in the later phases of a capital campaign is most commonly organized through a phonathon, in which volunteers gather in one location with many phone lines to make telephone calls on behalf of the campaign. Some phonathons last for three evenings, some as long as a week, some even longer.

Phonathons are a tidy way to complete the best remaining prospect solicitations. Many volunteers who feel intimidated by the idea of making face-to-face solicitations are willing to participate in phonathons. The phonathon process is more controlled, and many volunteers find it to be a comfortable way to help out in the campaign.

Phonathons often return more than money to the campaign. Through conversations with its constituency, an organization can get immediate feedback on its programs and learn firsthand about the prospects' interests and ideas.

Rather than using the staff time and energy that are needed to coordinate a phonathon, some organizations hire a telemarketing firm to conduct the telephone solicitations. Large organizations with tens of thousands of prospects use them regularly; small-to-midsized organizations must carefully weigh the costs and benefits of employing a telefundraising firm. For organizations with unsolicited prospect lists that are smaller than 6,000, using a telefundraising firm is probably not cost-effective.

Volunteer-staffed phonathons have three important advantages over those run by paid telemarketers.

1. Volunteers have a genuine and often heartfelt connection to the organization and enjoy sharing their stories about it with others.
2. Volunteers may also know the people whom they are calling, increasing the chances of obtaining a pledge.
3. Volunteer-staffed phonathons cost a fraction of that of hiring a telefundraising firm.

Organizing the Volunteer Phonathon

Determining Whom to Call

At this late stage in a capital campaign, phonathons are used to reach the most likely prospects among former donors who have not yet been solicited for the campaign. Often these donors will number in the thousands. Two or three hundred names may be those of individuals who were selected for face-to-face solicitation but whose cards were not selected. The rest will be names of donors who have given before but who were not targeted for personal solicitations. Although most organizations also have long lists of constituents who are not donors, these people are not usually included in campaign phonathons.

Lists of donors still to be contacted should be organized into categories ranging from most likely to least likely donors. Some organizations color code the prospect forms according to these categories so that the callers can easily see who should be contacted first.

Once the phonathon list has been determined, the staff must find the phone numbers to match the names. Some organizations regularly gather and update phone numbers from checks, pledge cards, or other information sources, and already have telephone numbers for the majority of their donors. Other organizations may have no phone numbers at all. Some organizations contract with an outside agency to provide phone numbers. Others have staff members and volunteers who are willing to look them up in the directory. On average, an organization will be able to find phone numbers for approximately 60 percent of the names on its list. The remainder of the prospects will have to be solicited by mail.

Recruiting Volunteers

Organizations are often able to recruit excellent phonathon volunteers during the concluding phases of a campaign. By this time, many people have solicited gifts face-to-face and have become more comfortable with the solicitation process. There are also many people who will agree to help because they are aware that they have not helped earlier and they are safe in the knowledge that their time commitment will be limited. The goal is near and people are often willing to sign on to help for the final push.

Anyone who is committed to the organization and is able to use the telephone can be an effective phonathon volunteer. Often board members, those who volunteer in other aspects of the organization's programs, staff members, professionals who have played a role in developing the campaign project (architects, graphic designers, attorneys, contractors, and so forth), and people who have volunteered for earlier phases of the campaign are willing to sign up for a calling session.

Campaign phonathons are often staff driven, although if the staff member plans far enough ahead, engaging the help of several volunteers may broaden and in some cases strengthen the phonathon. Volunteers may help the development staff member find an appropriate space, identify and enlist phonathon volunteers, and provide refreshments and prizes to motivate the callers. It is not unusual by the late stages in the campaign, when volun-

teers and staff members are weary, for a staff member not to rely on a volunteer committee to organize the phonathon. Some organizations even choose to hire a part-time staff person just to plan and coordinate the phonathon.

In any case, each calling session will require one set of volunteers to make the calls and another set of clerical volunteers to collect the paperwork, write notes, address envelopes, and keep track of gifts and pledges for the calling session. Generally, more callers and support people than needed should be recruited for each calling session to provide the necessary leeway for the two individuals who invariably don't show up.

Although there are many ways to recruit phonathon volunteers, many organizations recruit two phonathon chairs whose job it is to recruit the volunteers. The staff provides them with a list of those who have volunteered in the past, and the chairs set up the calling teams by dividing up the lists and contacting prospective volunteers. If time permits, it is also effective to circulate sign-up sheets showing the dates and times of each session with a blank space for each volunteer who is needed. The sign-up sheets might be circulated at board meetings, staff meetings, volunteer meetings, and campaign meetings. The staff should then thank each person who signs up for a slot and confirm their dates and times in writing. Staff members also often send a reminder notice or make a reminder call just prior to the date of the calling session.

Determining the Duration

The size and shape of the phonathon emerges from the number of solicitations to be made. We know from experience that on average, one volunteer can make approximately fifteen calls per hour. We also know that the average prospect will need to be called twice before being reached. So, if the staff has identified 750 names of people who should be called during the phonathon, the phonathon should be designed to make 1500 calls. In addition, most phonathons schedule calling sessions that last two hours, with an additional hour for training and distributing materials. Therefore, if each volunteer can make thirty calls in one calling session (15 calls × 2 hours = 30 calls per calling session) and if the organization has access to a good location with ten phone lines and ten desks, then the phonathon will require approximately five

---

A basic phonathon planning guide is that one volunteer makes an average of fifteen calls per hour, and each prospect will have to be called twice. Phonathon sessions are usually three hours long—one hour for training and two hours for calling.

calling sessions (1500 calls ÷ 300 calls per session = 5 calling sessions).

Setting Dates and Times

Campaign phonathons must be scheduled for just after the completion of all the face-to-face solicitations and so as not to conflict with the organization's regular annual giving program. Seasoned phonathon planners find the calling response rate best on midweek evenings, although some organizations also find Sunday evenings productive. A long phonathon, one requiring six or eight calling sessions, may be scheduled over two or even three weeks, with two or three calling sessions per week. Smaller phonathons are best scheduled during a one-week period to simplify the mailing of pledge forms and follow-up letters to those who were not reached and to focus the energy of staff and volunteers.

Calling sessions are often scheduled between 6:00 PM and 9:00 PM. This gives the volunteers a chance to assemble, receive their materials and training, and begin making calls by 7:00 PM.

Finding a Suitable Location

A suitable phonathon location has approximately ten telephone lines and twelve or more desks or tables assembled in an open space. Although organizing a phonathon on site is most convenient, many small nonprofits do not have the requisite large open area nor the multiple phone lines and desks, so they must borrow other space. Banks and insurance companies often have such configurations and are willing to donate the use of their space, as do travel agencies and other businesses that rely on phone sales.

A central and open space for phonathons creates the right mood. When staff and volunteers are close enough to communicate easily with one another, they can generate a sense of excitement and camaraderie. As they make calls and begin to get results, they can easily share information, celebrate successes, and laugh together over difficult calls.

Sending a Prephonathon Mail Appeal

Many organizations send every prospect a letter approximately two weeks before the phonathon. The letter summarizes the case for support in one or two brief paragraphs, suggests a giving range that the prospect might consider, and lets the prospect know that a volunteer will be calling during the week of the phonathon.

Opinion varies on whether to make it easy for people to respond to the letter by sending a gift and preempting a phone call. In its favor is the fact that some people would like to make a contribution but resent phone calls. Against this practice is the fact that people are likely to give larger gifts if they can be actively engaged in a conversation about the project.

Preparing Supporting Materials

Supporting materials include:

- prospect information forms
- pledge forms and response envelopes
- scripts, talking points, and common questions
- completed-call folders
- instructions for clerical volunteers
- instructions for solicitors

Simple, well-organized, color-coded materials help clarify the phonathon volunteers' tasks. Some of the material may be adapted from the campaign material that has already been designed, but some pieces will have to be created specifically for the phonathon. All of the material should highlight the campaign theme and logo, thereby distinguishing it from the organization's annual giving solicitations.

Prospect information forms should provide a place for name, address, telephone number, and giving history, as well as information, if any, about the relationship between the prospect and the organization. This information should be incorporated into a larger document (8½" × 11" works well) that provides space for the volunteer to keep track of what transpired during the call and also to take notes. Some organizations are able to design the form directly on the computer and print out a form for each prospect. Others design a form with a space for prospect labels, and then duplicate the forms and add the labels. Copying these forms onto

---

Off to a Strong Start

After going back and forth on whether we should send the pledge form along with the letter we sent out before the phonathon, we finally decided that we'd send both a pledge form and a return envelope. We even put a P.S. on the letter, telling people that if they didn't want to be called, they should send a gift by return mail. I didn't know what to expect, but I sure didn't expect what happened. We sent the letters on Friday. By the following Tuesday, we had received more than $10,000 back, and before the beginning of the phonathon people had sent in nearly $20,000! This turned out to be one-quarter of the total phonathon gifts, and at least one donor thanked me personally for giving her the mail option.

—Development Director, Hospice

color-coded paper according to request level provides the callers with a simple way of knowing whom to ask for what amount.

Pledge forms should be large enough to permit a brief handwritten note from a volunteer. These notes are often added the night of the calling session and sent out the next day. To facilitate the process, a volunteer also writes out by hand the address on a campaign envelope. Unlike annual giving phonathons, campaign phonathons encourage people to make multiyear pledges. The pledge form must reflect this option. In addition, more organizations today are finding that their donors are happy to use their credit cards to make pledges. Although this option will cost the organization a small percentage of the pledge, it will also prevent unpaid pledges—all in all a good investment!

Scripts help some volunteers who feel most comfortable with some appropriate written words to guide them through the call. Others find a script limiting and stilted and prefer to find their own words. To accommodate all styles, volunteers should be presented with a script, as well as a set of talking points and a set of common objections and the responses to them. Because every volunteer is likely to feel most comfortable with the information placed prominently in front of them while they make their calls, a place-mat size sheet, with the information well organized on it in large type, provides background support for volunteers as they make their calls. In this larger format, the information does not get lost among the other sheets of paper. It fits well on a desk, and it can be read at a glance.

Folders for completed calls help keep volunteer callers from feeling inundated by paper. A system of color-coded file folders helps callers keep their prospect forms organized. One might, for example, give each volunteer four folders—a green one for *complete pledges*, a red one for *rejections*, a blue one for prospects who *need more time or information*, and a yellow one for prospects whom the caller was *unable to reach*.

Written instructions help volunteers digest the material before they begin calling and help clarify any questions that they might have. Although the instructions are also covered verbally during the training session, some people absorb information more effectively when it is also in writing.

Solicitor training should precede each calling period. Usually these training sessions take approximately 30 to 45 minutes and are conducted by the development director or phonathon coordinator. They incorporate the following three elements.

1. Review basic instructions. Discuss the specifics of telephone operation, location of rest rooms, goals for the evening, dinner schedule, process and procedures, and prizes.
2. Review the telephone solicitation process. Discuss how to make a phone solicitation, the case for support, the pledge period, using a script, listening, summarizing from talking points, responding to common objections, and asking for the gift.
3. Review material. Distribute packets to each volunteer and then review the material, giving specific instructions about capturing and managing information.

Motivating Volunteers

There is nothing like food to help make people feel welcome. Because most phonathons take place over the dinner hour, organizations often provide pizza or sandwiches or other simple sustenance. Many people also use prizes to encourage the volunteers. Often, one volunteer is assigned the task of "cheerleader," whose job it is to dole out encouragement and prizes. The prizes are sometimes silly and simple, sometimes larger and more serious. Prizes are given for getting the highest number of gifts and the lowest number of gifts, for getting the most dollars and for getting no dollars at all, for completing the most calls or being the most cheerful, and so forth.

The cheerleader circulates around the room to collect forms from completed calls. This keeps the paper process moving throughout the period. Some development directors find it helpful to keep a running tally of the evening's progress on a large board in a central location.

Following Through

A great deal of the follow-up information can be prepared by the support staff during the calling period. Notes can be written directly on pledge forms, addresses handwritten on mailing envelopes, return envelopes enclosed, and even postage affixed so that those who have made a pledge will receive their confirmation within two days. Names of prospects who couldn't be reached should be placed back in the pile of calls to be made for the next night.

From the office the next day, letters should be sent to individuals who declined to make a contribution, thanking them for their time and if necessary, addressing any concerns that they may have articulated during the con-

---

On the last night of the phonathon, it's a nice touch to have each phonathon volunteer leave a thank-you note to the person whose desk they used.

versation with the caller. Thank-you notes should also be written to the volunteers, giving them a preliminary report of their accomplishments.

At the conclusion of the entire phonathon, letters should be sent to every prospect who was not reached. The letter should indicate that the organization was not able to reach them, and it should ask for a gift. This letter most certainly should include a prospect pledge card and a reply envelope.

After the phonathon, the staff must prepare the cumulative phonathon report, which includes each night's total and totals for the entire phonathon.

Reporting Results

Effective reporting practices are important not just for the staff, but also to let all the volunteers know what they have accomplished. The sample phonathon forms in Exhibit 9–2 help all involved to understand the results of the phonathon.

Exhibit 9–3 is a sample phonathon planning checklist.

Direct Mail and the Capital Campaign

Capital-campaign fund raising does not rely on mail as the primary method of soliciting gifts, yet the mail serves an important role throughout the campaign. Most, if not all, solicitations for campaign gifts begin as written proposals. The proposals are individualized, some are even unique. And at least as important, the mail transports multiple thank-you letters for every gift.

More and more people are using newer forms of communication such as e-mail and fax. However, "snail mail" still carries most solicitation letters, and these days truly personalized letters and envelopes stand out.

The great majority of the gifts made to a campaign are not made as a direct result of a mail solicitation; they result from personal contact made over the telephone and in face-to-face meetings. In fact, most gifts, particularly the larger ones, result from multiple contacts made in a variety of ways. Though it is rare for a campaign to keep track of the number of contacts it has taken to tie down each gift, such record-keeping would likely reveal that each significant gift (and some not-so-significant gifts) takes between five and ten contacts. Some, of course, require many more.

However, as the campaign draws to a conclusion, the mail solicitation acquires more importance. Throughout most of the campaign, staff members and volunteers do their utmost to maintain the initiative during the solicitation process. Each proposal letter begins what is often a long series of contacts and communications between the organization (through staff and volunteer) and the donor. Mail used at the end of the campaign turns the initiative over to the prospect. No longer are letters followed up with phone calls and visits. No more is the staff beginning a series of initiatives with every letter. At this stage in a campaign, letters close open-ended loops. They give people who have been solicited in one way or another earlier in the campaign one final chance to make a gift. And they reach out to people

Exhibit 9–2 Sample Phonathon Report Form

<table>
<tr><td colspan="2" align="center">Report of Dollars Raised and Expenses</td></tr>
<tr><td>Total Dollars Raised</td><td align="right">_____</td></tr>
<tr><td>Total Dollar Expenses</td><td></td></tr>
<tr><td> Printing</td><td align="center">_____</td></tr>
<tr><td> Postage</td><td align="center">_____</td></tr>
<tr><td> Food</td><td align="center">_____</td></tr>
<tr><td> Prizes</td><td align="center">_____</td></tr>
<tr><td> Phone</td><td align="center">_____</td></tr>
<tr><td>Net Return</td><td align="right">_____</td></tr>
<tr><td>Number of Prephonathon Letters Sent</td><td align="right">_____</td></tr>
<tr><td>Total Number of Gifts Pledged</td><td align="right">_____</td></tr>
<tr><td> No. of gifts sent prior to phoning period</td><td align="center">_____</td></tr>
<tr><td> No. of gifts made during phoning period</td><td align="center">_____</td></tr>
<tr><td> No. of gifts sent after phoning period</td><td align="center">_____</td></tr>
<tr><td>Average Dollar Amount Per Gift</td><td align="right">_____</td></tr>
<tr><td colspan="2" align="center">Report of Activity Levels</td></tr>
<tr><td>Total Number of Calls Made</td><td align="right">_____</td></tr>
<tr><td> Number of people reached</td><td align="center">_____</td></tr>
<tr><td> Number of people not reached</td><td align="center">_____</td></tr>
<tr><td> Number of rejections</td><td align="center">_____</td></tr>
<tr><td> Number of multiyear pledges</td><td align="center">_____</td></tr>
<tr><td> Number of gifts still pending</td><td align="center">_____</td></tr>
<tr><td>Total Number of Volunteers</td><td align="right">_____</td></tr>
<tr><td> Number of volunteer callers</td><td align="center">_____</td></tr>
<tr><td> Number of support volunteers</td><td align="center">_____</td></tr>
<tr><td>Total Number of Staff Hours Spent</td><td align="right">_____</td></tr>
</table>

more tangentially related to the organization who have not yet been solicited.

Why Mail?

The long and uncertain strands of prospect contacts that weave together during a campaign can frustrate even the most steadfast development-staff members. Early in the campaign, each contact invariably brings with it more work, more anxiety, and more bits of information to track, thus, staff members often feel relieved when they can begin to complete the giving exchanges.

Direct mail appeals late in a campaign serve four important purposes.

1. Letters provide a way to tie up loose ends.
2. Letters can reach people who were not reachable any other way.
3. Letters provide the organization's donors who were not solicited in any other way a chance to make a gift.
4. Letters enable an organization to broaden its base of support by reaching out to constituents who are not yet donors.

The solicitation process of many campaigns ends with a direct-mail appeal. Direct-mail appeals are typically sent to four types of prospects.

1. those who have been solicited but who haven't said yes or no
2. those who were not reached during the phonathon
3. those who are on the donor list but for whom a telephone number couldn't be located
4. everyone else on the mailing list who hasn't been solicited in another way

Occasionally, if the campaign is still some distance from its goal, letters will also be sent to those who have already made gifts but who might consider giving more or giving again.

Reaching Closure

Campaigns begin with a bang and inevitably end by petering out. The campaign has involved hundreds of volunteers, and thousands of prospects have been contacted; it is no wonder that as the campaign nears its goal, many people may feel ill-informed and out of the communications loop. Thank heaven for computers and

Exhibit 9–3 Phonathon Planning Check List

Prospect Names
- ❏ Select names
- ❏ Research phone numbers
- ❏ Prepare prospect forms

General Plan
- ❏ Determine number of prospects to be called
- ❏ Determine number of callers needed
- ❏ Determine number of calling periods
- ❏ Determine number of phone lines and desks needed
- ❏ Determine number of clerical volunteers per session

Location
- ❏ Check availability
- ❏ Review layout
- ❏ Determine available parking
- ❏ Check accessibility

Dates and Times
- ❏ Decide on times of day
- ❏ Select days of the week
- ❏ Determine duration of volunteer sessions
- ❏ Determine duration of calling periods

Recruiting Volunteers
- ❏ Recruit phonathon chairs
- ❏ Develop lists of volunteers to call
- ❏ Print sign-up sheets
- ❏ Prepare follow-up letters
- ❏ Plan reminder notices or calls

Prephonathon Mail Appeal
- ❏ Draft letter to send prior to phonathon

Support Materials
- ❏ Purchase folders
- ❏ Prepare prospect information forms
- ❏ Write telephone script
- ❏ Draft letter to be sent afterward to those not reached
- ❏ Outline talking points and common questions
- ❏ Prepare instructions for clerical volunteers
- ❏ Prepare instructions for solicitors
- ❏ Print pledge forms and response envelopes
- ❏ Print mailing envelopes

Training
- ❏ Outline training session
- ❏ Organize materials

Motivation
- ❏ Plan and arrange for refreshments
- ❏ Plan prizes

Follow up
- ❏ Send thank-you letters to volunteers
- ❏ Mail letters to those not reached
- ❏ Send pledge reminder notices
- ❏ Prepare phonathon summary report
- ❏ Send thank-you letters to location host and organizing committee

---

thank heaven for mail, because with those two helpers an organization can tidy up many loose ends, thereby helping staff, volunteers, donors, and prospects take part in the successful conclusion of the campaign.

Before turning to a broad direct-mail appeal, the development staff, campaign leaders, and executive director should take one last look at the names in the still-pending list. Are there people on that list who should be visited one more time? Are there people on the edge of a decision for whom an informal call from the chair would make the difference? Is there anyone on that list who really doesn't want to contribute but who could be helped to a resolution with a final personal contact? Is there someone important who for some reason hasn't been called?

As the pressure mounts to bring the campaign to a conclusion, a final review of the prospect lists will yield a set of people who should be called or visited rather than solicited by mail. These will be those who for some reason of history or financial capability have a larger-than-average stake in the project. Each of the cleanup visits should aim at closing the process, finding out if the individual intends to make a gift and getting the pledge or helping that person to say no. At this stage, each person is contacted as a courtesy so that the relationship between them and the organization can continue to be a healthy one—whether or not they make a gift.

Direct-mail appeals do have a place in most campaigns. However, their place is at the very end when the campaign goal is in sight. A campaign far from its goal will not be able to make up with a mailing what the face-to-face solicitation process has failed to accomplish. If a campaign has gone more slowly than expected, its conclusion should be delayed, and soliciting people one-to-one should continue until the campaign has concluded all solicitation except that at the very lowest level of giving. Then and only then has the time for direct mail arrived.

If the campaign has progressed well and the goal is within reach, as it should be, the direct-mail solicitation can benefit from the natural momentum that builds as the finish line draws near.

Refocusing the Case for Support

With success within reach, the case for supporting the campaign often shifts. No longer is there a question about whether the campaign will succeed, for success is virtually in hand. The final appeals invite people to help close the gap, to be among the heroes who made the cam-

> *The direct-mail campaign is an invitation to climb aboard a winning project.*

paign successful. Strange as it may seem, the opportunity to jump on board an enterprise that is sure to succeed motivates many people who, until momentum was high, had stood on the sidelines. The direct-mail campaign, then, is an invitation to climb aboard a winning project. Everyone who gives before the campaign is over will be able to feel his or her heart swell just a little bit when driving by the organization's new building or reading an article about the organization's success.

As the motivation shifts, the emphasis of the case for support moves from the project to the campaign itself. As the campaign draws to a close, the case shifts to emphasize its remarkable success to date and to tell donors how they can help take the campaign over the top. Of course, the real story for the project continues to be an important element in the case for support, but at this point it shares the stage.

When possible, these final appeals target a closing date for the campaign. This is easy when deadlines are determined by matching or challenge grants that impose the dates from the outside (so long as the dates are feasible). But when external deadlines are not imposed, an organization should determine an internal deadline, based on the date of a groundbreaking, a moving day, or some other visible event that will give the deadline credence.

When the end is in view, deadlines motivate staff, volunteers, and donors. Though they may complain and squirm under the pressure, if the deadlines are reasonable—tight enough to create some discomfort, but long enough to be doable—everyone will work more efficiently and cheerfully when they know exactly when the end really will arrive!

Special Characteristics of Direct Mail for Capital Campaign Appeals

In many ways, direct-mail appeals for campaigns are the same as direct mail used in annual giving, and an organization that is expert in this area should rely on their previous experience and knowledge to guide them in the specifics of writing, design, response pieces, mailings, and so forth. However, there are some ways that capital-campaign direct-mail appeals should be different from their annual appeal siblings.

First, the appeal should look different. Because the capital campaign is a distinct and special campaign, and because the donors should understand that it is different from annual giving, the campaign mail appeal should look and feel distinct. It should repeat the themes that were used in the rest of the campaign material. By engaging the same graphic designer who developed the campaign material to design the mail appeal, an organization can often give some added zip to that appeal.

Second, it should sound different. The writing style for a campaign appeal should have more punch and en-

ergy than many annual appeals manage even in their heroic attempts to stay fresh year after year. Capital-campaign appeals really are "once and done," and that very fact should inspire almost any author.

Third, it should ask for multiyear pledges. Unlike annual contributions, capital campaigns can ask donors to make gifts over as many as three, or even five years. Because many people are not in the habit of making multiyear pledges, this request should be highlighted in the letter, or perhaps included in the P.S., which most people actually do read. The multiyear pledge option should also be emphasized on the pledge form.

Fourth, it should ask prospects to consider gifts in a specific range or amount. Although some organizations use the practice of asking for specific gifts in their annual appeal, many do not. For the capital-campaign's direct mail, requesting a specific amount is even more important because it requests a multiyear pledge somewhat larger than gifts usually given to an annual campaign. This further separates it from the annual appeal. Someone who has given an organization $25 per year for the past ten years is likely to continue in that pattern unless specifically asked to change it. A specific request helps the prospect understand the "appropriate" level for a capital-campaign gift.

Finally, it should tell donors how they will be recognized. Because capital campaigns are often associated with building projects, donors of a certain amount may see their names on a permanent plaque. If the lowest amount for being listed on a plaque is within the range

---

The Last Minute . . . Is Now!

We were just $120,000 from our $1.8 million campaign goal and it was October. Our Kresge grant didn't have to be met until the following April, but another foundation challenged us to finish by November 1. We knew we wouldn't make their deadline, so we asked them if they would give us two more months and let us use their gift to highlight a December 30 deadline. The theme of the direct-mail appeal was "The last minute . . . is NOW!" We asked the people on our mailing list to help us get over the top by the end of the year. We sent out a large mailing the second week of December and were flooded by responses as the year drew to a close. When we were finally down to the wire, we found that we were still sixty dollars and fifty-eight cents short of our goal. We passed a hat at the staff meeting and went over the top!

—Executive Director

of possible direct-mail gifts, the appeal should be sure to mention this option. Although few people ever say that they want their names on a plaque, when they are listed, they are likely to point it out to their children, grandchildren, and friends when they walk by!

Segmenting the Mailing List

Many organizations today are quite sophisticated in the way in which they can segment their mailing lists so that they can send special letters targeted to specific groups. Effective capital-campaign mail appeals also rely on segmented lists so that every prospect receives a letter that fits his or her relationship to the campaign. A campaign mailing list might be segmented in the following four ways:

1. People who have been asked for a campaign gift but have not responded. These are truly cleanup calls and must be worded accordingly. A donor who has been solicited earlier and then receives a letter that does not acknowledge the prior solicitation is likely to become irritated. However, if the same donor understands that the organization is merely trying to find out whether or not he or she intends to give to the campaign, then the donor is likely to recognize that this letter will conclude the process and will therefore feel relieved!

2. Former donors who have not yet been asked for a campaign gift. One might further subdivide the list according to former giving patterns or according to specific relationships that the donors might have to the organization. For example, a school might choose to send a different letter to an alumnus than to an area businessman.

3. People who are on the organization's mailing list but who have never become donors. In this list are the seeds for future giving. Even if the organization does not ordinarily send its annual appeal letter to all these people (the numbers in this category are often large), an organization might use the campaign as an opportunity to reach them. Although this is not likely to bring in major gifts to the campaign, it may turn up new donors who will then continue on as donors to the organization for many years.

4. People who have already given a small gift of cash to the campaign. Some campaigns write to donors who have already given, asking them to extend their gift at the same level for each year of the pledge period. This second appeal offends some but works for others, and the decision about whether or not to use this approach will probably depend on how much money is yet to be raised.

Celebrate Success with a Last-Chance Appeal

As the campaign glides over the top, those with great stamina might send one last letter to all previous donors who have not yet given, inviting them to get on board before the celebrating begins. This letter should be short, low pressure, and light in tone. Responses to these very last appeals tend to trickle in over a remarkably long time.

Simple Reminders about Direct Mail

Direct mail appeals should be:

- Clear
- Attractive
- Distinctive
- Compelling
- Eye-catching
- Well written
- Focused
- Targeted
- Individualized
- Celebratory
- Upbeat
- Specific
- Easy to respond to

Most development directors are familiar with that mixed feeling of apprehension, excitement, and dread that greets the daily mail delivery following a broad-based appeal. At the conclusion of a capital campaign that has gone well in its early stages, these mail runs are often particularly exciting and rewarding. Each pledge form closes a relationship and helps close the distance to the goal. Every acknowledgment note brings with it a lighter heart and every dollar the anticipation of being closer to the goal.

Telephone and direct-mail fund raising provide excitement, relief, and comfort at the conclusion of a long and stressful campaign. Embedded in this low-end fund raising are often the seeds of a reinvigorated annual giving program for many years to come.

Reference

Blanton, Carol. 1994. The pitfalls and the promise of telephone fundraising. *Grassroots Fundraising Journal* 13 (December): 3–6.

Chapter 10
Special Events and the Capital Campaign

Chapter Outline
- Types of Events Used in Capital Campaigns
- The Organization and Design of Campaign Events
- More on Campaign Kickoff Events
- Making Campaigns Larger than Life

From beginning to end, special events play an important role in capital-campaign fund raising. Although campaigns rely on face-to-face solicitation as the primary method of generating contributions, events help organizations build relationships with many of the donors who will later be personally solicited for the campaign. Events also motivate volunteer solicitors, provide opportunities for media coverage, and recognize the many donors and volunteers who make campaigns successful. In addition, some campaigns incorporate actual fund-raising events into the final phases of their campaigns as a way of involving the broader community in the campaign effort.

Types of Events Used in Capital Campaigns

Small nonprofit organizations often rely almost exclusively on special events to raise money for their annual operating budgets. Although they may wish it were otherwise, many development directors are in reality special-events planners. Community-based organizations often conduct eight, ten, or even more special events each year just to stay afloat. These special events, combined with a direct-mail appeal, often make up an organization's entire fund-raising program.

In reality, however, special events are more effective for boosting an organization's image and increasing its constituents than they are for raising money. It is primarily because of these non-fund-raising purposes that they are important elements in a capital campaign.

Special events are used in five principal ways in a capital campaign.

1. for the cultivation of prospective donors
2. as a way to attract media attention
3. for recognizing and motivating volunteers and donors
4. for celebrating success
5. for raising funds

Of course, the same event may accomplish several of these goals simultaneously.

Cultivation

Long before a campaign takes shape, an organization should be preparing prospective donors so that they will be inclined make a donation to the organization. The phrase "to cultivate a donor" is one of those distasteful nonspecific phrases that is part of the fund-raising jargon. It gives a general idea of something that needs to be done, yet provides no clear idea of how, what, or when. It is easy to understand that donors must have real relationships with the organizations that they support. It is less easy to understand how to go about building such relationships without seeming—or in fact being—manipulative.

There are many ways for an organization to build relationships with prospective donors. Some people are drawn to an organization because of a natural or acquired interest in its mission. Others are brought in by a friend or acquaintance. Still others feel safer in a crowd and have their first contact by participating in a large gathering or gala event.

The most effective cultivation events are those in which a prospective donor is invited to learn more about an organization by someone who is already involved in it. Some executive directors regularly schedule one or two meetings every week with community leaders, prospective donors, new friends, or others in order to acquaint them with the organization. Although one-on-one cultivation of this sort does not build many relationships quickly, over time a director can accomplish a great deal with this simple strategy. A campaign that takes place after a director has met with, say, two different community leaders or donors every week for two years (that's about two hundred individuals) is likely to get underway with a knowledgeable and receptive audience of volunteers and donors.

Some directors are not comfortable in the role of host and prefer to meet with people in larger groups or to call on volunteers to identify and invite small groups of people to learn about the organization. Although small-group cultivation sessions, like the one-on-one meetings described above, are most effective when conducted regularly over a long period, this form of cultivation is often put into practice only when an organization begins to contemplate a capital campaign. In that context, small cultivation meetings might be structured as focus groups that inform the participants of the organization's plans and solicit their opinions about the proposed project.

These small-group cultivation sessions are often planned by an ad hoc committee of board members and community leaders who as a group are able to reach into different aspects of the community. Thus they can assemble lists of people to contact and determine who might host one or more meetings in a location that best matches the person, the organization, and the group. One country-club luncheon for six well-connected businessmen hosted by a well-respected community leader can sow the seeds of a successful campaign! Often the meetings are attended by a staff member who is thoroughly informed about the organization and the campaign project. These meetings are most successful when they cluster groups of friends or acquaintances and provide ample time for questions and discussion.

The Benefits of "Doing Lunch"

It was like pulling teeth trying to convince one of my clients, an executive director, to invite people to his organization for lunch. To make it easier for him, we assembled a list of people for him to cultivate and then sent letters inviting those individuals for lunch. He was supposed to follow up by telephone. But we could sense his distaste for this process—his fear of being rejected and his discomfort with being a host. However, his discomfort finally vanished when he realized that he was able through this process of one-on-one cultivation to make real contact with people and that these individuals, far from feeling put upon, felt honored to have been invited. Although we didn't do as much of this type of cultivation as we should have, every contact he made helped the campaign!

—Campaign Consultant

The Way to a Person's Heart

If our local country club was aware of the role that they played in our recent campaign, they'd probably be asking for a cut of our campaign proceeds! If it weren't for the luncheons we held in that club room, I'm not sure our campaign would have gone over the top. We must have had a dozen lunches there for business people and others in the community to talk about our project. Those unprepossessing luncheons got people involved better than anything else we did.

—Development Director

The protocol for picking up the tab for cultivation luncheons varies, depending on the preference of the volunteer and the culture of the organization. Sometimes the cost of the luncheon is borne by the hosting volunteer, other times the organization covers the cost, and occasionally it is appropriate for the participants to pay for their own meals. Whatever the payment arrangements, they should be determined beforehand in order to avoid awkwardness at the conclusion of the session.

A cocktail party or dinner for a select group at someone's home might also be incorporated into a cultivation plan. Such events work particularly well if they are hosted by someone whose home people would likely be interested in seeing or if the hosts are distinguished members of the community. It can be difficult to find the right combination of social interaction and cultivation at events like this, and without a clear schedule and plan that have been drawn up prior to the event, the evening is likely to become purely social and achieve little for the organization.

Receptions held in conjunction with another event can be used for cultivation as well. However, for such an event to be effective, both staff and volunteers will have to develop a very specific plan that involves their circulating among the guests, discussing pertinent topics, and gathering and reporting information about those in attendance. Frequently, organizations put on large receptions to cultivate people but don't develop a plan to find out more about the people who attend or to share specific information with them. To get the most out of an event like this, the staff and key volunteers might gather beforehand to review a list of those who will attend, and then assign guests to each staff member and volunteer. After the event, each staff member and volunteer is asked to write a report outlining any important information that they have learned. Sometimes this information is best gathered at a "postmortem" meeting of the event-planning committee.

These larger cultivation events are most successful when they incorporate a program that has been designed to interest those who have been invited. The "lure" should be in keeping with the character and mission of the organization, yet should appeal to the specific constituency that is being cultivated.

Many organizations incorporate a fund-raising gala into their annual calendar. These are cultivation events in the sense that people make a gift to attend the event, and by attending they affiliate themselves with the organization. Some organizations collaborate with another well-respected institution in their community to host a major event. This collaboration encourages donors to give to both organizations, and if done well, such an event can win significant support in the community.

Media Attention

Coverage in the news media is most important at specific times during a capital campaign, and although standard press releases sometimes produce satisfactory results, a well-orchestrated event is far more likely to yield column inches and air time.

The Power of Proper Planning

The Spanish-American Civic Center was in the midst of their first capital campaign to renovate and expand their facility. Because in the past they had relied heavily on government funding for many of their programs, they had not cultivated strong relationships with many area business people. The business-solicitation division decided that before they solicited gifts they would plan cultivation events that would take business people to the organization's rather dilapidated facilities. They engaged a human-resources consultant to present a brief, interactive diversity-training program at each of the sessions. The organization prepared very attractive and official-looking invitations to attend one of three sessions, planned for different days and different times, and these were sent to all of the area owners and leaders in the business community. About thirty people came to each session, and even now, seven years later, many of those who attended still remark about how powerful those meetings were. Everyone who attended learned something of importance and had an opportunity to visit the center and learn about its work before being solicited for a gift. This cultivation program built many relationships for the center that later resulted in campaign gifts.

Successful Collaboration

Every year we collaborate with our local theater to put on an evening of entertainment. Because our mission is the care of people who are dying and the theater is concerned about people with AIDS, our two organizations make an appropriate team. We invite the people and staff the event, while they select the entertainment and provide the venue for the show and the reception. Through our collaboration, the theater shows its support for our mission, and we for our part encourage our donors to become theater subscribers.

—Vice President, Hospice

The campaign kickoff marks the moment when a campaign moves from the so-called quiet phase into the public eye. Although the kickoff serves several purposes, it is often a media event designed to interest the press in a story about the capital campaign and the project it is to fund. The timing of the event is quite specific—it takes place after most if not all of the leadership gifts are in and after the solicitors for the midlevel gifts have been enlisted, but before they have begun to solicit those gifts. This event is designed to obtain media coverage in the broader community just before the solicitors begin to make their calls. A front-page article about the campaign and the project lends it credibility and visibility. And when the coverage hits the front page just a few days before the solicitors are to telephone their prospects, good press gives courage to the solicitors and also prepares their prospects to be solicited.

The campaign kickoff also inspires and motivates the campaign volunteers. A campaign kickoff is a curious sort of event in that it reports on the success of the campaign at the same time that it proclaims the campaign to be beginning. It's rather reminiscent of that Boston marathoner who sneaked a ride on the trolley to the fifteen-mile marker.

This seemingly cockeyed timing is actually a clever strategy for creating a sense of forward momentum and optimism at a crucial moment. The kickoff assembles a large and disparate group of campaign volunteers at one time and location around a shared goal, and uses that occasion to announce the specifics of the project to be funded and to recognize the campaign leaders who have already committed themselves to the success of the project. This all adds up to a compelling story for most community-newspaper editors.

In the case of building projects, the day the first shovelful of earth is turned is the visible beginning of forging tangible reality from the stuff of campaign dreams. If the groundbreaking occurs before the campaign has reached its goal, the ceremony presents yet another opportunity to raise the level of community confidence in the project. Once ground has been broken, the die is cast, the Rubicon crossed. There is no turning back. If the campaign has raised the better part of its goal by that date, the presence of the emerging building is likely to inspire additional gifts. Although the news media do not usually find ground-breakings particularly newsworthy, an important speaker combined with a thorough and persistent public-relations staff member will likely result in coverage.

In the same category as groundbreakings are the beginnings of any projects funded by a large and special campaign. Such events work best after the midlevel gifts have been raised but before the lower-level gifts have been solicited. In essence, the initiation of the project provides another push of visibility just before the broad-based solicitations.

Timing press coverage can be challenging, and even the best laid schemes can go awry if an overzealous reporter gets wind of a story before that story is ready for press. The best safeguard against untimely reporting is good relations with key reporters. In return for exclusive rights to the story when it is ready, a reporter may be able to head off premature coverage.

Occasionally, organizations find other opportunities for media coverage. It is tempting to reveal too much too soon and as a result not have the important stories when the campaign most needs them. Until the time is right, an organization should concentrate its public-relations efforts on highlighting the organization's ongoing services and the more of this the better.

Motivation

Events are effective ways to motivate volunteers and to build team spirit. Most people work harder and perform better when they are aware of being part of a larger organization and when other participants are people whom they recognize. Campaign events provide opportunities to bring the volunteers together around their common goal. Their collective energies and presence at an event builds a sense of confidence and enthusiasm.

Recognition and Celebration

Sometimes, trying to sign up volunteers is nearly impossible. But most people are very happy to take part in a celebration, and they are thrilled to be recognized for their accomplishments. Indeed, one of the signs of a first-rate development professional is the ability to acknowl-

edge people for even the smallest contributions. They have a way of seeing the best in other people and turning a blind eye to their vanities or hypocrisies. Campaign celebrations and recognition events are times for just this sort of recognition.

Organizations recognize donors in many ways, and these will be discussed in chapter 12. Recognition events and campaign celebrations are very important campaign events. Through them the trials and frustrations of months of hard work are transformed into a sense of accomplishment and triumph. Without them, frustrations often sour, leaving volunteers and staff feeling unsatisfied, even though the campaign went over its goal.

Celebration events should not be conceived of only as large, formal events with long speeches and the presentations of awards. At least as important are the celebrations that occur when the director shows up at the campaign chair's house to share a bottle of fine champagne, or the dozen roses that the campaign chair sends to the development director, or the final gathering of the campaign steering committee to review the final campaign count, or the handshake with the campaign consultant who has guided and driven and hounded everyone to success. Each of these mini-events privately recognizes individuals for what they did well and helps to heal the inevitable wounds and regrets of a campaign. These small events prepare an organization's insiders for a genuine public celebration.

Of course, to the extent that these small celebrations are not driven by genuine appreciation, they lose their effectiveness. But it is important that the campaign leadership understand the power and importance of such small gestures, and therefore make such gestures a way of life.

Waiting for the Right Time

A well-known gentleman in town sold us a large building at a price $700,000 below its market value. This was certainly news, and our benefactor would have been happy to have the publicity. However, our campaign was just in the planning stages and we didn't want to lose an opportunity for coverage later. So we asked him whether he would mind waiting several months until the campaign kickoff, when we could combine his gift with the gifts of many other community leaders. Together with the architect's renderings of the renovated building, we would have a story that could be a really big splash. Our donor agreed, and so long as the reporters don't decide to jump the gun, we'll be able to show him in a truly wonderful light!

—Campaign Director

Larger, more public celebrations are important at the end of a capital campaign. These are occasions for all the campaign volunteers, major donors, and staff to assemble and acknowledge the success of their individual and collective efforts. Some celebrations are simple and are held in the gymnasium of the local recreation center, for example; others are black-tie events in fancy restaurants. Some bring in nationally known speakers; others feature the campaign chair. No matter how lavish or simple, as much attention and effort should be devoted to campaign celebrations as was applied to the campaign kickoff. Although few people will ever say openly that they wish to be recognized, everyone who has helped to reach a goal wants to be acknowledged in some way, and an organization will benefit many times over from taking the time, money, and energy to celebrate the many ways in which people have contributed to the success of the campaign. This kind of after-the-fact recognition is without doubt the very best form of cultivation.

Fund Raising

Many do not recommend that organizations raise money for capital campaigns through special events. There are, however, some exceptions to this general proscription. Occasionally, a business or service organization in a community wishes to channel the income from their fund-raising event to an organization's capital campaign. The business may even be willing to commit to an event for each year of the campaign-pledge period. In such cases, and depending on the financial potential and the expectations of the organization, it may be wise to incorporate the event or at least the income from the event into the campaign.

Often, however, these "gifts" extract their pound of flesh in organization, volunteer coordination, and publicity; but if the stakes are high enough, the public visibility broad enough, and the occasion well-timed for the campaign, it may pay to collaborate with the business.

Some organizations may wish to use the excitement and energy that is generated by a campaign to revitalize a preexisting fund-raising event by designating those funds to the campaign. Although this may make sense, beware of averting staff and volunteer attention from the face-to-face solicitation process where it belongs during most of the campaign.

Particular individuals in a community may be willing to host fund raisers in their houses during the final stages of a campaign. In the context of these events, which might be house concerts, cocktail parties, dinners, or other types of gatherings, the hosts will extract campaign pledges from acquaintances who may have only a passing relationship with the organization. Sometimes the gifts are solicited with the invitation, with a signed pledge form

> *Beware of fund raising through special events for capital campaigns. They gobble up staff time. They are expensive. They are not often good cultivation events. They seldom raise significant amounts of money.*

being the required entry token. In other cases, pledge forms may be handed out during the event or sent out afterward. These events are sometimes successful in generating contributions that otherwise would not likely come in, but the cost in time and energy is often high.

In summary, beware of fund raising through special events for capital campaigns. They gobble up staff time. They are expensive. They often are not good cultivation events. They seldom raise significant amounts of money.

The Organization and Design of Campaign Events

The Special-Events Committee

Many campaigns incorporate a special-events committee into their structure (see chapter 6). The establishment of such a committee to plan and execute campaign events is usually an effective strategy in community-based campaigns.

For many campaigns, ad hoc subcommittees of the special-events committee plan and coordinate the campaign kickoff, the groundbreaking ceremony, and the final celebration. Committee members are given time-specific, clearly defined assignments, thus avoiding much of the special-events burnout that can result when the

The A-moo-zing Maze

A large, locally-owned grocery store in the middle of farm country was owned by the husband of a hospice nurse, and he wanted to do something to benefit the hospice campaign and at the same time enhance his store's visibility. So he came up with an unusual idea: In the spring, he planted corn in a field next to his store in the shape of a complex, cow-shaped maze. By fall the corn had grown "as high as an elephant's eye," and the grocer sold tickets to the maze—in the form of contributions to the campaign—to his customers and their children. He did this each year for three years, earning nearly $50,000 for the hospice campaign. The hospice staff helped with public relations and provided volunteers to help at the maze on weekends.

same committee members are responsible for multiple events.

The mere thought of a special event gives some people a four-aspirin headache. For them, special events mean lots of work with little reward. They shudder as they anticipate mediating endless disputes about table linens, and about whether it should be fish or chicken, chocolate mousse or tiramisu.

Others thrive on the complex logistical planning and plotting; the minuscule details; the haggling with caterers, florists, printers, public officials, and other key personnel; and recruiting underwriters for the event. These people may be exhausted when the event is over, yet after a good night's sleep they are ready to tie up the loose ends and move on to the next event with renewed enthusiasm.

It's usually easier to find a special events "natural" than a solicitation "natural." A person who hates special events should not be saddled with the task of planning them. Special events are demanding and time-consuming, and require a great deal of skill and know-how. Most communities have many such experts as potential volunteers. Organizations that do not have a special events natural in their ranks should take the time to cultivate one early in the campaign. The participation of such an individual can add zest and sparkle to an important aspect of the campaign.

General Considerations

Before planning a special event, an organization should consider the following suggestions.

First, clarify goals, objectives, and tasks. Every event should have clearly defined goals and objectives that have been understood and accepted by everyone who is working on the event. Before the first committee meeting, the staff should draft a statement that describes the purpose of the event and its function in the capital campaign. Such a statement will enable the volunteers to plan the event so that it will serve its intended purpose.

A statement of purpose for a campaign kickoff might look something like Exhibit 10–1.

This draft document should clarify the goals of the event and provide a framework from which the committee designs the specific character, type, and style of the event. Beginning the planning process with a written description of the event's purposes and limitations of time and money will help everyone work from the same set of assumptions, thereby smoothing the planning process.

A checklist of decisions to be made, such as the one in Exhibit 10–2, is sometimes helpful in presenting the questions and issues that must be addressed.

Second, develop a realistic budget and adhere to it. The process of building a budget will help an event-planning committee understand and explore realistic options.

Exhibit 10–1 Campaign Kickoff

> #### Planning Outline
> **Purposes:**
> - energize campaign volunteers
> - obtain press coverage for the campaign and the project that the campaign will fund
> - recognize the campaign's lead-gift donors
>
> **Timing:**
> - kickoff date
>
> **Suggested Attendees:**
> - major donors
> - major-gift prospects
> - community leaders
> - campaign volunteers
> - key staff members
>
> **Target Budget:** $15,000

The staff member who has been assigned to the project should present a preliminary budget or dollar range that fits within the budget for the entire campaign and then work with the committee to refine it as the event takes shape. This will put reasonable limits on the committee's decisions.

Third, attend to details.

"Who cares what color the napkins are?"

"We tested the slide projector when we visited the site two weeks ago. We don't need to test it again before the event."

"I don't think we need to worry about the seating arrangements."

"Everybody knows what's going on. We don't need to provide them with a printed program."

In planning any special event, it's the details that make all the difference. Many a well-conceived event has fallen short of its goals because its execution was sloppy. Taken one at a time, the myriad of detailed decisions seem relatively unimportant, but together they create the climate for the event. Guests often aren't conscious of every detail of appearance and organization, but they do absorb the overall ambiance, and they notice all too well when a number of little things are awry.

Fourth, thank and recognize event planners. Getting volunteers involved in special events is one of the best ways to solidify relationships with those volunteers. A volun-

> *Should organizations charge for campaign events? YES: Hosting a special event can be costly. NO: Kickoffs and celebrations are to acknowledge and thank people. Both arguments have validity, but it is better to plan a less lavish event than to charge people to attend.*

Exhibit 10–2 Sample Kickoff Checklist

Fundamentals	**Food and Drink**	❐ Displays
❐ Date	❐ Type of food	❐ Slide show or video
❐ Time	❐ Type of drinks	❐ Other
❐ Number of people	❐ Provider (caterers, local restau-	
❐ Guest list	rants, etc.)	**People Management**
❐ Description and timing of event	❐ Wait staff	❐ Volunteer roles
		❐ Welcome table
Location	**Set-up**	❐ Name tags
❐ Parking	❐ Linens	❐ Seating chart
❐ Handicapped accessibility	❐ Centerpieces	❐ Committee seating
❐ Size	❐ Flowers	❐ Prizes or other "take-homes"
❐ Appearance	❐ Table arrangements	
❐ Liquor license	❐ Chairs	**Cleanup**
❐ Insurance	❐ Stage	❐ Pack and cart materials
	❐ Linens	❐ Draft report on event
Invitations		❐ Final committee meeting
❐ Design	**Program**	❐ Thank-you to volunteers
❐ Production	❐ Speakers	
❐ Addressing	❐ Drafts of speeches	
❐ Date for mailing	❐ Presentations	
❐ Return mechanism	❐ Music	

teer may have worked hard for months to build a special event, and when that event succeeds, the volunteer feels a closer sense of belonging to the organization. However, these volunteers are not likely to put themselves forward to be recognized and rewarded at the event on which they have worked. Staff members, therefore, should make sure that all of the volunteers who worked on the event are properly thanked and recognized for their labors.

- Their names should be included in the printed program.
- There should be a special presentation to the event chair during the program.
- The event chair should be invited to make a brief speech during the program.
- Volunteers should be asked to stand and be recognized during the program.

Fifth, be true to the organization. Events should be in keeping with the style, capabilities, and traditions of the organization. Planners should not be carried away by the lavish event at the Metropolitan Museum of Art featured in the last issue of *Town and Country* when the organization lacks the experience, the resources, and the constituency to carry off such an elaborate production.

Sixth, involve volunteers and board members. Board members and volunteers are often responsible for the success of an event. They sell tickets and invite friends and colleagues, they provide in-kind donations, they make financial contributions toward the cost of the event, and they help run the event.

Seventh, reinforce the organization's message. While most of those who will attend campaign events are likely to know a good deal about the organization's mission and purpose, retelling the organization's story generates excitement and often shows the organization's work in a new light.

Finally, evaluate. After every event, the planners should take the time to evaluate its effectiveness. Evaluating an

A List Maker's Heaven

I am by nature a compulsive list maker, so I was in my element when it came to planning the campaign kickoff. I set up a form for the master to-do list on my computer—with a space for each job, who was going to do it, and when—and then left a space where we could check off each item as it was completed. The form could be easily updated and printed before each planning committee meeting so that everyone would know who was responsible for doing what.

Then I bought a big calendar for my wall and put each task in its proper place on the calendar. Keeping track of everything two different ways gave me an overall picture of the process while simultaneously letting me focus on each task as it needed to be done.

—Development Director

> *Kickoff events do more than announce a campaign. They motivate volunteers, reinforce the case for support, inform communities, and provide a forum for acknowledging leadership gifts and volunteers.*

1. The public dollar goal of the campaign is presented.
2. Major donors and other key people are recognized.
3. The campaign's progress to date is announced.
4. The case for the project is summarized (often with accompanying visual displays).

The guest list for a campaign kickoff usually includes the following:

- corporate, foundation, and individual donors and prospects
- former and current board members
- campaign volunteers
- public officials
- staff members

event and preparing a report are often useful when planning the next event.

For more on the nuts and bolts of event planning, see *Successful Special Events: Planning, Hosting, and Evaluating,* by Barbara R. Levy and Barbara Marion, another book in this series.

More on Campaign Kickoff Events

Once the campaign leadership has completed the quiet phase of the campaign by securing leadership gifts of 40 percent or more of the campaign goal, the organization is ready to announce the campaign publicly through a campaign kickoff.

Campaign kickoffs take many forms. Large institutions are likely to organize spectacular events with lavish theatrical productions written to dramatize the campaign themes. Small organizations sometimes choose to host a simple, low-cost, wine-and-cheese gathering for press and campaign volunteers. Regardless of the size, lavishness, or type of event that the organization decides to host, four things invariably happen during the kickoff.

Making Campaigns Larger than Life

Capital campaigns are composed of literally thousands of small meetings, each of which by itself is relatively insignificant. Yet the process by which these meetings are organized and the collective results that they achieve are major accomplishments. The large campaign events—the kickoff, groundbreaking, and final celebration—focus attention on the collective accomplishments of the campaign and in so doing, they lend credibility and importance to every small campaign meeting and phone call. These events move a campaign from phase to phase and create a public perception of forward movement and success that helps maintain or even increase the campaign's momentum.

Chapter 11
Campaign Materials

Chapter Outline

- Campaign Theme and Logo
- The Power of Campaign Letterhead
- Note Cards, Pledge Forms, Envelopes, and Mailing Labels
- Leadership Gift Solicitation Material
- The Campaign Brochure
- Does the Campaign Need a Videotape?
- Campaign Newsletters
- Miscellaneous Materials
- Direct-Mail Brochures
- Using a Graphic Designer
- The Power of Materials in Building a Campaign

Capital campaigns are symbolized by the materials that are developed for them. These materials give a campaign its unique style and appearance. They provide a distinctive character that helps focus the many elements of the campaign around a common theme. The materials that support the work of a capital campaign take many forms over the course of the campaign. They may not be the most important component of a campaign, but campaign materials provide a critical and concrete foundation that supports and facilitates the solicitation process as well as many other campaign activities.

This chapter will discuss the concepts behind all of the materials that might be used in a capital campaign, and how those materials can be effectively developed. It explores the function and importance of everything from the campaign logo and letterhead to the campaign brochure, pledge form, and note cards. This chapter opens the door to creative approaches to campaign materials and encourages its readers to be receptive to new ideas, styles, and formats.

Campaign Theme and Logo

The old adage, "One picture is worth a thousand words," expresses the spirit and importance of capturing the campaign theme in a simple and compelling logo. The logo might be a drawing or graphic image, or it might be a distinctive typeface that presents the campaign theme. Whatever the means, the logo should provide an image that encapsulates the concept behind the campaign. Although the logo or image should be in keeping with the standards of taste and style generally used by the organization, it should be distinct from the image of the organization itself.

The campaign logo is most often developed in conjunction with a campaign title, and the title emerges from the many discussions, drafts, and rewritings of the case for support. Gradually, through the development of the case for support, an organization clarifies the strongest, most compelling aspect of the campaign. It is that fundamental concept that should be captured in a campaign name and logo.

Examples of good campaign themes and logos abound, as seen in Figure 11–1.

- A Spanish American Civic Association chose the campaign title "Building Bridges" and used a multicolored rainbow as the campaign logo.
- A day-care center used an image of a child's hand print and entitled its campaign "The Campaign for the Next Generation."
- For the campaign to automate its card catalog, a library used the theme "Open Sesame" and developed an image in the form of a book-plate showing treasures behind a computer screen.
- For its building renovation campaign, a Planned Parenthood used the phrase "Moving Ahead with Our PLANned Parenthood" together with a simple image of a partially completed building.

Campaigns need names. Although it is easy to say, for instance, "I'm working on the campaign for the hospice," (and indeed, some organizations choose such simple and straightforward names), if a campaign has a compelling name that captures the essence of the project, that essential concept is promoted every time the name is mentioned. For example, it is far more powerful to speak of the Building Bridges campaign for the Spanish

Figure 11–1 Sample logos for capital campaigns.

Coming up with the right words or logo can be a great challenge. Sometimes the right words simply emerge from informal discussion. Sometimes they come from meetings that have been organized for the explicit purpose of determining the campaign theme. Yet other times a graphic designer or advertising firm will be hired to present a variety of ideas for an organization to choose from. Whatever the process, the theme and logo must be circulated among the key campaign volunteers and staff members before it is adopted. If someone in a leadership position strongly opposes the first choice, the organization should try again.

The most frustrating aspect of developing the theme and logo is that what rings true for one person might not entirely please another. This is yet another instance when one becomes aware that in capital campaigns not all opinions carry equal weight. The ins and outs of these decisions may require sensitive and politically astute maneuvering by the organization's staff. It is seldom a mistake, however, to engage in a great deal of communication. Even when some individual's opinion does not prevail, that person will have been pleased to have been included in the debate.

Once a campaign has settled on just the right theme, that theme can then be translated into a visual symbol or logo. Graphic designers are experts in this field. They understand the visual world in the same way many others understand the verbal world. Here are some simple guidelines to keep in mind when considering a campaign logo.

- It should be graphically simple enough so that it reads well even when rendered in a small size.
- It should read well in black and white, even if it will most often be depicted in three or more colors.
- It should have enough contrast to show well when run through a copier.
- It should be distinctive.
- It should be in character with the organization's culture and purpose.

The Power of Campaign Letterhead

Every campaign needs its own letterhead. Letterhead is the most basic of the campaign materials. Literally thousands of letters are sent during a campaign, and if it is designed well, the letterhead will itself send a powerful message, enhancing the impact of the text of the letter.

Campaign letterhead should include the campaign logo, title, name of the organization, address and phone number of the organization, and the names of those who serve on the campaign committee. Although it may at first seem insignificant,

> *In capital campaigns, not all opinions carry equal weight.*

American Civic Association than it is simply to mention the Spanish American Civic Association campaign. In the theme of bridges is embedded the powerful concept of creating opportunities for individuals in a minority culture to become integrated into mainstream society. Painfully aware of the problems that come from belonging to a ghettoized minority, the people who created that logo provided a simple image for a broad theme that helped motivate business leaders and other donors to contribute to the campaign.

Certain words and themes occur over and over in capital campaigns. Words like *cornerstone, foundation, century, opportunity,* and *investment* pop up in campaign after campaign. These words are used with such frequency because they are strong and powerful, though they tend to lose power over time due to overuse.

the letterhead is a powerful communicator, setting out the theme of the campaign, presenting the campaign's most important information, and establishing credibility by presenting the team of the campaign's most important players.

People will comment on a campaign brochure, yet they seldom comment on the campaign letterhead. Nonetheless, the importance of the letterhead is not to be underestimated, for it adds significant information to every piece of campaign correspondence and it communicates its message directly and with immediacy.

Several common issues often arise as the letterhead is being developed.

Listing the Names

The campaign letterhead should include the names of the campaign chairs and the names of those who serve on the campaign committee. It is a seemingly simple task, yet the listing of names always requires great care and attention. Not only does everyone have a particular preference as to how their names should be listed, but many people feel quite strongly indeed about exactly how their names are to appear. One person always uses a middle initial. Another never does. Connie wants to be addressed as Mrs. David Z. Kutler, Jr., while Susan will be certain to take offense if her name appears with her husband's surname; she is Susan Lansdown-Worthing—always has been, al-

ways will be. Such personal preferences are further complicated by the loosening of social conventions in recent years. What used to be guided by Emily Post is, in our post-Emily world, guided largely by personal preference.

The other question that arises in developing letterhead is whether or not to include the business affiliations of those whose names are listed. Including them makes for a text-heavy, cumbersome appearance, but the members' affiliations may well lend credibility to the campaign. In some cases, a blue-ribbon group will need no identification beyond their names. If business affiliations are included, one then struggles with the identification of those with the less prestigious identifiers. "Housewife" or "Community Volunteer" pales beside "Chief Operating Officer" or "Senior Vice President." One might choose to omit the affiliations of some while listing others. Finally, it is wise to check with each individual about how they want to be listed.

Although there is no right or wrong way to decide these issues, the decision should be based on the specific requirements of the planning committee and the organization. If the organization is struggling for credibility and the planning committee members are credible but not well-known in the community, their affiliations should be included. If the members are active community leaders whose names are often seen and recognized, then their affiliations may not be necessary.

Size

Occasionally an overzealous graphic designer will try too hard to make an organization's campaign materials stand out. One way that is often suggested to accomplish this laudable goal is to create square or oversized letterhead. Although this strategy does separate an organization from the pack, it can do so in a negative way. Standard business practice in the United States employs 8½" × 11" format almost exclusively. File folders, briefcases, business portfolios, and even most piles of papers on desks are designed to accommodate the standard size. Letterhead that is smaller or larger than the standard size loses a subtle sense of professionalism. Large-format letterhead may indeed attract attention, but having to fold it to fit into an envelope diminishes its appearance and may actually prove irritating. Smaller-than-normal letterhead, on the other hand, gets lost amid its standard-size brethren, and can accommodate only short letters without requiring a second page. Although the standard format may seem mundane, and mundane is not the ideal for capital campaign materials, this is one case in which the standard solution invariably works best.

Layout

Successful letterhead design leaves enough room for a reasonable amount of text. As obvious as that seems, in their search for good design or their desire to incorporate more and more material, some people forget the primary purpose of letterhead, which is to write letters.

By adhering to certain standards of layout, the letterhead can retain its function while still being attractive. In general, the logo and campaign title belong somewhere near the top of the page. Placing them anywhere on the page that will require special layout for the text of the letter is inconvenient and not worth the fuss. The list of names should be spaced down the left-hand margin and

Figure 11–2 Sample letterhead layouts.

should be set in a typeface and style that keeps the lines of type reasonably short. The address and phone number often appear near the top with the logo or title. If placed across the bottom, they should be well down on the page, leaving as much room as possible for text. See Figure 11–2 for sample layouts for successful letterhead.

Paper

The quality and color of the paper makes a big difference in the impression that the letterhead will make. All too often an organization will go to the time and trouble to procure well-designed letterhead and then decide to save a few dollars by printing it on poor quality paper. The look, feel, and weight of the letterhead affect people's perception of an organization. While there is no need for a modest institution to use the most elegant heavy paper stock—in fact that can be counterproductive—a

> *Before sending the letterhead to the printer, make several trial copies of the letterhead layout and print letters of different lengths on them to see how the letterhead will look when it is actually used.*

medium-weight paper of good quality is well worth the expense. The stock should be light enough in color so that photocopies will not look streaked or gray.

Note Cards, Pledge Forms, Envelopes, and Mailing Labels

If letterhead is the most important piece of campaign material, thank-you note cards come in a close second. Although many campaigns actually neglect the design and printing of these cards, printing special cards for campaign thank-you notes emphasizes most appropriately the fundamental importance of saying thank you. From the very beginning of the campaign planning to the bitter (well, not bitter we hope) end, there will be things to thank people for. Little things such as, "Thank you for attending that meeting." Big things such as, "Thank you for that half-million dollar gift," and all sorts of medium-sized things in between. By providing campaign thank-you notes for staff and volunteers, a campaign will send a strong signal to everyone who is involved that saying thank you is a vital part of the campaign.

The note cards should be reasonably small, so as to accommodate a *brief* note. They should be printed on a good-quality card stock that can be put through a laser printer but that also lends itself to handwritten notes. It should incorporate the campaign logo and theme so that those being thanked will know at once that the thanks is not just from the volunteer but that it represents a thank-you from the campaign as well.

Note cards sometimes double as invitations. If they can be run through a laser printer, such cards may serve as excellent invitations to small gatherings, or even as catchy reminder notices.

Every campaign requires pledge forms, although early in the campaign before the campaign material has been printed, it is common and acceptable to use laser-printed letters of agreement.

Printed pledge forms are generally used for most of the campaign gifts. The pledge form usually incorporates two types of information—information that instructs and assists the donor, and information that is received from the donor.

Information for the donor includes:

- a one-sentence statement of the goals of the campaign
- information about required gift size for being listed on the group plaque
- sample payment schedule for the pledge period and payment options for the campaign
- giving levels and giving categories, societies, or clubs (if relevant)
- specific information about how checks should be made out
- instructions for gifts of securities
- address and phone number of the organization

Information from the donor includes:

- total amount of the pledge
- number of years over which the gift will be paid
- reminder notice schedule preference
- date and year of first payment
- information about employer's matching gift program, if any
- information about how the donor wishes to be acknowledged
- printed name and signature
- date
- address
- phone number

Like letterhead, pledge forms have a specific function. It is always surprising therefore to see pledge forms that may look fine, but don't function well. By following some simple guidelines, an organization can make sure that their pledge form will work for the solicitors, the donors, and the organization.

The most effective pledge cards are large enough to accommodate all of the information listed above without looking crowded and confusing. The donor information space and signature line should be large enough so that someone can fill it out easily and legibly with a felt-tip pen.

A pledge card should be small enough so that together with a return envelope, it can be enclosed with a letter in a standard #10 business envelope.

Many donors are of middle age or older, and their eyesight is perhaps not what it was. The type on pledge forms should be large enough and dark enough to be read easily.

Both donors and solicitors generally prefer pledge forms that fold inward so that the information that the donor provides is concealed. This accommodates many people's sense that money is a private matter, and it helps solicitors control their urge to give the form a sidelong glance as the donor is handing it over.

The layout of material on a good pledge form looks simple. In fact, a great deal of disparate information must be carefully organized in a relatively small space. This is no task for amateurs. The pledge form should be designed by professionals who know how to use layout to lead a reader through complex material.

Every campaign needs envelopes—envelopes for mailing letters, return envelopes for pledge forms, envelopes for large proposals, envelopes for thank-you notes. Fortunately, campaign envelopes can and should be relatively simple and straightforward mailing envelopes. Campaigns generally do not use the window envelopes or response envelopes that are often employed in annual campaigns.

Many campaigns have found it worthwhile to print self-adhesive mailing labels that incorporate the campaign logo and theme. These may be used on large, unprinted mailing envelopes for proposals and other campaign materials. They can also serve double duty on unprinted folders, thereby creating campaign folders at little extra expense.

Leadership Gift Solicitation Material

The solicitation of lead gifts occurs early in the campaign, often before the campaign materials have been printed. While many people believe, quite understandably, that the solicitations for large gifts should be the most elaborate presentations, they in fact need not be at all elaborate; however, they must be comprehensible, professional, and personal. It is also a misconception to suppose that lead gift proposals must be long, or weighty, or composed entirely of polysyllabic, erudite, recondite, recherché, abstruse, and sesquipedalian words. The very best lead gift solicitation material is brief and simply stated.

The material used to precede or accompany most lead-gift solicitations is generally a brief proposal letter of one-to-three pages. The letter usually is addressed to the prospect from the campaign leadership. It contains a simple statement of specific and relevant information including:

- the amount of the gift being requested
- a brief statement of what the gift will accomplish
- a statement of the campaign dollar goal

- an indication of where a gift of the suggested size would fit into the campaign
- suggestions about how the donor might be recognized for the gift
- specific information about who will follow up on the proposal

Effective proposal letters are written to reflect the point of view of the prospect. Each is individualized, connecting relevant information about the donor and his or her interests to the project and the proposed gift. If a donor has given to the organization previously or has been involved in its work, the proposal letter usually makes reference to such prior involvement.

The proposal letter is often sent with a packet of background information, thus enabling the prospect to read the letter quickly, understand what is being requested, and determine whether or how to proceed. It also provides enough supporting information so that the prospect will be able to review material that will assist in making an informed decision. Supporting materials often include some or all of the following:

- case for support (the simple three- to five-page document that has been refined through the campaign planning process)
- list of the organization's board of directors
- list of the campaign planning committee (if this is not already presented on the letterhead)
- project budget
- project timetable
- small versions of project drawings (floor plans and renderings)
- list of naming opportunities, highlighting the suggested gift and showing which spaces have already been taken
- table of gifts for the campaign goal
- highlights of the organization's operations and programs
- audited financial statement

Much of this material may be generated on a computer and printed on a laser printer. It should be organized so that it is easy to understand. In some presentations the first sheet is an index to the material that is included. This enables the reader to skim the list and go directly to the most relevant material.

When an organization has gone to the expense of having a color rendering prepared for the project, a presentation might include a color copy or photo of that rendering.

Pocket folders work well for organizing this material. Some organizations go to the expense of printing folders with the campaign logo and theme. This makes an attractive presentation.

> *Once the package is complete, let it sit. Someone else should spend an hour looking it over. Be willing to fine-tune the materials one more time. That final review is always worth the effort.*

Before sealing and sending a leadership-gift proposal package, it's a good idea to take the time to review it as though one were a prospect looking at this material for the first time. Everything should be examined, beginning with the addressed envelope and continuing through each piece of material, viewing it all with a prospect's eyes.

First, put the completed package in its envelope on your desk. Does the envelope look professional? Are the name and address correct and accurate? Is the mailing label straight?

Second, pull out the packet. Is the proposal letter on top? Does it look inviting and easy to read? Does the folder look professional? Is the folder label personalized with the donor's name? Is the label on straight?

Third, read the proposal letter slowly and carefully. Is the salutation appropriate for the person who signed the letter? After reading the first paragraph do you know what it is about? Are there misspellings or other foolish errors? Has the letter been signed? Would you know how and when to respond?

Finally, open the folder. Can you see easily what information is included on each side of the folder? Does every piece of material look simple and clear? Does it all look professional? Do the numbers match? Is there anything that could be profitably omitted or simplified?

Such a thorough review seldom fails to turn up a need for last minute corrections or amendments. Not only will the process improve the proposal package, but it will also increase the peace of mind and confidence of the staff member who is responsible for the proposal.

The Campaign Brochure

The most visible and impressive of the campaign materials is the campaign brochure. It gathers and summarizes information about the project, the organization, and the campaign into an attractive and readable format. In images, captions, and headings, it should convey enough information so that someone with only a casual interest in the project can absorb its essence and importance after scanning the brochure for a minute or less.

Timing

Campaign brochures are usually unveiled and presented at the campaign kickoff, when the campaign is officially announced. The brochure presents the project and the campaign in their official format. By the time the brochure has gone to press, the building plans have been fine-tuned, the public goal for the campaign has been established, the campaign theme and logo have been settled, and the case for support has been finely honed. In some sense, the campaign brochure brings together in simple form the many months of work that went into preparing the project and the campaign.

Purpose

Campaign brochures are sent to prospective donors together with proposal letters. They are attractive, eye-catching, and easy to read. When the brochure arrives in the mail, together with a personal letter requesting a gift, it focuses the attention of the prospective donor on the project and the campaign.

Much more important, however, is the brochure's function as a tool for the volunteer solicitors. Volunteer solicitors are anxious—they are afraid that they don't know enough about the project, that they won't be able to make the case effectively, that they will get the facts wrong, or that they will forget what they are supposed to say. In short, many volunteers feel as though they are about to take an examination but haven't studied enough! The campaign brochure makes the solicitation process an open-book exam. It arms the solicitors with the facts, figures, words, and pictures to guide them through a successful solicitation visit.

These two functions—informing prospective donors and guiding solicitation meetings—overlap but are not the same. An understanding of both functions will have important consequences for design and layout. As a conveyor of information, the brochure should contain detailed information about the project, enabling a prospective donor to become thoroughly informed by reading the text. In its function as a solicitor's guide, it should be organized into talking points that will lead logically and smoothly through the solicitation process. Each point should be highlighted by headings in large type, with charts, drawings, or illustrations where they will graphically clarify or elucidate every concept to be covered during the solicitation.

Formats

The most common format for a campaign brochure is an 8½" × 11" stapled (saddle-stitched) booklet of eight to twelve pages. However, there are many brochure formats that work as well and may even be preferable for small or midsized campaigns. Brochures in traditional format usually work better as information pieces than they do as solicitors' guides. A prospective donor is able to sit and read or at least skim the booklet from cover to cover, absorbing the images and reading the headings and text. For a solicitor who is guiding a prospect, however, this format works less well since it requires the volunteer to turn pages while walking the prospect through the presentation. An easier solicitation format is one that opens to a larger size and presents all the important information on one page so that the volunteer can refer to particular topics and areas without having to flip back and forth.

Sometimes these campaign booklets are designed with pockets in the covers to hold pledge forms and other materials.

Occasionally, a graphic designer is able to develop a campaign brochure that accomplishes both ends equally well. One satisfactory format is 8½" × 34" and folded three times accordion style. This provides eight panels, and can either be held and read like a booklet or spread out to full length and placed on a table. Although this large size is difficult to produce, it functions extremely well.

Some campaigns use even larger formats that fold down to smaller sizes. These too can work well if the material is organized effectively. Examples of three formats are found in Figure 11–3.

Style

Campaign brochures range from extremely simple one- or two-color pieces all the way to elaborate four-color presentations. The only important determinant of style is that the format and degree of lavishness of the brochure match the mission and general values of the organization. Undoubtedly it is appropriate for an art museum to tip the scales on the artistic side, pulling out all of the stops for elegant design and high visual impact. On the other hand, the very same sort of brochure prepared for a small day-care center campaign would be inappropriate and consequently ineffective.

Social-service organizations are often afraid that their donors will disapprove of money spent on good design and printing. While this concern does contain a kernel of truth, a well-designed campaign brochure that is simple, clear, and attractive almost never engenders a donor's ire. Donors dislike wasted money, not well-designed brochures. Well-designed brochures, however, even if simple, require the assistance of excellent designers, good paper, and fine printers.

The use of poor photography often undermines what might otherwise be a strong campaign brochure. Sometimes, in the misguided effort at economy, an organization will elect to snap their own shots for the brochure. What usually results is a collection of stilted or uninteresting photos in washed-out tones of gray that communicate nothing specific about the case or the organization. Dollars spent on excellent photography are often some of the very best dollars spent. Although a picture sometimes is worth a thousand words, a bad picture is worth no words at all.

Figure 11–3 Examples of the accordian format, folded format, and booklet format for brochures.

Occasionally, an organization has an opportunity to highlight the work of a locally known artist in its campaign material. Although some brochures make powerful use of good photographs, others rely on artists' renderings and paintings. If an artist is well known in the community and willing to support the campaign, that individual might be willing to create a limited number of prints of the artwork that is used in the campaign brochure. Matted and framed, these make wonderful gifts for major donors and key campaign volunteers in appreciation for their part in the campaign.

Content

The content of the campaign brochure differs little from the information that is contained in a lead gift solicitation package. It contains information of three types.

1. Background information should include summary information about the organization's history, mission, programs, and goals; a board of directors list; the address and phone number of the organization; and the name of the executive director.
2. Information about the project should include the case for support, highlighted with headings; drawings of the building or project; floor plans; a map showing the project location; a project budget; and a timetable.
3. Information about the campaign should include the names of the campaign leadership, the names of the campaign planning committee, the campaign goal, the table of gifts, giving categories and donor-recognition opportunities, ways in which to make a gift (cash, pledges, securities), and a sample payment schedule.

The brochure should, of course, incorporate the campaign theme and logo into the design and where possible should clarify and emphasize, through photos, drawings, or other images.

Campaign brochures are sent to everyone who will be personally solicited for the campaign. Enough brochures should be printed for every solicitation, plus a healthy sur-

As you prepare for your campaign, collect campaign brochures. You will learn what is effective and what is not, preparing yourself to guide the development of a successful brochure for your campaign.

plus for various public-relations uses. Sometimes organizations print enough to send a brochure along with the direct-mail solicitation that concludes the campaign. More often, an organization will develop a different, smaller brochure for the end-of-campaign mailing. This smaller piece can create a final burst of energy and urgency by highlighting a looming deadline or the push for the end.

Does the Campaign Need a Videotape?

Videotapes are becoming more common in capital campaigns. Before deciding to invest in a videotape for a campaign, one must understand fully what they can and cannot accomplish.

Videotapes can

- present an organization in a lively and engaging fashion
- build credibility by using people who are well known and respected in the tape
- give a personal and human touch to the case for support
- create an easy way for a prospect to experience the case for support

Videotapes cannot

- solicit gifts
- replace face-to-face discussion

An organization that has many prospective donors who live far away should seriously consider developing a videotape for the campaign. Although a video is not nearly as good as a personal visit to the organization, a good videotape can do a respectable job of bringing the organization and the project to the donor in an engaging and entertaining fashion.

On the down side, video is a demanding and complex medium requiring specific expertise, technical sophistication, and elaborate equipment. Unless an organization is willing to spend the time and money that is necessary to develop a high-quality product, it would be better off not using video. Bad, boring video presentations are far worse than no videos at all.

Because of our experience with television and movies, people in our culture have come to expect professional-quality videos. We want attractive images, good lighting, clear color, well-timed dramatic effects, and professional graphics. And professional-quality videos are demanding, expensive, and time consuming to make.

If an organization is fortunate enough to have the resources to produce a high-quality videotape, its use should be carefully determined beforehand. No matter how good a video is, solicitors should not take it along to play during the solicitation meeting. Although a tape may be sent in advance or left with the prospect after the solicitation meeting, the time that the solicitor spends with the prospective donor should be used exclusively for active and personal interchange.

Campaign Newsletters

Campaign newsletters keep information flowing, and the flow of information builds energy and enthusiasm for the campaign. Campaigns often use two types of newsletters—informal, brief news bulletins for the campaign insiders, and more elaborate newsletters to communicate with all volunteers, donors, and other constituents.

Insider newsletters are often designed in-house and produced on the laser printer; these insider newsletters help keep the people closest to the campaign up to date about the campaign's progress. A wise development director will maintain a mailing list of those who have a special stake in the campaign and will be able to get out a bulletin in a short time and with limited effort. Actually preparing several sets of addressed envelopes to the insiders in advance facilitates the process even more.

These instant newsletters let people know about major gifts as they come in, progress or changes in the status of the project, special efforts that someone may have made on behalf of the campaign, or any other special and late-breaking campaign news. Some organizations have their graphic designer prepare a format for these communiqués that is in keeping with the other campaign material. Others simply use ad hoc formats. Attentive directors or campaign chairs may choose to add small personal notes to some of these small communications, helping people feel even more connected to the project.

If insider newsletters are distributed prior to the campaign kickoff, they should all be stamped CONFIDENTIAL to remind people that the campaign is not yet public and the information should not be broadcast.

Official campaign newsletters vary in number. Most campaigns produce at least four to six campaign newsletters. These are often designed to have a special campaign look that is different from that of the organization's regular newsletter. The campaign newsletter features the campaign logo and theme and presents only campaign-related information.

A series of campaign newsletters might cover the following material.

- Issue #1: Preannouncement of Campaign (one to two months before the campaign kickoff). Presents the organization's vision for the future, plans being developed to accomplish that vision, and plans for the campaign. This first issue should present the project and create a sense of anticipation.
- Issue #2: Campaign Kickoff (just after the campaign kickoff). Contains information about campaign organization, leadership, goal, and kickoff event. This second issue often acknowledges key campaign volunteers and contains more specific information about the project.
- Issue #3: Progress Report (two months after campaign kickoff). Reports on success and forward momentum of the campaign, including lead gifts and early results from the general solicitation process. This third issue contains news about volunteers and news about the project.
- Issue #4: Progress Report (two months after issue #3). Continues reporting on campaign progress. This fourth issue highlights special gifts or grants and creates a sense of urgency about reaching the goal.
- Issue #5: Victory Issue (when goal is achieved). Announces that the campaign has reached or gone over its goal. This fifth issue recognizes donors and volunteers, lists names of donors, and announces the campaign celebration.
- Issue #6: Wrap-Up Issue (after campaign celebration). Reports on the campaign celebration and the projects made possible by the campaign. The final issue provides a transition from the campaign communication back into the organization's standard communications pieces.

The content and timing of these broadly distributed campaign newsletters will vary from organization to organization depending on staff time and the funds that are available. Effective communication with donors, prospective donors, and volunteers is an important way to build team spirit and spread an aura of success and accomplishment.

Miscellaneous Materials

Many campaigns develop a whole host of other secondary materials to support the campaign. These may include campaign buttons, tote bags, T-shirts, paperweights, and banners. Although not necessary, these items can add enthusiasm and energy to a campaign. Before investing in any promotional items, the staff should develop a well-considered plan for distributing the items. Sometimes people get caught up in their own enthusiasm and decide to invest in one item or another only to find that they have no effective way of distributing them beyond a relatively few volunteers. It is not uncommon for boxes of campaign buttons or T-shirts to remain under a table in the workroom for years after the conclusion of the campaign.

Direct-Mail Brochures

For organizations that have a large mailing list that includes many who have not been personally solicited, it makes sense to develop a special direct-mail piece for the broad-base solicitation. By the direct-mail phase of the campaign, the remaining donor prospects usually have little or no direct connection with the organization. This list will include people who are low-level donors as well as those whose names are on the list but who have never given to the organization. Sending these people a complete campaign brochure is often inappropriate and expensive.

A specially designed, eye-catching, direct-mail solicitation will usually pay for itself many times over and will attract new donors to the organization.

Using a Graphic Designer

Graphic designers are the unsung heroes of campaign materials. A talented graphic designer is able to assemble concepts and images into a form that captures the spirit of the campaign within the value structure of the organization. They are trained to understand the language of visual images, type, and layout. Through their work, the themes that for most people are verbal are expressed and organized visually.

Although we seldom stop to reflect on it, the work of graphic designers permeates our culture. Advertisements, product packaging, billboards, and magazines are just a few of the many areas through which graphic designers shape the cultural environment.

Campaign materials are often designed by advertising or public-relations firms. And because these fields are so important in our society, most communities have a healthy selection of professionals to choose from. Every firm has its own particular style, so an organization is well advised to spend some time exploring the available talent pool and determining who is likely to work best for them.

Some firms want to be involved in the writing as well as the design. Others expect the organization to develop the text to fit their design. Still others design to fit existing text. Every firm is also likely to have different aesthetic sensibilities, and a review of their work on other projects will present a clear account of their preferences and styles.

Designers or Communicators

Effective graphic designers are more than artists, they are communicators as well. Not only do they understand how to add an image to an idea, but they are experts in the organization and flow of ideas—how they can be arranged on a page to encourage reading and increase comprehension. While many who work primarily in the verbal world add more words to elucidate and explain, graphic designers often pare away words, leaving only those that are essential to the concept that is being communicated.

In the authors' experience, graphic designers might be categorized according to whether they are primarily designers or primarily communicators. Some are wonderful designers but are less interested in communication and perhaps therefore less able to communicate clearly. Others understand the need to communicate, but, in doing so, they sometimes compromise their aesthetic standards. The ideal designer places equal value on both communication and design, and insists on doing them both well.

Two for One

Approximately 400,000 people have library cards in our county. When we automated the library system, we had to send each of our cardholders a new bar-coded library card. We decided to develop our final campaign appeal in conjunction with our library-card mailing. The appeal was actually the carrier for the new card, so everyone who received a new card also had an opportunity to fill out one flap of the flier and send it back in a return envelope with their gift to the campaign. This approach was very successful. It cost us very little, as we had to do the mailing anyway, and it combined the request with a tangible sign of what the new system would accomplish for the donors. Months later, we are still getting gifts from our library-card mailer. All together, we've added hundreds of new names to our donor lists and many of these people may continue as regular contributors!

—Library Director

The telltale signs of an artist who doesn't communicate well are:

- the use of small and light typefaces that look beautiful on the page but are difficult to read
- a propensity toward odd sizes and shapes that stand out visually but interfere with communication
- overprinting of one image or block of text onto another image in a way that is striking but confusing
- organization of the material on a page so that it looks elegant but on closer inspection does not flow logically.

The telltale signs of a communicator who compromises on the art are:

- text-heavy pages that flow well but are not visually inviting
- very little white space on each page
- sloppy spacing and placement of text blocks on the page
- lack of an overall unifying design concept

Tombstone Graphics

In recent years, with the spread of desktop publishing, the field of graphic design has become open to many people with little or no artistic training or ability. Beware of what is sometimes referred to as "tombstone graphics." This style, characterized by blocks of text bordered by single or double lined squares or rectangles, is typical of self-taught graphic designers and is generally not of a standard or quality that is suitable for the design of capital-campaign materials.

To review a designer's portfolio effectively, one must spend enough time to consider and read each piece. A quick glance at a glossy portfolio provides only the most cursory sense of the designer's style. A thorough examination—reading all the text and understanding the purpose of the piece—is likely to reveal the abilities of the designer. However, when reviewing a portfolio, an organization must be sure that they are examining the work of the person or team of people who will be responsible for their work. In larger firms, the portfolio might be a collection of work by various designers, none of whom will be working on the campaign materials.

Because capital campaigns involve the leadership of a community, it is not uncommon for design or advertising firms to donate design services for campaign materials, charging only their out-of-pocket expenses. This goodwill gesture helps spread the reputation of their firm.

Clarifying Responsibilities and Schedules

Before interviewing graphic designers, it is helpful to draft a list of the materials that they will be asked to develop and a preliminary timetable of when they will be needed. The list is likely to include the following pieces.

- campaign logo and theme
- campaign letterhead
- campaign brochure
- pledge form
- thank-you note cards
- mailing labels and/or campaign folders
- kickoff invitation
- format for an insiders' newsletter
- four to six issues of a campaign newsletter
- design for printing on promotional items
- celebration invitation
- direct-mail solicitation piece
- all necessary envelopes

Such a list will help the graphic designers understand the universe within which each piece will fit and prepare them to develop basic design concepts that can be adapted to a wide range of pieces.

The graphic designer usually coordinates all aspects of producing the materials. They select and collaborate with photographers, artists, typesetters, and printers. They recommend paper types and colors and help an organization understand the alternatives and benefits of one selection over another.

She Got the Message Right from the Start

We really lucked out. One of our PR committee members wanted to hire a small graphic design firm in town. They came to strut their stuff and just rubbed our director the wrong way. They didn't ask questions, and when he spoke they didn't listen. We almost hired them anyway because our volunteer had recommended them so highly, but at the last minute, I convinced the committee to interview a design firm that was located just a few miles away. The minute Elizabeth walked in, everyone (including the volunteer who had recommended the first firm) knew she was right for us. She had asked me many questions over the phone and came to the meeting having already developed a concept that just hit the mark. We hired her, and the materials she produced inspired volunteers and donors alike. The material also won several regional and even national design awards, which made us all feel proud!

—Director of Development, Planned Parenthood Center

The Power of Materials in Building a Campaign

When the graphic designer works collaboratively with the campaign leadership and together they arrive at a look and a feel that tell the tale and powerfully express the importance of the campaign in image and words, the campaign materials that arise from this collaboration greatly strengthen the campaign. With every written communication, the power of the case is restated. Through every image the unity of the campaign is reinforced.

While poor, unprofessional materials raise doubts and anxieties, excellent campaign materials empower and embolden staff members and volunteers. They symbolize the quality of the enterprise and the importance of the campaign's mission.

Campaign materials work hand in hand with the effective organization of volunteers, active face-to-face solicitation, responsible follow-through, and donor recognition to weave the strong fabric of commitment that is needed for successful campaigns.

Chapter 12
Practicing the Discipline of Gratitude

Chapter Outline
- The Discipline of Gratitude
- Saying Thank You
- Recognizing Donors and Volunteers Publicly
- Using Recognition to Further the Campaign
- Naming Opportunities
- Plaques
- Take-Home Mementos
- Recognition Ceremonies
- Reaping the Rewards of Gratitude

The Discipline of Gratitude

It may seem unusual to think about gratitude as a discipline to be practiced. But those who understand that gratitude is a discipline and that discipline requires practice learn to incorporate gratitude into their lives and the lives of their organizations. For these people, the discipline of gratitude yields constant and unexpected rewards. For them, the focus of a development program is as much about what they can give back to their donors as it is about what they can get from them. A genuine and disciplined emphasis on giving, surprisingly all too rare in the nonprofit world, creates an environment that encourages true philanthropy.

This chapter reviews many aspects of expressing gratitude in the context of a capital campaign. Campaign volunteers and donors can be thanked and recognized through means as simple and inexpensive as making thank-you phone calls and sending brief notes to techniques as complex and costly as installing donor plaques on a new building. In this chapter we will explore many aspects of a topic that all too often is assumed to involve nothing more than plain common sense. These topics may well be commonsense, but they are nonetheless far from obvious, and more than any other topic in fund raising, more than any technique for increasing gifts, more than any information about campaign structure, a disciplined approach to gratitude and recognition is a true investment in an organization's future.

Saying Thank You

The Many Places for "Thank You"

How many times a day does the average person say "thank you?" "Please" and "thank you" are certainly common occurrences in everyday parlance. We use these phrases to ask for and to acknowledge the small kindnesses that add so much to the quality of our lives. They are embedded in our speech patterns in much the same way as, "How are you?" or, "Good day." To thank someone is to express gratitude for something that they have done. Of course, using formulaic words of gratitude is often not the same thing as a sincere expression of appreciation. For example, we usually thank a sales clerk after making a purchase. We may be happy to have obtained the item, but we are not really grateful to the clerk for selling it to us. We may be grateful for efficient and businesslike behavior, but often we don't even have that to be grateful for. We often say, "thank you," simply because in our culture "thank you" is an acceptable way to indicate that a transaction has been completed.

Thank-you notes for gifts also bring a transaction to a close. They let the donor know that a check or pledge has been received and that someone in the organization has recorded it and responded to it. But the function of thank-you notes as indicating the completion of a transaction is just the beginning. Gratitude, real gratitude, connects people. It holds up and celebrates the best of human behavior and in doing so it reminds us of the ways in which we would like to behave. To practice the discipline of gratitude, one begins by looking for what is real and good in other people and figuring out ways to recognize and acknowledge it. Real thank-yous—the ones that inspire a tear or a lump in the throat—connect the gift and what it makes possible with what is special in the giver.

The Many Faces of "Thank You"

The variety of ways to thank people is limited only by the imagination. One need not succumb to the power of social conditioning that predisposes most people to act only within a limited range of options. Gratitude may be expressed effectively through something as simple as a casual thank you that is spoken in passing or as elaborately as a bronze plaque that dedicates a building in someone's name. The wide range of alternatives in between makes it possible to find just the right way to thank a specific donor for his or her particular contribution. Finding the right way to thank someone is just as personal and idiosyncratic as finding the right solicitor to ask for the right gift in just the right way.

A review of the most common ways of saying thank you yields a range of options from which one, two, or even more ways to thank a particular donor or volunteer can be selected. As readers review these familiar mechanisms of gratitude, their own creativity will help them find other ways to thank their donors and volunteers. Here are just some of the ways one might thank a donor for a gift.

- verbal thanks in person
- verbal thanks over the telephone
- handwritten thank-you notes
- typed thank-you notes or letters
- typed note with personal, handwritten note appended
- notes from the beneficiaries of the gift
- notes from the head of the institution
- notes from a friend
- personalized updates about the success of the project or program
- special humorous awards
- special serious awards
- personal invitations to dinner or another thank-you event
- flowers, candy, champagne, or some other extravagance
- personal invitation to visit the program or facility
- nonpersonalized tokens of appreciation
- personalized tokens of appreciation
- public acknowledgment from the podium
- public acknowledgment in the press
- permanent public acknowledgment (plaques, signs)
- a work of art commissioned to capture an image of the project
- artwork (photo, drawing, painting) of the building, mounted and framed along with personalized message

The Need for Honesty and Authenticity

In reviewing this far-ranging list of recognition techniques, it is important to remember that the effectiveness of a gesture is based more on the honesty and authenticity of the feelings that are motivating it than on

> *Honesty and authenticity are the sine qua non of effective gestures of gratitude.*

the lavishness of the gesture itself. An authentic expression of gratitude for a gift can make the smallest of thank-you gestures effective, while a vacant or dishonest gesture can diminish the value of even the grandest form of recognition.

Most people know only too well the disappointment that comes from a thank-you note that doesn't connect with its recipient. While most donors do not wish to be thanked excessively for a small- or medium-sized gift, most people do want to know that someone noticed that *they* gave!

Thanking Donors Personally

Without doubt, the most powerful forms of gratitude are personal gestures. Donors who are acknowledged by someone whom they know, in a way that reinforces the importance of their gifts, feel truly appreciated. Small and insignificant as they may seem, personal notes and phone calls specifically for the purposes of thanking a particular donor often leave a more lasting impression on a donor than the most deeply etched plaque.

Small notes, phone calls, or other gestures are effective when they are thoughtfully prepared. They need not take long or be particularly artistic, but they must come from the heart and reflect on specific characteristics of the donor. It is not enough, for example, to write a note that thanks the donor in a neutral, matter-of-fact way. It must mention something specific about the donor that

---

The Thank-You Note That Missed the Mark

I had just rotated off the board of a regional music festival, having served for six years. The following year, in response to a standard mailing, I made a medium-sized gift to the organization. I was disappointed, in fact angry, when some weeks later I received a formulaic thank-you note signed by the chairman of the board, whom I knew well. The letter was addressed, "Dear Mrs. Kihlstedt" and made no reference whatsoever to my long commitment and support of the organization. I understood that the failing was probably not meant as a personal slight, but I was hurt that no one had taken the time to recognize my gift personally. Because I was no longer on the board, for them I had simply ceased to exist! Not surprisingly, I gradually stopped giving to that organization.

—Campaign Consultant

bears on the gift and the organization. Such personalized comments let the donor know that the writer has actually thought about him or her as a particular individual. And knowing this, donor feels a personal sense of connection.

Consider, for example, the sample letters in Exhibits 12–1 and 12–2 that might be written by an executive director of a children's center to the son of a long-time supporter, now deceased.

Neither of these letters is bad, but the first one captures the spirit of Dave's father and in doing so, it lets Dave know that his gift will accomplish what he is really after—making sure that his father's memory is kept alive at the center. The second letter appropriately tells Dave that his gift will help the community and that it will help attract other gifts to the campaign, but it says nothing that lets him know that Dorothy really understood the motive behind the gift. The first letter is donor oriented, the second is organizationally oriented.

Writing donor-oriented thank-you letters is much easier when one knows the donor. With just a little practice and discipline, it is possible to put oneself in the shoes of the donor and envision the real reason that underlies the gift. Thank-you letters that actually address those underlying reasons often ring true and communicate effectively, even when the reasons are not the usual ones.

Consider, for example, the donor who gave a generous gift not because of the specific project, but because of who asked for the gift. The correspondence in Exhibits 12–3, 12–4, and 12–5, stands out because of its candor and good humor. The proper tone of a correspondence is established by the relationship between the donor and the organization. Ideally, every lead-gift donor has had an opportunity to build a relationship of trust and respect with the director of the organization, and the specific style and patterns of that relationship dictate the content and style of the letter more than any particular rules of fund raising.

These letters reflect a genuine relationship among Dave, Anne, and William. The first letter from Dave to William does not make more of the relationship between William and the center than is real, though it certainly expresses appropriate gratitude for the gift. The letter from Dave to Anne gives her credit for both her own and William's gifts; it lets Anne know that Dave is sensitive to her need to acknowledge her deceased husband through this gift, and it acknowledges the risk Anne took in asking William for such a large gift. The third letter from Anne to Dave lets him know that both her gift and William's were made because of her confidence in him.

Correspondence of this sort reflects honest relationships between the donor and an organization that have been built over a period of years. The gifts were really the culmination of these relationships, and the thank-you notes are strong in part because they recall the underlying motives all around.

Personally Thanking Donors One Doesn't Know

If one is not acquainted with the donor and knows nothing except their name, address, and gift amount, it is more difficult to write a letter that is donor oriented. Nevertheless, by sharing one's real feelings, it is possible to write a note that has a good chance of creating an authentic connection with the donor. Thank-you notes that reveal something personal about the author or something immediate about the organization, particularly as they relate to the gift, help the donor feel that he or she has not been relegated directly to the computer's form-letter software module.

The success of thank-you letters really does depend on their authenticity. Exhibits 12–6 and 12–7 illustrate simply the style and content typical of effective thank-you letters. Exhibit 12–8 is typical of a letter that doesn't work.

In Exhibit 12–6, even though Joan does not know Mr. Janus, her letter speaks directly to him. It highlights his rapid response time. It lets him know that his gift stood out. It also tells him that his gift made a difference to the emotional state of the staff as well as to the campaign itself. It informs him about how the campaign is doing and lets him know that Joan would like to meet him.

The letter in Exhibit 12–7 is simpler, but it still works. It acknowledges the gift and the special role it played when it was received. It lets the donor know that not only does her money count, but that her commitment to the center counts, and it looks ahead to a successful campaign.

The letter in Exhibit 12–8, which for many organizations is standard, falls well short of the mark. The word *generous* in the first line presumes information about the donor that the author does not have and thereby immediately strikes a false note. There is nothing in the letter that lets the donor know that Sonya Green specifically acknowledges this particular donor. Indeed, with a change of name this letter could be sent, and in fact probably was sent, to every campaign donor. Even though the letter is signed by Sonya Green, when Mr. Jamison reads it, he will have no sense that Sonya actually noticed his gift. This letter also reveals nothing about its author. In fact, it was probably written by the development director and simply signed by Ms. Green.

Campaign thank-you letters prepared by the staff for the campaign chairs to sign need not be so bloodless. If the staff takes the time to work with the campaign chairs to find the style and content that actually reflects their voices, even routine, staff-prepared letters can sing, and speak from the heart.

Exhibit 12–1 Donor-Oriented Thank-You Letter

Anytown Children's Center

535 Lewis Lane   Kidsville, Maryland 20917   Phone: (301) 555-6432

Dear Dave:

Your pledge to the campaign just arrived today, and it made my heart soar! I can't wait to tell Mary that you've decided to name the Center's library in memory of your father. He really believed that knowledge and information gave people power, and he spent countless hours reading to our children over the years. He would be so pleased to know that the library will be called the John Davison Memorial Library. How wonderful of you to help us all remember the lessons your father lived so well!

Thank you so very much for your gift. As we get a bit further along with the campaign, I'll call to set up an appointment so we can begin to talk about the specifics of naming the room.

Although words can't express the depth of my gratitude for this gift and what it means to me and the center, please know that your generosity has brought tears to my eyes both because of what it will do for the center and for the memories it brings back of your father!

With appreciation,

Dorothy

Exhibit 12–2 Organizational-Oriented Thank-You Letter

Anytown Children's Center

535 Lewis Lane   Kidsville, Maryland 20917   Phone: (301) 555-6432

Dear Dave:

Thank you so very much for your generous gift naming the center's library in memory of your father. Not only will the gift help renovate this important area of the center, but it will set the giving standard for the leadership division of our campaign.

The center continues to work to help young people in the community. The renovations will enable us to serve more than twice the number of families we have served in the past and your gift gets us off to a great start.

We are in the process of developing a plan for donor recognition and I will contact you soon to discuss the wording on the plaque for the center.

Sincerely,

Dorothy

Exhibit 12–3 Letter #1

Anytown Center

678 Capital Street   Some City, PA 17087   Phone: (718) 555-1234

Dear William:

Today in the mail I received your pledge for $250,000! Now I know that you are a generous person, and that collectively your gifts make possible much of what is good in our community, but I also know that you have no particular reason to be passionate about our organization. So you can imagine how surprised (and delighted) I was that a leadership gift should come from your foundation. I guess I really owe Anne a special thank-you as well. I knew she was taking you to lunch to call in some favors and I guess she did just that! Perhaps your real return from this gift is having evened the score with her! In a world where what goes around comes around, I guess you've made a full circle, and our organization is the thrilled beneficiary.

Thank you so much for your generous gift. It will go a long way toward providing a new fitness center in our community. People from all walks of life will have access to a well-equipped and furnished center. Older citizens will be able to use the new therapy pool and young children will be taken care of in the child-care center while their parents participate in our programs.

Perhaps you didn't know this, but the expanded gym will be fitted out for indoor tennis courts in the winter. When you come to visit, why don't you bring your racket and we can try it out!

Again, William, thank you so very much for your generous gift. We understand our good fortune and are indebted to you for it.

Sincerely,

Dave

Exhibit 12–4 Letter #2

Anytown Center

678 Capital Street   Some City, PA 17087   Phone: (718) 555-1234

Dear Anne:

You have certainly wrought a miracle! With just your gift and William's, we're about halfway toward our goal. What a true pleasure it is to know that someone is willing to go out on a limb for our center. Your lead gift got the ball rolling and your solicitation of William has set the standard for the entire campaign. I look forward to the day in not too many months when we can dedicate the new gymnasium to Sam's memory. That will be a day for all of us to celebrate the completion of a project that you really extended yourself for.

Thanks so very much.

Warmly,

Dave

Exhibit 12–5 Letter #3

Anne Markham Spencer
18 Montgomery Place
Some City, PA 17204

Dear Dave:

I've seldom had more fun than I did at lunch with William. I knew and he knew that he had asked me more than once for a big gift and that I had come through. He knew and I knew that I wanted a return favor for the center. I hemmed and he hawed, but in truth, I think it was done before we ever met for lunch. I guess I see myself as part of a small team in this county of people who are fortunate to have enough resources to give away. Those of us on the team really work together in an informal way to get the things done that are really important. So, although William and I seldom talk about it directly, we both know that we'll always help each other. That way, we both can accomplish even more!

Thanks so much, Dave, for being such a good manager and for making sure the center is worthy of our support. I, too, look forward to the dedication ceremonies. I wish Sam could be there to enjoy it too.

Sincerely,

Anne

The Number of Thank-Yous for Each Campaign Gift

Every campaign donor should be acknowledged at least three times soon after the receipt of the gift—the donor should receive an official thank you from the executive director that states the amount of the gift or pledge, a thank-you letter from the campaign chair, and a thank-you note from the person who solicited the gift.

Over a longer period of time, donors should be thanked in other ways as well. Thanks might be extended with personal notes that accompany periodic progress reports or newsletters. Or donors might be recognized in less personal ways at special events or in the organization's newsletter.

Personal thanks might also be extended through phone calls from board members to campaign donors. These calls, though inexpensive and easy to make, nonetheless send a powerful message to the donors. It gives them an opportunity to speak directly to one of the organization's leaders, ask questions, express their opinions, and feel personally acknowledged for their participation in the campaign.

Special Gifts and Lasting Mementos

Small gifts or gestures of appreciation that are given at unexpected times can sometimes have great meaning. Some people seem to have a particular knack for spotting just the right thing for the right person. Gifts and gestures must be appropriate to be effective. If they are either too lavish or given insincerely, the result can be worse than no gift at all.

Some campaigns go to the expense of creating mementos, often with the campaign logo, for volunteers and donors. Paperweights, tote bags, prints of fine art, tie tacks, pins, or even coffee mugs are sometimes presented to campaign workers and donors as tokens of thanks and as a remembrance of the campaign. For some campaigns, these items do indeed seem appropriate and well received, though for others they seem an unnecessary expense. The decision to invest in lasting mementos should be determined according to their appropriateness for the particular organization and whether the director and campaign chair feel comfortable with such an expenditure.

For donors of larger gifts, personalized tokens of appreciation that donors can display in their homes or offices are common, and they are usually appreciated.

Acknowledging Nondonors

Although it is often not done very well, thanking donors is commonplace. Less common is the practice of thanking nondonors, but much goodwill might be reaped by this simple gesture. In every campaign there are people who feel strongly about the organization but who for one reason or another are not sufficiently moved or just not able to make a campaign gift. It is tempting to view these people as stingy or as the organization's second-

Exhibit 12–6 Example #1: An Effective Thank-You to a Stranger

---

Campaign for the Arts

Dear Mr. Janus:

What a pleasure it was to find your pledge of $300.00 for our campaign in today's mail. Your gift was among the very first responses we had from the letters we mailed last week. You must have sent it by return mail! For us, therefore, your gift had extra significance. It meant that the letters actually got where they were supposed to go and people like you responded immediately.

The campaign is in its final stages. We still must raise $220,000 before the end of the year, but if the early response to this phase is any indication, we should be able to reach our goal in time.

Soon it will be time to plan a celebration. You'll get an invitation in the mail as soon as we've gone over the top!

I hope to meet you in the new year, and I send my sincere thanks for your pledge to our campaign.

Sincerely,

Joan Dresser
Executive Director

Exhibit 12–7 Example #2

Campaign for the Arts

Dear Mrs. Keener:

Thank you so very much for your pledge of $300.00 to the center's capital campaign. I was working with the architect to finalize the details of the new classroom when our deveopment director put it on my desk, and I felt reassured that money was coming in even as I was planning how to spend it!

Through these last five months when all of us here have worked so very hard to develop the building plans and manage the campaign, gifts like yours have buoyed our spirits. You remind us that there are people whom we haven't had the pleasure of meeting yet who care deeply about the center and give their hard-earned money to help us move ahead.

Thank you again. I look forward to writing to you before the end of the year to let you know that with your help, we've achieved our goal.

Sincerely,

Joan Dresser
Executive Director

Exhibit 12–8 Example #3

Campaign for the Arts

Dear Mr. Jamison:

Thank you very much for your generous pledge of $300.00 to the center's capital campaign. We are truly grateful for your support.

The campaign must raise another $230,000 to get us over the top. This money will fund the renovations to our building. This program will grow and be sustained by your generosity and that of many other donors.

I've enclosed an official receipt for your records. Thank you again for supporting the center's capital campaign.

Sincerely,

Sonya Green
Chair, Capital Campaign

---

class citizens. In truth, however, many nondonors wish to remain friends of the organization and may even become generous donors at another time. Post-campaign letters to nondonors help keep the door open for building stronger relationships in the future. Consider, for example, how a nondonor would feel receiving one of the letters in Exhibits 12–9, 12–10, or 12–11.

People who have written note after note in the course of their jobs as directors of agencies find that there are two ways in which one can accomplish this sometimes overwhelming task. One can think of it as a formal activity—one that simply needs to be done—or one can actually use it as a chance to connect with the many people who help in one way or another to make the organization strong. If one takes the former approach, one is relegating a substantial amount of one's time to routine work. If, however, one is able to grasp these small opportunities to communicate, the process of thanking people, though it need not take any more time, becomes a creative and personally rewarding assignment.

Recognizing Donors and Volunteers Publicly

Mixed Motives

The more public the recognition, the more mixed the motives for both the organization and the donors or volunteers. Organizations often recognize their most powerful donors and volunteers publicly because they want the community to know that these people have aligned themselves with their project. Many donors and volunteers are pleased to receive public recognition because it may increase their influence in the community. Other

donors and volunteers, though they may personally shy away from such coverage, understand its effect in the community and are willing to exert their influence to help the campaign.

However, *public* recognition is no substitute for *personal* recognition. Rather, public recognition most often stems from a collaboration between the donors and the organization to further the cause of the organization. When the donor is genuinely pleased with broad visibility, everyone wins. When the donor would rather remain private, their willingness to assume a public pres-

Artful Thanks

A day-care center decided to involve the center's children in the process of preparing the thank-you notes for their campaign. They gave pieces of card stock to each of the art teachers and asked them to have the three- to five-year-old children draw and paint on them. They then mounted these small works of art on brightly colored folded paper and glued white paper on the inside to use for handwritten thank-you notes. These were used as one type of thank-you note to campaign donors. Thus, in addition to an official typewritten thank-you letter, each donor received a handwritten thank-you note that came inside a unique work of art created by one of the children at the center. These notes brought the donor into contact with the children and gave the children a role to play in the campaign.

Exhibit 12–9 Letter #1

Campaign for the
Counseling Center

Dear Sue:

You've been such a good friend to the center for so many years that I thought you might want to join us for a tour of the newly renovated center on March 1 from 3:00– 4:00 P.M. We're inviting a small group of people who have been our long-time supporters to take a look at what we've accomplished and to see the amazing differences it will make in the way we are able to serve our patients. Please call Mary in the office (334- 8758) and let her know if you'll be able to join us.

I hope to see you then.

Sincerely,

Janet Moss
Executive Director

---

ence for a campaign is yet another reason for a private thank-you.

Public Recognition and Commitment

It is easy to forget the discomfort that comes with public visibility. On one hand, it is gratifying to be known for one's good works and generosity, but on the other hand, people in the public eye sometimes become the target for others' jealousies or irrational anger. By becoming publicly aligned with a particular campaign, one also accepts responsibility for its success or failure. If it fails, its failure will be your failure! If it succeeds, then of course that success is yours, too! People who have never experienced public visibility often overlook the downside and ignore the need to recognize donors and volunteers for their willingness to assume such a role.

Exhibit 12–10 Letter #2

Campaign for the
Counseling Center

Dear John:

I know you had reservations about the building project and chose not to give to it. And indeed, we really did go so far out on a limb with the project that even I felt uncomfortable at times. But now that it's over and the mission accomplished, I'd love to show you around and talk about how we might expand programming in the future. That's really your specialty and I hope to be able to pick your brain for some ideas.

I'll call you next week to set up an appointment. I look forward to speaking with you.

Sincerely,

Janet Moss
Executive Director

Exhibit 12–11 Letter #3

Campaign for the Counseling Center

Dear Ken:

I just wanted you to know how much I enjoyed our meeting yesterday. We've sat in the same boardroom for months and have seldom had a chance to get acquainted. So, finally to have a chance to learn about you and your extraordinary service in our community felt like a reward indeed. Although I am sorry you won't be able to join Doug and me in making a leadership gift to the center's campaign, your clear thinking and suggestions about developing the case for support have already gotten us going in the right direction. I hope you'll be willing to continue to guide me through this—it's my first campaign and I will truly need your advice!

Thanks so much for the many things you do for the center and for this community.

Sincerely,

Barbara McMillen
Campaign Chair

Sometimes the process of becoming a public figure actually helps an individual become more committed to the campaign. Such a person gradually becomes drawn in until finally his or her name and face have become publicly associated with a particular cause or campaign. And now, having publicly thrown in his lot with the campaign, this individual swallows all reservations and does whatever is needed to make sure the campaign succeeds.

Effective executive directors and development directors make sure that volunteers are presented in the very best light. They go to great lengths to get good photographs of key volunteers. They help draft public statements for campaign leadership. They work with volunteers to polish their presentations. And they do whatever is possible to protect volunteers from any negative coverage or publicity. Staff take the blame when things go awry and give credit to volunteers for what goes right.

The Desire for Anonymity

Some donors truly wish to remain anonymous. They don't want their names to appear on plaques or even in donor listings. Sometimes they don't want anyone but the campaign chair or executive director to know about their gift. More often, however, donors who wish anonymity are pleased to be recognized in nonpublic ways. While they shy away from publicity, they appreciate every personal thank you and gesture that lets them know just what their gift meant.

Misunderstandings around the expectations of the anonymous donor arise when the organization does not trouble itself to discuss these issues with the donor. Do they really want no one to know? Is it all right to share information about the gift with the organization's board and the campaign steering committee? A few specific questions posed to the donor will clarify their intentions and desires, which then should guide the way that donor is recognized. Lastly, it is well to remember that few if any donors—even the most anonymous—would prefer not to be thanked!

Say It with Chocolate

A development officer for an organization in Hershey, Pennsylvania started every meeting with a donor with a small gift of chocolate. Sometimes it was a large canister filled with Hershey Kisses and sometimes it was just a Hershey Bar. But, this small gift immediately set the donor into a good mood, started the meeting with a sincere and palatable thank you and allowed the development officer to leave a "sweet" reminder of her visit.

Staff take the blame when things go awry and give credit to volunteers for what goes right.

Using Recognition to Further the Campaign

Some campaigns honor an individual who is particularly beloved by an institution by naming a room or building in his or her honor. They then use that recognition to raise money from his friends and family for that area. This usually takes the form of a mini-campaign within a larger campaign structure. In a mini-campaign of this sort, a group of donors usually decide that they would like their gifts to be used to name a particular area—the Weisman Gymnasium, say—in honor of Abe Weisman, the basketball coach who lead the home team for more than twenty years. The initiating group of donors might negotiate with the organization for a dollar amount that they will have to raise to name the gym. They then work with the staff to organize a special campaign within the broader campaign. It is not uncommon in mini-campaigns that honor an individual for donors to make two campaign gifts—one to the general campaign and another to the special campaign.

While this strategy of recognizing someone to stimulate giving is often effective, it is also fraught with the complexities that come from mixed motives. The individual being "honored" and his or her family may feel compromised or awkward about the prospect of their friends and relatives being solicited on their behalf. In some campaigns, these subcampaigns create confusion as to who is to solicit whom, and they may even engender "turf" battles. However, many campaigns have successfully used this strategy as a way of raising money for an organization and honoring someone long associated with that organization, so it may be worth the struggles inherent in the concept.

When organizing mini-campaigns in honor of a particular individual, it is important to obtain the approval of the person being honored and/or the person's family. In some cases a spouse or children or even grandchildren will want to become actively involved in raising the money. Occasionally, the person and his family want no part of the project at all. Before proceeding with such a project, the executive director or development director must make sure that the family concurs with the concept and the plans.

Naming Opportunities

Many campaigns that raise funds for building projects—renovations or new buildings—offer wonderful opportunities for people to make gifts that enable them to have their names or the name of someone they care about inscribed on a plaque in a particular room or area. Although most people are quick to say that they have no interest in seeing their name "in lights," experience demonstrates otherwise. Though they may give to a campaign for reasons that have everything to do with the mission of the program and their desire to help the organization, a great many people also find pleasure in seeing their names or that of a loved one on the wall of a building.

Determining Giving Levels for Naming Opportunities

Contrary to popular belief, gifts made to name a specific room or space in a building do not actually pay for that particular space. Nor are the dollar amounts of those gifts determined by the cost of the space. Giving levels for naming opportunities are determined by the visibility, prestige, and emotional appeal of the space. Main lobbies are likely to have a higher price than even expensively equipped staff offices. The boardroom is likely to have a higher price than the training room. A chapel or meditation room is likely to be more valuable than a similar small meeting room.

The actual dollar amounts that are assigned to particular spaces should approximate the table of gifts being used in the campaign. The highest gift should correlate to the most prominent and prestigious space, the next two to the next most visible spaces, and so on.

The process of identifying spaces and assigning dollar values is generally accomplished by a small committee that includes the director, campaign leadership, and development director. The process works most simply if the development director prepares for everyone copies of the floor plans that indicate each of the rooms and spaces. Creativity is essential in preparing this list, for it is not only the standard rooms that can be named, but also flag poles, entry porticos, garden areas, fountains, and all sorts of other architectural elements. Sometimes there is more than one way to name a space or architectural element, for example, special stained- or etched-glass windows for which either the individual panes might be given by several moderate donors, or else one donor might donate the entire collection.

The discussions about what should be offered as a naming opportunity and how much it should be offered for are invariably interesting and lively and result in an understanding on the part of both staff and campaign leadership of the complex nature of naming rooms and spaces in buildings and the appeal of making a naming gift. Sometimes the process of determining the naming opportunities actually raises the sights of the campaign leaders about their own gifts.

Following the discussion, the development director is usually responsible for assembling all the opinions and collating them into a clear and reasonable list that gives the dollar amounts that have been assigned to rooms, spaces, and architectural elements in the building and provides spaces for donors to indicate their intention to "buy" a particular space. The list of naming opportunities is used during the solicitation of leadership gifts. It must be updated throughout the campaign as named spaces are spoken for.

Exhibit 12–12 is a sample naming-opportunity list that was presented to prospective donors to help them envision the size and location of the space they were being asked to consider.

Naming Opportunities and Low-Level Gifts

Although most naming opportunities are designed to stimulate mid- and upper-level gifts, some campaigns use naming opportunities for lower-level giving as well. Architectural elements such as tiles in walls or brick walkways or seats in auditoriums provide a chance to incorporate the names of many people who give relatively low-level gifts to the building.

Plaques

A Selling Tool or a Recognition Device?

Some campaigns and some solicitors use the list of naming opportunities as a primary solicitation tool. Others take a low-key approach and encourage donors to name a space only toward the conclusion of the campaign. The first approach capitalizes on an interest in having permanent recognition for a gift. The latter uses naming opportunities to strengthen relationships with people who are already donors, recognizing them in ways that they themselves might not have initiated.

Organizational Culture and the Role of Plaques

These different approaches often reflect variations in organizational culture. For some organizations, plaques and permanent recognition have always played an important role in the institution. A walk around the grounds and buildings of an organization is likely to turn up plaques of all kinds. In organizations with a "plaque culture," plaques tend to be well cared for and carefully displayed. Brass is polished, outdoor plaques are cleaned regularly, and photos and oil portraits of founding fa-

thers and mothers are proudly and prominently displayed.

In other organizations, one is struck by the occasional and haphazard use of plaques. There may be none at all, or there may be a few that are so poorly displayed that they radiate the organization's discomfort with the practice. Bronze is tarnished; one or two small plaques might hang by themselves in the middle of a large blank wall. Paintings of founders hang crookedly in their dirty frames.

If plaques are not a part of an organization's culture and history, it may be difficult for the leadership of that organization to commit the time, effort, and resources that it will take to use plaques effectively. Few things are more destructive to donor relationships than a promise of recognition that is not followed through with or that

Exhibit 12–12 Naming Opportunity List

List of Areas for Commemorative Plaques	
Entrance Vestibule	$300,000
Reception Area	150,000
Board Room	50,000
Indoor Garden	30,000
Large Conference Room	30,000
Small Conference Room (3)	15,000 each
Center for Living with Loss	
Entrance Vestibule	150,000
CLL Reception Area	75,000
Chapel/Solace Area (330 sq. ft.)	50,000
Multimedia Training Center	50,000
CLL Director's Office	30,000
Counseling Rooms (3)	15,000 each
Staff Lounge	30,000
Patio with Planters	15,000
Executive Director's Office	30,000
Chief Operating Officer's Office	30,000
Finance Office	30,000
Personnel Director's Office	15,000
Vice President's Offices (3)	15,000 each
Medical Director's Office	15,000
Medical Examination Room	15,000
Volunteer Area	30,000
Admissions Area	15,000
Development Office	15,000
Team Clusters (5)	15,000 each
North team	
South team	
East team	
West team	
Facility-based care team	
Window Panels	6,000 each

> *How would you feel if you had given $50,000 in honor of your father only to discover that your "plaque" is a small hand-lettered piece of plywood hung on the wall between the fire extinguisher and the exit sign?*

is carried out poorly, so the decision to use plaques should be made along with a long-term commitment for their display and upkeep.

In the short term, good plaques take thorough planning and a significant outlay of resources. It is not uncommon to spend $10,000 or more to design, prepare, and install donor plaques. Although plaques need not be of bronze or marble, they do need to be well designed, attractive, and well placed.

However, plaques are also for the long term, and any organization that decides to offer naming opportunities to its donors must accept the long-term responsibilities of maintaining the plaques in such a fashion that the donors whose names they honor and represent—and their descendants—will be proud to be a part of that institution.

Location and Design of Plaques

To develop a program for recognition through plaques that really works well, a campaign should begin during the planning process when the architects are planning the building. Alas, often plaques are mere afterthoughts. Not that they are conceived as development tools after the fact, but the specifics of their size, materials, design, and location are afterthoughts. Many a prestigious institution spends ample time poring over floor plans and assigning dollar values to spaces, but neglects to discuss the specifics of plaque size, design, and location with the architects or interior designers. Then, two months before the building dedication, the development director is assigned the task of getting plaques made for the building—a project far outside the expertise of most people in development. It is little wonder, then, that plaques often look out of character and ill placed.

Think ahead to avoid the problem of poorly planned plaques. One need only think ahead and incorporate a scheme for donor plaques into the design of the building. Qualified architects and interior designers, if given the assignment early in the design process, are capable of incorporating plaques into their design schemes in a way that pays respect to the donors and enhances (or at least does not diminish) the building design.

When the issues of size, design, and placement of plaques are sprung on architects and interior designers at the end of a project, these professionals are likely to see these plaques as detrimental to their design, so it's no wonder that they often relegate them to the fire ex-

tinguisher-exit sign cluster. Such conflict is less likely if expectations are presented early on and the designers have an opportunity to design around the needs of the campaign.

Just as people seldom think about plaques in a timely fashion, they also tend to ignore the need for incorporating directional and labeling signs for the building (both inside and out) until after the designers have completed their work. A building for which the design of both plaques and signs has been planned from the perspective of complementing the architecture is one that truly stands out. There is, however, nothing like tacked-up, poorly planned signs and plaques to make even the most competent building renovation look shoddy immediately.

In order to be able to inform donors accurately about just what it will mean to them to "buy" a naming plaque, the development director should work with the designers, director, and campaign leadership to determine policies about donor plaques. These policies should be outlined in writing as explicitly as possible during the planning phases of the campaign. They should include decisions about the following questions.

- **Group Plaques**
  Will there be a group plaque listing the names of all donors (except those who wish to remain anonymous) of gifts over a certain amount?
  How much must a donor give in order to be listed on the plaque?
  Will donors be listed according to gift amount or alphabetically within category?
  Will the amount of the gift be listed on the plaque?
  Where will the group plaque be located?
  What will it look like?
  Will donors be able to specify the wording of their name(s) on the group plaque?
- **Individual Plaques**
  What does it mean to "name a space"?
  Does naming imply any sort of ownership or proprietary benefits?
  Will donors be able to name spaces within wings named by other donors?
  Will the space actually be named for the donor? (e.g., the Weisman Room or the Stengle Chapel)
  How large will plaques be for each giving level?
  Who will determine the wording on each plaque?
  Will donors have a say in the design of their plaques?
  Will plaques be located within the named room or clustered with other plaques?
  What will plaques be made of and what will they look like?
  What will happen to the plaques and to the name of a particular space if the building is ever renovated or demolished?

Conflicting Goals

One of my clients recently presented their need to recognize donors on plaques to their design team just as construction was nearing completion. She was very surprised to find that the architects and interior designer found these plaques a distinct inconvenience. Their solution was to incorporate all the donor names into an etched window, which would minimize their visual impact in the overall building. Of course, that worked for the design team but distinctly did not work for my client, who realized that the donors expected their names to appear prominently on walls in or near the rooms they had designated. A prolonged and unpleasant battle ensued. The design team strongly objected to individual plaques, strewn, as they put it, all over the building. The development director felt strongly that every person who had given with the intent of naming a space should be recognized at or near that specific location. A satisfactory compromise was finally reached that clustered plaques that named the rooms in a particular wing on the wall of the entry to that wing. Great care was taken in informing the donors of the design decision, and, in the end, everyone was pleased. However, the road to compromise was littered with considerable argument and dissension.

Wording on Plaques

Wording on plaques is more difficult and sensitive than one might imagine. Group plaques often recognize all donors to a project who have given over a certain amount. This contribution level is often $1,000 but may be higher or lower depending on the size of the campaign and the number of donors. Most such plaques list donors by name alphabetically within giving categories. Some group plaques specify the dollar ranges indicated by the giving categories, but more often, the dollar range is omitted and the giving level is simply indicated by placing the highest giving category at the top of the plaque and listing the remaining giving categories in order of descending amount.

The wording of names is often suggested by the institution to the donors. It is often simpler to establish a preferred manner of listing and then to ask each of the donors if they are willing to be listed that way. By suggesting, for example, that every donor will be listed by first name, middle initial, last name, without titles such as Dr., Ms., Mr., or Mrs., one is able to develop relatively consistent text for the plaque. When someone wishes to include a

spouse, the organization should suggest the order and manner of the listing. A couple might, for example, be listed as:

- Mr. and Mrs. Anthony Partner,
- Susan B. and Anthony Partner,
- Anthony G. and Susan Partner,
- Susan Blain Partner and Anthony Partner, or
- Susan Blain and Anthony Partner.

Of course, decisions such as these must be guided as well by the preferences and standard practices of each couple, and one must not be rigid for the sake of consistency.

Most group plaques begin with an expression of thanks to the donors of the project. The wording should be relevant to the project, and should be an honest expression of gratitude. In general, simpler and shorter phrases are better than long, flowery ones.

Every group plaque should be dated and should state the name of the project or the campaign so that it will speak clearly throughout the future history of the organization.

Finding the right wording for individual plaques can be a challenge. For larger gifts, it is common to name a room for the donor and to indicate this by incorporating the donor's name into the building. So, for example,

But I Thought It Was My Wing

A major medical center put up a new building. One wing was dedicated to cancer research and a donor decided to name that wing by giving $1 million. The wing included many laboratories and offices. Using that lead gift to spark their campaign, the development officer and campaign leadership were able to raise many generous gifts from other donors to name each of the laboratories in the cancer-research wing. Everything seemed to be going well and on course until shortly before the building dedication, when the first donor visited the new building and was shocked to find other donors' names in "his" wing. In his mind, his million-dollar gift had actually bought that wing. And by selling off pieces of his wing, the campaign had diminished his gift. Now it looked as though he had not really donated the wing, but only in conjunction with all those other donors. If the donor had been better informed at the time that his gift was being solicited, then this problem never would have arisen. Of course, there would then have been the possibility that the donor might not have given such a large gift. He might, however, have given an additional $1 million to "buy up" all the real estate in his wing.

the waiting room might become the Arthur Judson Waiting Room, or the boardroom might have a sign on the transom that says "Bellows Boardroom." In some cases, the donor is further recognized with a plaque in the room as well as a sign that names the space.

When gifts are made in memory of loved ones, donors often have proprietary feelings about the message on the plaque. It is not uncommon to have a donor write a note with his pledge form asking that the plaque read something like the following:

> "In loving memory of Agnes, who was a wonderful wife and an outstanding mother. Her contributions to this agency over many years served to make it strong, and her unflagging enthusiasm provided hope for many of the patients served here.
>
> John Jamison, Cathe Jones,
> Jim Jamison, Jonathan Jamison,
> Mary Kreege, and Kristie Jamison Kelly."

Of course those heartfelt sentiments are lovely, but they are generally too long for a 6" × 8" plaque. Showing donors standard-wording options and plaque sizes early in their deliberations helps keep them from being disappointed or disillusioned later.

Approval from Donors

Donors must have a chance to see the wording, size, and design of their individual plaques in advance. They should have a chance to see a life-size drawing of their plaque and should be asked to indicate their approval. Some organizations send mockups of plaques to the donor with a response form that the donor is asked to sign and return. Other organizations invite donors to visit the site to review a mockup of the plaque in its proposed location.

Timing

Once the plaques have been designed, the process of finalizing the wording, checking with donors, and fabricating and installing the plaques can easily take two or three months of dedicated work. For plaques to be ready and installed by the building dedication, work should begin on plans for the plaques well before the building is complete.

Take-Home Mementos

In the effective practice of gratitude, every major donor should have a personal reminder of the gratitude of the organization. There are many ways to use take-home versions of plaques for donors. Some organizations actually have replicas of the plaques made for their donors. Others photograph donors with their plaques in the named room or building and then frame the photo with an inscription of gratitude. Still others assemble scrapbooks for donors showing the construction of the building and culminating with photos of the donor at the building dedication. Whatever the gift, it should be an appropriate one, and specific to the particular donor.

Recognition Ceremonies

Large institutions usually have the staff, facilities, budgets, and traditions that support effective recognition ceremonies. Unfortunately, it is common for smaller, lean-staffed organizations to make short shrift of recognition ceremonies. These organizations often find themselves so bogged down in moving and getting their new programs underway in the increased press of activity that often accompanies the completion of a major project that they overlook the importance of these ceremonies for both donors and staff.

These ceremonies provide both public and private opportunities for thanks and recognition. Donors and staff alike come together around a job well done. For such an event, they are no longer staff members or volunteers, rather they are people who have worked hard and have accomplished something significant for their community and their organization. These opportunities for recognition and gratitude are every bit as important as the plaques, thank-you letters, gifts, and mementos. They bring people together and give each of them a moment when they can enjoy knowing that their work counted.

Reaping the Rewards of Gratitude

The better one becomes at the discipline of gratitude, the easier it is to practice it! People who have made a habit of recognizing others for what they do well find that this practice repays them many times over. Not only does the practice of gratitude focus their vision of the world onto what people do that is good and right, which in itself is a gift, but they find that people who have worked with them want to do so again and again.

Fortunate is the staff member whose supervisor recognizes and acknowledges the many things he or she does for their organization. Fortunate is the director who works with a board chair who sees and cites his or her effectiveness. And fortunate are the donors and volunteers who help in a campaign where they are appreciated, whether or not every one of their calls brings in a gift!

The Best View in the State

Our campaign chair had his name on the reading room in the new library. When I took him up to check it out (on the day before the formal dedication), he stood in front of the window, got big tears in his eyes, and whispered, "This is the best view in the state." It is a beautiful view down the main green, past the chapel, and out toward the mountains. So, for his "thanks for being our chairman" gift, we had a photographer take a color photo of that view and make an 8" × 10" print. We had a calligrapher mount it on an 11" × 17" board and letter underneath our words of appreciation for everything he had done. The best part was that under the picture I had the artist letter, "The Best View in the State." We had it all matted and framed, and we gave it to him at the campaign celebration. He *loved* it. He still says it is the most meaningful thing he's ever been given.

—Development Director

Capital campaigns are strategic moments in the life of an organization. Although we tend to focus on the dollars that are raised through these campaigns, the long-term strength of the relationships that are built through a campaign have consequences far stronger than the money raised. The effective practice of the discipline of gratitude builds those relationships and strengthens the ties that shape an organization's future.

Chapter 13
Staff—The Unsung Heroes of Every Campaign

Chapter Outline
- Defining Staff Roles
- The Executive Director
- Roles of the Development Director and Development Assistant
- Preparing the Development Office
- Involving the Entire Staff
- Getting the Work Done
- The Rewards of Hard Work
- Ten Tips for Survival

Earlier chapters in this book discussed the leadership, commitment, generosity, and organization that is needed to build a capital campaign. We have highlighted and discussed in some detail the role of the board, the planning committee, and campaign volunteers. But behind the success of every campaign are hardworking and committed staff members. Few campaigns succeed without a competent, well-organized, and rock-solid staff. While their efforts are often invisible to those on the outside, and not always recognized even by those on the inside, the executive director, the development director, the development assistant, and even the clerical support staff are absolutely indispensible to a successful campaign.

The specific campaign responsibilities of the executive director, the development director and other development staff members vary from one organization to another. In some organizations the executive director plays a major role in fund raising and the development staff supports those efforts. In others, the executive director focuses almost exclusively on the program aspects of the organization's growth and leaves the fund-raising program to the development staff.

Because in a campaign the stakes are high and the potential for building important relationships is great, even those executive directors with only minor involvement in the annual giving program are often fully involved in many aspects of a capital campaign.

Defining Staff Roles

Typically, the campaign work of the executive director, development director, and development assistant falls into six general areas.

Preparation. Prior to the campaign, the staff makes sure that requisite development systems are in place to facilitate the campaign. They also gather and organize information on prospective donors and volunteers.

Planning. The staff works with the campaign consultant to develop a clear and workable structure for the campaign. They help design a campaign architecture that enables volunteers to work effectively toward shared ends, and they develop ways to communicate that structure effectively to all those working on the campaign.

Implementation. The executive director is often responsible for helping to enlist key volunteers and to solicit leadership gifts. Though these tasks are primarily assigned to leadership volunteers, the staff often participates in the process.

Coordination. Staff members pull together and manage all the pieces of the campaign; they keep track of every aspect of the campaign effort from beginning to end. They facilitate the hiring of outside professionals (graphic designer, printer, consultant, and sometimes even the architect) and make sure that these people have what they need to work effectively.

Information and Communication. Staff members manage both internal and external communication. They assemble information about the campaign—who is doing what, what gifts have come in, what gifts are pending, what is happening next, and so on, and they communicate with other staff members, volunteers, and donors to maintain a sense of clarity and forward momentum throughout the campaign. They also work with the public-relations staff and volunteers on communicating information about the project and the campaign to the community.

Support. Staff members support the efforts of everyone who is working on the campaign, simplifying and facilitating their jobs. They assemble and manage the paperwork that accompanies every solicitation. They establish internal systems to handle timely and effective donor and volunteer recognition. They call meetings, send follow-up notes, make reminder calls, encourage, nag, and when necessary, browbeat.

Recognizing the Organizational Culture

The roles of the executive director and the development director vary significantly from one organization to another. At one end of the spectrum are organizations whose executive director has delegated all fund-raising responsibilities to the development director. These executive directors see their job as running an agency, not raising money. They believe that the board, supported by the development director, should be responsible for securing financial resources. In many organizations of this type, the development director relies almost exclusively on staff-driven fund-raising strategies like direct mail and special events, and shies away from major-gift fund raising.

At the other end of the spectrum are organizations whose executive directors play the role of chief fund raiser. These directors set the agenda and tone for the entire development effort. They rely on the board to help identify, cultivate, and solicit prospects and on development directors to support, coordinate, and track their efforts as well as to implement the standard direct-mail and special-events fund raising that is typical of most nonprofit development programs.

Many small- to medium-sized organizations fall somewhere in between these two poles. The roles of executive director and development director in fund raising reflect the history and culture of the organization and are shaped by the particular skills and personalities that the individuals bring to their jobs.

Shifting Staff Roles

The period just before a capital campaign is an excellent time for an organization to reevaluate and shift staff roles in fund raising. Organizations that are short on staff in their development programs might consider adding a new staff member to take over some of the responsibilities for annual giving, thereby freeing some of the development director's time for the campaign. Or they might use the prospect of a campaign to replace a lower level development professional with someone more experienced.

It is not uncommon for capital campaigns in smaller nonprofits to inspire staff changes. As executive directors and development directors begin to experience the pressures, they realize that the demands of their jobs will soar during the campaign period. Those who are weak of heart or lacking in commitment may jump ship, but those who feel excited by challenge, grasp a campaign as an opportunity for learning and promotion. Some executive directors who have never been interested in fund raising suddenly begin to play a more active role. Development directors who have confined their activities to direct mail, phonathons, and special-events fund raising find the courage to shift their sights to major-gift fund raising. Usually, such transitions take place early in the campaign planning process, but sometimes they occur in midstream, causing significant interruptions in the work of the campaign.

Although these turnovers and shifts are often painful, most organizations become stronger because of them. If a campaign is viewed as an opportunity to raise an organization's level of fund-raising ambition and sophistication, it is reasonable to assume that it will be a time either to develop and promote fund-raising staff or to institute changes in this area.

Tasks Handled by Staff

Because many smaller nonprofits have never before conducted a campaign and because staff members take on campaigns in addition to their ongoing work, it is often difficult to predict accurately just how staff functions should best be handled. Even with careful and effective planning, staff members generally need to feel their way into this process, guided by the needs of the campaign, the ongoing demands of the organization, and their own abilities and zeal for the work.

For many smaller nonprofits, a team approach to staffing works well. A campaign team might include the executive director, the development director, and the campaign consultant. It might also include a development assistant or public-relations staff member. Together they learn, discuss, brainstorm, and explore every aspect of campaign planning and implementation. As it becomes clear that specific tasks are necessary, these are allocated to particular staff members or volunteers whose expertise best suits the need. Such a team approach, though time consuming, supports learning, lowers the pressure on any one staff person, and creates a group of individuals who are informed and excited about the campaign.

Although it is difficult to assign staff roles that will fit every organization, it is possible to develop an organized list of the tasks and responsibilities that are part of every campaign and to indicate the staff person who most often handles each task. One possible division of labor is shown in Exhibit 13–1. Sometimes these tasks are taken on by one primary staff member and sometimes they are shared by a group of people, but for every campaign these are the tasks that generally fall to staff members to accomplish. Even though many of them are behind the

Exhibit 13–1 Campaign Responsibilities

Campaign Tasks	Executive Director	Development Director	Development Assistant	Campaign Consultant
Planning				
Recruit volunteers	✓	✓		
Solicit gifts	✓			
Design campaign strategies	✓	✓		✓
Plan project	✓			
Develop internal case for project	✓	✓		✓
Plan work of campaign steering committee	✓	✓		✓
Preparation				
Gather information about prospects	✓	✓	✓	
Identify and cultivate donors and volunteers	✓	✓		
Organize prospect rating sessions		✓	✓	
Assess development office systems		✓	✓	
Engage consultant, designer, etc.	✓	✓		
Implementation				
Recruit campaign leadership	✓			
Recruit campaign volunteers	✓	✓		
Train solicitors		✓		✓
Solicit gifts	✓	✓		
Coordination				
Coordinate work of outside professionals		✓	✓	
Coordinate campaign materials		✓	✓	
Coordinate public relations		✓	✓	
Coordinate campaign events		✓	✓	
Coordinate campaign newsletters		✓	✓	
Coordinate internal flow of information		✓	✓	
Coordinate direct-mail campaign		✓	✓	
Coordinate phonathon		✓	✓	
Coordinate staff campaign		✓	✓	
Coordinate donor recognition		✓	✓	
Coordinate plaque preparation		✓	✓	
Information and Communication				
Manage data and computer systems		✓	✓	
Keep donor records		✓	✓	
Thank donors	✓	✓	✓	
Track and report solicitation progress		✓	✓	
Track and report campaign progress	✓	✓		✓
Disseminate campaign information	✓	✓		
Schedule and present speeches	✓	✓		
Communicate with solicitors	✓	✓	✓	
Communicate with volunteers	✓	✓	✓	
Communicate with campaign leadership	✓	✓		
Communicate with staff about the campaign	✓	✓		
Prepare and distribute meeting notes			✓	
Support				
Schedule appointments	✓	✓	✓	
Schedule meetings		✓	✓	
Attend to details of meeting setup		✓	✓	
Follow up after meetings		✓	✓	
Send reminder notices			✓	
Make follow-up phone calls			✓	
Draft proposals	✓	✓		
Prepare proposals			✓	
Handle and coordinate all campaign paperwork		✓	✓	
Encourage and motivate	✓	✓		

scenes and seemingly insignificant, collectively they are critical to the success of a campaign.

Anticipating Campaign Workloads

The intensity of staff work for a campaign varies from one phase of a campaign to another. During some phases, the executive director finds that it is necessary to work almost full time on the campaign. During other phases, the bulk of the responsibility shifts to the development director and development assistant. Figure 13–1 shows patterns of work flow that are typical to a campaign for a small nonprofit organization. It assumes that the organization has a full-time executive director, development director, and development assistant.

The executive director should anticipate spending considerable time working on the campaign during both the planning and the quiet phases. Most executive directors play an active role in soliciting major gifts and gifts from former board members and founders. They often work with the campaign chair and board chair or other volunteers during the quiet phase of the campaign. Directors are also often involved in the planning of the campaign kickoff. After the campaign kickoff, the director may continue to work on lead-gift or major-gift solicita-

tions—following up on pending solicitations and initiating new solicitations if needed. During the latter half of the campaign, the total time that the director spends on the campaign often decreases. By this time in the campaign, the key volunteers are usually in place and functioning well, and the development staff understands the campaign process. Now the building project clamors for the director's attention.

During the early phases of the campaign, the development director and development assistant spend time assessing and strengthening the development department, making sure that the computer system is adequate for the campaign, checking records, updating donor research, reviewing lists of donor prospects to be used in rating sessions, reviewing and fine-tuning the processes for thanking donors, recording contributions, and preparing and sending receipts. During this early campaign period, a development director might review the plans for annual giving to make certain that those plans can be carried out efficiently and with a minimum of extra effort during the campaign period.

In many smaller nonprofits, the early campaign planning is usually carried out by the executive director in conjunction with the board chair and the consultant. A

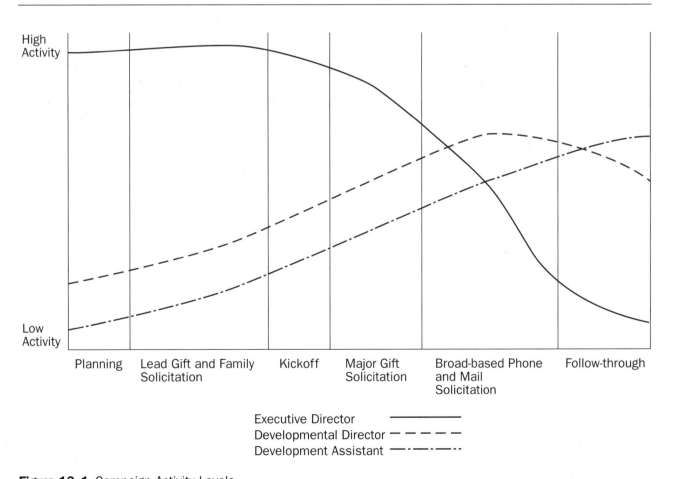

Figure 13–1 Campaign Activity Levels

development director who is excluded from the early campaign planning may feel left out and uninformed. It is easy for an executive director who is spending hour after hour and day after day outlining campaign strategies with the consultant and meeting with key volunteers to neglect to inform the appropriate staff members about the content and progress being made in those meetings. For the development director and development assistant, who know that the campaign will place great but unspecified burdens on their workload, a sense that they have not been included in the planning process can give rise to anxiety and resentment. A wise executive director will bring these individuals into the planning process early in the campaign.

As the campaign progresses, the burden of work gradually shifts onto the shoulders of the development director and development assistant. The number of volunteer solicitors increases, the volume of solicitations mushrooms, and the development director and assistant often spend nearly all their time managing and communicating with volunteers and preparing and organizing the proposals and other paperwork that are needed to support the solicitation process.

Campaigns seldom go exactly as planned, so, during this post-kickoff phase, the executive director works with the campaign chairs to make sure that the campaign is progressing as it should and to institute changes as necessary. This requires frequent progress updates, review of solicitations in progress, and regular analysis of projections.

The Executive Director

The Roles of the Executive Director

Executive directors play complicated and demanding roles during a campaign period. Internally, they lead from in front, bearing aloft the campaign standard for the entire staff. Externally, they lead from behind, keeping themselves in the background, supporting the efforts of the key volunteers and ensuring their success while making sure that the actual work of the campaign is accomplished effectively. These tasks, of course, are added to the executive director's full-time responsibilities of running the organization.

Leading from the Front

Whether or not the executive director has been through a campaign before, the staff looks to the executive direc-

tor to establish the tenor of the campaign. Optimism and enthusiasm combined with an insistence on high quality, hard work, and a healthy dose of good humor set the internal tone for a campaign. Both the development director and the development assistant take their cues from the standard of behavior set by the executive director. Although it is natural for even the most steadfast and experienced of executive directors to experience moments of anxiety, during campaigns—invariably times of change and stress—wise directors will use their will, courage, and determination to create the pattern for success.

Internally, when beginning a capital campaign, executive directors are usually managing organizations that are in transition and must lead already stressed agencies into new and demanding fund-raising territory as well. For example, an organization that is contemplating a major building project usually finds its staff in overcrowded and poor working conditions. In a cramped environment, rising noise levels, and work overloads, the prospect of adding a capital campaign to the mix is often greeted with something less than ardent enthusiasm.

Internally then, the executive director must support and motivate staff members to stretch themselves to navigate a successful campaign, which after all will be the means whereby many of their difficulties will be al-

---

The Glass Half Empty

I'm an enthusiastic person. I guess I was born that way. So when the organization I worked for as development director decided to launch a campaign, I really got on board. The idea of having larger and better facilities, which we really needed, excited me, and the thought of increasing the fund-raising ambitions of the organization, well, it made me anxious, but I was even excited about that.

Our executive director was not an enthusiast. I suppose he saw himself as a pragmatist. I saw him as a pessimist! Throughout the whole campaign, when it came to enthusiasm, we were polar opposites. A gift would come in, and I would jump up and down with glee while he worried that it should have been bigger. A donor would call and leave a message—I would be sure the call was about a gift, he was sure there was a problem. We would tally campaign progress—I would see how far we had come. He would see how far we had to go.

I guess we balanced each other, but I sure felt that at least half of my energies were wasted just by countering his "realism." In truth, if his views had been the realistic ones, we would never have reached our goal!

—Former Development Director

leviated. This takes patience, open-mindedness, and a willingness to lead by setting examples for hard work, steadfastness, and commitment.

The internal discomforts of a campaign are often exacerbated by the lack of campaign experience. Not only have most development directors and assistants never before been through a capital campaign, but the majority of executive directors are new to the campaign process as well. For them, anxiety is usually high and every step of planning and implementation requires excruciating attention to detail.

Leading from Behind

Externally, the executive director leads from behind. The visible positions in the campaign are occupied by the volunteer leaders, but without the effective behind-the-scenes leadership of the executive director, campaign volunteers are likely to lose momentum. The executive director, along with the development director, provides the structure and support that are necessary for the campaign leadership to do its best. The staff finds just the right way to accommodate the needs of each of the volunteer leaders. Some may need specific and detailed written instructions to guide their every move. Others may want to play a larger role in designing the campaign.

Effective executive directors are willing to accept the blame for problems and give credit to their campaign volunteers when there is success. Because many people struggle with their own insecurities and vulnerabilities, this practice proves challenging for even the most seasoned of leaders.

Roles of the Development Director and Development Assistant

Organizational Mavens

Campaigns require the concentrated attention of staff members who are not only willing and able to carry out each and every organizational detail but who also have the will and fortitude to follow up on every loose end. Although big visions and careful design are extremely important, all of the planning in the world will come to naught without someone who can implement every aspect of the plan.

The development director and development assistant often work in tandem to carry out the campaign plan. Once a meeting date is set, the development director and development assistant make sure it occurs just as it should. They think through every detail, develop the materials needed to support the work of the group, and make sure that the people who could not attend are brought up to date after the meeting. Once one meeting has been successfully navigated, the staff members follow up on every detail and begin to plan for the next step in the campaign.

Managing the Campaign from the Middle

The development director and development assistant often find themselves playing challenging roles in managing the campaign from the inside. They often must keep their executive directors in line, making sure that they are well informed and using their time where it is best spent. They also have considerable contact with campaign volunteers, calling to set up meetings, answering questions, and checking to make sure volunteers have completed their assignments. The development director

Cementing the Campaign Together

I came into the agency's capital campaign about six months before it was scheduled to be completed. I was replacing the development director, who had held the job for about six months before being fired a month prior to my coming on board. The campaign had stalled. The chair and planning committee were struggling to complete their solicitations. The executive director was feeling the pressure of completing the campaign in order to fulfill the conditions of a major grant. The support staff was functioning without direction. Everyone was angry and confused by the mess that had been left by the development director, and there was no one around to sort it all out.

With the help of our consultant, we assessed where we were in the process and put together a six-month plan that would lead to the completion of the program. One of my biggest challenges, though, was figuring out who was who. I wasn't familiar with the community, so donors' names meant nothing to me. I was recruiting volunteers based on the recommendations of others but with no personal experience of their abilities. And everyone was carrying some significant emotional baggage because they hadn't been treated well or effectively communicated with earlier in the campaign.

I put my ego aside wherever possible and was willing to look a little foolish as I stumbled through the process. I was fortunate that I had a solid consultant, a responsive exec, and incredibly committed campaign leadership, who were all motivated to make the campaign happen. But it made me very aware of the role that a development director plays in cementing the campaign together and keeping everyone on track—not by being in the lead, but by providing information, encouragement, and follow-up.

—Interim Development Director

and the development assistant are the people who develop firsthand knowledge of the donor data base, knowing who has given and who has not, remembering obscure tidbits of information about one person or another that will be important to a solicitor, and being able to manipulate the software so it will churn out mailing labels, proposal letters, thank-you notes, and myriad other pieces of campaign material. Finally, they are the people who are responsible for making sure that all of the internal systems that support the campaign work smoothly.

Preparing the Development Office

Although staff roles in the campaign are many and diverse, most of them require a well-organized internal system to manage information. Before the campaign, the development staff should evaluate and analyze the management information systems that are in use in the development office to be sure that they will accomplish the tasks of the campaign such as:

- donor information and tracking
- volunteer information
- gift processing
- gift acknowledgment
- gift accounting
- computer and printer capabilities

Evaluating Development Systems

Some organizations conduct an internal review of their development systems. It is sometimes difficult to see the problems because one has learned to work around them, so it may be wise to hire an outside consultant to audit these systems and make recommendations as to how they might be strengthened in preparation for the campaign.

A traditional development audit conducted by a consultant usually evaluates the development programs, personnel, and internal communication as well as the information management systems. The following questions have been designed to guide a development director though an assessment of each system in the development office. These systems should function well for the annual giving program, but it often takes the impetus of a capital campaign to motivate the development staff to make sure that each area works as well as it should. Well-conceived internal development practices and systems will benefit both a capital campaign and an organization's ongoing development program. The authors recommend that the development director take the time to write a report that addresses these questions. Such an exercise will help clarify the structure and function of the development systems and will also serve as a useful tool to inform the campaign consultant and executive director, as well as the campaign chairs.

Through answering these questions the development director should become more aware of the capabilities and weaknesses in the development systems. He or she may wish to share the reports with the campaign consultant, who may be able to make specific suggestions about ways to strengthen the systems.

Gift Processing

Checks. Write a step-by-step description of what happens to a contribution check from the time it arrives in the mail until it is deposited in the bank.

- Who opens the envelope?
- What is done with the envelope and any note or other enclosures?
- Who records the gift amount?
- Is the pledge form or remittance enclosure saved with a copy of the check?
- Is the gift amount credited to the specific fund-raising program that generated it?
- What other information is recorded from the check?
- Is the address checked against the donor files and recorded if new?
- Is the phone number checked and recorded?
- In whose name is the gift acknowledged?
- Whose name is used if the check is in two names and the note in only one?
- What name is used if the check comes from a business or foundation?
- How are memorial gifts credited, to operating or endowment?
- Is there a policy that guides to what fund bequests are credited?
- Who records specific donor instructions, and where are they recorded?
- Do at least two people record the amount of the check?
- How are the receipt figures reconciled?
- How often are they reconciled?
- Is a copy of the check made before it is deposited?
- Are checks of every amount processed in the same way?
- Is the development director notified when a large gift is received?
- What qualifies as a large gift?
- How many days elapse between the receipt and deposit of a check?

Pledges. Prepare a written description of the procedures for handling pledges.

- Who records the pledge?
- Is the total amount of the pledge recorded?
- How are future payments recorded?
- Is there a system for sending payment-reminder notices?
- Are reminder notices used to convey other information about the organization?

Securities. Prepare a written description of the procedures for handling a gift of securities.

- Where is the organization's brokerage account?
- Who is the organization's broker?
- Who pays the broker's commission?
- Who is responsible for overseeing the transfer of securities?
- How do the finance department and the development department interact with regard to the transfer of securities?
- What is the mechanism for tracking securities that have been transferred to the organization's brokerage account without a donor name?
- Is the information that the donor needs to transfer securities (name of the organization's broker, federal ID number, and account number) easily accessible?

Gift Acknowledgment

Describe the procedures and policies for acknowledging gifts in your organization.

- Does every donor receive a gift receipt?
- If not, who receives a receipt and who does not?
- What information is included in the receipt?
- Is the receipt information incorporated into the thank-you letter format?
- How many thank-you notes does the donor receive?
- Who writes thank-you notes?
- Who signs thank-you notes?
- Are some thank-you notes individualized?
- Are some thank-you notes handwritten?
- Do some typed letters have handwritten personal notes added to them?
- Are there different thank-you note policies for gifts of different sizes?
- Are donors of gifts of certain sizes called on the telephone? If so, who calls them?
- What internal mechanisms trigger thank-you notes and/or phone calls?
- Is the family member notified of the receipt of a memorial gift?
- Are donors of memorial gifts thanked in a special way?
- If a gift was solicited in person, how is the solicitor informed of its receipt?
- How many days elapse between the receipt of a gift and mailing the first thank-you note?
- If a donor is to receive more than one thank-you note, how are the notes scheduled?
- How are donors of in-kind gifts recognized?
- Are donor names published in the annual report?
- Are donors listed alphabetically in the report or alphabetically within a giving category?
- Who keeps track of donor names for the annual report?
- Do donors have an opportunity to request that their names not be listed?
- How does the organization determine the way in which each name should be listed?
- Are records kept or copies made of thank-you letters sent to donors?
- What determines when a hard-copy file on a donor is opened?
- Are donors recognized for cumulative lifetime giving?
- Are donors specifically thanked at the end of the year for their cumulative contributions for the year?
- Is any sort of memento used for recognizing donors at different giving levels?

Gift Accounting

Describe the policies that guide how and when gifts are counted toward specific fund-raising goals.

- Who tallies the gifts that come in to the annual giving program?
- Are there specific starting and stopping dates for gifts that are counted for annual giving? for the capital campaign?
- Is the full amount of a pledge counted in the year it is received?
- What is the policy on writing off unfulfilled pledges?
- How are gifts of stock or other securities valued?
- How are gifts of life insurance counted? How are deferred gifts counted?
- Is there a mechanism for recording and counting in-kind gifts?

Donor Information

Describe in written form the system for gathering, updating, and tracking information about donors.

- Who is responsible for gathering information about donors?
- Who gathers information about donors from the newspapers and other media?
- How is donor information captured and stored?
- How is the mailing list updated?
- Is the mailing list periodically purged of nonresponders?
- How often is the mailing list purged?
- What guidelines are used to purge the mailing list?
- Are names added to the list?
- Where do new names come from?
- Whose job is it to assemble them?
- How are addresses updated?
- What percentage of the donor names have telephone numbers?

- What percentage of the donor records include information beyond the basic name, address, and phone number?
- Does the system have a place for both business and home addresses?
- Is there a way to store a wide range of donor information such as hobbies, alma mater, children's names, gifts to other organizations, and birthdays?
- Can total donor giving be easily retrieved?
- Can the system show the number and size of gifts made in any specified year?
- What are the mechanisms for obtaining information from the donors themselves?
- What information should be gathered?

Volunteer Information

Describe the ways in which information about volunteers is gathered and stored.

- Are accurate records of all volunteer involvement maintained and updated?
- What information about volunteer activity is systematically recorded?
- Are the dates on which people volunteered, the tasks they performed, and the number of hours they worked tracked?
- Can volunteers be sorted by specific activity?
- Can volunteers be sorted by date of involvement?
- Do staff members evaluate volunteers after each assignment?
- Are such staff evaluations summarized or indicated in any way in the volunteers' records?

Computer and Printer Capabilities

- Is the computer easy to use?
- Does the development office have at least one dedicated terminal for its use?
- Is the system powerful enough to handle the entire mailing list?
- Is someone in the development office fluent with the development software?
- Is it possible to design multiple reports without engaging a computer specialist?
- Is it possible to store appropriate salutations for letters to be signed by the board chair, executive director, and campaign chair?
- Is it possible to individualize letters using the mail-merge feature of the software?
- Is it possible to edit individual letters while performing a mail-merge?
- Is it easy to mail-merge and print envelopes?
- Does the printer produce clean and professional-looking letters?

- Is it easy to feed letterhead and envelopes through the printer?
- Will the printer handle mailing labels and/or oversized envelopes?
- Does the software have the capability to flag special donors?
- Can donors be coded in special categories?
- Does the software enable donors to be given a primary affiliation?
- Can the donors be flagged for special acknowledgments?
- Can the software track pledges?

It is not necessary that an organization have systems in place that cover everything noted above, but, if after answering all these questions the development staff becomes aware that its systems fall far short of the ideal, the organization should consider investing the time and resources to develop systems for the areas found lacking and to acquire the hardware and software necessary to implement them efficiently and effectively.

At the very least, an organization must be able to sort donor names by the categories under which they will be solicited. The system must contain accurate and accessible information about donor names, addresses, and phone numbers, as well as records of giving and other information that document the donor's relationship with the organization. The system must be able to merge segmented donor lists into letters in which at least three pieces of information will vary from letter to letter. The system should include a laser printer that produces clean, clear copies, and that sheet-feeds both letterhead and envelopes quickly and easily.

Selecting Development Software

Although decades of development professionals based their campaigns on index cards, inexpensive and effective computing systems have rendered these rudimentary systems obsolete. Indeed, today even small nonprofits are able to afford computers and dedicated development software.

The vast array of products and vendors and the rapidity of change in the field make the process of selecting a development system almost overwhelming. Large institutions often engage computer-development consultants to help them assess their computer needs, select the right systems, and train the staff after the system is installed. Although small organizations need not invest in an expert, they should do their homework before embarking on a search for a development system. This homework should include knowing the organization's needs, talking to colleagues, and gathering information from vendors.

First comes an assessment of the organization's needs. A determination must be made of how many names the software program must be able to handle. This estimate should project three to five years ahead. Information should be assembled about the software programs already in use within the organization so that the development software that is selected will at least have a compatible word-processing program. Although it is helpful to know what types of reports the development director will want to generate, in reality, few who have not had experience with development software will be able to anticipate those needs.

Second comes talking to one's colleagues. The topic of computers invariably arises at professional meetings, "What kind of development software does your office use? Do you like it? Is it effective? Was it worth the investment?" Development professionals are seldom shy about voicing their praises or complaints about their computer software, and one can learn a great deal from other organizations' mistakes.

A campaign consultant is often a good source for software recommendations. Working in many different organizations, they have an opportunity to compare the strengths and weaknesses of different systems.

Third comes gathering vendor information. Information from four to six software vendors should be compiled. It is a good idea to find out whether a neighboring organization is using the software that is under consideration. If so, a visit to that organization allows the development officer to see the product in actual use in a development setting and to ask the users about their experience with the program and the vendor. Some vendors will send a salesperson to the organization to demonstrate their product.

In assessing hardware and software the following questions will yield valuable information.

- What kinds of technical support are available? How is it billed? How long does it typically take the technical-support person to call back with an answer?
- What kinds of training are available?
- How often are upgrades issued? How are they priced?
- How long has the vendor been in business?
- Who are the vendor's clients?
- Will the vendor convert the organization's present data? What is the fee for conversion?
- Is it possible to see a copy of the software manual? (Look for a manual with an extensive index that is free of techno-jargon and easy to understand for a computer nonexpert.)
- Is the software compatible with the organization's existing hardware?
- Is the software compatible with the organization's word-processing software, so that letters and other documents can be merged and produced easily?

Purchasing a software system should take place at least six to twelve months prior to the start of the quiet phase of the campaign. This will provide enough time to convert and enter data, train the development staff to use the program, and to work out the bugs and be able to use the software fluently.

Staffing Requirements

Truly skilled development professionals are rare. They combine an ability to see the big picture with an enviable talent for the punctilious handling of details. They are able to work with the rich and powerful, and at the same time are willing to pitch in at any level to help get a job done. They think clearly and write well, and—perhaps their most important quality—they bring perspective and humor to even the most stressful situations.

Forgetting a Crucial Question

One of my clients was planning to purchase new software prior to their campaign. They asked me to draft a list of questions for them to take along when they went to visit the vendors of the software that they were considering. I came up with a long list of items that I thought the program should be able to accomplish for the development office. My client then went to see the vendors and returned having made a purchase. They had been assured that the program could do everything I had specified plus many other, more sophisticated things. I was in high spirits.

It turned out that although the system could do what we needed, getting even the simplest report or segmentation of the database required the assistance of an experienced computer programmer. The system could perform every task on my list, but at what cost in time, effort, and money? Their system had no flexibility, so the development director couldn't do anything that wasn't vanilla without engaging expert help. And often even with such help, it was difficult to get what we needed. Although my questions had been good ones, I neglected to ask a fundamental question: "Is the system user-friendly and flexible enough so that the development director will be able to design her own reports and get what she needs without the help of a programmer?"

—Campaign Consultant

Although it is often difficult to find this combination of characteristics in one person, most organizations are able to cover all these bases by combining the skills of a number of individuals into an effective development team. The most common configuration for a development team that is capable of conducting a capital campaign is an executive director who is able to free up approximately one-half of his or her time for the campaign, a full-time development director, and a full-time development assistant. With this level of staffing, it should be possible to maintain an annual giving program while planning and implementing a capital campaign.

Someone must be a stickler for details. Even well-organized campaigns flounder if the details are not right. At least one member of the development team must be detail oriented. Proposals must be letter-perfect. Donor records must be accurate, and every salutation, name spelling, and dollar amount must be absolutely correct. As the piles of paperwork mount during a campaign, such a high standard of quality becomes more and more difficult to adhere to. However, while from inside the

> *Errors that result from mail-merging are common. Only the eagle eye of a dedicated error-catcher will pick up the small inconsistencies and inaccuracies.*

development office a particular proposal letter may be just one among hundreds that are being prepared, to the donor that letter is often his or her first contact with the campaign. An incorrect salutation or a misspelled name reminds the donor that he or she is just one among many in a sloppy solicitation process—not the message any campaign would like to convey.

Someone must be creative, flexible, and visionary. Attention to detail is not enough to run a successful campaign. Someone on the development team must be able to see the broader campaign picture and be creative and flexible enough to design and redesign throughout the campaign process. Although campaigns begin with the development of a clear plan, inevitably the plan requires adjustment as pieces fall by the wayside here and there. Perhaps a lead gift falls through, or perhaps a campaign chair becomes ill, or perhaps the zoning for the building project is not approved. At every turn and with every unanticipated change, the development team must respond with creativity, flexibility, and resilience. In these situations, they must set a standard for creative problem solving that maintains the energy and enthusiasm of staff and volunteer leadership alike—even in the face of setbacks.

Someone must have excellent "people" skills. One or more individuals on the development team must be very good at dealing with people. They must be well spoken, friendly, and encouraging. Their style in dress and appearance must be appealing to all sorts of people. And they must have the courage and ability to persist in their efforts until they achieve their goals.

Staffing Alternatives

For some smaller organizations, it may not be possible to have the ideal campaign staffing that was discussed earlier in this chapter—one-half of the executive director's time, a full-time development director, and a full-time development assistant. Many successful campaigns have used other models. Sometimes the executive director runs a campaign with only clerical support, some campaigns are managed by teams of staff members each of whom oversees specific aspects of the campaign. In some cases, a committed volunteer might run the campaign instead of paid staff members or volunteers might participate as part of an in-house campaign-management team.

Sometimes an executive director will take on the challenge of running the campaign. He or she will use a va-

More for Less

When early in the campaign it became clear that the development director was on his way out, I wondered to myself just how the campaign was going to succeed. The library director wanted to use the campaign to learn more about fund raising and she decided that she and her assistant could pull it off. And they did! Kathy, the director's assistant, worked like mad to master the intricacies of the fund-raising software that had been developed by the departed development director. Mary, the director, delegated as much of the work of running the library as she could to her colleagues. Together Mary and Kathy dove into the campaign. They worked days and they worked nights. They set up meetings, cajoled volunteers and donors, and managed reams of campaign paper. When it was over, not only had the campaign succeeded, but the library functioned better than ever. Other staff members had learned new responsibilities. Mary had developed strong relationships with the funding leadership of the community. Kathy had become a first-rate development staff member who now handles the entire annual giving program. Although the two were more than happy to take their vacations after the campaign was done, they both feel that they got back more than they gave, both for themselves and for their library.

riety of clerical assistants to manage the paperwork and the flow of information, but the planning and implementation of the campaign will be tightly held by the person at the top. Given the right person, this strategy can be successful, but it takes its toll on the executive director, and more than a few directors have burned themselves out through the effort. Sometimes, however, if the director is able to delegate other pieces of the job to effective staff members and find a first-rate support person to work with, this arrangement can work well.

Often organizations have staff members who collectively possess all the talents and capabilities that are required for the campaign staff, but no one person has them all. Although the team approach to campaign staffing takes time and coordination, an organization in which the executive director and the development director are willing to share the staff leadership for the campaign may be able to create a campaign team that will be able to accomplish more than any one or two staff members could on their own. To manage this effectively requires a strong commitment to conscious team building and communication.

In small organizations, it is sometimes possible to conduct a capital campaign using volunteers in lieu of paid staff. Although the heyday of the "professional volunteer" is long gone, sometimes an organization is fortunate to have a first-rate volunteer who is willing to take on the challenge of running a capital campaign. Such arrangements have inherent difficulties, but occasionally, if they are well structured in advance, they can work to the advantage of both the volunteer and the organization.

But beware of the well-meaning volunteer who offers his or her services to manage the campaign but who has little understanding of what the task will entail. In fact, the volunteer may have strong feelings about fund raising that are quite antithetical to sound campaign practice and may even be antithetical to the ethos and style of the organization. And, as anyone who has worked with volunteers knows, they can be difficult to guide and impossible to fire.

To ensure that a capital campaign being conducted by a well-meaning volunteer doesn't become a glorified bake sale and fall far short of its goal, the staff must spend considerable time educating the volunteer campaign director about capital campaigns prior to passing over the leadership torch. The director and the volunteer should discuss fund-raising approaches and determine whether they can agree on a sound campaign strategy. The director might assign the volunteer some small preliminary tasks to evaluate this person's competence and effectiveness.

Many retired people who volunteer for such a task begin with wonderful intentions but don't realize that the campaign effort is likely to extend for a year or longer—right through that planned trip to Florida and the skiing vacation at Snowmass.

The Worst of Both Worlds

Midway through our campaign, the development director left and was replaced with someone new. One of our best campaign volunteers, who had been intimately involved with the campaign, offered to serve as campaign director so that the campaign would be less disrupted by the change in staff. I was very pleased and thought that I had the best of both worlds. Alas, I was sadly wrong. The new development director turned out to be very territorial and resented what she viewed as the intrusion of the volunteer onto her turf! The volunteer ended up spending less and less time in the office because the new director made her time there so unpleasant, but the new development director was neither able nor willing to pick up those campaign responsibilities. We ended up with the worst of both worlds.

—A Frustrated Executive Director

Nonetheless, the perfect volunteer does surface now and again. And as long as both the volunteer and the organization clearly understand the tasks and responsibilities, the likely timetable and duration, and the fund-raising strategies that are required for sound capital campaign fund raising, there is no reason not to take advantage of a mutually beneficial situation.

A more common model for campaign staffing is the organization that has a full-time development director who is able to find two or three part-time volunteers to assist with the campaign. Although the paid staff member is responsible for campaign direction and leadership, competent volunteers might well serve in well-defined support roles. Of course, in this situation as well, all roles must be spelled out with precision to avoid unmet expectations, and volunteers should be tested in other, less crucial roles before being given major campaign responsibilities.

Involving the Entire Staff

Upstairs/Downstairs

Many organizations struggle with a division between the "upstairs" staff members, those who raise and process the money and handle the upper-level administrative tasks of the organization, and the "downstairs" staff members—the service providers. Downstairs people feel that they do all the work but that the management, or upstairs, folks get to wear the suits and earn more money. And the more the executive director's job takes him or her in the direction of money, the more the development staff has access to the director and the more the workers in the trenches feel left out.

Petty jealousies, misunderstandings, and especially a general lack of communication between these two groups tend to plague organizations, especially when they are growing rapidly. When an organization is small and intimate, everyone has access to the director and information tends to flow easily. As the organization grows, easy access and open communication among the staff are often among the first casualties. Since many campaigns follow periods of rapid growth, it is not uncommon for the campaign to be an added burden upon an organization that is already coping with internal stresses. If not treated carefully, the campaign is likely to exacerbate the stresses and widen the breach between the upstairs and the downstairs staff.

As the executive director becomes more and more consumed with the tasks and responsibilities of the campaign, he or she usually has less time for internal issues, yet is often unable or unwilling to delegate such responsibility to others. Downstairs staff members can no longer get the attention and resources they need to maintain their programs. Upstairs staff members realize that the campaign will afford them an opportunity to move themselves and their organization into a much more powerful sphere in the community. The power and potential of new contacts and opportunities are usually so compelling (and anxiety producing) that the executive staff

---

Campaign consultants often interact only with the major players, understand the organization's program only superficially, and are insensitive to the stresses caused by the campaign in other areas of the organization.

---

tend to lose touch with what's really going on downstairs. To compound the problem, the director is usually spending money on what might be thought of as upstairs priorities (the campaign and the plans for the new project) while holding a tight rein on downstairs spending (staff and equipment for direct services). It's no wonder, then, that friction grows and tempers flare!

Informing the Staff about the Campaign

Although some upstairs-downstairs stress is inevitable, keeping the downstairs staff informed about the campaign does help. They should understand what the campaign is, how and when it will be conducted, how it will affect them, and what its outcome is likely to be. Staff members appreciate the opportunity to meet in small groups with the campaign consultant to hear about the process and ask questions. This process also helps the consultant learn more about the actual function of the organization and explore with the downstairs staff ways in which they might help and support the fund-raising process.

In some cases, the problem goes deeper. Development priorities are set, money is raised, and projects are funded, often without direct (or even indirect) consultation with those who will have to live with those decisions and who are the real experts to boot. The head of information systems may not know about a grant for a new computing system; the head nurse may not be consulted on the design for the renovated nursing stations, and so forth. If the direct-service staff has not had opportunities to provide input into the planning of the project, it should come as no surprise if the downstairs staff resents and does not support the capital campaign.

As the campaign progresses through the quiet phase, there are several ways to keep staff members informed. Many organizations have small, weekly newsletters designed just for staff. Stories or campaign updates help build support for the campaign among the staff and help keep the downstairs staff from feeling out of the information loop.

The Staff Campaign

Not only does one hope to ease the tensions among the various factions of the staff, but every campaign should provide an opportunity for every staff member to make a campaign contribution. In many organizations, the staff campaign is the most sensitive facet of

---

Friends or Strangers?

We were concerned that the development office wasn't able to gather enough information about patients who might be prospective donors. So we decided to conduct a series of small-group meetings with the service providers to explore how we might improve the information flow. Those meetings turned out to be important and rewarding in ways we had never expected. At the most basic level, staff members had a chance to find out who we were. They had seen us around two or three days a month huddling with their leaders but didn't know who we were or what we were doing. It had made them a bit anxious. The meetings also gave them a chance to learn more about fund raising and to begin to understand it as an opportunity for donors rather than as a repugnant form of arm-twisting. Finally, it gave us a chance to ask them how we should approach the design of a staff campaign within the larger campaign. After every meeting we got feedback from the staff about how pleased they were to have been included in the process.

—Campaign Consultants

---

the entire campaign. Staff members who are already smarting from perceived slights are easily outraged by any hint of being pressured into making a campaign gift. This is particularly true in social-service organizations, which are often staffed by people who feel that they already give their lives to the organization and receive little remuneration for their work.

Despite such sensitivities, a staff campaign should be part of every campaign for several reasons.

- Among most staffs there are some people who are able and eager to make significant gifts to a campaign.
- A well-designed staff campaign can help build spirit and enthusiasm for the campaign and the project that it will fund.
- Staff giving is yet another important gauge of an organization's health, and a strong showing in a staff campaign sends powerful messages to other funding sources.
- Every staff campaign should be designed to provide a way to enable every staff member to participate, no matter what their financial situation, but in no way should it pressure them to do so.

The most successful staff campaign involves key staff members in designing the campaign. It should be spearheaded by the development director (not the executive director) and should involve a handful of nonmanagerial representatives from the various parts of the staff. The selection procedure depends in part on the strength of the relationship between the development director and the rest of the staff. Some development directors ask each division of the staff to appoint a representative to help develop a staff campaign. Others select the individuals whom they think would do the best job and be the most enthusiastic cheerleaders for the campaign. The staff-campaign coordinating committee determines goals for the staff campaign and develops a number of ways in which staff members can become involved. They also report to other members of their divisions and serve as spokespeople for them.

Many staff campaigns adopt dual goals. They determine a dollar goal that they believe is attainable but generous, and they adopt a goal for the percentage of staff participation in the staff campaign, which includes both financial contributions and campaign assistance. Adopting both dollar and activity goals defuses the pressure to make a financial contribution while providing other acceptable ways to give.

Successful staff campaigns often incorporate three aspects: (1) direct solicitation, (2) staff-sponsored events whose proceeds are designated for the campaign, and (3) individual initiatives to raise campaign funds.

Although staff members in management positions might well be personally solicited for the campaign, in no instance should a staff person be solicited by anyone who has managerial responsibilities over them. The staff-solicitation process should be organized so that staff members are solicited by their peers, not by their supervisors.

The executive director should make as generous a contribution as possible to the campaign. Because of the complicated politics of soliciting the executive director, a responsible and sensitive executive director will make his or her gift early in the campaign without being solicited.

The development director, working with the staff-campaign coordinating committee, then reviews the names of all staff members and determines those who should be personally solicited and the person most appropriate to conduct the solicitation. Every staff member who will not be solicited in person should receive a letter from the coordinating committee providing the opportunity to make a pledge to the campaign should they wish to do so. However, the letter should take care not to exert any pressure.

Some organizations give their employees the option of having their campaign gift deducted from their paychecks. This offers a convenient way for a staff member to make a pledge for a number of years. Other organizations believe that this method brings with it a pressure to give that they feel is inappropriate.

Many staff groups are experts on planning special activities. These might take the form of office bake sales, production and sale of a staff cookbook, bulb sales, a used-book exchange, or any number of other fund-raising projects. Some staffs design activities that are limited to the staff, others organize activities to raise funds from the community on behalf of their organization.

Sign On for Sit-Ups

One of our staff members—a slightly rotund, middle-aged woman—decided that she was going to raise money and get herself in better shape at the same time, so she organized her own sit-up campaign. She developed a sign-up sheet and asked everyone in the office to sponsor her. Each sponsor agreed to donate 25¢ to the campaign for each sit-up she could do at the office on a particular Friday morning four weeks hence. Then she set to work at home building up her abdominal muscles. By the day of her sit-up performance, everyone gathered to watch while she got down on the floor and began to do sit-ups—twenty-five, fifty, one hundred and ten sit-ups! When all of the money was collected from the thirty sponsors she had signed up, she had raised nearly $500 for the campaign.

Beating the Board

The board of our organization decided on a board-giving goal of $100,000 for the campaign. When the committee designed our staff campaign, they decided on a giving goal of $80,000. As the campaign moved along, the board crept toward their goal, but the staff campaign really caught on and in a few months we had gone over the staff goal. At one of our campaign-coordinating meetings, one of our members, disgusted at how slowly the board was moving, said, "I'll bet the staff can beat the board goal. That'd show them something!" So, we took that idea to the whole staff, and some months later the staff had indeed raised more money than the board. The effort brought a great camaraderie to the staff and I think it embarrassed the board.

Some staff members prefer to design their own fundraising activities to support the campaign. These individual efforts add to the general excitement that is generated by the staff campaign and often add a touch of humor as well.

Because staff members are part of a closed system, establishing deadlines, reporting progress, and celebrating success are extremely important. Establishing and clearly communicating a calendar for the staff campaign helps build activity timelines and staff expectations. Periodic reporting throughout the campaign period builds momentum as the campaign edges closer to its goals. And of course there are few better ways to develop team spirit among a staff than to support the process of celebrating once the goal has been achieved.

Getting the Work Done

Organize the Paper

Campaigns generate paper—lots of paper. Managing all this paper is a challenge to even the most organized. Through years of watching executive directors, development directors, development assistants, and campaign volunteers struggle with campaign paper, the authors have come to believe that every campaign should maintain two filing systems—one in file folders and the other in a three-ring notebook. In the file folders can be kept the inevitable duplicate copies of material that might be needed later in the campaign. Papers can be put in and taken out as necessary throughout the campaign. In the three-ring notebooks should be filed one copy of every piece of paper generated for the campaign. Once something has been filed in a notebook, it should not be taken out. These notebooks then become the permanent record

of the campaign. The file headings might be organized as follows:

- Co-conspirators Planning Meeting
- Campaign Planning Committee
- Campaign Plan
- Plaques and Donor Recognition
- Campaign Steering Committee
- Public Relations Committee
  —Campaign Materials
  —Press Releases
- Lead Gift Division
- Family Division
  —Board
  —Former Board
  —Staff
  —Former Staff
  —Volunteers
  —Former Volunteers
- Special Events Committee
  —Cultivation Events
  —Campaign Kickoff
- Major Gifts Division
- Phonathon
- Direct-Mail Campaign
- Campaign Cleanup
- Campaign Evaluation

In a typical campaign, one might fill two or three large three-ring binders with paper, but if the dual system is maintained with discipline, it will minimize the amount of time that campaign workers spend looking for the papers they need.

More Paper Management Tips

Every document that is produced for the campaign should bear a date. Campaigns often go through many drafts of every document. Plans change, cases for support are edited and updated, timetables are revised, and unless every piece of paper is dated, it is difficult to know which paper represents the most recent version.

The computer file name for each document should be added to the document itself. Few things are more frustrating than not remembering how a particular document was filed in the computer and having to open dozens of files to find it.

Several inexpensive three-hole punches should be purchased and left in strategic places. The three-hole binder system fails most often because the three-hole punch is hidden under paper or has been borrowed by another department. Once a large three-hole binder has been littered with unpunched pages sticking out in all directions, the motivation and discipline to maintain it quickly evaporate.

One Step at a Time

A campaign is a monumental undertaking and an immense challenge to all but the most imperturbable. While one always wants to know what lies ahead, it can often be enough to restrict one's gaze merely to the next step . . . and the next . . . and the next—until finally one does get to the end. Anyone who is a runner knows the power of just putting one foot in front of the other as a way of combating fatigue and loss of heart. The success of completing each small step inspires the next one. Particularly in the early phases of a campaign, when the job seems so monumental and uncertain, there is comfort and encouragement in focusing on the next task and being sure that one does it thoroughly and well.

Look Ahead

At the same time, quick glances a longer distance ahead are necessary to make sure that the campaign stays on course. Often the campaign consultant will take the role of looking ahead, designing and redesigning the best path to bring the campaign to a successful conclusion. Throughout the campaign, looking ahead becomes more and more effective. In the early phases, with too much uncertainty, one might focus on tomorrow's task, but as the campaign gets close to its goal, its very proximity draws one ahead and motivates staff members and volunteers alike.

Set Realistic Deadlines

Realistic and reasonable deadlines motivate both staff and volunteers, so:

- Get input from other people when setting deadlines. Deadlines that are set with input from the people who will be responsible for meeting them tend to be more successful than deadlines that are imposed from above.
- Use deadlines to take advantage of different people's working patterns. For example, if a person works better under pressure, their schedule should plan to put them to work on the task just shortly before the deadline. Or if the campaign chair is always late in fulfilling his commitments, the staff might set up a meeting with him to review his progress several days before the actual deadline.
- Schedule meetings to create interim deadlines. Meetings spur people to complete their assigned tasks. Schedule short meetings frequently to move a project along.
- Be flexible. Occasionally deadlines must be changed. People don't always run according to plan. Stick to deadlines when they make sense and set new ones when they don't.

Tips for Working Smart

Take time to reorganize your office. As a campaign heats up, working smart becomes critical. Take time to look around your office. Is it set up for efficiency? Is there a computer terminal at your desk? Are file drawers within easy reach? Can you close the door and have a quiet place to concentrate? Have the names and numbers of the people who are involved in the campaign been entered in your Rolodex? Is it possible to clear a desk or table just for the campaign? Just one day spent reorganizing and rearranging to make your life easier and help you become more efficient will pay off in many hours saved during the campaign.

Practice immediacy. Most people procrastinate, and in doing so they spend more time delaying than doing. Campaigns require staff members to carry out many small tasks every day—making telephone calls, writing notes, following up with staff members, drafting agendas, preparing proposals, and then making more telephone calls. If one uses the campaign to practice the art of doing things immediately, it is possible to increase one's efficiency, reduce anxiety, and create a clear sense of forward momentum. Campaigns in which the staff acts and responds quickly tend also to be campaigns with effective volunteers.

Practicing immediacy is particularly important because the anxiety that is inherent in making many campaign

> *As the campaign gets close to its goal, its very proximity draws one ahead.*

calls tends to foster procrastination at all levels. If one can get in an "action" frame of mind for the duration of the campaign, that attitude will inspire and fuel the entire campaign.

Do what's important. As campaign pressures mount, the staff must learn to work strategically, doing what is needed to get the job done well and not spending time where it is not needed. For example, some volunteers and donors require extra time and attention, others are perfectly happy with an occasional phone call. Be sure to differentiate between them so that you will be able to use your time wisely.

Although in some respects every aspect of a capital campaign is important, lead gifts and their donors are the most important! If you are not able to accomplish everything, be sure to manage the lead-gift cultivation and solicitation process well. Indeed, success in this aspect of the campaign will bring success in every other.

Ask others to help. Don't forget the double value of asking others to help. When you ask someone to help, not only does it help get the work done, but it broadens the ownership of the campaign.

The Rewards of Hard Work

Many development directors in small- to medium-sized organizations have never participated in a campaign before and feel apprehensive about their own abilities in this new and overwhelming enterprise. Perhaps for the first time in their careers they are expected to interact with board members and community leaders and are expected to help solicit large gifts. Both the risks and expectations are high.

Take comfort in the opportunities for learning that accompany all capital campaigns. A consultant can serve as a teacher or mentor. An experienced campaign chair is often happy to share ideas and experiences to help a young or inexperienced staff member. The lessons are many and immediate, and in capital campaigns occasional mistakes are allowed and hard work is rewarded.

The chances to learn and experience the real power of fund raising through a capital campaign are unmatched in any other type of fund raising. The wise development director or assistant will jump at the chance to work on a campaign. In doing so, they expand their contacts in the community, learn and practice important skills in fund raising, and prepare themselves for moving up the development career ladder.

Ten Tips for Survival

1. Find a confidant. Every person who works on a capital campaign needs someone to confide in. No matter how successful the campaign, frustrations and discouragement are part of the process. A confidant outside of the organization will provide an outlet for fears, frustrations, and anxieties that will not negatively affect the campaign.

2. Pamper yourself. Capital campaigns are high-stress times. Counter the stress by treating yourself often to the special things you like. Take a yoga class, find a masseuse, get a facial, take a hot-air balloon ride. Do good things for yourself in the midst of the campaign.

3. Celebrate every success. Campaigns are full of small successes that all too often go by without remark. Do something to celebrate every success, whether the celebration is simply a trip to the lunchroom for a fresh cup of coffee, a round of applause by the development staff, or a nice lunch at a downtown restaurant. Notice success more than you notice failure.

4. Build team spirit. Team spirit doesn't just happen, it is built. Think of ways to listen to every member of the team. Remember their birthdays, celebrate their successes, share the leadership with them, encourage them to be creative risk takers by rewarding their successes. By working at building team spirit, the entire campaign will be more fun and effective.

5. Lighten up. Campaigns are serious business, but even campaigns must have their lighter moments. Find the part of your mind that sees the humor in things and use it well throughout the campaign.

6. Juggle your schedule. Sometimes it pays to take days off during the week and work on weekends. If it works for you, do it.

7. Share stories. Find opportunities for people in the office to share their most recent campaign experience or story. Telling stories creates bonds among people, helps them see the humor in their situations, and makes the campaign human and interesting.

8. Laugh a little. Silliness has its place in a campaign—even sometimes with the most powerful of leaders, for they too are people and may enjoy a good laugh.

9. Listen to your inner voices. Most of us have inner voices. Sometimes they tell us things that are right, and sometimes they are wrong. In a campaign, when they nag about something again and again, chances are they are right!

10. Don't look back. An allowance for a good deal of failure is built into every campaign. If one begins to look back and second-guess why one thing or another didn't happen just the way you wanted it to, one begins casting blame. Far healthier is the process of involving people in figuring out how to make the next day successful.

Chapter 14
It's a Wrap!

Chapter Outline
- Finishing the Campaign
- Evaluation, Reporting, and Stewardship
- For the Record
- Institutionalizing the Power of the Campaign
- Looking Ahead
- Campaign Lessons

Finishing the Campaign

While for the volunteers the campaign wrap-up celebration signals the end, for the development staff it is merely a transition. After the champagne has been drunk and the streamers cleared away, there is still much work for the development staff in cleaning up odds and ends and making sure that pledge-payment systems are working. It is also time for the development staff to begin thinking about how to incorporate lessons from the campaign into the organization's ongoing development program.

This final campaign period, which often lasts several months, provides a transition for both staff and board during which the excitement and struggles of the campaign gradually take their place in the history of the organization and the organization begins once again to look to the future. This transition period is often ignored, but if consciously incorporated into organizational planning, it will provide a healthy conclusion to an important episode in the life of the organization.

Is It Ever Really Over?

It is far easier to know when a campaign begins than when it ends. Most campaigns seem to go on and on and on. Even campaigns that have struggled hard to reach their goals seem loath to stop soliciting merely because the goal has been reached. There are always more calls to be completed and more people to be solicited. In fact, in the last weeks of the campaign, it is quite common for a foot-dragging executive director, campaign chair, or development director to find "campaign religion." Perhaps the certain success of the campaign emboldens them, or per-

haps their guilt about their earlier procrastination finally motivates them. Whatever the reason, many campaign workers find new zeal in the last days of the campaign that often carries them along until one or even two months after the official end of the campaign.

In some sense, the campaign can be considered to be over when the staff and volunteers wind down and when every solicitation that was initiated during the campaign has been completed either in person, or by telephone or mail. But this ending is just one of many, for long after the final solicitation has been accomplished, the development staff still collects pledges, thanks donors and volunteers, and prepares final reports on the campaign for the staff and board. And even when all of the cleanup activity is over, the campaign doesn't really end until the staff and board can begin to move on and once again begin to plan their organization's future.

Gifts and Pledges Just Keep Coming

Although the torrent of gifts and pledges that come in as the campaign reaches its goal gradually subsides, it is common for gifts to trickle in for months after the campaign has concluded. One by one, all those donors who had put off writing their checks or filling in their pledge forms find the time to sort through the stacks of papers on their desks, and then they finally get around to doing what they had always intended to do. To many donors, the decision to give is made when an organization's pledge form and envelope are put on the to-do pile rather than deposited in the circular file. The timing of their gifts depends on their internal timekeepers rather than the campaign schedule. Most of these late-arriving gifts are small, but occasionally a large gift comes in as well. Although these gifts after the fact often seem like magic, they are nonetheless the result of the cumulative efforts of everyone who worked on the campaign.

When the campaign has gone over its goal

> *It is far easier to know when a campaign begins than when it ends.*

and donors keep sending gifts, the organization may elect to let these donors know of the extra things that their gifts will make possible. Some campaigns use such an "extras" strategy to squeeze the last bit out of the campaign. They write a brief case for the extras—perhaps landscaping or furnishing a specific area or something else that wasn't included in the original budget, and then write to everyone who has not yet given, soliciting a special final gift.

Collecting Pledges

Verbal pledges are common in capital campaigns. An individual promises to make a contribution but then never sends in the pledge forms. If left unresolved, this incomplete transaction is likely to irritate both parties. The donor feels uneasy, the development director annoyed—both would like to complete the process one way or the other. Before a campaign is over, the solicitor, director, or campaign chair should call to check on every pending gift. The context of concluding the campaign often enables a solicitor to focus on completing the request rather than on pressuring the donor into a gift. This change in focus often gives the donor the requisite feeling of autonomy to actually make a gift.

A system to track pledges and send reminder notices should already be in place by the time the solicitation of gifts draws to a close. Most development software tracks outstanding balances and pledge payments, and once a system is set up, pledge reminders and thank-you letters become a standard part of the office staff's work.

Once the active portion of the campaign is over, an organization might consider using its pledge reminders and thank-you notes as opportunities to keep their donors informed about the progress of the project that their gift is helping to create. A simple update that is changed every month might be enclosed with each pledge reminder and thank-you note, or receipts for checks that are received might incorporate some specific information about the project. The long-distance telephone company Working Assets uses their monthly invoices as an opportunity to inform their customers about issues they support. This idea can be applied to the billing process for capital campaign pledges.

Defaults occur in every campaign when a small group of donors do not make good on their pledges. Some people just pay late and though they may have missed their quarterly payments, at year's end they send in the entire amount due. Others make pledges but then never send in any payments at all. Most organizations send second notices and even third notices, and when the donor still fails to respond, the executive calls the donor to discuss the situation. Organizations seldom resort to the courts to resolve these situations and rely instead on moral suasion, and if that doesn't work, they write the pledge off. The great percentage of gift defaults are for relatively small gifts, so even if the number of defaulting donors seems large, the dollar value of such pledges seldom amounts to as much as 5 percent of the total amount of campaign gifts and pledges.

Pledging is a practice most campaigns encourage. Donors make their contributions over a period of several years (three to five years is the most common range), but pledge payments are likely to arrive in a somewhat different pattern. Although the specifics of payment will vary according to the vagaries of the individual donor, the donors for every campaign fall into three categories—those who prepay their pledges, those who pay exactly as they have indicated on the pledge form, and those who pay later than they indicated. Figure 14–1 illustrates a common pattern of actual payments for a campaign with a three-year pledge period. Keep in mind that this typical pattern may be skewed substantially by one or more major donors who select a different payment schedule.

Celebrating the End of the Campaign

After the goal has been reached and the solicitation and cleanup activity has died down, it is important to

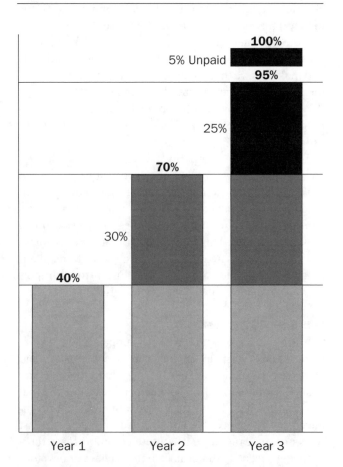

Figure 14–1 Common Payment Projections for a Three-Year Campaign

> **The Defaulting Donor**
>
> It doesn't happen often, but every once in a while a major donor defaults. For our campaign to expand our day-care center, our principal donor was a philanthropic leader in our community. The head of an international corporation headquartered in our community, he had established himself as a generous patron of many of our community's arts and social-service organizations. True to form, he pledged the lead gift to our campaign. We raised the rest of the money and thought we were sitting pretty, until one day we opened the newspaper to learn that our benefactor had been exposed as a scam artist and that the house of cards he had constructed over the years had collapsed, almost taking a major British armaments company down with him. His pledge to us was worthless, and we wound up $50,000 short. The gentleman in question has since taken up residence in a federal penitentiary.

spend time and resources to celebrate the campaign's success. For many campaign volunteers, the celebration marks the end of the campaign. This is the time for small acknowledgments, special lunches, bottles of campaign champagne, and for large parties that help draw a campaign to a successful close, completing the long journey for staff, donors, and volunteers. These activities highlight all the many positive aspects of the campaign. They recognize volunteers for their hard work, they applaud donors for their generosity, and they acknowledge staff members for the thousands of hours of organization and coordination that made it all possible. Such gestures help coalesce all the many acts of commitment that make a campaign successful, and in so doing they erase the memory of the things that didn't go quite right.

Campaign celebrations serve another important function. As the campaign draws to a close, staff members and volunteers often experience a sense of emptiness and loss. Suddenly the overwhelming burden and anxiety of the campaign has evaporated, the phone is quieter, the to-do lists are shorter, and meetings are less frequent. Celebrations help staff and volunteers wind down constructively. They can put their energies and minds into one more campaign event, one that brings a sense of completion.

Campaign celebration parties are primarily for all the staff members and campaign volunteers who helped to make the campaign a success. Of course, the celebration should include all the major donors as well. Often such parties take place at an elegant restaurant or country club. But inexpensive celebrations in simple locations work well too.

As with any special event, planning the campaign celebration requires a great deal of time and attention to detail. Because most nonprofits are expert at planning special events and because events are covered in some detail in chapter 9, what follows are only some ideas and guidelines specific to campaign celebrations.

The guest list should focus on the campaign staff, volunteers, and major donors. This is not the time for a huge event attended by every donor.

A location should be chosen that will not offend people. If the country club has exclusive membership policies, it may not be wise to use it for the campaign celebration.

A memento from the campaign is a nice way to recognize all those who helped it succeed. For the rank and file one might give printed tote bags, T-shirts, or mugs. Some organizations prefer the more traditional engraved paperweights, certificates, wall plaques, or coffee-table statues.

The best presents for campaign chairs are those that are specific to them and their role in the campaign.

A new beginning comes with the campaign celebration, which marks the end of the campaign for donors and volunteers. The end also begins a new phase in donors' relationships with the organization. Every organization should use the celebration event to engage donors and volunteers in the process of looking beyond the campaign. The celebration should thank them for their help and paint a picture of a future exciting enough to get them thinking about wanting to stay on board.

A short and sweet program works best. Thanks and speeches are an important part of these events, but it doesn't take long before they become stale to a large crowd who would rather be socializing.

Evaluation, Reporting, and Stewardship

No campaign is complete without an evaluation of the results and a report on its successes. A structured evaluation process provides the opportunity to reflect on what actually took place and analyze the results. A judiciously worded report can solidify and reinforce the organization's image and reputation in the community.

Taking time to think critically about the campaign after it is over may seem a daunting task, but it is nevertheless a key component in ensuring that the lessons learned during the campaign carry over into the organization's development program, strengthening it and preparing it for the organization's next phase of growth. Usually the develop-

> *A judiciously worded report can solidify and reinforce the organization's image and reputation in the community.*

ment director manages the evaluation process, with the assistance of the campaign consultant.

Evaluation

Campaign evaluation has two components—the objective collection of facts and information, and the subjective analysis of what worked well and what worked less well. Both are important pieces of a complete evaluation and should be assembled into a report that will be included in the written documentation of the campaign. (See more on that subject later in this chapter.)

At the conclusion of the campaign, the development staff should prepare a report that documents the quantifiable results of the campaign. Sometimes assembling this document produces surprises for both staff and board, revealing patterns of giving that previously had been only hunches.

The campaign evaluation should contain at least the pattern of campaign gifts, categorizing of gifts by donor type, the number of gifts, the number of gifts made by volunteers, and the campaign costs.

Find the pattern of campaign gifts by using the original table of gifts as a model. Giving information should be collated to show how many gifts actually came in at which giving levels. This process requires some interpolation, as actual gift amounts seldom coincide exactly with the amounts on the table of gifts, but with a bit of stretching and contracting one way or another it is usually possible to compare the actual results of the campaign with those projected on the gift table. Exhibit 14–1 shows an example of a final report on the pattern of campaign gifts.

Examining the final pattern of giving in this way directs attention to specific areas of the campaign. The table below shows a campaign in which the lead gifts and general gifts exceeded the original expectations, but where the midlevel gifts fell short of the target goals. A pattern like this may reflect a structural weakness in the campaign—perhaps a division head who didn't follow through, or relationships with midlevel donors that had not sufficiently matured prior to the campaign, or some other specific cause that, if known, might be helpful in pointing the way to strengthening the organization's development program.

One might also choose to analyze the reasons for the campaign's success in the leadership-gift area. The strong showing of leadership gifts came from the fact that the two campaign chairs both made leadership gifts themselves and through their own commitments were able to leverage gifts from other major foundations and individuals in the community. The success of the bottom end of the campaign resulted from a major foundation that challenged the community to match their substantial pledge two-to-one before they would actually commit their money. This challenge, coupled with an excellent direct-mail package, brought in a significant number of gifts of under $500.

A discussion and analysis of the actual giving pattern helped the campaign staff and leadership understand the correlations between their work and the pattern in which the gifts came in.

Categorizing gifts by donor type is also an instructive way to analyze a campaign. Talleying the amount of money raised from each type of donor—board, staff, volunteers, former donors, new donors, businesses, and foundations—indicates strengths and opportunities for future development initiatives. Various organizations are likely to categorize gifts in different ways. A school, for example, might look at alumni, parents, and grandparents; a medical facility at patients and patient families; a library at regular borrowers and volunteers.

Exhibit 14–1 Actual Pattern of Gifts

Number of Gifts	Amount of Each Gift	Actual Number of Gifts	Projected Amount from Level	Actual Amount From Level
1	$150,000	1	$150,000	$150,000
1	75,000	2	75,000	150,000
2	50,000	2	100,000	115,530
6	25,000	7	150,000	177,486
10	10,000	7	100,000	69,843
20	5,000	14	100,000	71,345
40	2,500	23	100,000	57,500
80	1,000	46	80,000	46,622
160	500	76	80,000	39,520
many	under $500	436	65,000	143,423
	Totals:	614	$1,000,000	$1,021,269

It is often helpful to know the total number of gifts and pledges that were made to the campaign and how many of these were made as one-time gifts and how many as multiyear pledges. In addition, one may wish to look at how many gifts were received from regular donors, how many from lapsed donors, how many from new donors, and how many from campaign volunteers.

Volunteer activity and campaign gifts are often revealing (and surprising). Some organizations that are good at gathering information report not only on how many volunteers actually worked on the campaign and how many campaign gifts they made, but they also estimate how many volunteer hours were spent.

The objective evaluation part of the report should also summarize the actual cost of the campaign. It is often helpful to compare actual campaign costs with those that were budgeted. Consistency is important in this analysis. Many questions often arise about what does or does not count as a campaign cost. For example, an organization that has combined its campaign newsletter with the regular newsletter must determine what portion of the newsletter costs to apportion to the campaign and what to its regular operating costs. Another gray area is whether and at what level to allot a portion of the salaries of the executive director, development director, and development assistant to the campaign. Colleges and universities have tried to standardize the practices by which organizations determine their campaign costs. However, simplicity, clarity, and internal consistency in reporting guide the practices of most smaller institutions.

Subjective opinions are an important component of the campaign process. The campaign evaluation should also incorporate feedback from the primary campaign volunteers. Some campaigns ask each campaign chair, committee chair, and division head to fill out a written evaluation of their portion of the campaign. The types of questions that are asked might include some of the following generic questions, as well as others that reflect the specific campaign.

- General evaluation questions
  1. Did you understand what would be expected of you when you accepted your campaign role?
  2. Did the staff support you in carrying out your tasks?
  3. Overall, was this campaign a positive experience for you?
  4. Do you feel that campaign meetings were well organized and productive?
  5. What would you have needed in order to carry out your responsibilities more efficiently?
  6. Which were the most challenging aspects of your tasks?
     — enlisting volunteers to help you

     — rating prospects
     — soliciting prospects
     — keeping in touch with other solicitors in your division
     — working with the staff
     — other
  7. What were the most rewarding aspects of your involvement?
     — furthering the organization's cause
     — making new friends
     — learning about capital campaigns and fund raising
     — getting recognition and visibility for your work on the campaign
     — other
- Campaign materials and public relations
  1. Do you feel that the campaign materials were clear?
  2. In your opinion, were they well written and attractive?
  3. Do you think that they presented the case effectively?
  4. Was the pledge form easy to understand and use?
  5. Did you want to read the newsletters?
  6. Do you feel that the campaign received adequate publicity?
- Solicitation training
  1. Did the trainer present the material thoroughly?
  2. Was the training too long? Too short?
  3. Was it engaging and interesting?
  4. Did it provide the information that your volunteers needed to solicit their prospects?
- Follow-up
  1. Were you and your volunteers well informed about the results of your solicitations?
  2. Was material sent out to prospects and volunteers in a timely fashion?
- Campaign events
  1. Were campaign events consistent with the character of the organization?
  2. Did they add to the momentum of the campaign?
  3. Were you provided with the materials that you needed to do your job thoroughly?

Written evaluations from the campaign consultant often provide a broader perspective. At the conclusion of the campaign, the campaign consultant should be asked to submit a final written report. Most consultants do this as a matter of course, but because consultants sometimes conclude their work with an organization before the conclusion of the campaign, the consultant's report and the campaign's end sometimes do not dovetail. Because consultants are outside the organization and have experience with many other campaigns, their opinions are often valuable additions to the final report. Some organizations actually contract with their consultants to help design and manage the entire evaluation process.

Finally, the staff often helps in evaluating the campaign. The role of staff is often complicated by the political realities in an organization. It is not uncommon for a staff member to have been dissatisfied with the performance of a colleague throughout the campaign. Perhaps the development director believes that the executive director did not pull her weight during the campaign, or perhaps the executive director despaired about the development director's lack of follow-through or inattention to detail. It is equally common for staff members to blame the board for any weaknesses of the campaign.

The campaign-evaluation report is not the appropriate mechanism in which to raise these issues. Rather, an executive director might incorporate these discussions into the regular performance evaluations with staff or discuss board issues in the course of private meetings with the board chair.

Of course, staff members should be invited to contribute their ideas about the campaign and the lessons learned from it that might be incorporated into the culture of the organization.

Some campaigns prefer to gather information from their campaign leaders and key volunteers through a meeting called specifically to discuss various aspects of the campaign. Although an informal evaluation meeting is often a good way to help complete the campaign experience for both staff and volunteers, such a meeting must be organized to focus attention on the positive rather than providing a forum for chewing over the negative. An evaluation meeting might pose questions such as:

- What are the most important things you have learned through this campaign?
- What are the lessons this organization should take from the campaign?
- How can we apply the lessons of the campaign to the future of the organization?
- Which campaign volunteers would be good candidates to involve further in our organization?
- How in the future might our organization do a better job of involving volunteers?
- What have you learned about your own strengths through this campaign?

Some organizations ask key campaign volunteers to fill out written forms and then use the collective results and feedback as a basis for group discussion.

Reporting

A written evaluation report should be prepared and shared with the staff members who worked on the campaign, with the board, and with the campaign leadership. The written report should frame weaknesses and criticisms as opportunities for learning and growth, using them to guide the organization into the future rather than trying to affix blame for past transgressions.

Once key staff members and campaign volunteers have had a chance to review the report, the staff should determine in what form to report the campaign evaluation to the full board, campaign planning and steering committees, and other campaign volunteers. Some organizations distribute the complete evaluation report, others excerpt from it and distribute a summary report.

Because various constituencies have differing interests and goals, an organization might excerpt different elements from the report for different groups. For example, a campaign-evaluation report for the full board might summarize the campaign statistics, board giving, and opportunities for strengthening the development program or other aspects of the report that they might use in the future. A report for the campaign steering committee might focus in greater detail on the successes of the campaign and the involvement of volunteers.

The results of the campaign should be reported more broadly as well. Every volunteer who worked on the campaign and every donor should be informed that they were part of a winning team. As the reporting process broadens beyond the leadership, the message must be tightened and the medium must be more focused. Although a campaign volunteer who made five solicitation calls wants to be informed of the success of the campaign and to be recognized for his part in that success, that volunteer does not want to read pages of text analyzing the campaign. Rather, such an individual would be happy with a simple letter, note, or card telling him that the campaign has gone over the goal and thanking him for his contribution to the campaign's success.

Campaign Reporting and the Annual Report

Most organizations also produce final campaign reports that list all the donors by giving category. These are generally printed reports similar to an organization's annual report. Some organizations produce a separate report for the campaign, others combine the campaign report into the annual report, including special articles about the campaign and a separate list of campaign donors. A combined report might highlight the campaign, using the campaign logo and theme on the cover and giving the campaign priority billing.

Many organizations miss the chance to get the most out of their successful campaigns because they run out of steam

> *Many organizations miss the chance to get the most out of their successful campaigns because they run out of steam at the final lap.*

at the final lap. A successful campaign casts the glow of success and accomplishment over the entire organization, often boosting its stature and reputation in the community. The success of the campaign should therefore be announced as broadly as possible in the community. This takes just a bit more time and energy just as other future-oriented pressures begin to mount. But even though they may be tired and ready to be done with the campaign, the public-relations staff and committee should muster one final blitz of the local media to spread news of the organization's triumph and the consequences of the campaign's success throughout the community.

As the money that was raised is applied to the campaign project, the organization must keep its donors informed of its progress, letting them know that the organization has been and continues to be a good steward of their money. Informing donors of the consequences (both short- and long-term) of their gifts is every bit as important as thanking them. If done well, it will solidify the relationship between donor and organization and begin preparing every donor to contribute to the next campaign. Good stewards report not only on how the money has been used but also on the consequences of their investment to the community.

For the Record

What to Include

When all the celebrating, evaluating, and reporting are done, the development director and executive director have one final task. It is up to them to store the campaign for future reference. This requires going through and cleaning out campaign files, storing what's important, discarding what's not, and assembling a paper record that will make sense years and even decades later to those who have had no contact whatsoever with the campaign.

All pledge cards and copies of checks should be dated and stored for a period of five years.

Even if these records are maintained on the computer, the hard-copy record of the campaign should include a list of all donors to the campaign and the amount of each gift or pledge.

Records of all substantive correspondence with every donor should be kept, as well as copies of all correspondence with donors of middle- and upper-level gifts. The organization should determine the dollar levels for which all donor correspondence is kept.

The record should contain documents that describe the plan for the campaign. These should include the campaign structure, names of campaign leaders and planning committee members, campaign policies, campaign timetables, case for support, and division and committee planning documents.

The record should include one copy of each piece of campaign material: letterhead, envelopes, brochure, invitations, note cards, announcements, newsletters, internal newsletters, campaign reports, and so forth.

Also to be included are the campaign evaluation and the mechanisms used to report on the campaign to the various constituencies.

The names of the staff members who worked on the campaign should be included, as well as the length of their work on the campaign and the positions that they held.

A three-ring binder with front and back pockets is an effective mechanism for assembling the campaign record. It should be clearly titled with the name and dates of the campaign and organized into effective categories so that someone who has played no role in the campaign can learn about the campaign without undue difficulty just by paging through the notebook.

What Not to Include

Not every piece of paper kept in the campaign notebooks must be preserved for the long-term file. Meeting agendas, hand-scrawled notes, multiple copies, early drafts, and interim progress reports might well be discarded as part of the effort to consolidate the final record into a meaningful and effective historical document.

Institutionalizing the Power of the Campaign

Changes Brought about by a Capital Campaign

Capital campaigns are usually times of organizational change. Not only are organizations often rapidly growing or evolving when they consider a campaign, but campaigns usually push organizations to a more effective level of operation. Volunteers must be involved at exceptional levels of performance and with greater intensity. Executive directors and development directors must face any latent fears about major-gift fund raising and learn to ask courageously for large gifts. Donors of major gifts often begin to help shape the future direction of the organization. Everyone works harder and as a result either becomes more committed to the organzation or decides that it's time to leave.

Although staff and volunteers are happy to see the end of the increased tensions and greater workloads that accompanied the campaign, many of the changes wrought by the campaign greatly strengthen the organization and should be incorporated into its ongoing life and development patterns. The following are some of the changes that many smaller nonprofits seek to make in their operations.

Major gift fund-raising. Most smaller nonprofit organizations shy away from major-gift fund raising until they are forced into it by a capital campaign. Through the campaign experience, many executive directors and development directors not only lose their fear but even become impatient with the bottom-end fund raising that has until now shaped the bulk of their annual giving campaigns. Suddenly, the potential for requesting and receiving larger gifts for specific programs or needs alters the focus of the development effort.

Role of the executive director. It is also quite common for an executive director who has had little or no interest in fund raising to learn through the campaign that major-gift fund raising is an avenue to power and potential for the director as well as the organization. Suddenly, the executive director becomes a hands-on development person, looking for special projects to be funded, building relationships with individuals in the community who can help make them happen, and participating in activities in the community that make him or her more visible. This change in roles necessitates a change in the relationship between the executive director and the development director. No longer do they operate quite so independently of each other. After a campaign, they often become partners in the process of major-gift fund raising.

Reframing the operating budget. With new attention turned to major-gift fund raising, the design of the operating budget takes on new meaning. No longer does an organization see the budget simply as line items and dollar amounts, but the budgeting process becomes a way to find opportunities for major donors. The standard line for equipment now translates into a form that might interest a donor. For example, the amount that is budgeted for new playground equipment might be higher than otherwise if a donor can be identified who would love to purchase something special that catches her fancy. The line item for the organization's radio program now looks different because the director knows that a donor is particularly interested in helping to spread the word about a particular program over the airwaves. No longer is lack of money an acceptable reason for why things can't happen. The reason now that some things don't happen is that the executive director and the development director just haven't yet found the right person to give the money that will make it possible.

Donor recognition and stewardship. The campaign having created a group of major donors, each with considerable clout, an organization can no longer afford a hit-or-miss attitude toward donor recognition and stewardship. Major donors want to know that their gifts are appreciated and being used well. One result of a capital campaign is that most organizations become far more sensitive to this aspect of their development program.

Board building. Capital campaigns push many organizations to build stronger boards. No longer are they content with their working boards. After a campaign, not only do the staff and board leadership understand far better the potential of a fund-raising board, but they have also had an opportunity to develop relationships with excellent candidates for future board membership.

Relationship building. After a campaign, development professionals begin to understand the importance of building relationships with individuals who can affect the future of their organizations. Gone are the days when a director could run the organization as a sole-proprietor enterprise. Moreover, today's directors are under considerable pressure to serve as advocates for their organizations, constantly seeking new friends and developing new contacts.

Our Board Didn't Do Fund Raising

One of the most important lessons that I learned from my organization's capital campaign was the importance of a board that was willing to raise money. Our board didn't do much fund raising during the campaign. As the campaign progressed, our volunteer solicitors resented doing all the "hard" work of asking for gifts while the board did none. As a result of that lesson, we are now recruiting new board members who understand and embrace their roles as fund raisers. While this process will take some time, we will be better prepared, at least from a board perspective, for our next campaign.

—Development Director

Redesigning the Annual Giving Program

All the changes mentioned above have profound consequences for an organization's annual giving program. No longer can it rely on letters and a few special events. Those bottom-end fund-raising methods must now serve the larger goals of identifying and cultivating donors for a major-gifts program. Moreover, the major-gifts program should become the centerpiece of the entire annual-giving initiative. A new focus on major-gift fund raising will compel an organization to redesign its annual giving program. Sometimes this requires reformulating the composition and function of the development committee. It may even require a change of development staff. But if the annual giving program is not redesigned to accommodate the new focus on major gifts that the capital campaign has made possible, those important lessons will be lost within one or two years, and the organization will fall back to its former reliance on bottom-end fund raising.

Looking Ahead

Planning

When a campaign draws to a close and staff and volunteers breathe sighs of relief, it is time to begin looking ahead. No longer are the projects funded by the campaign out in some hazy future. They are at hand, and the future once again beckons! Following a break that is long enough to let staff and volunteers recharge, an organization should begin developing a long-range, or strategic, plan. Without doubt, the best and most exciting fund raising is always done as an organization moves ahead. Effective fund raisers have little time to rest on their laurels. Indeed, in effective organizations, there is little time for repose of any sort. Organizations must always be looking ahead, not necessarily to grow, but to remain vital, changing with the times to improve programs and find ever better ways to serve their constituencies and their communities.

Another Campaign?

For many staff members who have just completed a campaign, the very thought of another campaign is unthinkable, but with good planning and stewardship, a community organization might consider conducting a second campaign within a ten-year period. Many colleges and universities, for whom capital campaigns are a way of life, schedule their campaigns more tightly, planning the next campaign even as an earlier one concludes.

> *The best and most exciting fund raising is always done as an organization moves ahead.*

But unless there is a compelling reason to move more quickly, smaller, community-based organizations should probably let at least three or four years elapse between the end of the pledge period and the start of planning for the next campaign.

A breathing period between campaigns provides a time for community donors to take care of some of their other favorite organizations and keeps an organization from appearing greedy in the eyes of those donors who are expected to fund most of the capital campaigns in their community. It also enables the organization to build new relationships and to institutionalize the lessons of the campaign.

Campaign Lessons

Capital campaigns are replete with many of the lessons for life that people learn again and again. Campaigns are based on enabling people to use their resources effectively to accomplish something important and lasting in their community. Through campaigns, organizations build relationships and make friendships that endure far beyond the duration of the campaign itself. In many cases, friendships among staff members, volunteers, and donors begun during a capital campaign last a lifetime and evolve and grow through other campaigns and other organizations.

The lessons of a campaign are simple lessons that remind us of the power of positive human interaction. They call on each of us to find and share our own humanity, our commitment to helping others, and our ability to be generous in many ways. The lessons are many and varied. But they are important lessons that if taken seriously and practiced steadfastly will enrich our lives.

Involving Other People

Although the simplest course is often to work alone on a project, the results of solo work are seldom as effective as those obtained if one takes the time and finds the patience to ask for the help of others. In doing so, one will learn about other viewpoints and become exposed to new ideas. Through the collaborative process, one's own ideas are led into new, richer channels.

Sharing the Ownership

The more one shares ownership, the more of a project one owns, for one cannot share something one does not own. Sharing ownership also increases the chances of success, for people seldom accept ownership of something that they don't wish to see succeed.

Practicing Gratitude

The practice of gratitude brings powerful returns to its practitioners and to its recipients. The grateful person has the opportunity to observe and remark on a worthy act. The person who is recognized for a worthy act knows that he or she has had a positive impact on someone's life.

Looking Ahead

There is more to be gained from looking ahead than from looking back. Looking back encourages one to place blame on things that didn't go well, while looking ahead encourages the projecting of the positive lessons of the past into the future. People are usually happy to become part of an organization that is moving ahead, and happy to abandon one that is not.

Celebrating Success

All too often in life we chew over our failures and discredit our successes, but the balance between success and failure can be radically altered by recognizing and celebrating every success and acknowledging and learning from and then letting go of every failure.

Trusting Others

It is difficult to learn to trust volunteers and donors to make the right decisions for themselvees. How many times do we choose not to ask someone to do something because we are afraid of the answer they will give.

If we trust people to make the decisions that are right for them and then respect those decisions, asking becomes far easier. Through trusting others we share the burdens of decision making and together work for shared goals and values.

Recognizing Your Own Power

As you harness the abilities of other people around a common goal, you will come to recognize your own power. Because of our insecurities, we all too often forget that by our actions, efforts, and commitments we have the power to make our organizations strong. Many staff members come to recognize and understand their own power and potential through their work in a capital campaign, and this new awareness can have far-reaching consequences.

Doing the Right Thing

Successful capital campaigns and successful lives are built on honesty and integrity. When in doubt about how to present something or how to act, always make the choice that will let you sleep at night. Those choices may cause short-term stresses. They may even cost your organization a major gift or you your job, but the long-term returns will be worth the short-term costs.

Appendix
Troubleshooting Guide to Capital Campaigns

No matter how carefully one plans and prepares a capital campaign, challenges always arise, and although one would like to think they should not happen, when they do occur, one would wish for guidance in designing a constructive solution. The authors have relied on their own experiences and that of many other professionals in the field to determine the most commonly encountered campaign difficulties to include in a troubleshooting guide. Most of the situations described below are complex and confusing and seem to have no *right* answer. However, in every case, opportunities are hidden in the obstacles and a positive approach that looks for and magnifies those hidden opportunities will be the key to developing an action plan.

Perhaps one of the greatest lessons to be learned through capital-campaign fund raising is that very few obstacles and challenges are big enough to stop a campaign. Persistence, good humor, and an unflagging commitment to making the campaign succeed can carry one through, under, around, or over virtually any brick wall. When one stops seeing brick walls as obstacles and begins seeing them as life-enriching puzzles, then one is able to continue forward with glee even when presented with what would otherwise seem to be insurmountable challenges.

The collection of challenges below have been adapted from real campaigns.

Campaign challenges fall roughly into seven major categories.

1. dollar goals
2. people (volunteers, staff, and donors)
3. specific gifts
4. public relations
5. organizational issues
6. project difficulties
7. national calamities or acts of God

A general discussion each category follows, along with a variety of specific stories adapted from real campaign

difficulties and food for thought about how one might deal with each. The authors present no formulaic answers, but they do offer ideas that might help clarify the issues in hopes of stimulating the reader to find his or her own solutions to fit the actual situation, specific personalities, and tolerances of the people involved.

The reflections below are intended to encourage the development professional to explore creative ways to approach each challenge. There is no one correct solution to any of the situations, and very few solutions are absolutely wrong. If one is guided by a commitment to honesty and integrity, if one is willing to communicate openly, and if one has the patience to evaluate results over the longer term, the paths taken through the complex terrain of a capital campaign will almost inevitably lead to a successful conclusion.

Campaign Goal Challenges

"We are not interested in the possibilities of defeat."
Queen Victoria

Problems relating to campaign goals fall into two categories. Sometimes goals appear to have been set too high, other times too low. Of course goal difficulties are merely the reflection of a campaign that has not progressed as anticipated. In the case of the too-high goal, the campaign has not raised as much money as was originally targeted; if goals have been set too low, the campaign did better than anticipated.

The real goal of every capital campaign should be to raise as much money as possible to accomplish a specific project in a way that develops strong and healthy relationships among the organization, its donors, and its community. The dollar goal, then, is just one aspect of a campaign goal, and although the dollar goal is the one most commonly highlighted, every decision about goals must be considered in its broader framework.

Story #1. The Campaign Is Just a Little Short

Our campaign has gone well. We hired a consultant, recruited a good campaign chair, and developed a strong case. We were to have finished the campaign by December 30 and indeed by mid-November we had completed the lead-gift and major-gift solicitations and were busy soliciting the broad base of donors in our community. But it's December 20, and we are still about $60,000 shy of our $1.5 million goal. What should we do?

- A torrent of gifts often come in at the very end of the year. The $60,000 may still roll in before the deadline.
- The shortfall provides a wonderful opportunity to breathe a final spark of energy into the campaign. Meetings with several major donors asking them to close the gap might do just that. Or a letter inviting all donors who have made one-time gifts to extend their gifts with a second- or third-year pledge may yield strong results.
- The shortfall also enables a campaign to go back to donors who have been solicited but have not yet made a commitment and let them know that they have an opportunity take the campaign over the top.
- Although specific deadlines are important for a campaign, within reason, people are far less concerned about the specific date than about the overall success of the campaign. If December 30 comes and goes and the campaign has not quite reached its goal, it does not mean that the campaign has failed. Especially over the holiday season when people are busy, mail is even slower than usual, and staff is burdened, campaign leaders are generally happy even if the campaign doesn't actually go over its goal for two or three weeks after the deadline.
- Relatively small distances to the end of the campaign provide opportunities to create a hero! In one of our campaigns, the steering committee met just before the end when there was still a $30,000 gap. At that meeting, the steering committee member who had made the very first gift to the campaign pulled out his checkbook and wrote a check for $30,000 saying that he would have to refinance his mortgage to cover the check but would do so if necessary. He asked every person in the room to do their part in closing the gap, but said that his check would close the gap if need be! His generosity sparked others to increase their gifts and in the end although the donor did not have to go to the mortgage company his commitment made him one of the heroes of our campaign.

- As the finish line of a race approaches, spectators cheer, runners go faster, and enthusiasm builds. It is possible to build the same momentum and enthusiasm for a campaign even though people are not standing at the finish line to actually witness the end. To do so, however, the organization must keep as many people as possible informed as the campaign runs toward its goal.

Story #2. The Campaign Is Far Short of Its Goal

Most of the donors have been solicited and the projected end of the campaign is in sight, but the campaign has raised only $700,000 of its $1.2 million goal. Volunteers and staff are disheartened and tired.

- The situation described above is probably the result of poor campaign preparation and planning. If the campaign is short because it missed some major leadership gifts, either the goal should have been lowered before the campaign became public or the kickoff should have been delayed until more leadership gifts could have been secured. If the campaign was successful in raising its leadership gifts but fell short in soliciting midlevel and lower-level gifts, the table of gifts probably did not accurately reflect the realities of the organization. Nonetheless, organizations do find themselves in situation like this and staff and board members must find creative and constructive ways to turn potential failure into success.
- If one sees virtually no prospects of finding the remaining dollars, one must stop weeping and begging and take stock! Assess just where you are and your various options, and develop a plan that is embraced by the steering committee and the board. Grasping at straws saps energy and destroys an organization's credibility. But since everyone who has been involved in the campaign would like it to succeed, they will be relieved to understand the options and embrace a new plan that will enable the campaign to succeed even if on a different timetable and for modified goals.
- An organization might hire an outside expert to take stock of the realities of the situation by interviewing key donors, staff, and board members; look at what has and has not been accomplished through the campaign and work with a group of committed volunteers to fashion a plan. The plan might include developing phases, lowering the goal, extending the time frame, and/or exploring other ways to finance the project.

- Along with the need to develop a well-conceived plan to get beyond being stuck, the organization will need a public-relations plan to reposition the campaign and the project in the eye of the broader community. While the campaign may have fallen short of its goal, it should be possible to focus attention on the first phase of the construction project rather than on the campaign's failure.

- It is *not* wise to throw the campaign on the mercy of the community. It is tempting to believe that people will send in money if they know an organization is in trouble. The reality is that while people will often send money if they read a heart-wrenching story about *people* in trouble, they are seldom inclined to support a failing campaign or a failing organization.

- If major donors have given well short of their abilities, many donors have not yet been solicited, and/or many solicitations have not been completed, it may be possible to raise the remaining money without going back to the drawing board. One might go back to committed leadership donors to ask them to increase and/or extend their commitments. One might extend the campaign time line and organize another solicitation effort. Or one might find other solicitors or approaches to help close pending solicitations.

Story #3. The Campaign Reaches Its Goal before Everyone Has Been Solicited

Although our building was projected to cost nearly $4 million, our consultant estimated that we wouldn't be able to raise more than $2 million, so we adopted that number as our campaign goal and arranged for long-term financing to cover the rest. Everything went pretty much as planned. We raised $1.2 million in leadership gifts, announced a $2 million goal, and set to work soliciting the midlevel gifts. But not long after the campaign kick-off, one of our solicitors asked a prospect who had given small gifts to us for many years for a pledge of $15,000 and came back with a gift of $500,000! Suddenly we have raised more than $1.7 million, we've just barely scratched the surface of the midlevel solicitations or the lower-level giving, and our campaign is scheduled to continue for another six months. What should we do?

- Because the project costs exceed the goal by $2 million, the organization might shift the campaign emphasis from the campaign goal to the project costs. It would be compelling for donors to know that the remarkable generosity of the community has enabled the organization to shoot for raising the entire amount of the project cost, leaving the organization debt free.

- One might consider asking the donor to frame the $500,000 gift as a challenge grant, requiring the organization to raise $1 or even $2 in new money for every one of hers by a certain date. This approach engages the donor in stimulating additional gifts from the community and would result in at least $3.2 million.

- Another approach would be to discuss with the donor the possibility of using her gift to create a special endowment fund that would support a particular aspect of the new facility, thereby separating it from the stated campaign goal.

People Problems

> "What really matters is what you do with what you have."
>
> *Shirley Lord*

Some of the most challenging and common campaign problems arise from the idiosyncrasies and varying capabilities of both staff members and campaign volunteers. Without doubt, the most common cause of all people problems is poor communication. People often simply don't communicate, and when they do, they often communicate incompletely or inaccurately. As we have discussed in earlier sections of this book, communications difficulties are two-sided, being as much the fault of the receiver as the fault of the sender. Not only do many people not organize and impart information effectively, but most people don't read or listen carefully, often missing a large percentage of the material that has been presented.

But people problems are not just a result of poor communication. They also result from people who are unable to follow through on commitments that they have made in an effective and timely way. These performance problems are compounded by a common tendency not to accept responsibility for one's own weaknesses. It is quite common, for example, for a staff member or volunteer who has not done his job to assign blame for his own poor performance to someone else.

Sometimes people problems arise from more extreme causes—a staff member quits, a campaign chair dies, a donor winds up in jail. These events cause unanticipated and often unpreventable disruptions to the flow of a campaign, and as unlikely as they seem at the start, these extraordinary events occur in more campaigns than one might imagine.

All of these people problems have profound consequences on capital campaigns, but whether the effect on the campaign is beneficial or adverse depends on how they are handled.

Story #1. The Campaign Chair Doesn't Solicit His Prospects

Our campaign chair does a wonderful job of presenting the campaign and the organization in public. He is handsome, speaks well, knows the organization thoroughly, and is a real advocate for the cause. Unfortunately, he does less well soliciting gifts. Actually he would do it very well if he ever got around to it, but the calls he's supposed to make just get put off and put off. What should we do?

- Some years ago when Andrea was nagging an unresponsive volunteer more and more, a sage advisor gave her the following advice: "Andrea" he said, "turning up the volume is fine for a start, but if it doesn't work, try changing the channel." So, one might begin by making a couple of follow-up calls to the chair asking him if he has a solicitation date yet, if he would like you to go along, or if you can send a proposal letter to the prospect. But once he starts avoiding your calls, turning up the volume is no longer working.
- To change the channel you might ask a peer of his who is already involved in the campaign to offer to make the calls with him. Or you might ask the chair if he would feel more comfortable if you reassigned the prospects.
- Some people only work to deadlines, so it might help to call a lead-gift report meeting of all of those volunteers who are making leadership-gift solicitations. Most people will produce when it gets to the wire and they know that they will have to report to their peers. The down side of this strategy is that if the chair doesn't perform his tasks before the meeting his nonperformance will negatively affect the momentum of the entire group.
- Scolding generally doesn't work. People who put themselves in a position of being nagged or scolded generally do so because it satisfies something in them. At some subconscious level, the attention of the scolding itself is often a greater reward than the completion of the task.

Story #2. The Executive Director Doesn't Perform

As we began to plan the campaign, it soon became clear that our executive director was better at finding reasons *not* to do campaign assignments than she was in figuring out how *to* do them. Every time the consultant or a board member suggests an action, the director either derails the idea or says that she doesn't have time to carry it out. Often others pick up the slack for her, but gradually we all see what is going on and little by little we become less willing to work hard ourselves. The poor campaign consultant is stuck in the middle. Suggestions?

- Usually when a staff member doesn't perform effectively during a capital campaign his or her behavior is merely an exaggerated form of the way that person has been performing the rest of the time. During normal times, however, it is possible to overlook mediocre performance. During campaigns it is not.
- As the campaign heats up, and the conflicts with the consultant grow, the director is likely to be less and less comfortable in the role and may leave of his or her own accord.
- There are at least two ways to deal with every staff problem. One can try to change the source of the problem—either by strengthening or replacing the nonperforming staff member or by shifting the staff member's responsibilities away from the tasks of critical importance and reassigning the responsibilities to someone more effective.

In a real-life situation like the example above, the consultant pushed and pushed the director. Her nagging produced an intolerable tension between the two of them, and the director up and quit, much to the relief of the consultant and the board.

Story #3. A Board Member Rebels

We've been planning our building renovation for years. Various committees of the board have worked actively on many aspects of the project. We developed architectural plans, conducted a feasibility study, and are nearing the successful conclusion of our campaign. The board has been informed at every turn and officially approved the campaign and the building project. Last week our campaign chair (a former board chair), who solicited each board member in person, followed up with one board member who had not yet made his gift. At that meeting the board member informed the campaign chair that he had given the building project careful thought and not only had he decided not to make a campaign gift, but he was going to make a motion at the next board meeting to put the renovation project on hold for an indefinite period while the climate around the medical professions stabilized. What should the campaign chair do?

- The real risk of this situation is that this board member will unnerve other board members, and, if he works hard to bring people to his opinion, he might be able to derail the project. But if the current board chair is solidly behind the project, such a dire consequence is unlikely.
- The campaign chair might express his disappointment that the board member will not make a gift and might suggest that the board member contact the current board chair to discuss his views well before the next board meeting. The campaign chair should then call the board chair to alert him or her to the views of the board member.
- In the real situation from which this story was taken the executive director documented all board involvement with the building project—at which meetings it was presented, what votes were taken, and when board members had opportunities to discuss the project. His documentation was extensive and reminded the board that they had owned the project at every step. He distributed his list to board members at their meeting. By the time of that meeting, the dissenting board member elected not to say a word.

Story #4. A Major Donor Dies

Our campaign chair was a wonderful and generous man. Early in the campaign planning process, he let us know that he intended to make a gift of $250,000 to name the chapel in the new facility. We were thrilled and proceeded with the campaign, which went quite well until our chairman became ill and was diagnosed with leukemia. To us it seemed that all of a sudden he went downhill. He seemed well one day and deathly ill the next. In fact, he died within six weeks of being diagnosed. During that time, we realized that we did not have a signed pledge form for his gift, but once he was so ill, we felt uncomfortable asking him to sign one and he died without having done so. What should we have done?

- It's not uncommon for those closest to a campaign to be too relaxed about filling out pledge forms. Because these people are in constant touch with the organization, handling pledge forms for other donors all the time, and meeting perhaps daily with the executive director or development director, once the amount of the gift has been established verbally, everyone simply assumes that the corroborating paperwork either has been or will be submitted.
- In these situations executive directors are often uncomfortable asking the chair to sign a pledge form because of what might be perceived as an underlying mistrust.
- Once a donor has become critically ill, it becomes even more difficult to ask them to sign a pledge form. Suddenly one is aware that their priorities might have changed and that the solicitor might appear to be a waiting vulture even by bringing up the subject with the donor or the family.
- It is easier to discuss these issues from the perspective of wanting to be able to fulfill the donor's wishes rather than wanting the donor to make good on his or her pledge.
- This organization was fortunate that the family was willing to honor a verbal commitment for such a large amount. That is probably the exception rather than the rule. However, signed pledge forms for specific gift amounts are considered obligations against the estate in most states.
- The campaign has an excellent opportunity to create a lasting memorial to the deceased donor. Not only would this be a fitting and appropriate gesture for the organization, but it would help build a relationship between the organization and the donor's family.

Story #5. We Can't Find a Campaign Chair

We spent hours deciding who to invite to serve as campaign chair and planning our approach to our nominees. We came up with three people who would make excellent campaign chairs, but as we made the rounds, one by one, they all said they'd help with the campaign but they would not serve as chair. We have no choice, we have to move ahead. The building project is underway, the campaign is being planned, momentum is building . . . but no campaign chair! What do we do?

- One might consider the team approach to campaign leadership. If the burden of chairing the campaign is too heavy for one individual, a shared responsibility might be more manageable. Perhaps a former board chair or even a current board chair might agree to cochair the campaign and then invite one of the others to join him.
- One needs to guard against panic, which leads to dipping deeper and deeper into the well. Stop! Take stock

of the situation. Examine why the first three said no. Consider what you really need from a campaign chair. Before you ask another person, raise your sights. Just because the first three said no doesn't mean that everyone of their stature or even higher stature will say no. In fact, someone of greater stature in the community may have more wisdom and say yes!

Story #6. We Can't Recruit Enough Volunteers to Solicit All of the Prospects

We did fine gathering the people to solicit leadership gifts and the family division. Those solicitors were the people who were actively involved in planning the campaign and who are in our organization. But when we began to broaden the effort and enlist the teams for the community division we came up short. We had a hard time finding team captains and the team captains had a very difficult time finding enough solicitors. In the end, we managed to get enough volunteers to solicit only about half of the prospects whom we had identified for that phase of the campaign. Are there things we might have done to increase the number of volunteers? And how should we deal with the shortfall?

- With two-income families, who have less time for volunteer activities, and with more and more campaigns looking for solicitors, many organizations are having difficulty finding volunteer solicitors. The farther in advance an organization begins to enlist volunteers, the more they will be able to find. Not only does planning ahead provide more time for the enlistment process, but the longer the time between asking someone to do something and the date on which it must be performed, the greater is the likelihood that the person will say yes.
- The best way to build a base of solicitors is by involving potential solicitors in the life of the organization well before the actual campaign. Organizations with large and vital volunteer programs tend to have an easier time than those who do not regularly use volunteers.
- All is not lost because enough volunteers couldn't be found. One might ask each solicitor to take more cards. Or, once the solicitors have completed their first round of solicitation calls, one might invite those who have been successful to take another set of cards.
- If the division will not be able to solicit all of the prospects who have been identified, it becomes more important to highlight the cards of those prospects who are most likely to make a gift so that the personal solicitations are used to maximum effect.

- The cards that are not selected even after a second pass might be targeted for priority attention in the phonathon. Generally it is easier to enlist volunteers for a phonathon than it is for personal solicitations. And the better the prospects who are left for the phonathon, the better its results.

Story #7. Board Members Resent the Campaign Steering Committee

When we were able to recruit some really powerful people for our campaign steering committee, I was sure the board would be thrilled. Here, finally, we had been able to involve some of our community's largest donors and most credible names in shaping the future of our organization. I could just taste the long-range potential, not only to our campaign, but to our entire organization! So I was taken aback when board members began to question the decisions of the steering committee and even question the wisdom of the whole campaign. I think that the board members were actually jealous of the steering committee. The obvious power discrepancy between the board and the steering committee made board members feel as though they were being phased out, and some of them didn't want to go! What might we have done?

- This situation is not unusual, although it is often overlooked and almost never discussed.
- Most people are uncomfortable with others of dissimilar backgrounds, financial resources, and levels of power. So it is not surprising that a working board would feel uncomfortable when paired with a fund-raising board. This organization might have avoided some of the problems had they taken steps early in the campaign planning process to make sure that the two groups interacted in some way and that key members of the board felt included in the campaign.
- Perhaps the campaign chair and two or three other board members well respected by the rest of the board should have been included in the campaign planning committee. Early in the campaign, the board might have hosted a cocktail party or other event for the full board and steering committee to thank the steering committee members for their assistance and to facilitate some informal communication among members of both groups.
- Some of the steering committee members might have created a task force with some board members to explore ways in which the board might actively participate in the campaign.

- Boards of directors are often not well informed about campaigns, and in a vacuum of thorough information they become anxious. They are painfully aware that the results of a failed campaign will end up in their laps—not the laps of the steering committee—and are therefore anxious about the progress of the campaign. The campaign chair, working in coordination with the board chair and the executive director, should put special effort into keeping the board informed. This might be done at regular board meetings, at periodic special meetings, or in writing.
- No matter what the steering committee accomplishes, never forget that the board of directors is really responsible for the health of the organization.
- If an executive director is frustrated with his or her board it would be easy for him to express those frustrations to the more powerful members of the steering committee. The director must remember, however, that the steering committee is actually an ad hoc group with no authority. The director must resist the temptation to talk down the board to the steering committee.

Gift Problems

"All that glitters is not gold."

Some campaigns face difficult and even embarrassing situations that stem from difficulty around specific gifts—anticipated gifts that don't materialize, multiple gifts intended to name the same area or room, or the gift with strings attached.

Worries about specific gifts have kept many development directors and campaign chairs awake at night. When all of the process of the campaign—the committees and divisions and solicitation teams—is done, the success of the campaign hinges on whether or not the gifts come in. And a problem around one of the top-ten campaign gifts has the power to tip the balance from success to failure or vice versa.

Most gift problems arise because of misunderstandings. But sometimes donors make commitments that they are unable to make good on and sometimes organizations do the same.

Story #1. The Retracted Major Gift

A donor gave a major gift to our institution and to confirm the gift he sent a signed letter stating his intentions. All was well and the campaign proceeded according to schedule. At the campaign kickoff we announced our goal and publicly honored our donor for his leadership gift. About a month later, while the general phase of the campaign was in full swing, the donor was diagnosed with cancer and his wife sent us a letter saying that in light of his illness he would be unable to honor his commitment. What should we do?

- Although written pledges giving the date, signature of the donor, amount of the gift, and terms of payment usually serve as legal contracts and in most states stand up in court, most community-based organizations hesitate to use the legal system as a way of forcing payment. The consequences of negative publicity and ill will caused by an aggressive approach are often seen as being too detrimental to the long-term reputation of the institution.
- The organization might try to meet with both the donor and his wife to review the commitment letter, discuss the gift, and determine the donor's intentions. If, at such a meeting, it becomes clear that the donor himself has had a change of heart and would like to change the gift, it may be possible to find a way for him to change the type or terms of the gift so that they work better for him in his current circumstances.
- One might involve other people in the community who have a close relationship with the donor and his spouse to learn more about the facts of the case. Is the wife estranged from her husband? Is she being pressured by children who are hungry for the estate? Are there real financial hardships? An organization would be better able to find a workable solution if it had a thorough grasp of the situation. Unfortunately, when a family is in distress, the facts may be colored by emotion that is difficult to unravel.

Story #2. The Wealthy Campaign Chair Who Makes a Small Gift

We were so pleased when one of the wealthiest members of our community agreed to chair our campaign. Although he did not have a strong history of giving, his family had been active in our organization's programs. We did not know him well, but we felt that the ties were strong enough to make him a reasonable campaign chair. When we recruited him, we talked about the importance of his making a leadership gift though we were not specific about the actual dollar amount of the gift. We were shocked when, early in the campaign he sent in his pledge form making a gift of just $10,000 toward our goal of $2.2 million. His stature in the community and his perceived wealth made that gift seem like a slap in the face to us and we are worried about how effective he will be as a lead-gift solicitor.

- There are few things more disheartening than receiving a small gift from a wealthy campaign chair early in the campaign. We suggest a good night's sleep before starting the search for the best way to turn this disaster into an opportunity. Then consider the following as just a few of the many ways one might choose to proceed.
- Meet with him to discuss the strategic importance of his gift and figure out a way to serve both his financial situation and the campaign. He may increase his gift by extending the pledge period, make an entirely different kind of gift, delay his gift, or simply increase it. Just remember that he may not have thought through the negative effect of his gift. Do not make assumptions! Talk clearly and openly and listen carefully! Together you and the chair will probably be able to turn the problem around.
- Suggest that he hold off on his gift until later when some of the other lead gifts have been solicited. Then make sure that several of the major gifts are in before soliciting him. Some of the large donors might participate in the solicitation and ask him to match their gifts.
- Meet with some of his family members who have been actively involved in the organization to find out whether they would consider pitching in to make his gift part of a larger family gift.
- The table of gifts for the campaign can serve as an excellent tool to help facilitate the discussion of his gift.
- This story reminds us once again of the importance of early and specific discussions about the role of campaign leaders—before they sign on.
- The fact that the important money matters were not discussed in advance does not mean that they cannot be discussed later. Clear, nonassumptive, open discussion about the campaign, the role of campaign leaders, and his interests and intentions can often solve such problems. Indeed, through the discussions, the campaign chair is likely to learn to be an effective solicitor—and that's the silk purse that might be gotten from the sow's ear!

Story #3. The "Sure" Gift That Didn't Come In

For many years our largest gift had come from one donor. Year after year she supported our organization to the tune of approximately $10,000 each year. She had told us clearly that she preferred giving away her money while she still lived. When we began our campaign she was in her nineties and her health was beginning to fail. We went to her in the spring to ask for a campaign gift of $100,000. In her usual fashion, she listened and told us that

she would consult her attorney and let us know by September. September came and went but we received no word from our donor. Our board chair knew her attorney and called him only to learn that he was concerned about our donor's declining health and need for round-the-clock care and was advising her against making any more large gifts. It looked like our sure leadership gift was not so sure after all.

- The frustrations of this story are twofold. Not only has the gift not been made as anticipated, but there is simply no clear word at all.
- Sometimes elderly people become virtual prisoners of their caregivers, attorneys, and accountants. It would help to gather as much information as possible about her situation from the community grapevine. Is she making large gifts to other organizations? Are other organizations getting the same feedback? Is she still seeing people? Does she still like company even though her health is not good? How much of a say does she still have in giving away her money? Unless one knows the answers to these and other questions it is difficult to determine the appropriate strategy.
- Sometimes one does miss a gift because of timing. If her health is truly failing and she has decided not to make a gift, the organization might shift its focus from trying to tie down a campaign commitment to doing nice things for her that will help enrich and soften the end of her life. Even in campaign times, organizations should not lose track of what is right—and if right is letting go of the gift and supporting a generous old friend, that is what you should do.

Story #4. The Lead-Gift Donor Doesn't Pay Up

Our campaign went over its goal and we celebrated with great glee. We then heaved a sigh of relief and dove headfirst into constructing the addition to our building. All was fine until several months later when one of our major donors missed his first payment of $10,000 on a $50,000 pledge. At first I thought it was just an oversight, but when my calls weren't returned and no check showed up, I began to think that he made his contribution for show and has no intention of making good on it. How would you handle this?

- People generally behave consistently, so it might help to track down some other information about this donor's patterns. You certainly do not want to assume that he is defaulting on his gift if in reality he intends to pay. By checking around with other organizations and other people in the community, you might find that he has done the same thing before only to pay off the whole amount in one lump sum at the end of the year. Or, you may find that he has defaulted on other gifts. Whatever the pattern, knowing it might help you determine the best course of action.

- When someone makes a commitment for a campaign gift in writing, in most states that document serves as a contract under the law and one might consider bringing suit against him for the gift. Although for large gifts this is certainly a strategy to consider, sometimes even then the ill will that such an action engenders and the time and energy it takes may not be worth the return.

- Sometimes people default on or delay payment of gifts because their financial situation has suffered an unforeseen blow. It is not uncommon for people who have fallen on hard times to be sensitive and awkward about their reduced means. If this is the case, your donor may appreciate a face-saving strategy. You might send a letter inviting him to redesign his gift to the organization. He might choose to alter the payment schedule or even lower the amount of the gift. By offering him a way out, you might retain him as a donor even though you may not get the full gift.

- If you get no response from the donor, it is sometimes possible to engineer a conversation with his spouse or other family member to try to get more information about what is going on. If someone in your organization is friends with the donor or the spouse, you might share the basics of the situation with them and ask if they could try to find out what is going on. One must use careful judgment about what information to share and what should be kept confidential. The grapevine is often a good source of information and a few well-placed queries might unearth answers to many of the questions.

Story #5. The Campaign That Received Two Gifts to Name One Library

In the course of soliciting lead gifts we invited three people to consider making gifts that would name the library in our building. We thought we would be lucky if one of the three donors would make a gift of the size it would take to name that space, so we were surprised, delighted, *and* dismayed when two of the donors promptly responded with pledges to name that space. How should we have dealt with the situation?

- Most people are flexible in their preferences for naming a space. You might open a conversation about alternative spaces with the donor who has the strongest ties to the organization. Often when presented with a quandary of this sort, a donor who cares about the organization is likely to be thrilled that another donor has made a large gift and be perfectly willing to select an alternate space.

- On rare occasions, both donors may have strong reasons for selecting the library. Perhaps one gift was to be in honor of the donor's librarian mother, for example, and the other arose out of a strong conviction of the need for such a library. If both donors are adamant about naming the library, one might consider naming different aspects of the library. Perhaps the collections might be named for one donor and the reading area for another. Or, one might suggest naming the library after both donors—The Smithson-Kirk Library.

- The key to resolving all of these cases is to communicate fully and openly with the donors, involving them in the process of determining a solution that they are both happy (or at least willing) to live with.

- Covering up or obscuring the problem and/or delaying contacting the donors is likely only to create more difficulties. Clarity, honesty, and immediacy are the best approaches to this issue—as they are to many others as well.

Story #6. The Gift That Might Have Been Tied to a Contract

We knew that one of our lead gifts might come from an area company that was one of several bidders on a major contract that our organization had put out for bids just as the campaign was progressing. Because of the timing of the campaign, we asked for the gift well before our organization had to make the contract decision, but the corporation delayed their response to our request. We suspected that they were waiting to see if they received the contract. We were fortunate that the company, though not the low bidder, provided services that most closely fit what we were looking for and our committee decided to award them the contract. Approximately one month later, we received their signed pledge form for the amount we had requested. We were uncomfortable about the potential conflicts (both actual and perceived) in that process. Were there specific steps we might have taken to lessen the potential for the appearance of unethical behavior?

- These issues arise in one form or another in many campaigns. In fact, many companies in that situation would not make a campaign gift if they were not awarded the contract. This behavior often makes good sense and represents no conflict of interest at all. Consider that the business may have had no contact with the organization prior to submitting the proposal, and would probably have no ongoing relationship were they not to get the contract and therefore would not be likely to have the motivation to make the gift. Most organizations, however, consider it sound business practice to support client organizations.
- More troublesome is the possibility that a contract may be awarded by a nonprofit not because of the quality of work or the cost quoted in the proposal but as a way of influencing a gift. This practice is most certainly to be discouraged. During a campaign period, an organization would be well served to use the most rigorous of business practices when requesting proposals from businesses with whom they are considering doing business. Every business that is being considered should be treated in the same way, and the process to review proposals should be conducted by a committee that has been instructed to use objective, written standards to select the firm.
- In a similar situation that we encountered recently, the delay actually helped our client. Between the time we had asked them for their gift of $75,000 and the time the contract was awarded, our other major corporate donor had increased its campaign gift from $75,000 to $125,000. This gave us a wonderful opportunity to go back to the company that had kept us waiting and ask them to match the larger gift, which they did.

Public-Relations Nightmares

> "Don't agonize. Organize."
>
> *Florynce Kennedy*

Scandals that surface within an organization in the middle of a campaign definitely cause trouble. One needn't look very far to find scandals: murder, rape, allegations of sexual harassment, internal schisms, and labor disputes are just a few of the things that happen to organizations and are particularly challenging if they happen in the middle of a capital campaign.

Story #1. The Symphony Campaign and the Musicians' Strike

There I was scheduled to have lunch with my friend to ask him for a large campaign gift to build a new symphony hall and the headlines of the morning paper are about the musicians' strike. What timing!

- What timing, indeed. But canceling the lunch is quite certainly not the appropriate response. In fact, over drinks or lunch, the solicitor may agree with the prospect to discuss the labor situation at the symphony but to postpone their discussion of a gift to the campaign until the labor issues are resolved.
- However, because the strike presumably has to do with the operating budget and short-term issues and the construction of a new symphony hall has longer consequences, the prospect may not be put off at all.
- The solicitor should be sensitive to the mood and reaction of the prospect before determining the best strategy.

Story #2. National Fund-Raising Scandals

Within a couple of short years, the misuse of money at the United Way and the exposure of the fraud at the New Era Foundation seemed to undermine donors' faith in the nonprofit community. Our organization was a United Way member and had both given to and received money from the New Era Foundation. We are planning a campaign and wonder how these facts will affect our prospects.

- Both the United Way and the New Era scandals did undermine peoples' belief and trust in the nonprofit world at a national level. Local nonprofits that have built strong relationships with people in their community are often unaffected by such erosions of confidence.
- Some organizations that lost money in the New Era debacle actually garnered positive public relations by making full and complete disclosures about what happened and by inviting local donors to make contributions to make up for the funding deficits caused by the default of New Era funds. Because the New Era story was of such interest to the press, organizations that managed the press coverage well actually attracted a great number of new donors.
- National scandals encourage local giving. In fact, local, community-based nonprofits may benefit as more donors decide to increase their support to local organizations and decrease their gifts to larger national causes.

Story #3. Potential Public-Relations Problems

Our campaign was in full swing when one of our former patients decided to sue us for malpractice.

Although from our perspective the staff had behaved conscientiously and professionally, the patient had encountered medical complications weeks after leaving our care and was turning over every stone to assign blame. We had accurate and careful documentation that we thought would clear us should the case come to trial, but nonetheless we were concerned that the story might be covered badly in the paper just before our campaign kickoff.

- Preparation and planning in case of a public-relations disaster can go a long way toward preventing or at least minimizing the damage. When a potential problem like this one is in the wind, an organization should develop a strategy for dealing with the press. Draft a press release stating the situation in a clear, honest, unemotional way.
- Assign one person to be the spokesperson for the organization should the problem become a target for the press. Inform everyone else who is closely associated with the organization and the campaign about the situation and the strategy for handling it. Provide key volunteers (board members and campaign leaders) with specific written instructions about what to say should they be called by the local newspaper, radio, or television media.
- Should the media become involved, early and full disclosure is almost always the best strategy. Openness defuses the media, defensiveness and covert behavior only whet the appetite of most journalists.
- Make sure that key campaign volunteers are thoroughly informed early, so they don't get caught short hearing about the potential problem from someone outside the organization. It is truly embarrassing to learn about a brewing scandal while one is soliciting a prospect.

Story #4. The Board Chair Who Was Accused of Shoplifting

We were just beginning to talk about a capital campaign when the chairman of our board was arrested for shoplifting! He maintained that he had been exchanging shirts that he had purchased at the store earlier but that as he went to pick up the new sizes, the floorwalker accused him of trying to steal the two shirts. Our chairman couldn't produce his receipt for the original purchase and the store detectives turned him over to the local law-enforcement officials. The local newspaper photographed him being led away by the police in handcuffs and the next day they ran the photo in the paper. How, if at all, should this affect our campaign planning?

- Whether or not the chairman is actually guilty of shoplifting, the image of him in handcuffs will undoubtedly undermine his credibility in the community and his tarnished image may well affect the reputation of the organization while he is chairman of the board.
- Conversely, however, an organization should stand up for what it believes to be right, and steady support for the chairman through his problems may be the right thing to do even if it is not the short-term best public-relations stance.
- Most certainly the chairman should be involved and not excluded from discussions about how, if at all, the organization should react. Although it might be tempting to exclude the chairman from discussions of his situation, this would only further complicate the situation.

Errors and Mistakes

"If I had my life to live over again, I'd dare to make more mistakes next time."

Nadine Stair

Like it or not, errors do occur. The most common campaign errors occur around counting gifts and pledges. This seemingly simple task is actually quite complex and many campaigns find themselves at some time or another during the course of the campaign having counted one gift twice or having not counted a gift because it wasn't entered properly in the system or even having lost a pledge. There are, of course, other errors as well. Leaving out people's names, misspelling names, or including the names of people who wished to be anonymous. It is also common, even in the era of computer spell-check programs, to send out major gift proposals with spelling or grammatical errors. Most of these errors are small and do not warrant specific stories, a few reminders and suggestions may put them in their proper perspective.

Story #1. We Thought We Had . . . But We Hadn't

We got to the end of our campaign, sneaking over our goal by just a few hundred dollars. Even though it was by inches and not miles that we succeeded, succeed we did! And in our jubilation at completing what had been a very challenging campaign, we called all of our leaders, primary campaign workers, major donors, and a good number of other people who in one way or another had made the campaign a success. We were thrilled. They were thrilled.

The day after all of our calls were made and my feet once again were nearing the ground, the development assistant who also logged gifts and kept track of campaign counting crept into my office, her head low, to tell me that she had found an error. She had recorded one $15,000 gift twice and had, therefore, credited the campaign with $15,000 more than it had raised. We were not $436 dollars over goal. Rather we were $14,564 short! My feet landed back on the ground with a harsh thump!

- This issue raises three related topics: how to correct the error and ensure that there are no more like it in the system; how to make up the shortfall as quickly as possible; and who to tell and who not to tell.
- Although confessing one's errors is often an impressive and effective way to begin correcting the problem, there are times when one should do so broadly and times when only a few people need know. In this case, one might inform the campaign chair and board chair and involve them in developing and carrying out a strategy to close the gap quickly. If this can be done, there is no reason to interrupt the celebratory mood among the organization's constituents.
- It is sometimes difficult to know when to communicate about one's errors broadly and when to keep them in the family. These are important issues of judgment, and if the error is large, these judgments should be determined in collaboration with the campaign leadership.

Story #2. Sometimes Careless Errors Help

We worked like mad to meet the deadline of a major foundation that we were asking for a challenge grant. We prepared what we thought was a good proposal and sent it off thinking that we had asked for a challenge grant that had to be met by June of 1994. We were most surprised, therefore, when we got notice that our proposal had been accepted and we had until June of 1995 to meet their challenge. When we went back to the proposal we realized that in one place we had put the first date and in another place we had mistakenly put the later date.

- It just goes to show that most people read what we send them far less carefully than we write it. Gener-

ally small errors are not even spotted by the readers of our letters and proposals. However, people do read their own names carefully! As a general rule of thumb, we suggest not pointing out or correcting small errors in written material after the fact, but if you learn that you have misspelled someone's name or used the wrong name, you may wish to send a follow-up apology note.

Story #3. The Editing Prospect

We sent a leadership-gift package to a major donor in our area whom we knew quite well. Within three days we had the package on our desk with several corrections and suggestions about how we might make it more succinct. There was no comment or letter about our request, just his suggestions for how it might be better. What should we have done?

- Most written material can be made better, and a sharp pencil and an astute editing eye is something most organizations could well use. How fortunate this organization is to have a donor prospect with those skills. If that were our prospect, we would not hesitate to incorporate the prospect's suggestions, checking carefully for typos and the like and send it back to him as soon as possible with a note of thanks for his part in improving the solicitation material that will be used as a model for many other requests. We bet that the exchange will help solidify the prospect's gift.
- Of course, to err is human. In fact, when most of us find an error in someone else's work, if they are genuinely pleased to have it pointed out so they can correct it, we, the error finders, feel as though we have made a positive contribution to the process.
- The difficult part of foolish errors is that once we learn that we have made them we indeed do feel foolish. And foolish is not what we think we are hired to be, so we get defensive and behave in ways that are often counterproductive.
- The ability to embrace one's errors, communicate clearly about them and correct them with pride is a wonderful strength to be recognized and applauded. Of all of the strengths one could list, this is one of the most difficult and least common.
- Open, nondefensive responses usually save the day.

Organizational and Project Problems

"Heaven sends us misfortunes as a moral tonic."
Lady Marguerite Blessington

Because capital campaigns and the projects they fund take many months to complete, many unforeseen events occur during those periods. Most of those occurrences are minor, but occasionally minor problems mushroom into full-blown disasters, and because capital campaigns and organizations need the confidence of their donors and constituents to thrive, these disasters often have important consequences.

Story #1. The Bottom Fell Out of Our Market in the Middle of the Campaign

Our organization had been financially strong for several years. Our market boomed and money flowed. As a consequence we began a capital campaign so that we could renovate a new larger site to accommodate our rapid growth. But as the campaign began, our market collapsed for reasons that had little or nothing to do with how we were conducting our business. We went from having a profit of nearly $500,000 in one year to losing $700,000 the next. Our campaign leadership and committee members had all joined us in part because of our financial strength and we were afraid to tell them what was going on.

- Most campaign leaders are savvy business leaders who are willing to call on their experience to help solve problems. Leaving them out of the loop is a dangerous and potentially damaging strategy.
- Fear has stopped many people from doing what they should.
- As long as the organization can develop a convincing and careful plan to show how the short-term difficulties can be overcome and that the organization has the funds to cover the immediate future, the problem may be quite acceptable to the leadership.
- Be sure that it is wise to continue. Sometimes organizations in a campaign mode blindly continue for fear of losing face. If the project itself no longer makes sense for the organization, stop to reevaluate rather than letting momentum carry you along.
- To be confronted with such a problem by a prospect during a solicitation and not have adequate information to discuss the issue is an unforgivable slap in the face to the campaign leadership.

Story #2. The Zoning Board Turned Us Down

We live in a small town and have lots of good will in the community, so when we decided to expand our center we assumed that we could get it through the zoning board without any problem. Unfortunately, at the zoning hearing one of our neighbors decided that she didn't want us to expand and she organized forces against us. To our horror they turned us down flat. The project for which we had already raised half the money couldn't be built!

- This is a time for planning and communications. Presumably the center must still expand. Perhaps it will build a satellite site elsewhere, perhaps it will redesign the expansion to make it more acceptable. Maybe the entire center will move to a new building. While the organization regroups and explores other alternatives, donors must be informed.
- In general, when people are well informed, they are quite reasonable. Most donors to the campaign will be willing to wait until the goals of the campaign are met as long as they know what is going on. But the organization must bend over backward to keep them informed month by month or even weekly as the planning progresses. No one who has made a gift should have to wonder what has or will become of their money.
- Building bridges is especially important in a small community. One might invite the person who led the charge against the zoning change to be part of the discussions to figure out how to provide a bigger center to serve the community.

Story #3. It Cost More Than We Anticipated

We set out to raise $750,000 and we did. Then we built our building. When it came to furnishing the building, I just couldn't keep the costs down. In fact, I knew that if I didn't do it right this time, I'd probably never get the chance again. When the project was completed I had spent nearly $250,000 more than we had planned for, but the building was just right.

- Don't let the cost overruns spoil the success of the campaign. This organization was very successful, but if one is not careful, it would be easy to have them feel that they failed. The energy that comes from a successful campaign is one of its most important aspects. Don't lose it.
- Unless the ways to raise that money are apparent, consider taking out a mortgage on the building rather than beating the donors to extend the campaign. Then let a few years go by and launch a new

campaign that incorporates paying off the mortgage as one of its goals.

- Plan better. Boards tend to get a bit testy when they feel that their arms have been twisted. Involving them in the decision process up front usually leads to better long-term results. If you don't trust their judgments and decisions, either work with them, give in to them, or resign.

National Disasters or Acts of God

"The only people who never fail are those who never try."

Ilka Chase

We all like to think of ourselves as being more or less in control of our lives and the destinies of our organizations. And living in a country that has not been touched directly by a major war, we can easily fool ourselves into believing that to be the case. In reality, awful things way beyond our power to control do occur, and when they do, they have a profound effect on our ability to raise funds.

The authors have been fortunate not to have encountered such situations directly, but we believe that no trouble-shooting section would be complete without an acknowledgment that such things do happen. Extraordinary events like wars, bombs, earthquakes, floods, and famines in our country or our communities do require extraordinary reactions on the part of our volunteers and our donors. These disasters don't consider the timetables of our capital campaigns and when they occur, they may well disrupt and even ruin what we have spent years building.

Although we would choose not to have to accommodate them, accommodate them we must, and the more generously we are able to put our own self-interests and those of our organizations aside and lend our support to the larger community good, the stronger we are likely to emerge when life returns to normal.

Bibliography

Alexander, G. Douglass. "Setting Campaign Goals: A Tricky Business," *NSFRE Journal*, Summer 1991, 16–18.

American Association of Fund Raising Counsel Trust for Philanthropy. *Giving USA: The Annual Report on Philanthropy for the Year 1994*. New York: American Association of Fund Raising Counsel, 1995.

Bailey, Trevor. "How Visions Take Shape." *Hoke Communications* 18, no. 4 (1987): 52.

Bayley, Ted. *The Fundraiser's Guide to Successful Campaigns*. New York: McGraw-Hill, 1988.

Broce, Thomas. *The Guide to Raising Money from Private Sources*. Norman, OK: University of Oklahoma Press, 1979.

Cheney, Carol. "Designing the Campaign." *Currents* (Nov/Dec 1995): 34–38.

Ciconte, Barbara Kushner and Jeanne Jacob. *Fund Raising Basics: A Complete Guide*. Gaithersburg, MD: Aspen Publishers, Inc., 1997.

Craig, Donald. "The Askable Moment." *CASE Currents*, December 1991, 30–33.

Crawford, Jean, and Judith Potts. "How to Survive a Capital Campaign," *Fund Raising Management*, July 1986, 39–46.

Dailey, B. "From Zero to Millions, The Anatomy of a Major Gift Solicitation, from Identification to Follow-Up," *CASE Currents*, November/December 1990.

Dove, Kent E. *Conducting a Successful Capital Campaign: A Comprehensive Fundraising Guide for Nonprofit Organizations*. Arlington, VA: Volunteer—The National Center, 1988.

Geever, Jane C. "How to Select and Use Fund Raising Consultants." In *Achieving Excellence in Fund Raising*, edited by H. A. Rosso and Associates. San Francisco: Jossey-Bass, 1991.

Giese, T. Robert and J. Richard Murray. "Planned Giving in a Capital Campaign." *Hoke Communications* 18, no. 12 (1988).

Gough, Samuel N., Jr. *Major Gift Programs: Practical Implementation*. Gaithersburg, MD: Aspen Publishers, Inc., 1997.

Grace, Kay Sprinkel. "Managing for Results." In *Achieving Excellence in Fund Raising*, edited by H. A. Rosso and Associates. San Francisco: Jossey-Bass Publishers, 1991.

Gurin, Maurice G. *What Volunteers Should Know for Successful Fund-Raising*. New York: Stein and Day, 1982.

Hall, Holly. "Raising More Money by Doing Research on Contributors," *The Chronicle of Philanthropy*, 12 January 1993, 32–34.

———. "The Long and Short of Writing Letters to Raise Money," *The Chronicle of Philanthropy*, 9 February 1993.

———. "Direct-Mail Fund Raising Bounces Back," *The Chronicle of Philanthropy*, 23 February 1993, 30–34.

———. "What Fund Raisers Do When Donors Object to Making a Gift." *The Chronicle of Philanthropy*, 10 August 1993, 36–38.

———. "How Small Charities Can Borrow Big Ideas for Capital Campaigns," *The Chronicle of Philanthropy*, 21 September 1993, 39–40.

———. "How to Avoid Pitfalls in Picking the Chair of a Capital Campaign." *The Chronicle of Philanthropy*, 8 March 1994, 40–42.

Hall, Johanne. "Intuition or Intellect: How to Recognize the Askable Moment," *CASE Currents*, December 1991, 34–36.

Hartsook, Robert F. "What To Do When the Campaign Is Over." *Fund Raising Management* (November 1995): 32–33.

Hauman, David J. *The Capital Campaign Handbook*. Washington, DC: The Taft Group, 1987.

Joyaux, Simone P. *Strategic Fund Development: Building Profitable Relationships that Last*. Gaithersburg, MD: Aspen Publishers, 1997.

Klein, Kim. *Fundraising for Social Change*. Inverness, CA: Chardon Press, 1988.

Levy, Barbara R. and Barbara Marion. *Successful Special Events: Planning, Hosting, and Evaluating*. Gaithersburg, MD: Aspen Publishers, Inc., 1997.

McGrath, Kevin. "Cultivating the Long-Term Donor," *NonProfit Times*, 21 October 1993.

Moore, Jennifer. "Donor Details on the Net," *The Chronicle of Philanthropy*, 10 August 1995, 29–32.

———. "Fund Raisers Debate Where to Draw the Line in Digging Up Personal Data on Potential Donors," *The Chronicle of Philanthropy*, 8 September 1992, 23.

Quigg, H. Gerald. *The Successful Capital Campaign from Planning to Victory Celebration*. Washington, DC: Council for the Advancement and Support of Education, 1986.

Reid, Russ. "Why Do People Give?" *Reid Report* (occasional undated newsletter): 1.

Rosso, Henry A. "Asset Building Through Capital Fund Raising." In *Achieving Excellence in Fund Raising*, edited by H. A. Rosso and Associates. San Francisco: Jossey-Bass Publishers, 1991.

———. "Preparing a Case that Empowers Fund Raising." In *Achieving Excellence in Fund Raising*, edited by H. A. Rosso and Associates. San Francisco: Jossey-Bass Publishers, 1991.

Scanlan, Eugene A. *Corporate and Foundation Fund Raising: A Complete Guide from the Inside*. Gaithersburg, MD: Aspen Publishers, Inc., 1997.

Scott, Miranda D. "Using Online Databases for Prospect Research," *Fund Raising Management* 28, no. 8 (1993): 44–49.

Schneiter, Paul H. *The Art of Asking: How to Solicit Philanthropic Gifts*. Ambler, PA: Fund Raising Institute, 1985.

Sheldon, K. Scott. "Foundations as a Source of Support." In *Achieving Excellence in Fund Raising*, edited by H. A. Rosso and Associates. San Francisco: Jossey-Bass Publishers, 1991.

Warwick, Mal. "How to Raise $1,000 Gifts by Mail," *NonProfit Times*, February 1993, 41–43.

Whitley, Frank V. "The 15 Worst Errors in Community Capital Campaigns," *Fund Raising Management*, September 1992, 43–46.

Williams, M. Jane. *Capital Ideas: Step by Step: How to Solicit Major Gifts from Private Sources*. Ambler, PA: Fund Raising Institute, 1979.

Williams, M. Jane. *Big Gifts*. Rockville, MD: Fund Raising Institute, 1991.

Index

About the Authors

ANDREA KIHLSTEDT has earned her reputation as a capital campaign consultant by guiding one campaign after another to a successful conclusion. Her firm, The Kihlstedt Group, is known for its creative and participatory approach to planning and fund raising. The firm works with small and mid-sized social service, educational, and cultural institutions.

Ms. Kihlstedt is a founding member of The Consultants' Alliance, an association of independent consulting firms that assist non-profit organizations. She also founded the New Generation Concert Series and served as its director for ten years.

Ms. Kihlstedt holds a Bachelors degree from the University of Pennsylvania and a Masters in Philosophy from Brown University. She is a Johns Hopkins Fellow in Change Management and a graduate of the Small Group Facilitators Intensive Program. She and her husband, a college professor, have two daughters who both earn their livings in the arts—one an actress, the other a musician.

CATHERINE SCHWARTZ has more than a decade of experience in capital campaigns, planned and annual giving, prospect research, and grantsmanship. She has served as the director of development in a number of nonprofit organizations including the Theatre Project Company, Capitol College, and the Alban Institute.

She has written several articles on fund raising in community-based organizations.

Ms. Schwartz is a graduate of Washington University in St. Louis.